# ROBERT OWEN

# Robert Owen

## SOCIAL VISIONARY

### Ian Donnachie

JOHN DONALD

First published in Great Britain in 2000 by Tuckwell Press
This edition published in 2005 by
John Donald an imprint of Birlinn Ltd
West Newington House
10 Newington Road
Edinburgh EH9 1QS
www.birlinn.co.uk

Reprinted with a revised preface 2011

ISBN 13: 978 0 85976 615 9

*British Library Cataloguing in Publication Data*
A catalogue record for this book is available
on request from the British Library

The author and publisher are grateful to the Friends of New Lanark
for supporting the publication of this edition.

Typeset by Palimpsest Book Production Limited,
Falkirk, Stirlingshire
Printed and bound in Britain by
Bell and Bain Ltd, Glasgow

# Contents

# List of Illustrations

# Preface

Robert Owen was one of the most controversial figures of his generation. Born in Wales in 1771 he lived through the later stages of the Enlightenment and the whole Age of Revolutions. Maturing into a perceptive and dynamic individual, he was greatly affected by both the ideas and the dramatic changes which characterised that era. He profited enormously during the first half of his life from the rise of industry, and then devoted his time to promoting a social and economic philosophy which he saw as a corrective to the excesses and evils of progress. Much of this derived from his experience and strongly emphasised the importance of education, environment, and ultimately co-operation. He gained fame, even notoriety, as a social reformer, and long after his death in 1858 his ideas continued to inspire others. The subsequent hagiography generated by his followers did neither his name nor his reputation much good, since they transformed the 'Social Father' of Owenism into the 'Father of Socialism', a sobriquet that ill fits him, yet sticks to this day.

In this biography, the first for fifty years, I review Owen's remarkable life and set it in the wider context of his time. Starting with the acknowledged scholarship I have synthesised practically everything of any importance that has been written about Owen, and examined most of the major archival collections in Britain and the United States containing Owen material. Since the book was first published there has been a remarkable upsurge of interest in Owen and his ideas and a flood of further publications has followed. This includes edited collections of pamphlets by or about Owen, many of which can also be accessed on the internet. I have updated the bibliography accordingly.

Given the established facts of Owen's long and eventful life, it is suprising that new material keeps coming to light in the form of letters, diaries, and travelogues, often in private keeping, or other material tucked away in forgotten corners of archives and libraries. A substantial amount of new evidence is emerging from digitised newspaper reports of Owen's activities and the frantic timetable maintained almost until his death. For example, more about his European tour of 1818 is being revealed by digitisation of French newspapers, though the censorship which prevailed under the Restoration may prove an impediment. In this connection whether or not Owen was as welcome in Paris as he claims is open to dispute! Thanks to searches of Irish newspapers much more is known about his Irish tour of 1822–23 than was reported in the British press and so his itinerary and liaisons with landowners, clergy and the political elite are better understood. Some research has also been undertaken on his Mexican adventure, 1828–29, and while this remains unpublished I am sure there is much more to be discovered.

Owen continues to motivate and puzzle in equal measure and there are many intriguing questions that arise. For example, recent research confirms that Owen's father-in-law, David Dale, the founder of New Lanark, had already made the community famous long before Owen set eyes on the place. So what did Owen himself actually achieve at New Lanark, why did it become even more famous and what really intrigued the thousands of visitors about Owen's 'arrangements' in the place? I believe it is because Owen was remarkably successful in integrating workplace and community reforms for the common good. The fact that New Lanark became a test-bed for Owen's ambitious plans for planned communities designed to solve the problems of his time also raises questions about whether or not it was an appropriate model when removed from its context as a manufacturing village.

How much did his 'Village Plan' derive from New Lanark and Owen's essays? Population, presumably controlled by contraception or abstention, was to be much the same, the architecture of the earliest designs close, though the planning and layout were very different. The social arrangements might be similar but the economic structure differed substantially. Unfortunately Owen was at his weakest transposing capitalism into co-operation if such a move was then possible. How would all this work, people asked, how would labour be valued, how would property be shared, if at all? What would happen if people wanted to leave?

Education was another key issue in Owen's campaigns, but like factory reform it had much wider implications given the crusade for social and moral regeneration signalled in the essays. If character formation was to work it would be most effective from infancy, hence the importance attached to early childhood education. But Owen's interest extended to all ages, ultimately delivering a progressive curriculum with innovative methods derived partly from Joseph Lancaster and Johann Heinrich Pestalozzi. The evening schools and uplifting lectures were also open to adults, so reforming of character that started in infancy and childhood could be pursued into adult life. Interestingly Owen himself, when called upon to reflect on his career, said that the schools were his biggest achievement at New Lanark. Perhaps he absorbed something of the Scottish democratic tradition in education, to contradict those who asked why the poor should be educated?

Owen's attitudes towards religion raise many questions. The rejection of religion was not unusual for someone personally touched by Enlightenment thought, becoming a deist (or perhaps an agnostic). He evidently believed he had been called by some divine force to lead a crusade of social and moral reformation. He consistently resorted to religious and even millennial language. Owen's attack was not on religion but on sectarianism, as he was generally careful to make clear, since the clergy remained highly influential and he needed their support as much as other elites. And while local ministers of the Scottish Kirk pursued Owen because they thought he was treading on their toes, many clergy seemed to have been interested in his ideas about the relief of the poor and parochial education, which beyond the gospel and moral order, were the prime concerns of their parish ministries. His support of religious worship at New Lanark seems contradictory, though it could be seen as another means of social control. Owen's clerical connections were impressive, including theology professors in the Scottish universities, the Archbishop of Canterbury, many senior bishops in England and Ireland, leading dissenters, even members of the Catholic hierarchy whom he addressed at Maynooth during the Irish tour of 1822–23. However, there is no question that after 1817, when he first pronounced on religion, the sectarian and secular issues constantly got Owen into trouble and muddied the waters of Owenism during his many campaigns. Quite why he did this, given his obsession with the social reform agenda, is hard to fathom.

Another great puzzle in the Owen story is the role of slavery in wealth creation and his attitude toward it. As far as we can tell, he seemed hardly aware of its contribution to the profitability of the cotton industry and, like Dale, could apparently distance this from the moral repugnance both probably felt. Dale himself, it has recently been discovered, was active in the anti-slavery movement, an extension of his philanthropy in Glasgow and beyond. Owen said little about slavery while at New Harmony, which seems odd given that Kentucky, a slave state, lay just across the Ohio. He thought plantation slaves he encountered in the West Indies were better off than factory workers back in Britain.

Owen and women, as the reader will discover, is an intriguing subject, though difficult to de-code. There can be little doubt that he was a charismatic man, apparently attractive to women, who flocked in large numbers to New Lanark and to his lectures. It is impossible to tell whether such women were more interested in his ideas than the man himself. But I have arrived at the conclusion that his advocacy of birth control, his promotion of more liberal attitudes to marriage, and the on-going rumours, true or not, about free-love among the Owenites, were great crowd pullers. More generally, gender is omni-present, though given the context of the time, women and women's roles in Owen's life and schemes are inevitably subverted to those of men. That said, Owen encountered many powerful women: his wife, Caroline Dale, and others, including the educator Marie Fretageot, the prison reformer Elizabeth Fry, the writer Fanny Trollope, and the feminist and emancipist Fanny Wright, among them. And although under constant public scrutiny he may well have had liaisons with women he met on his endless travels, Helen Fisher being a case in point. We can only speculate and, as with slavery, recognise that modern values on gender cannot be applied to Owen's era.

It is often said that Owen was only interested in promoting New Lanark and his New View of Society nationally and internationally. But the evidence suggests extensive community involvement in Lanark county, Old Lanark and district, and in Glasgow, where he donned the mantle of the philanthropic Dale. Three illustrations of this are: his *Report to the County of Lanark* (1820), which proved to be the most comprehensive statement of his economic ideas; his donations for poor relief in Lanark burgh, further extending his philanthropic reach; and his promotion of a concert and ball at the New Lanark Institute in aid of a school in the nearby village of Nemphlar.

As I write we are entering a period which will see extensive reference to Owen's ideas, as expressed in *A New View of Society*, and many bi-centennial events celebrating the publication of the first essay in 1812. Widely circulated, all four essays were published in a single volume in 1816, by which time Owen was famous, promoting himself as a social reformer, and people interested in both the man and his ideas flocked to view the community on the Clyde. The essays have remained in print ever since, and world-wide interest in Owen's ideas has been enhanced by New Lanark's World Heritage status. Much of his agenda on issues like education, citizenship, co-operation, sustainability, and environment are immediately relevant to modern society and likely to remain so in future. Historical analogies are always dangerous but Owen's solutions to the problems of his time, by default or design, are remarkably similar to those being adopted by western democracies at the present day.

Ian Donnachie
2011

# Acknowledgements

D uring the time this book has been in the making I have received help and kindness from many individuals and organisations. I am very grateful to The Open University, which several times released me from daily routines to undertake research, and also assisted financially both in Britain and the United States. Professors Arthur Marwick, Ruth Finnegan and other colleagues have been highly supportive. My friends at the New Lanark Conservation Trust, notably Jim Arnold and Lorna Davidson, have shown great interest in the project throughout. At New Harmony I have accumulated many debts but in particular to Jane and Kenneth Dale Owen for their kindness and hospitality. Jane Dale Owen, whose energy is inspiring, encouraged me to persist when my own was flagging.

I am deeply indebted to the staffs of numerous archives and libraries I have consulted in the course of research, including: (in Scotland) Blair Castle, Blair Atholl; Edinburgh University Library; Glasgow University Archives, Business Records Centre; Grand Lodge of Scotland; Highland Council Archive, Inverness; Lindsay Institute, Lanark; Mitchell Library, Glasgow; Motherwell Heritage Centre (formerly Motherwell District Library); National Archives of Scotland; the National Library of Scotland; North Lanarkshire Council; Royal Commission on the Ancient and Historical Monuments of Scotland; St Andrews University Library; Signet Library, Edinburgh; South Lanarkshire Council; and the former Strathclyde Regional Archive; (in England) Bodleian Library, Oxford; the British Library; Co-operative Union, Manchester; Devon County Record Office; Friends House Library, London; Goldsmiths Library, University of London; Lincoln County Library; and Nuffield College, Oxford; (in Wales) the National Library of Wales; and the Robert Owen Memorial Museum, Newtown; (in Ireland) the National Library of Ireland; National University of Ireland, Maynooth (formerly St Patrick's College); (in the US) John Carter Brown Library, Brown University; Illinois Historic Survey, University of Illinois, Urbana-Champaign; Indiana Historical Society; Indiana State Library; Library of Congress; National Archives, Washington, D.C.; University of Southern Indiana, Centre for Communal Studies; and the Workingmens' Institute and Library, New Harmony; and (in Switzerland) Burgerbliothek, Bern.

Many people have assisted me individually, notably:

Jane Anderson at Blair Castle for help with research there; Paul

Archibald, for his kindness in making material available from the Lindsay Institute's collection; Joyce Brown, Stamford Library, for references to McGuffog, Owen's employer there; Anthony Cooke, who generously pointed me in the direction of the Owen correspondence in the Atholl Papers and shared with me his deep knowledge of the Stanley enterprise; John H. Davidson, Hon. Curator of the Robert Owen Memorial Museum, for his assistance and very helpful observations on Owen's upbringing; Dr Andrea Duncan, who provided information on the Applegarth family; Josephine Elliott for advice and help in the archives at New Harmony; Michael Fry for some useful references; Dr George Hewitt for helping me with the New Lanark book, and indirectly with this; John Hoffmann for his help in researching the Bestor Papers at the Illinois Historic Survey; Gillian Lonergan for assistance and providing copies from the Owen Collection at the Co-operative Union; Dr David Maclaren, for sharing ideas about David Dale and about New Harmony; Professor Donald Pitzer of the University of Southern Indiana for hospitality, ideas and help; Robert Steward for making available the Inverness Burgh Records; my colleague, Dr W.T.R. Pryce, for so generously sharing ideas and providing references to the linguistic geography of Wales and to mid-Wales and Newtown in the eighteenth century. I have bored many people with Robert Owen, notably David Crabbe and Professor Christopher Whatley, but I am grateful to them for listening and providing a sounding-board for ideas. I would also like to thank Ian and Caroline Ferguson for their hospitality in Washington, D.C. Lillian Porch undertook a great deal of painstaking work on the text prior to publication. Finally, I am mindful of how much I have learned from students in my British and American history classes over the years. To them and others I have neglected to mention, I am very grateful.

For help with illustrations I wish to thank Jaqueline Bonnemains, Curator, Collection Charles-Alexandre Lesueur, Museum d'Histoire Naturelle, Le Havre; Helen Watson, Scottish National Portrait Gallery; and staff in the Research Library, National Portrait Gallery and the British Museum, Department of Prints and Drawings.

A version of the first chapter was originally published in the *Montgomeryshire Collections* (1998) and I am grateful to the editors for permission to use it. For several of the later chapters, with due acknowledgement, I have drawn liberally on the study of New Lanark I wrote with Dr George Hewitt, and published by Edinburgh University Press. Chapter Nine, in particular, derives partially altered from the New Lanark study. I hope this book matches the standard of the last and that the two will be seen to complement each other in the future.

Claire contributed many ideas and in recognition the book is dedicated to her with gratitude and love.

# ONE

# Childhood in Wales

R obert Owen might with justification be described as one of the most
famous Welshmen of his time though surprisingly much that is
said of him in Wales seems to take little account of the influence his
background exercised on his subsequent ideas about social psychology,
education and social reform. His own character and outlook, about which
he talked and wrote at length, were shaped by his Welsh roots, by his
Welsh linguistic and cultural heritage, by the Welshness of his schooling
and religious upbringing, by his immediate family and kin, and by
the environment of Montgomeryshire, specifically of Newtown and its
surroundings.[1]

Even so, Owen's early life has never been explored in any detail, and
biographers, including Frank Podmore and G.D.H. and Margaret Cole, all
gave a very sketchy account of his boyhood.[2] Of the more recent works
J.F.C. Harrison's monumental study was understandably concerned less
with Owen's life and more with his ideas and the movement he inspired,
while the major bi-centennial studies tended to concentrate on previously
unexplored aspects of his business career, his social psychology, educational practice and impact on working class movements.[3] Anne Taylor's
important study of millenarianism, which compares developments at
New Lanark and New Harmony, alludes to the circumstances of his
youth, but only in passing.[4] For Owen's origins almost every account
before and since Podmore has relied exclusively and selectively on
Owen's autobiography, which, written at different times by an old man of
fading memory in tandem with an amanuensis who was perhaps less than
accurate, is inevitably disjointed and confused about the details of people,
places, dates and events during an exceedingly long life.[5] As Claeys found
in researching his invaluable annotations to the latest edition of the *Life*,
and the present writer can confirm, there were also many mistakes or
printer's errors which escaped notice prior to publication.[6] More seriously,
much that Owen later wrote about his boyhood has previously been taken
at face-value and none of his biographers, with the possible exception of
Podmore, apparently bothered to verify even the most obvious details
and follow up the story of his early life and upbringing in mid Wales.

For all their weaknesses, however, Owen's memories of his childhood
do give some clues to a more complex and influential early life than
he himself probably believed (or cared to remember) in adulthood and
indeed narrated so many years later. While his recollections are practically

all that we have to go on, no one has unpacked or deconstructed them in a systematic manner nor attempted to compare them with other potentially illuminating sources about his upbringing in Newtown and elsewhere. A useful archive relating to Owen's life and some valuable memorabilia have been collected over the years by the Robert Owen Memorial Museum, and these documents and artifacts can help us to fill in more of the details about his family background and early life.[7] Amazingly, given the influence that Owen claimed for environmental forces on his own and others' characters, earlier scholars apparently attached little significance to Newtown and its surroundings in the making of the young Owen. As others have demonstrated conclusively, the area of Montgomeryshire in which Newtown is located experienced considerable economic, social, cultural and linguistic change during the closing decades of the eighteenth century and provided the backdrop for what was evidently a rather unusual upbringing for someone in Owen's class of society. In general little detailed attention has previously been paid to his family background, his schooling or the people with whom he associated – yet these and other boyhood influences were clearly of vital significance to his subsequent career, attitudes and ideas.

Robert Owen, as the parish records confirm, was born on 14 May 1771 in the house above his father's shop in the Broad Street of Newtown. The simply furnished room, as depicted in a later watercolour preserved in the Robert Owen Memorial Museum, had a lowish, beamed ceiling and to the left of the door was a fireplace with its small cast iron grate. The room was at the back of the house and looked out on the leafy gardens that ran behind the properties, in some cases as far as the gates of the local estate, Newtown Hall. Beyond could be seen the rich, rolling countryside typical of this part of the upper Severn valley.[8] His father, also Robert Owen, had been born in Welshpool, about fifteen miles distant, in either 1739 or 1741.[9] Owen senior's family were reasonably well-off farmers, who had fallen on hard times and according to one source had become landlords of the 'White Lion' inn and an adjacent malt house in Welshpool.[10] Certainly small farmers often became inn-keepers and brewers, because of the obvious link the raw materials of beer provided between the two occupations. As was common practice when many families had multiple occupations, the Owens may have combined farming with inn-keeping, but there is no way that this can be substantiated. At any rate it seems that Owen senior, being one of the younger sons and unlikely to inherit such assets as the family still possessed, was bound as a saddler's apprentice.[11] Throughout the age of horse transport, and in both town and countryside, this was a vital and potentially lucrative occupation; not every saddler made a fortune, perhaps, but few would ever be out of work or starve. When he had served his time and was about to embark on his own career he married Anne Williams, who had been born in 1735, and was said by

Owen to have been the daughter of a farmer in the neighbourhood of Newtown, though other Williamses were grocers, bakers, coopers and tailors in the town.[12] According to Owen they were among the most respectable farming folk in the district, and his mother, the eldest sister of the family, was 'deemed beautiful . . . and for her class, superior in mind and manner'.[13] Whether or not his family were esteemed locally is impossible to tell, but his memories of his mother are certainly important since he was at pains to emphasise her intelligence and good character. Owen senior, probably with some help from his wife's family, set himself up in business as a saddler, which he soon combined successfully with another trade, retail ironmongery. Moreover he subsequently became the post-master and a churchwarden, positions of some responsibility in the town and neighbourhood, demanding both integrity and at least some modest administrative and financial skills. Neither of these official positions, however, was particularly remunerative. The post-master of Newtown was a sub-deputy to the post-master at Bristol before 1791, when the office was made a head post office, and the salary of the post-master was fixed at £10 a year. So his earlier salary must have been even lower.[14] His father thus combined craft skills with two official appointments which required appropriate levels of numeracy and literacy (presumably in both Welsh and English). Such practical skills, transferred from father to son, were potentially useful to a child who had apparently also inherited his mother's intelligence. Robert Owen was the youngest but one of a family of seven, two of whom died in infancy. The survivors were William, at least ten years older, Anne and John, who were also older, and a younger brother, Richard. William helped Robert in his career but little is known about Richard.[15] Three of Owen's sons, maintaining the family tradition, were presumably named after them. John was two years older than Robert. His sister, Anne, was born in 1765.[16] According to the parish register Robert himself was baptised in the ancient church of St Mary's by the edge of the Severn on 12 June 1771.[17]

At that time Newtown was a small market town in the upper Severn valley, and according to Owen's recollections 'a neat, clean, beautifully situated country village, rather than a town, not containing more than one thousand inhabitants, with the ordinary trades, but no manufactures except a very few flannel looms'.[18] Newtown was one of several emergent flannel making locations in central Wales at that time – an industry grafted on to the small towns that had long established themselves as modest market centres, including nearby Welshpool, Llanidloes and Llanfair Caereinion.[19] In Newtown's case the loom-shops were to be found mainly in a suburb or extension of the town located on the other bank of the Severn in the parish of Llanllwchaiarn. This was later to become a thriving, teeming warren of industrial activity, with small woollen factories, more like workshops than

anything grander, occupying the topmost stories of the compressed hud-
dle of blocks which clung to the slope above the river, with the workers
living in the multitudinous press of cottages below.[20] While it is tempting
to make something of his early acquaintance with proto-industrialisation
in the textile trade of Newtown through seeing these looms at work, it
was rather the general ambience of the place which probably had the
greater impact on young Owen. Both the splendid riverside setting and
the lush rolling countryside of farms and small hamlets interspersed with
woodland, where nature could be appreciated in all its infinite variety,
greatly attracted him and were to prove enduring influences both on his
own outlook and his social psychology.[21]

Apart from the influence of the environment in this part of Wales
on his early life and his later views about social development and
education, his Welshness also gifted him with considerable linguistic
skills. We do not know for certain if Robert spoke Welsh at home
during his boyhood, but it seems possible. He was almost certainly
bilingual from infancy, a facility reflecting the linguistic geography
of this area of mid Wales.[22] While Newtown is not regarded as an
integral part of the Welsh Marches, it is in close proximity to the
borderlands of England in nearby Shropshire. Certainly because of its
regional location, the upper Severn valley was anglicised from early
times. It faces east, towards the English lowlands and West Midlands,
and the broad open vale of the upper Severn provided an easy routeway
for the diffusion of English speaking into inner Wales. These anglicising
influences came primarily from the English Midlands, especially from
Shropshire, for although Cheshire and Lancashire to the north were
growing in importance economically they were too far from the main-
stream of movement before the era of industrialisation. While Welsh
was still widely spoken in the surrounding district during the second
half the eighteenth century, English was becoming the language of
commerce and finding its way slowly into the everyday language of
the people – even some of the country folk in this part of the upper
Severn valley.[23] Writing to the SPCK (Society for the Promotion of
Christian Knowledge) in 1730, Sir John Pryce of Newtown requested
that if the society was sending further books for distribution among
the poor in the town and adjacent parishes they should be in English
rather than Welsh. 'Most people' he pointed out, 'understand English
much better than Welsh, so that Welsh books . . . are wholly useless'.[24]
This linguistic dilution clearly did not meet with the full approval
of the rural dean who made a tour of inspection on behalf of the
bishop and diocese of St Asaph, visiting the neighbouring parish of
Llanllwchaiarn in 1749. He apparently felt that too much English had
been introduced into church worship there, though interestingly, as
he and others remarked, this was not so among the Dissenters and

Methodists.[25] A search of the burial grounds of both Newtown and Llanllwchaiarn confirms a trend towards English becoming the 'official' language of the established church – much as it did about the same time in parts of Gaelic-speaking Ireland and the Scottish Highlands – for there are few tombstones of the period to be found in Welsh. Newtown represented, in fact, a pocket of predominantly English speakers, almost surrounded, except to the east, by bilingualism.[26] In Robert's time in Newtown both Welsh and English were in daily use with English dominant, so it is more than likely that as a boy he could understand and perhaps spoke Welsh to his father's customers. In his youth, particularly reflecting on his early years in Manchester, he claimed to be 'ill-educated and awkward, speaking ungrammatically, a kind of Welsh English, in consequence of the imperfect language spoken in Newtown, which was an imperfect mixture of both languages'. It seems unlikely, given his enthusiasm for his roots, that this was a slight on his Welshness, but like much else that he says about his early life, Owen's memories of himself are suspect. Rather than specifically deprecating his Welshness, it seems he deliberately exaggerated the image of himself as an untutored youth in order to emphasise the prominence he had achieved from such apparently humble origins.

Another significant skill which Robert possibly owed to his Welshness was his power over speech, though he claimed in his autobiography to have been much intimidated by his early experiences of speaking in public. As a boy Owen had ample opportunity to hear language, probably both in English and Welsh, used to good effect in the everyday conversation of his father's shop, in the more formal setting of the schoolroom, and in church, as a member of the congregation at St Mary's. There he could hear the clergyman in full flow, preaching a sermon embroidered with the kind of messianic language typical of the period, and which he would come to use himself in his writings and speeches. Indeed Welsh has a word which aptly describes this phenomenon, 'hwyl', meaning a sail, and suggesting a ship sailing along in a fine breeze. So the preacher and his congregation would be carried away in a great flow of language communicating a powerful and persuasive argument. Owen, the propagandist, would often be in what is still known as the 'hwyl' as he hammered home his message of reform on public platforms.

We might just note that in his role as manager at New Lanark Owen was at first scathing of the laziness and immorality of the workforce, though later he specifically expressed considerable sympathy for the Highlanders of the community and encouraged their language and dress, as well as their religious preferences. Indeed, not long after arriving as managing partner at New Lanark he toured the central and eastern Highlands as far as Sutherland, where on his father-in-law, David Dale's behalf, he inspected the most northerly outpost of the British cotton industry, a small mill at Spinningdale on the Dornoch Firth.[27] He and his companion, George Mackintosh, were duly entertained in some style by the authorities in Inverness, where they were honoured with civic freedoms.[28] Owen specifically mentions the many Gaelic speakers they encountered and it is just possible that he learned at least something of the language – and indeed communicated in it with the New Lanark workforce. These are aspects of his attitude and management skills which can be viewed from a very different perspective than that attributed to him by the majority of his contemporary critics. His Celtic origins, perhaps even his understanding of something of the Gaelic language, combined with a toleration of different cultures and wide-ranging religious views gained in his childhood, were to prove as alien to many Scottish Lowlanders, especially the ministers of the established Presbyterian kirk, as they were to his numerous and voluble English critics.

Robert's formal education began early, probably between four and five years of age. We cannot be certain exactly when this was for in his autobiography he claimed, quite understandably, to have no recollection of his first days at school and no records have survived which could confirm the date.[29] The school itself was in the apartments of the nearby Newtown Hall, then the property and residence of the local landowner, the eccentric and unfortunate Sir John Powell Pryce, who had lost his sight in an accident and was so plagued by debts, probably through mismanagement of his affairs, that he eventually died in penury.[30] Podmore later described Newtown Hall as 'a low, rambling, unpretentious building', but if he was not actually describing outbuildings where the school might well have been accommodated, the hall itself was, in fact, originally a fine Jacobean house of many gables and splendid carved panelling and timbers, which could claim a modest historical association, since Charles I had been hospitably entertained there for two days and nights after the battle of Naseby and on his way to Chester in 1645.[31] The master who was to take charge of his education was William Thickens, mistakenly, and perhaps jokingly, recalled by Owen many years later under the improbable name of Mr Thickness, possibly the master's nick-name.[32] Robert was nevertheless an enthusiastic scholar and typical of many high achievers was always anxious to be first in the school and first home. He and the other boys invariably had a race of about 300 yards from the school to the town and being a fast runner Robert was 'almost always the first at school in the morning ... and usually at home the first'. On one occasion, as he later related, his haste almost resulted in his early demise:

I used to have for breakfast a basin of flummery, a food prepared in Wales from flour, and eaten with milk, and which is usually given to children as the Scotch use oatmeal porridge. It is pleasant and nutritious, and is generally liked by young persons. I requested that this breakfast might be always ready when I returned from school, so that I might eat it speedily, in order to be the first back again at school. One morning, when about five years old, I ran home as usual from school, found my basin of flummery ready, and as I supposed sufficiently cooled for eating, for no heat appeared to rise from it. It had skimmed over as when quite cold; but on my hastily taking a spoonful of it, I found it was quite scalding hot, the body of it retaining all its heat. The consequence was an instant fainting, from the stomach being scalded. In that state I remained so long, that my parents thought life was extinct.

Fortunately Robert revived but the accident evidently left its mark both physically and psychologically. From then on he was able to digest only small quantities of food at any one time and this, he said, made him cautious about his 'changed constitution' and his diet. It gave him, he claimed, 'the habit of close observation and continual reflection'. 'I have always thought', he later wrote, 'that this accident had a great influence in forming my character'.[33] Certainly it was the first of several such incidents in his early life which may have indicated to observers but perhaps not to himself that his impetuosity made him, if not vulnerable, then at the very least accident prone. Another consequence of the scalding incident, he recalled, was that from that time onwards he had to watch his diet and 'notice the effects produced by different kinds of food' on his constitution. 'I could not eat and drink as others of my age, and was thus compelled to live in some respects the life of a hermit as regards temperance'.[34] This remark evidently relates to his diet as a boy and he says that he continued to be careful about what he ate in his youth. In later life Owen, though appalled by drunkenness, certainly took a drink, for, according to his own recollections and those of others including his eldest son, Robert Dale, sherry, wine and whisky, at least in modest quantities, were known to pass his lips on occasion.[35] He certainly kept a well-stocked wine cellar in his house at Braxfield near New Lanark. So as regards alcohol, as he was later to discover for himself during the journey to the Scottish Highlands, his constitution was certainly not permanently damaged by the accident of eating the hot flummery.[36]

Robert's education at the feet of Thickens embraced no more than the three 'Rs' for in small towns like Newtown 'it was considered a good education if one could read fluently, write a legible hand, and understand the first four rules of arithmetic'. This apparently presented him with few problems and, again by his own account, he had acquired 'these small rudiments of learning' by the age of seven. Thickens must have recognised his obvious talents because he approached his father offering the young Robert, then (so he says) about eight years of age, the post of 'assistant and usher' in return for a free education during the rest of his schooling.[37]

Quite what his role as assistant and usher to William Thickens involved is hard to determine, but Owen evidently had more responsibilities than simply filling ink wells or fetching and carrying writing slates or books. It probably resembled the post of monitor which was created in some early nineteenth-century schools modelling themselves on the ideas of educational reformers like the Scot, Dr Andrew Bell, the Quaker, Joseph Lancaster and others, and indeed later adopted by Owen himself in the school at New Lanark. The principle was that of the Factory System applied to education, whereby specially selected and generally clever senior pupils, passed on learning by rote to their juniors, and often in large numbers – what became known in France and on the Continent more generally as 'instruction mutuel'.[38] During the next two years Robert 'acquired the habit of teaching others what [he] knew' and this experience probably gave him early responsibilities for the care, supervision, and education of others, presumably, but not necessarily younger than himself.[39] It also gave him some knowledge, albeit limited at that age, of the elementary school curriculum, which would later prove very useful. At the very least he gained some first-hand experience of teaching and this might well have influenced his ideas about education in the way that his retail experience in Stamford, London and Manchester evidently affected his business strategy.[40]

While he later felt that his period as an assistant in the classroom at Newtown was lost to him in terms of further formal instruction, his literary, religious and social education was carried beyond the schoolroom by a variety of means. 'At this period', he says, 'I was fond of and had a strong passion for reading everything which fell in my way' and indeed in the community he was already regarded as a bookish and clever boy. This fact and his family's position in the community opened up to him the libraries of the learned in the town – the clergyman, doctor and lawyer – 'with permission to take home any volume' that he liked.[41] His reading matter, as a result, included many classics of the time, for as he tells us:

> Among the books I selected at this period were Robinson Crusoe, Philip Quarle, Pilgrim's Progress, Paradise Lost, Harvey's Medi-tations among the Tombs, Young's Night Thoughts, Richardson's, and all other standard novels . . . Then I read Cook's and all the circumnavigators' voyages, – the history of the world, – Rollin's ancient history, – all the lives I could meet with of the philosophers and great men.

He was deeply interested in all he read, generally finishing a volume every day. Not only this, he apparently took the maxims of these books to heart, which in the instances of both *The Pilgrim's Progress* and *Robinson Crusoe* was particularly significant in the longer term development of his attitudes in life – particularly regarding religion and enterprise. The former had a considerable impact on the religious susceptibilities of the boy; while the latter, so he claims, stayed in his memory for the rest of his life and he continued even as an adult to identify closely with its famous shipwrecked hero cast upon his desert island. *Robinson Crusoe*, of course, was more than just a romantic adventure of danger and triumph, likely to capture young Robert's imagination, for it was also a highly moral tale, with strong religious, environmental and economic messages. 'We do not read it', as, the literary scholar, Angus Ross, has observed, 'only in order to escape into an exciting world of danger and triumph. We read it rather in order to follow with meticulous interest and constant self-identification the hero's success in building up, step by step, out of whatever materials came to hand, a physical and moral replica of the world he had left behind him'.[42] New Lanark, the place Owen was later to make internationally famous, became, in a sense, his 'island', much like the one he had read about as a child many years before. There, like his hero, he used what came to hand, both in the physical environment and in what he himself later called the 'human capital'. Nor given Owen's first-hand experience of shopkeeping in the family business and those of its neighbours were Crusoe's financial and commercial dealings likely to have gone unnoted. One can understand that stories of exploration and history, like those of that great hero of the day, Captain Cook, would also prove attractive to an apparently thoughtful youngster like Robert, but whether or not the actual ideas of the Enlightenment, which underpinned many such works, had any impact on his thinking at that age is impossible to determine. They were certainly to be encountered, if randomly, in his subsequent publications.

While young Robert clearly loved reading it seems strange that in later life he exhibited to both his wife and children and to some of those who had reason to challenge the educational notions practised at New Lanark and articulated in his many writings, a strong disdain for books. Possibly this reflected an impatience over the time it actually took to read some of them, a trait common in busy people or other self-made and self-taught individuals, but by no means unique to them, or a fundamental disagreement with the subject matter if it did not accord directly with his own views. Owen was always intolerant of those who disagreed with him in print, though strangely the contrary was often the case in face-to-face meetings or even in the numerous public debates into which he found himself drawn in later life.

Of those in the town and district who lent Robert books from their libraries, the person he refers to as Parson Drake seems to have exercised considerable influence, perhaps strengthening for a while his Church of England parentage. The Revd. Samuel Drake, vicar of the neighbouring parish of Llanllwchaiarn from 1773, was the son of Dr Samuel Drake, Rector of Treeton, then a rural parish in south Yorkshire between Sheffield and Rotherham. Born in 1738 Drake was educated at Sedbergh and St John's College, Cambridge, before entering the church. He was a curate in Northamptonshire and Yorkshire before moving to Montgomeryshire.[43] Drake and his wife, Ann, had a young family, including three sons, about Robert's age; a fourth son dying in infancy about the time the young Robert set out from Newtown to earn his living in the wider world.[44] Drake seems to have befriended Robert and encouraged his literary education; while the boy's regular walks to Drake's vicarage took him along the splendid wooded banks of the Severn as it pursued its course downstream of his home, so further enhancing his knowledge of and enthusiasm for his natural surroundings. Drake clearly was himself something of an eccentric, but if Owen's story about him is anything to go on he must at least have been very sure of his position in the community, for his living came from the Bishop's patronage.

> He took me to church with him one Sunday after he had a difference
> with the squire of the parish, and to my surprise and the astonish-
> ment of the congregation he gave a most severe personal lecture
> to the squire during the sermon, – so personal and severe, that
> before its conclusion the squire, who was present with his family,
> became extremely uneasy in his very conspicuous pew, and at length
> prepared to leave it, when Mr Drake stopped, and looking towards
> him, said, 'don't be in a hurry, I shall have done soon and you had
> better sit quiet'.

'This scene', Owen recalled, 'made a deep impression on me, and never left my memory'.[45] Whether this showed him the effect of organised religion, particularly the self-discipline it engendered in the individual, is unclear, but again it certainly illustrated the power of rhetoric and persuasion which were to prove strong features of his own character in adult life.

Robert's attendance at church and his relationship with the Revd. Drake were not the only exposures to religion during his childhood, for when he was about eight or nine three Methodist ladies, near neighbours, though they cannot be identified, became friendly with the Owens and, presumably with parental approval, lent Robert some of their books and tracts to read. The first wave of Calvinistic Methodism hit Montgomeryshire in the 1740s but collapsed soon after 1751. However this sect began to take hold again from 1770 and entered a period of sustained growth, coinciding with Owen's boyhood.[46] According to Owen, the ladies, knowing him to be religiously inclined were anxious to convert him to what he called 'their peculiar faith'. He evidently studied 'with great attention' all the books and tracts they lent him but as he read he was at first surprised then became increasingly sceptical 'at the opposition between the different sects of Christians, afterwards at the deadly hatred between the Jews, Christians, Mahomedans [sic], Hindoos, Chinese &c., &c., and between these and what they call Pagans and Infidels. The study of these contending faiths, and their deadly hatred to each other, began to create doubts in my mind respecting the truth of any one of these divisions'.[47] Whether or not a boy of Robert's age could have been expected to absorb much of the various beliefs he mentioned is hard to credit, but at the very least he would have been puzzled by their diversity and role in social conflict.

While the Methodists, those 'diabolical seducers' to the mind of many a contemporary (at least in the Established Church), did not actually succeed in converting Robert he evidently went through a profoundly religious phase 'studying and thinking with great earnestness upon these subjects' – even composing three 'sermons' and earning the nick-name (whether only in the family or beyond its ranks, he does not record) of the 'Little Parson'. He kept these, so he said, until he read the works of Laurence Sterne (best known for his *Sentimental Journey*, published in 1768), probably *The Sermons of Mr Yorick*, where, much to his surprise he found three very like them 'in idea and turn of mind'. Thinking he might be accused of plagiarism he hastily threw them on the fire. This he later regretted because he thought on reflection that it would have been interesting to know 'how I then thought and expressed myself on such subjects'. Although this is an interesting and revealing incident, we have no way of knowing whether or not it actually occurred while he was still living at home in Newtown; he may well have ascribed it to his boyhood rather than some later period. Others certainly thought him religious; and many years later in 1826 a nephew, Robert Owen Davies, wrote to a newspaper to vindicate his uncle from the charges of atheism then current, noting that 'as a boy Robert Owen slept alone, because his elder brother (presumably John) was always beating him for saying his prayers upon his knees at the bedside: and afterwards when a youth he was very remarked for his strict attention to his religious duties'.[48]

Although apparently a serious and contemplative individual, young Robert also threw himself with enthusiasm into normal boyish pursuits like the games played by boys everywhere – marbles, hand ball and football. By his own account he was a good runner and claimed to be the best 'runner and leaper, both as to height and distance' in the school, even outpacing boys two or three years older. This enthusiasm for exercise may well have influenced him in his reforms at New Lanark, especially the emphasis on military drill for the boys in the school there. Other extra-curricular pursuits were also to have a longer-term influence, particularly dancing and music. He attended a local dancing school for a time and also attempted to learn music, playing the clarinet. He much enjoyed dancing, which despite his youth, afforded a pleasant opportunity to meet members of the opposite sex. Because he was the best dancer, or so he relates, he was never short of a partner, though he says he found the contest for partners among the girls both amusing and distressing. It caused him to reflect in later life that 'the mind and feelings of young children are seldom duly considered or attended to, and that if adults would patiently encourage them to express candidly what they thought and felt, much suffering would be saved to the children, and much useful knowledge of human nature would be gained by the adults'. 'I am now conscious', he added, 'that there was much real suffering in that dancing room, which had there been more knowledge of human nature in the dancing master and in the parents of the children, might have been avoided'. He continued to take lessons until he left Newtown. Practising in his father's back shop, his rendition on the clarinet of 'God Save the King' and other tunes could be heard up and down the street, but the good folk of Newtown were evidently forgiving since he was such a great favourite with everyone – too much so for his own good he later observed.[49] An enthusiasm for dancing and music was to stay with him throughout his youth and manhood and ultimately both came to play significant roles in his social philosophy and in the social life of both communities at New Lanark and New Harmony.[50]

For a summer when he was about eight or nine Robert associated with an older and better educated youth, James Donne, who had come to visit relatives in Newtown. Donne was from Radnorshire and was destined to follow in Drake's footsteps to St John's College in Cambridge with a view to entering the Church. He later graduated M.A. (1792), and entering teaching, subsequently became headmaster of Oswestry Grammar School in Shropshire, a post he held for 36 years.[51] He evidently maintained a correspondence with Owen perhaps dating back to 1817, but unfortunately only later correspondence has survived. Donne, then about sixteen, became Owen's 'every-day companion' on rambles 'about the woods and lanes and higher grounds to examine the scenery in all directions'. 'These excursions with a man of cultivated taste and superior conversation', Owen recalled, 'awakened in me a sense of pleasure which I ever afterwards experienced in observing nature in its every variety – a pleasure which as I advanced in years continued and increased'. Although he did not realise it at the time, the surroundings of Newtown undoubtedly instilled in someone who was to spend much of his life in urban contexts, notably in Manchester, Glasgow, and London, an enduring love of the natural environment and the countryside. When Owen came to articulate his views about education it is not surprising that the influence of environment on human character and the study of the natural world figured so prominently.

His cousin, Richard Williams, though a year younger, was another companion whom Robert regarded highly and as someone else to be emulated. He met him regularly during the school holidays, when visits were paid to three families of his mother's relations – two aunts and an uncle – all farmers in the Newtown neighbourhood. Richard senior had prospered, moving from Vaynor, one and half miles south west of Newtown, to a larger farm at Old Hall, near the present day hamlet of Sarn in Kerry Parish. The Williamses were considered 'a superior family of their class' and Owen thought his aunt 'one of the best of women I ever saw in her rank of life'. 'Everyone who knew her, loved her', he recalled, 'and every one liked to enjoy the hospitality of the family, which was well known over the country to a considerable distance.' One of Owen's earliest recollections of his grandfather was seeing him sitting by the fireside at his cousin's house. Robert and Richard were always great friends, 'much attached to each other and delighted to be together'. His cousin Richard, he later recalled, 'had the finest qualities I have ever seen in any youth' and the advantages of something he possibly envied, 'a superior education at a distant boarding school'. Although a year younger, he was superior 'in almost everything, for in whatever he attempted he far excelled all of his age'. Moreover Richard seemed to be 'unconscious of his own extraordinary powers'. Owen tells of how, in company with Richard, he learned more of the virtues of hard work, when:

> One very hot day in hay harvest-time we felt ourselves, being over-clothed, quite overcome with heat while we sauntered from the house towards a large field where numerous hay-makers were actively at work. They appeared to us, who had been doing nothing and yet were overcome with heat, to be cool and comfortable. I said, 'Richard! how is this? These active workpeople are not heated, but are pleasantly cool, and do not suffer as we do from the heat. There must be some secret in this. Let us try to find out. Let us do exactly as they do, and work with them'. He willingly agreed. We observed that all the men were without their coats and waistcoats and had their shirts open. We adopted the same practice.

Fetching rakes and forks, Robert and Richard, having taken off their heavy clothing 'led the field for several hours' and were 'cooler and less fatigued' than when they were 'idle and wasting [their] time'. 'This became ever afterwards', Owen remembered, 'a good *experience* and *lesson* to both; for we found ourselves much more comfortable with active employment than when we were idle.'[52] While this experience convinced Robert that work had greater merit than idleness, he was certainly to remember his friendship with Richard in later life and ultimately to give his cousin's name to one of his sons.

Members of shopkeeping families invariably worked together to reduce expenses and the Owens were no exception. Robert, from an early age, helped his father in the shop as well as running errands and it was on one such errand that he again almost came to grief. He had been sent to fetch his father's favourite cream coloured mare from her pasture on the other side of the Severn which was then reached by a narrow wooden bridge. He takes up the story thus:

> When returning from the field mounted on this mare, I was passing homeward over the bridge, but before I was half over, a wagon had made some progress from the opposite side. There was not room for me to pass without my legs coming in contact with the wheels of this wagon or with the rails of the bridge. I had not sense enough to turn back, and endeavoured to pass the wagon. I soon found that my leg was in danger of being grazed by the wheels, and I threw it over the saddle , and in consequence I fell on the opposite side, but in falling I was so alarmed lest I should drop into the river or should strike against the bridge, that I lost all recollection. How I escaped I know not; but on recovering I found myself on the footpath of the bridge, the mare standing quietly near me, and the wagon had fairly passed, and I was unhurt.

This incident, so he says, left him with a special liking for cream coloured horses.[53]

When Robert was older he also helped at a neighbouring shop belonging to two maiden ladies, the Misses Tilsley, who kept 'a superior country shop for the sale of drapery and haberdashery'. When one of the ladies married John Moore, another shopkeeper, grocer and mercer, the business was expanded to embrace wholesale as well as retail. Owen was initially 'borrowed' to help out on busy market and fair days and then more permanently when Moore asked his father for Robert 'to be with them every day of the week'. He seems to have embraced this opportunity with enthusiasm since by that time he had spent two years as an usher 'learning nothing but how to teach'.

In his old age he vividly recalled another accident which befell – on this occasion – a school friend, John Stanley, a boy about his own age whose father kept a grocer's shop in the town. John's father had run out of molasses, 'an article then much in demand', and John was sent to Moore's with a tub to purchase as much as it would hold. The molasses was kept in a cellar under the shop which was reached by a trap-door and steps. Young Stanley, Owen relates, had filled his tub to the top and on coming up the steps knocked one of the handles against the edge of the trap door. Inevitably the tub tipped and its contents ran over hair which happened to be specially thick. 'The molasses', says Owen, 'ran down over the whole of his clothes and person, making him one of the most laughable and at the same time pitiable figures that the imagination could paint'. What sort of reception poor Stanley got at home beggars description, but, wrote Owen, 'the disaster was always remembered to his annoyance by our neighbours as long as I remained in Newtown'.[54]

His work in his father's and neighbour's shops undoubtedly gave Robert basic retail experience, and coincidentally, some knowledge of the different qualities and prices of various goods, significantly relative to his later career, in drapery and haberdashery. He might also have gained some appreciation of simple accounts, which would not have been difficult if, as he claims, he had mastered the basic elements of arithmetic to such a level that he could teach them to others. Moreover, and perhaps of greater importance in the short to medium term, the social mix in Newtown in and out of the shop gave the young Robert a confidence in dealing with customers, especially those above him on the social scale – limited though this inevitably was in a place like Newtown. Learning how to deal with his betters, like Sir John Powell Pryce, who apparently called regularly to speak to his father, was especially important.

Incidentally, Sir John's misfortune in losing his sight, falling into debt 'by want of prudence', and ending his life in the melancholy surroundings of the King's Bench Prison, was to become universal knowledge through-out the town and district – a real-life moral tale about the fate of someone who both abused his advantages in life and squandered his means. Also useful to Robert was an awareness of how his parents and others of their rank handled their equals and those further down the social ladder of the town and district. Contrary to what we might expect, he later claimed an innate shyness in his dealings with his betters, and indeed, the opposite sex, that does not reconcile easily with the apparent confidence of his childhood and early youth, far less his adult life.[55]

There are other aspects of the Owen family's situation which probably influenced him. As church warden and later as post-master his father was called upon to undertake a wide range of local administrative duties. These involved basic clerical work, such as sorting letters and papers, form filling, attention to detailed record keeping and dealing with small sums of money. Quite likely Robert assisted his father on occasion. At the social rather than the practical level because of his father's position he and his family were well known in the town and neighbourhood. Owen himself recalled the advantages this gave him personally, for in the modest circles in which he moved in and around Newtown he was apparently well known and well liked both by his peers and their seniors. This, of course, could have been a reflection of his personality, rather than his social position.

Only once in his childhood, when he was about seven, could Owen remember being punished, for in his memoirs he claims he was an obedient boy. The incident arose from a misunderstanding with his mother, who asked him rather indistinctly to do something for her.

Robert thought the answer should be 'no' and said so, 'supposing [he] was meeting her wishes'. When she spoke more sharply Robert again said 'no', 'but without any idea of disobeying her' and thinking that he would be lying if he changed his response to 'yes'. His mother then spoke more angrily for he had never before disobeyed her and was very surprised and annoyed when he repeated that he would not do as he had been told. His father was then summoned to punish him and he soon felt the whip every time he refused to do what his mother asked, till eventually he said quietly but firmly, 'You may kill me, but I will not do it', and this, he claimed, 'decided the contest'. After this incident, so he recalls, he soon made up with his parents and 'continued the favorite I had always been'. If we are to believe this and other assertions, Robert seems to have been precocious but nevertheless well liked both by family and friends.

How far contemporary events in the world beyond Newtown, then still one of the most rural places in southern Britain, impinged on Owen's consciousness at this young age is hard to gauge. There was certainly plenty going on in the world beyond Newtown during the 1770s and early '80s. The year 1775 alone saw two events which in different ways were greatly to influence Robert's life: closest to home at Matthew Boulton's Birmingham works James Watt perfected his most significant improvements to the steam engine, making possible, among other applications, its use in textile mills; while on the other side of the Atlantic, which Owen was to cross many times in later life, the opening shots were fired in the War of American Independence, leading to the defeat of the British at Lexington and Concord, followed rapidly by the meeting of the Second Continental Congress in Philadelphia and the appointment of George Washington as Commander in Chief of the American forces. Apart from conversation or gossip with customers, newspapers would be the most obvious medium likely to keep the Owens in touch with the outside world, but we do not know whether they were ever to be found in the household. Given Owen senior's position it seems quite likely, and Owen himself later became an avid newspaper reader, mainly, it seems, because he was too busy to read books.[56]

On the economic front the effects of industrialisation in the West Midlands, Shropshire and Lancashire were felt primarily in enhanced demand for agricultural produce, but despite improvements in the turnpike roads leading to Oswestry and Shrewsbury, transport remained something of a problem until eased by the cutting of the Montgomery Canal after 1794, though it did not reach Newtown itself until many years later. While Newtown benefited from its status as a small but rapidly growing market centre, it clearly did not offer diverse enough economic opportunities for all its inhabitants, for if the Owen family can be taken as typical, three of the sons, including Robert, were forced to migrate and seek their livelihoods elsewhere. It could be that their parents and they themselves realised the limitations of the place, and certainly by this time migration, even over quite long distances, had become a familiar feature of life in many rural districts, particularly those adjacent to larger and rapidly expanding urban industrial centres. Robert's departure from his native town was preceded by that of his eldest brother William, who had made his way to London, and probably also by that of John, his other elder brother, who also went to England but eventually emigrated across the Atlantic and settled in Canada.[57] Certainly by the time Robert himself left Newtown, when he was probably about ten or eleven, he could be seen to have had a practical and by no means uneducated upbringing, laced with limited but nevertheless potentially useful social skills, which would open doors to employment in the wider world of commerce and industry. He would carry in his baggage memories of a Welsh childhood spent among a hard-working, religious-minded, shopkeeping family, and of life in an enviable rural environment to which in his subconscious he would always long to return.

## NOTES

1. I am most grateful to Dr W.T.R. Pryce, The Open University in Wales and to John H. Davidson of the Robert Owen Memorial Museum for comments on a draft of this chapter and for helpful references which had escaped my attention.
2. F. Podmore, *Robert Owen* London, 1906, vol. 1, pp. 1–14.; G.D.H. Cole, *Life of Robert Owen* London, 1925, 3rd ed. 1965, pp. 36–45; M. Cole, *Robert Owen of New Lanark*, London, 1953, pp. 4–11.
3. J.F.C. Harrison, *Robert Owen and the Owenites in Britain and North America* London, 1969; J. Butt (ed.) *Robert Owen. Prince of Cotton Spinners* Newton Abbot, 1971; S. Pollard and J. Salt, *Robert Owen. Prophet of the Poor*, London, 1971.
4. Anne Taylor, *Visions of Harmony. A Study in Nineteenth Century Millenarianism*, Oxford, 1987, pp. 54–55.
5. R. Owen, *The Life of Robert Owen Written By Himself*, London, 1857. The reprint of 1971 with an introduction by J. Butt is referred to here. It retains the original pagination.
6. G. Claeys (ed.) *Selected Works of Robert Owen vol 4. The Life of Robert Owen*, London, 1993.
7. A detailed inventory of holdings, archives and memorabilia, can be inspected at the Robert Owen Memorial Museum.
8. The watercolour of Robert Owen's birthroom (Item 2) is displayed in the museum. Podmore (opp. p. 22) reproduces a photograph of the birthplace, adjoining the house in which he died on 11 November 1858.
9. Owen senior's age at his death on 14 March 1804 is given as 65 on his tombstone. Other authorities claim he was younger. Claeys gives 1741 in a footnote to *Life*, p. 51.

10. R. Owen, 'Welshpool Landmarks', *Montgomeryshire Collections*, 38, 1918, pp. 153–184.
11. Owen claims that the 'estate' to which his father alluded was worth £500 per annum. *Life*, p. 1.
12. Claeys in footnote, p. 51.
13. *Life*, p. 1.
14. Podmore, p. 2.
15. For further details see Claeys, footnote, p. 52.
16. Owen kept in touch with his sister, Anne (1765–1844), after the death of his parents. She married first Thomas Davies and second Joseph Weaver. Owen apparently passed remittances to her via Dr James Donne, his childhood companion.
17. Robert Owen Memorial Museum, item 3/2, copy of parish register.
18. *Life*, p. 2. Owen's estimate of the population at the time of his upbringing was reasonably accurate. By 1801 the population of Newtown and Llanllwchaiarn together was 1665. See Lyn Williams, 'A Case Study of Newtown, Montgomeryshire: The Socio-Economic Structure of a Small Industrial Town in the Mid-Nineteenth Century', *Montgomeryshire Collections*, 64, 1976.
19. For the context and background see J.G. Jenkins, *The Welsh Woollen Industry*, Cardiff, 1969, pp. 116–69, especially pp. 127 *et seq* gives a very good treatment of Newtown as an emerging industrial centre.
20. J.G. Jenkins, 'Newtown and the Woollen Industry', *Journal of Industrial Archaeology*, Vol 2 No 1,1964, pp. 26–32; M. Richards, *An Outline of the Newtown Woollen Industry* London, 1971.
21. See, for example, his references in *Life*, pp. 14, 18, 39, 73–4, etc.
22. *Life*, p. 31, where he says the language spoken in Newtown was 'an imperfect mixture' of Welsh and English.
23. For a definitive view of the bilingual-English divide at this period see W.T.R. Pryce, 'Welsh and English in Wales, 1750–1971: A Spatial Analysis Based on the Linguistic Affiliation of Parochial Communities', *The Bulletin of the Board of Celtic Studies*, vol. XXVIII, 1978, pp. 1–33.
24. M.Clement, *Correspondence and Minutes of the SPCK relating to Wales,* Cardiff, 1952, extract 10800, 3 June 1730. I am grateful to Dr. T.M. Humphreys for drawing this to my attention.
25. Quoted in W.T.R. Pryce, 'Wales as a Culture Region: Patterns of Change 1750–1971', *Transactions of the Honourable Society of Cymmrodorion*, 1978, pp. 229–261.
26. Pryce, *op. cit.*, 'Welsh and English', p. 11–13.
27. The visit to the Highlands is described in *Life*, pp. 72–76.
28. Highland Council Archive, Burgh of Inverness, Treasurer's Accounts 1797–1822, 'Entertainments for the Honor and Interest of the Burgh', 1801–2.
29. *Life*, p. 2.
30. On Pryce see R. Williams, 'Montgomeryshire Worthies', *Montgomeryshire Collections*, 16, 1883, pp. 35–70; and his 'An Episode in the History of Newtown', *Montgomeryshire Collections*, 23, 1889, pp. 315–320.
31. Podmore, *Robert Owen*, pp. 4–5.
32. Claeys, footnote in *Life*, p. 52.
33. *Life*, p. 3.
34. ibid, p. 4, a point he reiterates on p. 22.

35. R.D. Owen, *Threading My Way. Twenty-Seven Years of Autobiography*, London, 1874, p. 69.
36. *Life*, p. 74.
37. Ibid, p. 3.
38. For a recent discussion of the rival monitorial systems see R. D. Anderson, *Education and the Scottish People 1750–1918*, Oxford, 1995, pp. 35–36, 144–46. On the system adopted at New Lanark, I. Donnachie and G. Hewitt, *Historic New Lanark. The Dale and Owen Industrial Community since 1785*, Edinburgh, 1993, pp. 96–107, 116–117.
39. *Life*, pp. 3 and 9.
40. On the development of his educational ideas see M. Browning, 'Owen as an Educator', in Butt, pp. 52–75; H. Silver, 'Owen's Reputation as an Educationist', in Pollard and Salt, pp. 65–83; and more recently, D.J. Mclaren, 'Robert Owen, William Maclure and New Harmony', *History of Education*, 25, 1996, pp. 223–233.
41. *Life*, p. 3.
42. A. Ross in introduction to *The Life and Adventures of Robinson Crusoe*, Harmondsworth, 1985, p. 7.
43. *Alumni Cantabrigienses Part II 1752–1900*, Vol II, Cambridge, 1944, p. 335.
44. See memorial to Drake and family in Llanllwchaiarn church.
45. *Life*, p. 5.
46. Details of the progress of this movement and earlier forms of Dissent in the area are given in M. Humphreys, *the Crisis of Community: Montgomeryshire, 1680–1815* Cardiff, 1996. See also I.G. Jones 'Patterns of Religious Worship in Montgomeryshire in the Mid-Nineteenth Century', *Montgomeryshire Collections*, vol. 68, 1980, pp 93–118.
47. *Life*, pp. 3–4.
48. *St James's Chronicle*, Dec. 1826, quoted in Podmore, p. 8.
49. *Life*, pp. 9–10.
50. C.K. Sluder and R.S. Hahn, 'A Survey of Musical Activities in New Lanark Under Robert Owen's Management', paper presented at Utopian Thought and Communal Experience Conference, New Lanark, 1988; Donnachie and Hewitt, pp. 106–107.
51. *Alumni Cantabrigienses*, p. 319.
52. *Life*, pp. 6–7.
53. Ibid, p. 8.
54. Ibid, p. 9.
55. See, for example, *Life*, pp. 31 and 38 describing how uncomfortable he felt with strangers and speaking in public.
56. R.D. Owen, *Threading My Way*, p. 67.
57. *Life*, p. 11.

# TWO

# Shop Assistant

In the industrialised world modern attitudes to children working are bound up with perceptions of both child labour and the drive towards compulsory education. In the last quarter of the eighteenth century industrialisation was beginning to impose new patterns of life and labour both on individuals and on families who had often worked together on farms, in small workshops, or in shop-keeping. Child labour was taken for granted, an accepted and acceptable aspect of life – as it remains today throughout much of the developing world. The Factory System brought with it more rigorously enforced time discipline, while economic necessity, both in nuclear and one-parent families, formalised child labour, for the more hands a family could deploy the greater its income.[1] Education was not much of a priority and the opportunities for the majority of the labouring class, in any case, were generally very limited, and only marginally better for trades folk like the Owens. Robert's family might have been exceptional, for both his mother and father were probably better educated than others of their class. His mother, in his own view, was certainly 'superior', and his father's various official positions suggest someone who was more than simply literate and numerate. His parents, and possibly his brothers, especially William, did much to encourage Robert's education, though their means did not stretch far enough to take him beyond the elementary stage offered in Newtown.

While this was an era when children began work or were apprenticed very early in life, it was also a time when migration in search of better job opportunities, as we saw, had become much more significant than before, particularly from the countryside to the town and from the town to the city. Robert's various step-wise moves in search of employment and advancement at such a young age were certainly not unusual. He had wanted to leave when he was about nine-and-a-half, for, as he recalled, 'having by this period read much of other countries and other proceedings, and, with my habits of reflection and extreme temperance, not liking the habits and manners of a small country town', he 'began to desire a different field of action' and asked his parents if he could go to London, presumably to join his brother. He was not allowed to do so on the grounds of age, but Robert, if his memory so late in life is taken at face value, managed to persuade his parents to let him leave home when he was ten.[2] It seems unlikely that they would have agreed to letting someone so young leave home had not his older brother, William, been willing to take him in and make arrangements to find him an apprenticeship. Meantime Robert pursued his job as a shop assistant – as well as continuing with his reading and taking dancing lessons. If we are to believe what he says in his memoirs his parents valued his judgement for they used to consult him 'when any matter of importance was to be decided'. He claims that he did not know why they asked his opinion and was not aware that he could give any useful advice.

In the traditional fairy tale, the younger son has to go out into the world and seek his fortune, inevitably breaking with home and family. He is usually given something, often by an outside agency, to help him on his way. And so it was with Robert. Before he left Newtown he called on everyone he knew to say goodbye. As was customary he was given keepsakes, and, from the more wealthy, money to tide him over till he found employment. So, with the stage-coach fare already paid for him and with forty shillings in his pocket, he felt he was 'amply provided to seek [his] fortune'.[3] His father took him to Welshpool, and from there he caught a coach to Shrewsbury, then the nearest place to Newtown with a direct connection to London. He was to take the night coach and Robert's father had arranged with the proprietor that he should travel as an inside passenger. Unluckily for him 'some ill-tempered man' discovered that Robert's father had only paid for an outside place and refused to allow him to travel inside. 'It was dark, and I could not see the objector, nor discover how crowded the coach might be', he recalled, 'for coaches then carried six inside'. He never found out who the man was and could not be angry with him, as he felt he should have been 'for refusing admission to a child'. 'I then had not fully learned the principles of the formation of character, and the influences of circumstances over all that have life, or I should not have been angry or surprised at such conduct', he later observed. Thus he travelled to the metropolis,'a journey which in the then state of the roads was thought formidable for grown persons', far less a ten-year-old. But Robert soon became a seasoned traveller, and in later life travel seemed almost to become an obsession.

He arrived safely in London and was warmly welcomed by his brother, who had evidently always had a soft spot for him, and this seems also to have been so of his sister-in-law. William Owen had done well for himself. After working with his father, he had decided to go to London, and taken a job with another saddler, a Mr Reynolds, who ran his business from premises at 84 High Holborn. In the interim Reynolds had died and William had not only taken over the business, but had also made a fortuitous marriage with the widow. Possibly the intention was that William would make arrangements for his brother, but as events transpired it was Robert's father and the neighbour, Moore, who used their connections to secure an opening for the boy. Robert's father had written to a friend, Robert Heptinstall, who was a partner in a haberdashery business at 6 Ludgate Hill, and subsequently became a cotton master in Nottingham; while Moore had corresponded with William Tilsley, a relative of his wife, who kept a large drapery in Newgate Street.[4] Heptinstall may have agreed to take Robert into his own business, but having no immediate vacancies, apparently wasted little time in securing an apprenticeship elsewhere. Within six weeks of arriving at his brother's Heptinstall had arranged a situation for Robert with James McGuffog, a successful and prosperous retail linen and woollen draper in Stamford, Lincolnshire. He was promised employment for three years, the first without pay, the second with a salary of eight pounds, and the third with ten pounds, 'with board, lodging, and washing in the house'. Since he was 'well found with clothes to last more than a year' he felt this was a good opportunity: from then on, or so he tells us, he maintained himself without asking his family for any further financial assistance. It seems a reasonable enough claim for in this and subsequent apprenticeships in London and Manchester he had his modest, though gradually increasing salary, and, as was quite common in the circumstances, 'all found' in both lodging and meals.[5]

By any standard Stamford was an excellent choice for a business selling female garments to the well-to-do. One of the finest mediaeval towns in Europe, it became socially desirable in the eighteenth century due to the large number of country houses in its vicinity and its proximity to the Great North Road, giving ready access to the metropolis. Indeed Stamford was a notable staging post for the coaches – both south and north bound – that day and night brought travellers seeking refreshment and accommodation at its numerous inns and hotels. The George Hotel, one of the original coaching inns, still boasts two rooms, labelled 'London' and 'York', which were waiting rooms for stagecoach passengers. Stamford also owed its continuing prosperity to its function as an important market town at the centre of a prosperous agricultural district embracing parts of Lincolnshire, Leicestershire, Rutland, Northamptonshire and Huntingdon. Much of the surrounding area had been in the vanguard of agricultural improvement, which together with rising rents, had greatly increased the fortunes of local gentry, farmers and merchants. This wealth was reflected not only in the many fine estates and country seats to be found in the neighbourhood, but also in the outstanding quality of some of Stamford's eighteenth-century public buildings, including a splendid town hall and a theatre. Much systematic rebuilding was undertaken by the ninth Earl of Exeter, who, as it happened, Robert was to see frequently walking in the grounds of nearby Burghley Park. The growing prosperity of the merchants and professional men also resulted in many fine houses being built. The town continued to grow apace and by the early 1780s probably had a population of over 4,000. It was certainly a place where any enterprising shopkeeper selling goods of quality could reasonably expect to enjoy an expanding market and do well for himself.[6]

Arriving in Stamford, Robert found that McGuffog did indeed have a 'large business for a provincial town' and that the house where he was to become a lodger was very respectable and comfortable. Robert soon realised that here he had made a fortunate start in life. McGuffog, a Scot, born in 1747, was in every sense a self-made man, who told Robert he had begun his business with half-a-crown in his pocket and 'laid it out in the purchase of some things for sale, and hawked them in a basket'. He gradually built up his trade, changing his basket for a pack, building up his stock until he was able to do his rounds on a horse and then with a horse and covered van. Whether or not McGuffog began in Scotland and then moved south to Lincolnshire is unclear but when Owen picked up the story his employer was making 'regular rounds among customers of the first respectability' in the county and surrounding districts selling the 'best and finest articles of female wear' and in the process building up a profitable business. His goods were in such demand that he was prevailed upon by his customers, who included the local gentry and farmers, to open a shop in Stamford and this had proved such a success that by the time Robert arrived on the scene as an assistant McGuffog was 'so independent that he made all his purchases with ready money and was becoming wealthy'. Robert found McGuffog 'thoroughly honest, a good man of business, very methodical, kind and liberal, and much respected by his neighbours and customers'. He was noted for his good sense, particularly by those from whom he obtained his supplies of linen and haberdashery. Like Robert's brother, William, McGuffog had made a good marriage to Mary, the daughter of a 'well-doing middle class person', and both were industrious 'always attending to their business, yet respectable at all times in their persons, and altogether superior as respectable trades people, being quite the aristocracy of that class, without its usual weak vanities'. According to Robert's recollections, McGuffog, 'much respected for his honesty and plain dealing', also acted as a sort of 'country banker', extending credit and perhaps even making small loans to the local aristocracy, including Sir William Lowther, later Earl of Lonsdale. There were, it seems, some quite striking parallels in the business and private lives of both McGuffog and another Scot who was to have an even greater influence on Robert's career, the more successful and celebrated textile entrepreneur, turned banker, David Dale, who eighteen years later was to become his father-in-law.[7]

Despite their obvious prosperity, McGuffog and his wife remained closely involved in the family business. Robert was soon initiated into the routine, being encouraged to pay great attention to detail and to become accustomed to 'great order and accuracy' in his work. Indeed, McGuffog ran the shop with 'system and good order', and there was never any evidence of confusion even when the place was busy. The rule of the house was 'never to bring on the counter a second article until the first was returned and neatly put in its proper place'. When the customers had left there was little to do 'for everything was in order'.[8] McGuffog was a judicious buyer and his stock was the best that money could buy, the 'finest and most choice qualities that could be procured from all the markets of the world'. He made regular trips to London to procure the finest Irish linen, then the most expensive that could be had. He also bought from Samuel Oldknow, the Stockport cotton spinner, who in 1781 pioneered the manufacture of British muslins, which gradually came to match the quality of those imported from the East Indies. Indeed so good was Oldknow's muslin that McGuffog 'could not obtain a supply equal to his demand'. The results spoke for themselves as McGuffog's shop had rapidly become a 'kind of general rendezvous of the higher class nobility' and often six or seven carriages waited for their wealthy owners by the kerbside. Always a great name-dropper, Owen could not resist listing in his autobiography the noble families he maintained he had once served: among others, the Burghleys, Westmorelands, Lowthers, Ancasters, Broughtons, Noels and by an interesting quirk of fate, the Trollopes, one of whom, the famous Mrs Frances Trollope, he was to meet in later life during his stay in the United States and who wrote about him in her widely acclaimed (and heavily criticised) book on the *Domestic Manners of the Americans*. In all of this there were some important lessons for Robert about business efficiency (which could also be readily applied to personnel management), greater familiarity with the quality and price of the finest fabrics, and as far as social skills mattered to someone of his age, enhanced opportunities for observing the manners and conduct of the middle class and gentry and overhearing their conversation, whether discussing matters of moment or engaging in mere tittle-tattle.[9]

Apart from the tact and efficiency with which James McGuffog evidently ran his business catering for the well-to-do, Robert was able to observe another side of his master's character, his honesty. He would settle for a reasonable profit, recalled Owen, and never take advantage of anyone. An example of what Owen afterwards described as 'stubborn honesty' greatly amused him but also made a big impression on him and apparently taught him something he had previously not realised about the 'waywardness' of human nature:

> One of the rich Lincolnshire families – and many of them were wealthy at this period died – and left his widow and family more wealth than they knew how advantageously to spend. The widow was desirous of buying a piece of the finest Irish linen for chemises that he had for sale. Mr McGuffog brought her one of the finest pieces that he had purchased, and the finest that could then be made by any manufacturer. The price was eight shillings the yard, allowing

him his usual moderate profit. The lady looked and looked again at
this fabric, and said, 'Have you no finer than this piece, which is not
fine enough for my purpose?' Mr McGuffog was much surprised at
this speech, for he knew it was fine enough to satisfy the wants of
the first duchess in the land.

McGuffog, 'with his usual knowledge of character', said that he thought
he had a finer piece in his upper warehouse, went upstairs, and returned
with an identical piece of cloth to the one he had already shown the
customer, saying, 'I have found one, but the price is ten shillings per
yard, and is perhaps higher than you would wish to give'. The customer
examined the piece of cloth and said this was the very thing she was
looking for and that the price was perfectly acceptable. McGuffog, as
Owen put it, 'smiled within himself', knowing that the cloth was being
valued by its price and 'not for its intrinsic worth'. However, Owen
observed, McGuffog 'would never take advantage of the ignorance or
want of experience in rich or poor' and charged her only eight shillings,
saying he would not charge her more, because 'at that price it afforded him
a fair profit'. Lessons about fair dealing, honesty and character could be
learned from this incident, certainly, but since the customer never returned
it might have been in McGuffog's best interests in the long run to have
charged what she was prepared to pay.[10]
As was sometimes the case with apprentices or assistants in trade
lucky enough to have found congenial employers, Robert felt he was
part of an extended family. One of the assistants, a boy about Robert's
age, was McGuffog's nephew; the other, David Sloane, a bachelor in his
mid thirties, who also lived in, had been employed by Mcguffog for some
years. Robert felt that he was treated more like the McGuffog's own child
rather than as 'a stranger come from afar'. If, as was apparently the case,
the McGuffogs had no family of their own, the affection in which both
their nephew and Robert himself were held is perfectly understandable,
and it was something he remembered with gratitude for the rest of his life.
Later, in the second year of his apprenticeship at Stamford, other relatives
of Mary McGuffog, a sister of nineteen and a niece (presumably daughter
of another sister who had perhaps died) about Robert's own age, arrived
to swell the household. 'Our pleasure was increased', he recalled, 'for
there was a mutual good feeling among all the members of the family'.
The niece, in particular, seems to have been greatly attracted to Robert, or
so at least (he says) she told him when they met many years later, causing
him to speculate that had he stayed with the McGuffogs he might have
become a member of the family and inherited the business. Certainly, the
situation in which he found himself might have been some recompense
for the separation from his own family, which he certainly missed.
According to his autobiography in all the time he spent in Stamford

he never met anyone he had previously known, but he remembered a telling incident, when:

> One day as I was passing the George Inn, the principal hotel in the place, I saw a person at the entrance talking to a gentleman, and who was so like my father, that I concluded it must be he, and while the conversation continued I walked past them and returned several times, being more and more convinced it must be my father. At length the conversation terminated, and I then came very near to my supposed father, so as to catch his eye and draw his attention to me, but there was no sign of recognition on his part.

While the resemblance was quite striking, Robert realised his mistake and was greatly disappointed to find that the man was not his father after all. Taken at face value his account of this incident, like others before and after, as well as his many positive comments about his relations in general, tend to confirm the continuing importance of family ties to the young exile. It also raises interesting questions about his subsequent family life and his attitude towards his parents, his wife and her relations and indeed his own children.[11]

In his autobiography Owen recalled another incident which may have taught him something else about himself and perhaps about human character in general. The principal actor was Sloane, who despite the apparent congeniality of working at McGuffog's was 'least satisfied with himself and others' and, Owen remembered, 'seemed jealous of the general kindness shown to me by all members of the family'. Another thing that evidently upset Sloane was that customers preferred to be served by Robert rather than by him. But although Sloane's jealousy might have been obvious to Robert, it was his 'penurious habits' that made him the object of more general derision. Sloane slept in a room adjoining the wholesale department, and when it was full some of the stock was kept in his room. On this occasion some high quality and expensive items were left on a table in the room. Sloane looked after his clothes carefully, and having just bought a pair of new breeches put them on the table before going to bed. As he put out the candle before falling asleep sparks or snuffing seem to have fallen on the clothes and as Sloane slept some of them, including the breeches, were burned. The smell of the fire woke the McGuffogs, who immediately raised the alarm, and everyone 'hastily arose in their night clothes'. The smoke was found coming from Sloane's room, he was quickly wakened and the fire put out. 'When the danger was over', recalled Owen, 'all parties began to look at each other, but David was the conspicuous figure'. He stood by the table in his night shirt and coloured cap, 'looking most woefully', and picking up some buttons and the charred remains of his clothes exclaimed, 'Oh my new breeches! Oh my new breeches!', apparently regardless either of the danger he had caused or the consequent loss to McGuffog. Nothing else could be got from Sloane, so, says Owen, 'the scene became so farcical and ludicrous that no one could avoid laughing at him, and he was left, looking most miserable, to his own reflections until the morning'. It was a scene that was never forgotten, especially by poor Sloane, who became a recurrent victim of jokes made about himself and his breeches.[12]

Robert worked from ten in the morning till four in the afternoon, which by the standards of the time and of most factory work in the early stages of mass production, a twelve hour day or more being the norm, seems relatively congenial. He spent much of his leisure time reading and for the duration of his stay in Stamford claimed to have read for an average of five hours a day. This assertion may be true but needs to be treated with some caution for again is somewhat at odds with his apparent lack of interest in books in later life. McGuffog certainly had a 'well selected' library where Robert could browse and which he could freely use, carrying off selected volumes either to his room or to Burghley Park, where he was apparently free to 'walk, read, think, and study, in those noble avenues which were then numerous in it'.[13] Although we do not know for certain whether the public was permitted to roam at large in the grounds of Burghley, or at least those close to the town, it seems unlikely. Nevertheless Robert tells us that during the summer when the weather permitted he was often in the park in the early morning and again in the evening until it was nearly dark. He said that he transcribed some of Seneca's moral precepts into a pocket book and though it might seem unusual for a teenager, pondering over them in the park was apparently one of his favourite pastimes. The work to which he refers was almost certainly the *Select Epistles on Several Moral Subjects*, published in 1739. Like other Stoics, Seneca taught that wisdom held the key to goodness, and that true virtue was possible only by rising above pain, pleasure, fear and desire. In particular his advocacy of benevolence to all may well have had some influence on Owen's longer-term views.[14] Robert made the park his study and read (although unspecified) 'many volumes of the most useful works' he could lay his hands on. He says he regularly saw the Earl of Exeter, who had so influenced Stamford's regeneration, taking his morning walk, though whether he actually made his acquaintance he does not say. He was greatly struck by the earl's habits, for, as Robert observed, he was always up and about as soon as he woke, and stuck rigidly to his daily routine, evidently dining punctually at three o'clock in the afternoon each day without waiting for other members of the household or guests who might have been late. This behaviour, which was presumably common knowledge in the community and the subject of gossip, might strike us as eccentric, but whether it seemed so at the time to Robert we cannot tell. Certainly, if he is to believed, Robert's own regime was unusual for a boy of his age – for he frequently 'hailed the rising sun, and in the evening watched its setting and the rising of the moon'. The 'happy healthy hours' spent in the park were, he recalled, beneficial to both body and mind, and probably set a pattern which he was to follow for the rest of his life.[15] If we take what he says at face value his love of the countryside and the natural environment, embedded in his mind during childhood in rural mid-Wales, was thus further re-inforced by the splendid surroundings of Stamford.

Altogether more complex is the question about what influence, if any, religion played in shaping his views at this time. Because the McGuffog's were regular churchgoers, religion undoubtedly continued to play a role in Robert's life. As had been the case earlier in Newtown he was exposed to contrasting views, for James McGuffog was a staunch Presbyterian, said by Owen to be a member of the Church of Scotland, while his wife was an Anglican. McGuffog was probably a member of one of the non-conformist or congregational chapels in the town and any potential conflict between his wife and himself was resolved by attending both conformist and non-conformist services, one in the morning, the other in the afternoon. There was apparently never any dispute in the family about these arrangements and Robert was therefore regularly taken to listen to the 'contending sermons', which, he recalled, they most generally were 'either in reference to their own sectarian notions, or in opposition to some of the opposing sects'.[16] In his memoirs he says that during his time in Stamford he was 'very religiously inclined' and 'all the time trying to find out *the true religion*'. This was not without its problems for Robert was very puzzled by the discovery that every sect throughout the globe claimed to be an advocate of '*the true religion*'. Robert studied and studied, anxious, as he put it, 'to be in the right way'. All sects seemed to have the same roots and this led him to question how Christianity could be the only true faith. While he claims he concluded at that time that all religions should be rejected it seems more likely that this phase of self-analysis and doubt about his religiosity occurred later in his youth or early manhood, rather than his boyhood. Had he articulated these views, which in any case would be surprising coming from someone of his age, it seems unlikely that he would have been as popular as he claimed to be in the McGuffog household. Something that confirms Robert's adherence to Christianity during his early teens is the story he tells about writing to William Pitt, who became Prime Minister in 1783, the subject of the letter being 'the sacredness of the Christian Sabbath', apparently 'much disregarded' in Stamford. Robert 'stated the desecration which was going forward in Stamford, and expressed a hope that the Government would adopt some measures to enforce a better observance of the Sabbath'. This very subject had been debated from time to time in parliament since 1781, was of concern to the authorities and to church-goers, and possibly was discussed in the McGuffog household. At any rate, Robert had taken a while to write his letter and after he had handed it over at the post office the McGuffogs asked him what he had been so interested in. Robert said, 'I have been writing a letter to Mr Pitt'. 'To Mr Pitt!', they exclaimed with astonishment, 'What could you have to say to Mr Pitt?' Robert replied that it was about 'the Sabbath being so shamefully employed as it was by many in Stamford, some of whom even kept their shops open on that day'. The McGuffogs looked at each other and smiled but Robert apparently thought there was 'nothing extraordinary in it'.

Eight or ten days later, or so the story goes, McGuffog brought in a London newspaper and said to Robert, 'Here is an answer to your letter to Mr Pitt'. Robert, never expecting a reply, was taken by surprise and blushed. He asked what the answer was and was told that parliament had just issued 'a long proclamation recommending all parties to keep the Sabbath more strictly'. Robert thought his letter would have ended up in the waste bin, and while recognising that the occasion of his writing and the issuing of the proclamation were mere coincidence, was very pleased at the outcome. The McGuffogs were evidently amazed. If nothing else this story, which, since his letter to Pitt cannot be traced, we can only presume to be true, further emphasises Robert's precociousness at that age and certainly makes it difficult to believe his claim that he suffered from shyness in his later youth and early manhood. It also highlights his piety and suggests that his scepticism was a later development.[17]

When he was about fourteen or fifteen Robert had finished his term with McGuffog, and though there is some confusion about whether this had lasted three or four years (probably the former), his master evidently asked him to stay on as an assistant for another year. Owen later recollected that while he had enjoyed working and living with the McGuffogs and probably could have stayed as long as liked, he felt he had 'acquired as much knowledge of the business as the situation afforded' and that what he really wanted was 'more knowledge and an enlarged field of action'. True or false, he had certainly been well treated by the McGuffogs, who tried to persuade him to stay, but when he ultimately left gave him a good reference. Subsequently James McGuffog was to prove a useful contact, probably as important to his career as the actual experience he gained in the business or the confidence and social skills he had acquired in the process.

There was thus a break in Robert's career for he left Stamford and returned to London to stay with his brother. He spent several months sightseeing and getting to know his way around. On Sundays, accompanied by his brother and sister-in-law, he wandered in the parks, particularly in Kensington Gardens, where, no doubt, he had further opportunities to observe the various social classes at leisure. This sojourn, at a time when he would have been much more aware of his surroundings than during his earlier stay, would undoubtedly help to put him at ease with the city, already knowing his way around when he had cause to visit it in the future, either on business or when his public career began. Robert also visited his parents and relatives in Wales, the first time he had been home since leaving three or four years earlier. Although he records that he was 'uncommonly well received by all parties', he does not say how he himself reacted to being back with his relations. He spent some time with his cousin and boyhood friend, Richard Williams, at his father's farm, Old Hall, near Kerry, about three miles from Newtown, and also visited his sister Anne, who had married Thomas Davies, and was living in nearby Radnorshire. Since his cash was limited he only stayed in Wales for a short time and, evidently keen to get back to work, returned to his brother's in London.[18]

There, thanks to McGuffog's recommendation, he was taken on as an assistant with Flint and Palmer, an old-established and respected firm of haberdashers, whose premises were located at 324 Borough, London Bridge, Southwark. William Flint had begun the business with one Sebire in 1776, being joined in the partnership by Benjamin Palmer in 1781 or 1782.[19] The business had prospered, Flint had made what was then considered a fortune for a retailer, while Palmer, 'a very respectable and gentlemanly person for his position, and an honest and practical man of business', had married Flint's only daughter. When Flint died his share of the business and its 'large capital' were left to his widow, daughter, and son-in-law. Like Robert's brother, Palmer had made a judicious marriage, and perhaps there was a lesson to be learned there. Certainly as far as business practice was concerned there was much to be learned from the enterprise for, according to Owen, Flint and Palmer was one of the first haberdashers to 'sell at a small profit for ready money only', and when he went to work there had become so prosperous that all stock was also bought with cash. As far as his personal finances were concerned, over and above board and lodging Robert had salary of £25 per annum and in consequence thought he was 'rich and independent', able to supply all his personal wants from his income.[20]

However, the contrast with his previous place of employment could not have been greater, and unfortunately for Robert, he found he had joined the firm just before the spring rush and that this was 'a very different situation to the one [he] had enjoyed in Stamford'. The scale of the operation was greater and the place was more like a department store with a large number of assistants, male and female. The clientele, because of their lower class, bought at cut prices for cash only, for, as he recalled:

The customers were of an inferior class – they were treated differently. Not much time was allowed for bargaining, a price being fixed for everything, and, compared with other houses, cheap. If any demur was made, or much hesitation, the article asked for was withdrawn, and, as the shop was generally full from morning till late in the evening, another customer was attended to.

This was an altogether different environment which clearly gave Robert experience of working in a business with a large and rapid turnover. Compared to McGuffog's the regime was frenetic and the assistants regularly worked long hours. They were up, had breakfast, dressed and ready to serve customers by eight o'clock. Dressing then was 'no slight affair' and Robert had to wait his turn to have the hairdresser powder, pomatum and curl his hair, which was done up in a pigtail with two large curls on either side. 'Until all this was very nicely and systematically done', he remembered, 'no one could think of appearing before a customer'.[21] Between eight and nine customers flooded into the shop, which although large, was soon packed. This continued all day and into the evening, as late as ten or ten-thirty. Meals were gulped down when time allowed, the only regular meal being breakfast, except on Sundays when 'a good dinner was always provided, and very much enjoyed'. When the customers ultimately left, often as late as eleven at night, the stock was invariably 'tossed and tumbled and unfolded in the utmost confusion and disorder' and by the time this had been rectified ready for the next day's business it was sometimes two o'clock in the morning. Poor Robert had been on his feet since eight the previous morning and found that he was 'scarcely able with the aid of the banisters to go upstairs to bed'. Even then he might get only five hours sleep. It was soon clear that 'this hurried work and slavery of every day', despite teaching him 'habits of quickness in business, and of great industry', was more than his constitution could stand for long, so he again asked Robert Heptinstall if he could look out for a suitable vacancy for him.

Coincidentally the rush eased off and the work gradually became less demanding. Despite the longish hours the assistants could at least take their meals in a civilised fashion and get to bed by eleven or twelve. Robert found that he could hardly complain since, all in all, he was very well treated by his employers. Palmer had two brothers who worked in the business and Robert became good friends with the younger, William, who was roughly his own age. William, 'a fine youth' with good habits and pleasing manners, got on well with Robert and they became good friends. On Sundays they went on outings together and as work in the shop eased off 'began to enjoy our leisure hours in out of door exercise or in reading', for either of which, understandably, Robert had had little time since he joined Flint and Palmer. As things settled down he was actually beginning to enjoy himself, so when his brother told him that Heptinstall had got him the offer of another job it was like a bolt out of the blue. Heptinstall had done all he could for Robert who was offered a 'very good situation' as an assistant to John Satterfield & Co, a firm of silk mercers and linen drapers in Manchester, with a salary of £40 per annum and all found. Robert felt he could hardly turn down such an offer, especially since Heptinstall had recommended him to Satterfield, and so he reluctantly handed in his notice to Palmer. Despite his short stay (we do not know how long exactly) Robert must have made a good impression and they parted company, at least so he says, with 'mutual regret', especially since he knew he would miss his friend, William. Although he would increase his salary he could not have been aware just how significant a step he was about to take in his career.

As far as we know Robert left London for Manchester in 1788 when he was about seventeen. He arrived in a town which in size and appearance was more like a city, the product of rapid expansion in the era of manufactures. In Lancashire industrialisation in much of the eighteenth century meant to a large extent the expansion of domestic industries in rural areas, but with the growth of the port of Liverpool and the development of Manchester as a commercial and manufacturing centre, the process was beginning to become more concentrated and urbanised. Manchester itself experienced phenomenal growth, the town's population of around 29,000 in 1773 increasing to 50,000 or more by the time Robert arrived there.[22] Much of the town's growth historically was explained by textiles, the proto-industrial or domestic stages of their manufacture having being largely orchestrated by Manchester merchants whose wide-ranging connections stretched well beyond Lancashire, adjoining parts of Cheshire and the West Riding, indeed, as far as London. The traditional linens and fustians were rapidly being eclipsed by cotton, which had long been imported via London, but was by then being shipped in greater bulk through Liverpool, which like Bristol and Glasgow had expanded rapidly thanks to the surge in colonial trade. While factories employing large numbers of spinners or weavers were still exceptional, major innovations in spinning technology, notably Hargreave's spinning jenny, Arkwright's water frame and Crompton's mule, had already begun to demonstrate the potential for mass production, particularly where those inventions could be harnessed up to water wheels or steam engines. The latter had increasing value to cotton spinners anxious to mechanise thanks to James Watt's improvements during the 1780s, notably rotary motion, achieved by the sun-and-planet gear, the double-acting engine, parallel motion, the centrifugal governor, to control the speed of the engine, and culminating in 1790 with the pressure gauge, which together made the engines more efficient and reliable. While waterpower and water itself remained important to the textile masters of Manchester it was the steam engine which led to the development of the factory system. Many of these units, however, remained small, more on the scale of their rural counterparts.[23] The commercial as opposed to the manufacturing side was evidenced in a wide range of enterprises dealing with textiles at every stage of their production, the business that Robert joined being typical. Like Stamford, but on an altogether larger scale, he soon found that Manchester had a growing middle class, so there was a ready and expanding clientele for high quality material and clothing.

John Satterfield had established Satterfield & Co, a firm of silk merchants and drapers, located at 5 St Ann's Square, in 1775. Satterfield was appointed Royal linen draper for Manchester in 1791 after attending and displaying his wares to George III, Queen Charlotte and the five princesses.[24] Robert therefore reckoned, quite rightly, that Satterfield ran 'a first rate house' both wholesale and retail, though it was more successful in the latter. In contrast to McGuffog, he remembered Satterfield as an indifferent buyer but an excellent salesman, a view confirmed by his master's subsequent success in front of royalty. However, as Owen reflected, there was a further lesson to be learned in comparing the business skills of his masters, for:

> When goods are well and judiciously purchased for a local trade, they almost sell themselves, and give little trouble to the seller; while if they are not bought with judgement, the trouble of sale is greatly increased. The good buyer also is almost sure to gain success to his business; while indifferent buyers scarcely ever succeed in accumulating independence.

McGuffog was able to retire from his business (about 1805) with substantial capital and when he died in 1829 leave his widow a thousand a year. Satterfield, on the other hand, even running a much larger enterprise and working much harder, could only clear his way, 'unable to purchase except on credit'. His son, Joshua, was evidently more successful.[25]

Robert discovered that he had again made a judicious move. The customers, while not in quite the same league as McGuffog's, were certainly an improvement on those in London, generally, as he himself said, of the upper middle class, manufacturers' and merchants' wives and families. So, he claimed, he could become acquainted with the ideas and habits of this class. His fellow assistants came from respectable families and were well behaved and their working and living conditions were good. He says he soon became reconciled to the change and with his salary of £40 with board, lodging and washing thrown in, thought he was well off. His temperate habits (he said) meant that, in any case, he ate simply and modestly and had never touched strong drink. He might well have become further reconciled to this apparently comfortable existence as a sales assistant had he not met John Jones, probably another Welshman, described in 1794 as a machine-maker of 58 Water Street, but then a wiremaker supplying Satterfield with wire frames for ladies' bonnets. Every week Jones called at the shop with a supply of wire[26] frames which Robert generally took in. Jones told Robert of 'the great and extraordinary discoveries that were beginning to be introduced into Manchester for spinning cotton by new and curious machinery'. He was trying to see it and find out how it worked and if successful 'could make a very good business out of it'.[27]

The likelihood is that the machinery in question was a variant of Samuel Crompton's spinning mule, the 'muslin wheel' or hand mule, which solved the problem of spinning a light and strong yarn capable of being woven into superior fabrics like muslin or cambric. Crompton had developed a proto-type of his machine, a combination of the water frame and the jenny, in 1779 and continued to improve it during the subsequent decade. While patents were jealously guarded and much secrecy surrounded early factories, it is difficult to believe that Jones, who evidently dealt regularly with the textile trade, or Robert himself, for that matter, had such a limited knowledge of current developments in the industry which dominated Manchester's economy. However, Jones, deploying what Owen in his memoirs condescendingly described as his 'small inventive powers' yet 'very active mind', eventually saw the machines working and was convinced he could build and make them work himself. Since it was difficult to enforce patents and piracy of machinery like Crompton's was widespread, Jones anticipated a good return on any business manufacturing the machines, but he lacked the necessary capital to get started. Jones said that if Robert could find £100 they would set up a partnership and 'soon accumulate capital sufficient to proceed'. Robert was convinced that Jones had got hold of 'a great secret' and wrote to his brother, William, asking if he would lend him a £100. When this duly arrived he gave in his notice, evidently to Satterfield's disappointment for despite his relatively short time with the firm, Robert had become 'a useful and steady assistant and a favourite server with his principal customers'.[28]

How had Robert used the gifts which his background and family had bestowed on him? Like his parents he was industrious and pious and despite the obvious limits of his formal schooling he was probably much better educated than others of his age.

If he had read as widely as he later claimed, together with his assertion that he regularly wrote down even simple lines copied from whatever book he happened to be reading, he must have been equipped with better than average literacy and vocabulary. Robert was by no means the untutored youth he later claimed. Apart from an inclination to hard work and acquiring a better education he had other opportunities to build on what he had learned at home. While there was nothing unusual about Robert's career up to that point, he had, in fact, acquired a great deal of experience in a relatively short time. He had accumulated a good all-round knowledge of the retail clothing trade, some basic business skills, and perhaps most important of all the necessary social skills to deal successfully with people from different backgrounds. If we give any credence to his views about the importance of childhood and adolescence in forming character his experience as a shop assistant might well have helped him grasp the inner truths about human relationships. He learned 'the due deference and gentility while serving McGuffog's grand customers' which enabled him later to mix on practically equal terms with Scottish lairds, with royal dukes, with diplomats, and with aristocratic and occasionally radical cabinet ministers.[29] His experience with Flint and Palmer introduced him to a lower class, and during his stay in London he acquired wider business experience in a harsher environment, and possibly a deeper understanding of humanity. When he moved to Manchester, certainly a significant step, he found himself serving Satterfield's middle-class customers, some of whom he would meet again when he began to associate with the town's cultural and scientific elite. It could be, as Butt has observed, that it was his virtually indefinable quality of successful human relationships, often disregarded and put down to good luck, which gives coherence to his success in business and his influence on social movements. He may have been a gawky, retiring youth, as he purports to have been in his *Life*, but his progress and direction were clear. Above all, Owen, as we will now call him, showed that he had considerable initiative and promise.[30] As it happened Manchester, with its dynamic cotton industry, provided the ideal environment for these qualities to flourish.

## NOTES

1. See Pollard, 'Factory Discipline'.
2. *Life*, p. 9.
3. *Life*, p. 10.
4. *Life*, p. 12; Claeys, footnotes in *Life*, p. 62.
5. *Life*, p. 12. He often emphasised his independence from this early age.
6. On the growth of Stamford see N.R.Wright, *Lincolnshire Towns and Industry 1700–1914*, Lincoln, 1982, pp. 87–94; And A. Rogers (ed.) *the Making of Stamford*, Leicester, 1965, p. 85.
7. Claeys, footnotes in *Life*, pp. 62–3; *Stamford Mercury*, 24 July 1801; 30 July 1802; 22 March 1805. McGuffog's death notice 14 August, 1829.
8. *Life*, p. 20.
9. *Life*, p. 13.

10. *Life*, pp. 20–21.
11. *Life*, pp. 17–18.
12. *Life*, pp. 14–15.
13. *Life*, p. 13.
14. Claeys, 'Introduction', *Selected Works*, Vol. 1, xvi.
15. *Life*, pp. 13–14.
16. *Life*, pp. 15–16.
17. The story is re-told in *Life*, pp. 16–17.
18. *Life*, p. 18. He says he only ever returned to Newtown once, probably in 1803. See Atholl Mss, Owen to Craig 23 April 1803; 24 May 1803.
19. Claeys, note to *Life*, p. 69.
20. *Life*, p. 18.
21. *Life*, pp. 19–20.
22. On Manchester's growth see R. Scola, *Feeding the Victorian City: The Food Supply of Manchester*, Manchester, 1992, pp. 16–19.
23. The context of this is well described in R. Lloyd Jones and M.J.Lewis, *Manchester and the Age of the Factory*, London, 1988.
24. Claeys, note to *Life*, p. 71.
25. *Life*, pp. 21–22.
26. Claeys, footnote to *Life*, p. 73.
27. *Life*, p. 22.
28. *Life*, pp. 22–3.
29. Butt in 'Introduction' to *Life*, viii.
30. Claeys, 'Introduction', xvi.

# THREE

# Machine-Maker and Mill Manager

R obinson Crusoe, as Owen never forgot, survived using whatever came to hand. So, with slender resources and slighter experience, Jones and Owen, late in 1790 or early in 1791 began machine making for the cotton industry.[1] The apparently modest capital which was required would need to be multiplied many times over to arrive at a modern equivalent, but nevertheless was typical of entry levels for a small business during the early Industrial Revolution, especially one in which craft skills were still as important as machinery. They were also lucky in that particularly easy credit conditions prevailed between 1789 and 1793.[2] While Owen was working out his notice at Satterfield's he and his partner agreed to rent a 'large machine workshop', also containing some rooms for cotton spinners, and specially constructed for them by a local builder.[3] Soon they had about forty men at work, purchasing their raw materials of iron, wood and brass on credit. Their business was duly advertised in the issues of the *Manchester Mercury* for 18 and 25 January 1791:

## JONES AND OWEN

Respectfully inform the Public, that they have opened a Warehouse near the New Bridge, Dolefield, for making WATER PREPARATION and MULE MACHINES, and flatter themselves from their strict Attention to Business, and the experienced Hands they employ, that they shall be able to finish work in such a manner as will merit the future Favours of those that employ them.

The above Machines are made upon the most approved Plans, and all orders punctually executed to the Time engaged for.

Owen claims that he had not 'the slightest knowledge' of the machinery and had never seen it work, but it is difficult to believe that he would have agreed to be Jones's partner without first verifying his story and familiarising himself with their potential products. Whatever the truth of this, their main line was spinning mules, while it seems likely that the 'water preparation machines' were roving frames (which prepared cotton wool to the stage immediately before it was spun into yarn). They also employed three spinners spinning yarn from rovings which Owen bought. The firm then began to produce its own roving for sale to mule spinners and buy their yarn back from them, as announced in the *Manchester Mercury* of 8 February 1791:

## TO MULE SPINNERS

GOOD MULE SPINNERS may be supplied with Roving Weekly,
and the Twist bought in Return, by applying to Jones and Owen,
Machine Makers, near the New Bridge, Dole Field, Manchester.

So from being highly specialised and involving little in the way of
coordination, the firm had quickly diversified, albeit in a small way,
into yarn production and marketing.

Quite what Owen's role in the firm was is difficult to determine, because
his declarations and opinions about his career in Manchester can be found
wanting in significant respects. He says he soon found out that Jones was
'a mere working mechanic, without any idea how to manage workmen,
or how to conduct business on the scale on which he had commenced',
so he himself took over the book-keeping, all other financial matters
and the oversight and payment of the men. However, assuming Jones
was a competent mechanic it would have seemed reasonable on any
sensible division of labour for Owen, who at least had some basic
business skills, to take charge of buying and selling and look after the
firm's books. He watched what the men were doing and 'by intensely
observing everything, maintained order and regularity throughout the
establishment'. Things went better than he had anticipated, so Jones
must have used his engineering skills in the production department
effectively. Indeed Owen's suggestion that Jones had absolutely no sense
of management and business acumen is contradicted by the fact that
despite subsequent partnership changes and financial difficulties Jones
and Company survived for some time after Owen retired from the firm.
Jones was still working as a machine maker in 1794.[4]

Whoever was responsible for the success of the partnership it attracted
another investor, whom Owen, strangely, does not name. This individual
had ready capital at his disposal and seemed to think the firm had good
prospects. He asked Jones if he would take him on as a partner, apparently
in place of Owen, who might be induced to pull out if a good offer was
made. Since Owen 'proceeded with fear and trembling' given his doubts
about Jones he seems to have been only too glad to sever his connection
with the enterprise, no matter how good its prospects. He must also have
been thinking about his brother's loan which would need to be repaid at
some point. Owen was promised as compensation for his share in the
partnership 'six mule machines such as we were making for sale, a reel,
and a making up machine, with which to pack the yarn when finished
in skeins into bundles for sale'.[5] In actual fact he only received three of
the six mules, but, nothing daunted, he rented from a builder and land
surveyor named Christopher Woodroofe of Ancoats Lane 'a large newly
erected building, or factory, as such places were beginning to be called'.
Here he started on his own 'in a small part of one of the rooms in this

large building'. The split between Robert Owen and John Jones cannot be dated exactly.

There was no announcement of the dissolution of the partnership in the *Manchester Mercury* and Owen merely says that he did not stay with Jones for many months. Later, in April 1792, Owen was to tell his future employer, Peter Drinkwater, that he was making £300 a year in his business as a yarn manufacturer and dealer, which suggests that he had at any rate between three and six months experience of working on his own. This would indicate that he severed his connection with Jones during the latter half of 1791.[6]

Until then Owen, as an apprentice or assistant, had lived with his masters but when he left Satterfield he had to look for lodgings. Luck again seemed to be on his side for he found somewhere eminently suitable in nearby St Ann's Square: the house of an elderly widow who took in lodgers. His description of his lodgings, at half a guinea a week, gives us an insight into the relatively comfortable surroundings he could evidently afford even at that stage in his career:

> Here were two respectable travellers already established when I applied, and I found I could have a bedroom to myself, a sitting room fronting the square, in company with these gentlemen travelling for some respectable manufacturing houses, and board such as they had, for half a guinea a week. I accepted it, found the house clean, the attendance good, – tea or coffee, etc, for breakfast, – a hot joint well cooked, and a pudding or pie daily for dinner, tea in the afternoon, – and good bread and cheese and butter, and a glass of ale, at supper, – and I do not recollect ever living, as mere living, better, or more to my satisfaction.

Although provisions were cheap and 'manufacturing luxury had not commenced' he could never understand quite how the widow managed to make a living out of her lodgers, but she always appeared 'cheerful and satisfied'. Owen thought the rate very reasonable and could evidently afford to spend about £30 of his annual income on his lodgings. If the daily routine was as he described, it suggests Owen was able to come home for tea in the afternoon, although we do not know his hours of work and this may just have been at weekends. However his stay in St Ann's Square did not last long for after he set up on his own, and perhaps with economy in mind, he lodged for a time with Woodroofe.[7]

While Owen was still in partnership with Jones another interesting opportunity presented itself, for unexpectedly, McGuffog wrote asking him to join his business. Not only would McGuffog put up the capital and give Owen fifty per cent of the profits, but also make over the business to him after a few years. This was a strong temptation but Owen declined. It is difficult to know, of course, exactly why he turned down McGuffog's offer, but it is perhaps indicative of his growing self-confidence that he decided to stay where he was, presumably having already made up his mind to quit his association with Jones and set up on his own. Perhaps he could sense that the heady atmosphere of business and commercial life in Manchester was already more to his taste than tranquil Stamford. His brother's loan might again have been a factor in this decision: a significant one, because had he changed direction he could have married McGuffog's niece and 'lived and died a rich Stamford linen draper'.

Owen took on three men to operate the spinning mules, and since he had no machinery to make them himself, purchased the roving from local suppliers. When the men had spun the yarn it was wound on cops, or conical balls on spindles, which, using the reeling machine, Owen made up into hanks of 840yds in length. He then made the hanks up into bundles weighing 5lbs each, wrapping them neatly in paper. One of his main customers was an individual named Mitchell, the agent for several Glasgow manufacturers, who either sold the yarn on to muslin weavers, or worked it up themselves. Thus the Scottish connection in Owen's career established by his apprenticeship with McGuffog continued to be significant in his first solo venture. It was further emphasised by the fact that the main supplier of his rovings was the firm of Sandfords, McConnel and Kennedy which, like Jones and Owen, had been established in 1791 by two young industrious Scots, James McConnel and John Kennedy. Using their accumulated capital of £700, a great deal more than Owen and his partner could scrape together, they began as machine builders and mule spinners, creating what was to become one of the largest businesses of its kind in Manchester. Owen was 'one of their first and most regular customers', for as he recalled, '*they* could then only make the rovings without finishing the thread; and I could only *finish* the thread, without being competent to make the *rovings*'.

According to Owen, Jones and his new partner were soon in difficulty and told him they 'could not make good their engagement' with him. He realised that he would be unlikely to get the other three mules he had been promised. Whether he had expected these to materialise or not, he had no option but to press on regardless, perhaps another instance of his tendency to exaggerate his success against difficult odds. If he is to be believed the business was certainly prospering, for cotton bought as roving for 12 shillings (60p) was fetching 22 shillings (£1.10) when sold as yarn. He reckoned that on his weekly sales to Mitchell he was making a profit of £6 per week, for he had been fortunate to let the rest of the large building he occupied and in the process covered his own rent.[8] He thought he was doing well for someone just starting out and he may well have been right because even from modest beginnings there were certainly fortunes to be made in the cotton industry. Another like-minded individual was Peter Drinkwater, a leading Manchester merchant, who had already invested heavily in cotton spinning.

Drinkwater was a major figure among the town's merchant elite and had become so thanks to his success in fustian manufacture and later as a textile middleman and exporter. Between 1784–6 he subscribed 40 guineas to the Committee of the Fustian Trade set up in Manchester to lobby for the repeal of Pitt's 'impolitic, odious and oppressive tax upon the cotton manufacture, and for preventing the ruin attendant upon passing the Irish Propositions into law'. The former was bad enough, but the latter, by proposing to establish a free interchange of goods between Britain and Ireland, threatened to flood the British market with cheap goods, notably linen, an industry which had expanded almost as dramatically as cotton, mainly but not exclusively in Ulster. These views were alarmist, but not wholly unrealistic. Drinkwater's importance in the campaign against taxation and free trade can be gauged by the fact that only he and Arkwright contributed the substantial sum of 40 guineas (£42). Oldknow by comparison contributed only 5 guineas (£5.25). In November 1785 he chaired a meeting at the Exchange coffee house 'to consider the best means of giving proper and effectual support to that useful and highly necessary institution, the General Chamber of Manufacturers of Great Britain' and he was to become one of the founding members of the Manchester 'Commercial Society of Merchants trading on the Continent of Europe' on its formation in 1794. Later in 1791 he supported, in pacifist terms, Pitt's policies on Anglo-Russian relations and the following year was appointed a local Justice of the Peace.[9]

Government policy was not the only thing that posed a threat to the expansion of the cotton industry, because Arkwright's patents on preparatory machinery, though widely evaded, were also irksome. It was Drinkwater's brother-in-law, Serjeant Bolton, who examined Thomas Highs as counsel for the Crown in the famous case of Rex v Arkwright in the Court of the King's Bench, when the Lancashire cotton spinners successfully opposed the validity of Arkwright's second patent of 1775 for carding, drawing and roving machines. Highs claimed that Arkwright filched both the idea of spinning by rollers and the device of the cylinders in the roving frames from him. It seems likely that Drinkwater's connection with Bolton may have worked to the Lancashire spinners' advantage and, according to Edward Baines, Highs was supported in his old age by payments from Drinkwater and others. The outcome of the case was certainly highly significant and it may very well have convinced Drinkwater that, with another impediment removed, it was time to invest more heavily in cotton. He did so, some time before 1789, by purchasing or setting up a water-powered factory housing Arkwright-type machinery at Northwich in Cheshire, and early in 1789 starting to build in Manchester a second factory, popularly known as Bank Top Mill, and to those involved in it as the Piccadilly Factory. According to Owen, Drinkwater was 'totally ignorant of everything connected with cotton spinning' but all the evidence indicates that in his realisation of the potential of steam power and his attention to its installation in his new mill the truth was otherwise.[10] When Owen arrived on the scene, the Piccadilly Factory, off London Road, familiar enough from the outside, no doubt, contained the most up-to-date plant producing some of the finest yarn yet manufactured.

For a short time before Owen took over, the Piccadilly Factory was managed on Drinkwater's behalf by George Augustus Lee, a former clerk in the Northwich mill. Lee himself had taken over at short notice in 1791 following the death of Richard Slack, 'one of the first [ie, best] practical spinners of that day', who if not actually Drinkwater's partner, had, according to correspondence in the Boulton and Watt papers, 'a very considerable interest' in the enterprise and 'sole conducting of it'.[11] Lee rather shabbily decided to leave Drinkwater in order to go into partnership with a rival, George (later Sir George) Phillips, in another large cotton mill in Salford. As MP for Ilchester, Phillips was later to oppose Peel's efforts to regulate child labour in the cotton industry and was a member of the select committee to which both Owen and Lee gave evidence.[12] At any rate Lee gave in his notice and according to Owen's recollections Drinkwater 'had to advertise for a manager to undertake the superintendence [sic] of this mill, now in progress'. Owen continued:

> His advertisement appeared on a Saturday in the Manchester papers, but I had not seen or heard of it until I went to my factory on the Monday morning following, when, as entered the room where my spinning machines were, one of the spinners said – 'Mr Lee has left Mr Drinkwater, and he has advertised for a manager'.[13]

In the well known account of his interview with Drinkwater concerning the post, Owen alleged that he replied to Drinkwater's question about how old he was by saying 'Twenty in May this year' which would place the event in 1791. In actual fact Drinkwater's advertisement appeared exactly a year after Owen said. The advertisement first appeared in the *Manchester Chronicle* for 14 April 1792, was repeated in the *Manchester Mercury* on the 17th, and later appeared in the Radical *Manchester Herald* on Saturday 21 with slight alterations. The last insertion was date-lined 'King-street, 19 April' indicating that the vacancy was not then filled. It is impossible to say which one Owen saw, but it may very well have been that in the *Manchester Herald*. The original advertisement ran:

## SUPERINTENDENCY OF A FACTORY WANTED

A PERSON to superintend and conduct an extensive MULE FAC-
TORY, to whom any salary will be allowed proportionate to Merit.

No one need apply, whose Character, in regard to Morals, as well
as Capacity and Steadiness, is not in every way respectable.

For particulars apply to Mr Drinkwater, at his Warehouse in
Manchester, on Tuesdays, Thursdays or Saturdays from eleven to
two o'clock.

This would pinpoint the date of the interview with Drinkwater to Monday
23 April 1792 but unfortunately if we take the advertisement at face value
Drinkwater would not have been interviewing applicants for the post on
a *Monday* morning, although Owen says he had been doing so. Typical
of his directness he may simply have jumped the queue.

The story of how Owen persuaded Drinkwater to appoint him as manager of the Piccadilly factory is worth repeating. Evidently, Drinkwater's
interviewing technique included asking applicants how often in the week
they were drunk, to which Owen, 'blushing scarlet at this unexpected
question', indignantly replied that he had never been drunk in his life.
Strange though it may seem Drinkwater does not appear to have asked
Owen about his actual experience in the textile trade or of cotton spinning,
though he did ask for references from former employers. When asked
what salary he expected Owen replied, 'Three hundred a year'. 'What?',
retorted Drinkwater, 'Three hundred a year! I have had this morning I
know not how many seeking the situation, and I do not think that all
their askings together would amount to what you require.' 'I cannot
be governed by what others ask', said Owen, 'and I cannot take less. I
am now making that sum by my own business.' He could prove it, he
said, if Drinkwater looked at his premises in Ancoats Lane and inspected
the books, which they duly did. Drinkwater seemed convinced and after
following up Owen's references offered him the job at £300 per annum.
He also bought his machinery at cost price, which suggests that it was
a condition of Owen's employment that he cease trading and devote all
his time to managing Drinkwater's mill. Owen may have been lucky, for
the boom in spinning meant that there were very few individuals with
the necessary expertise to take on the job. But if he just happened to be
in the right place at the right time, it paid off and, as he later observed,
'the circumstances made a lasting impression . . . because they led to
important future consequences'.[14]

Owen was rather taken aback when he saw 500 workers, men, women
and children, and the new machines in Drinkwater's large modern factory.
'Had I seen the establishment before I applied to manage it', he wrote,
'I should never have thought of doing an act so truly presumptuous'.

Drinkwater had not even bothered to show him over the plant on his appointment and Lee had apparently left the day before. 'Well, there I was, to undertake this task', Owen remembered, and like Crusoe on his island, 'no one to give me any assistance'. However, after keeping his eyes open and his mouth shut for six weeks he concluded, as was to become usual, that he was master of all he surveyed and 'ready to give directions in every department'. He felt that his background, especially with McGuffog, had given him considerable knowledge of fine cloth, and he set about trying to improve the quality of yarns. Lee, 'a man of high genius', who 'possessed great talent as a scientific machinist and engineer' had managed to produce yarn 'of extraordinary fineness', what was technically known as 120 hanks to the pound, but it was of variable quality. Owen examined the drawings and calculations Lee had left behind and then felt able to adjust and improve the 'correctness which was required in making certain parts of the machinery'.

It is hard to tell exactly what Owen achieved in his first six months as Drinkwater's manager, but rather than greatly increasing the fineness of the yarn at that stage he probably managed to improve overall quality control. More generally, having 'perceived defects in the various processes' he re-arranged the factory and 'always had it kept in superior order, so that at all times it was in a state to be inspected by any parties'. He could only have meant Drinkwater and his immediate associates because the Piccadilly factory, like most cotton mills, was 'closed against all strangers'. Owen may have changed the existing rules and regulations for the conduct of workers, but since he would not have had the authority to do so without consulting Drinkwater it seems unlikely. According to Lee the hours of work were from 6am to 8pm, an hour longer than in Arkwright's mills at Cromford or, indeed, in Drinkwater's other mill at Northwich. The latter also worked at night, though no children were employed on this shift. Apparently there were other mills in Manchester that worked similar hours, especially where hand spinning prevailed. However, Owen says quite specifically that in his first six months he paid as much attention to the 'living machinery' as he did to the dead and had completely won over the workforce to his regime, even if it was no different from what prevailed before he took over. Thus, he recalled, 'the order and discipline exceeded that of any other [factory] in or near Manchester' and 'for regularity and sobriety an example which none could imitate'. While Owen was personally appalled by drunkenness in the mills, sobriety was essential for business efficiency in the quality of the yarn and the safety of the workers.[15]

While there is little doubt that Owen was already beginning to demonstrate considerable technical and managerial ability he singularly failed to explain the advantages the Piccadilly factory possessed and the state-of-the-art plant with which it was equipped. Nor did he acknowledge the fact that Drinkwater had personally supervised the smallest detail of the mill's construction and the installation of its steam engine, supplied by the famous Boulton and Watt. Drinkwater's contract with the engineers, ante-dated to 1 April 1789, shows that it was a rotary engine with a 16 inch cylinder, a piston with a 4 foot stroke, capable of generating 8 horse power. The annual premium was £40 and the engine was to be used for 'preparing and carding cotton and for such other purposes as may be required'. But Drinkwater stated quite specifically in a letter of 3 April that he did not intend to use it for spinning cotton. He tried to negotiate a lower premium by attempting to persuade the engineers that the engine would not be working to full capacity because the mill would not be 'immediately filled with machinery and people'. Although the engineers had probably heard such special pleading before, Drinkwater, sometime later in the year, had been favoured with a visit from the great Matthew Boulton himself, who promised, among other improvements, that the engine would be fitted with Watt's new governor, a device which would not 'permit 2 strokes per minute of increase of velocity though all the work were taken away at once'. What this meant was that even if all the machinery was working at the same time it would still run smoothly, a point that had not escaped Drinkwater. In spite of his alleged ignorance of steam engines and cotton manufacture he wrote in November 1789 after Boulton's visit:

> . . . among these inventions one, I understand, is of nature solely calculated to secure more effectually an equable motion under different degrees of heat from the fire – a property so extremely essential in preparing cotton to work into *fine* yarn that I would on no account have you deny [me] the use of this instrument.

Watt agreed to fit his governor to Drinkwater's engine, but added a strong warning about showing it to anyone else. Undoubtedly it was this innovation which helped Slack, Lee and then Owen produce the high quality roving needed for fine yarn production on hand mules and at a later date on machines driven by the engine. Even before Owen began his attempts to spin finer yarn, the factory was geared up for experimentation and presumably many of its workers were already skilled machinists familiar with the techniques of fine spinning.[16]

Drinkwater also insisted that the new mill should be as light and airy as possible and had a running battle with Boulton and Watt about the engine house which he feared would block up too many windows. He wanted, he said, 'to give the building its greatest possible convenience' with a 'continued series of windows' to maximise the natural light falling on the machinery and improve ventilation. Owen's master was equally concerned about sanitation, asking the engineers to 'introduce 4 small single necessaries – one for each room, to be placed neatly one over another, and so, if possible, to be managed as neither to be offensive or endanger the health of the people at work'. Boulton and Watt suggested water closets, which Drinkwater for a time resisted partly on the grounds of expense and partly because he believed 'the poor ignorant workpeople and children' could not be relied upon 'to turn and manage the cocks, etc without the closets running into a state of disorder and nastiness'. But the engineers got their way and to make sure that the lavatories were kept clean Drinkwater ordered that they be flushed out with 'a strong stream of water from the great wooden cistern of the engine . . . when the rain collected from the roof and through a leaden pipe does not do the business sufficiently'. In making such arrangements, Drinkwater wrote, 'the object of keeping the factory sweet and wholesome is a matter which I cannot help considering of the utmost importance, whether as regards decency, convenience or humanity'. While these sanitary arrangements and sentiments were by no means unique, they set a standard which in future Owen himself would try to emulate, most notably at New Lanark.[17]

Although youthful managers were common in the cotton industry, news of Owen's appointment was evidently greeted with disbelief in Manchester. Drinkwater was said to have lost his senses by employing 'a mere boy without experience' to run a mill which was reckoned to be 'one of the wonders of the mechanical and manufacturing world'.[18] Despite what must have been a substantial investment in this 'rather expensive' factory Owen claims his employer hardly ever visited it, which seems odd since his business office or counting house was in York Street just round the corner from his town house in Fountain Street, both ten minutes walk from London Road. He seems to have visited it only three times, once to show it to John Pemberton Heyhood of Lincoln's Inn, a future son-in-law, and on another occasion to Sir William Herschel, the famous astronomer. Rather confusingly Owen says on three separate occasions that Drinkwater 'never came to the mill', meaning he was not in the habit of doing so, that 'he came only three times during the four years I retained management of it', and that 'Mr Drinkwater . . . for three years had once only been to his factory in Manchester'.[19] However, during the summer Drinkwater lived at his country dwelling, Irwell House, near Agecroft Bridge, and went to the office twice a week, when Owen was generally on call to brief him on developments at the factory. Owen brought Drinkwater 'specimens of the manufacture', the quality of which gradually improved, and, he was able to report, was more popular than the old stock left unsold since Lee departed. Drinkwater had heard good reports about Owen's work, particularly his attention to detail and enforcement of discipline, and 'became week by week more satisfied with the boy he had taken in opposition to public opinion to manage his new factory'. Sometime in the autumn Drinkwater, aware of the 'progress and change' that had been made at the factory since Owen took over, asked him to Irwell House to discuss his future. Somewhat nervously Owen listened as Drinkwater said, 'Mr Owen, I have sent for you to propose a matter of business important to you and me. I have watched your proceedings, and know them well, since you came into my service, and I am well pleased with all you have done. I now wish you to make up your mind to remain permanently with me'. He said that if Owen stayed with him his salary would be increased to £400 for the next year, £500 for the third and in the autumn of 1795 he would become a partner in the business with Thomas and John Drinkwater, the merchant's two young sons, and share a quarter of the profits. 'You know now what they are likely to be', added Drinkwater, who then asked, 'What do you say to this proposal?' Owen replied, 'I think it most liberal, and willingly agree to it'. Owen and his employer immediately signed an agreement on these terms.[20]

His future secure, Owen continued his experiments, and within a year of taking over management had succeeded in producing twist of the fineness of 160 hanks to the pound. We do not know when or exactly how but he ultimately managed to spin to 300 hanks to the pound. He tells us that a measure of his initial success was the fact that the finer yarns fetched 10 per cent above the list price, while those left over from Lee's regime 'sold slowly at the list price'. When he had more experience and had enhanced his 'knowledge of the qualities of cotton, improved the accuracy of the machinery used, and the correctness of all the processes through which the material had to pass' the Piccadilly factory was producing yarns which on occasion fetched 50 per cent above the list price. He put much of his success down to judicious buying of raw materials, which was something of a gamble for the unwary because of inconsistent quality. According to Owen cotton from mainland North America could not be spun very effectively on the machinery then available and the bulk of his supply came from the West Indies and South America, the finest yarn being made with fibre from the French West Indies, known as Orleans cotton. Owen was naturally anxious to claim credit for the finer yarn, and in a move typical of his self-promotion later in life, sought and obtained Drinkwater's permission to have his name stamped on the bundles of thread before dispatch to the firm's customers.[21]

Owen claimed to be the first to spin American Sea Island cotton on the 'new machinery through rollers, instead of from the distaff or hand card', by which he meant roving machinery and mules. The cotton was supplied by one of Drinkwater's brokers, Robert Spear, a partner in the firm of Clegg and Spear, cotton merchants and fustian manufacturers in Crow Lane.[22] It had been sent by an American planter via his Liverpool agent with the request that a competent spinner be found to work it up and estimate its quality and value. Loosely packed, the cotton was half full of seeds (a problem solved by Eli Whitney's cotton gin, patented soon after in 1794), but Owen had it cleaned and spun into yarn. While it was a dingy colour compared to the French West Indian or Orleans cotton and hence 'less attractive to the eye' it produced a much better thread. Owen sold it to a Scottish merchant, James Craig (who coincidentally was Dale's neighbour in Charlotte Street, Glasgow), settling for a lower price because of the colour.[23] Craig may well have been one of the first to use American cotton yarn in muslin, and when he appeared back in Manchester looking for further supplies was disappointed to find that it had all been sold. Owen was rather surprised and said he would be happy to supply the whiter yarn at the usual price, but Craig told him that the dingy yarn was the best quality he had ever seen and the colour was no problem because it bleached much better than the white yarn. This experience made Owen appreciate the quality and potential of long staple American Sea Island cotton, which was to become the main raw material of the cotton spinning industry until machinery was developed to spin the shorter staples grown in the inland plantations of the American South. Craig was not the only Scottish merchant-manufacturer to buy Drinkwater's yarn and according to Owen the Scots were his main customers. Alexander Speirs, a successful Kilbarchan merchant and muslin and cambric manufacturer, who, with others, already employed as many as 360 looms in 1782, was another who dealt with Drinkwater. Speirs, so Owen's story goes, bought yarn at a count of 250 spun from cotton which Owen had purchased for 5 shillings (25p) a pound for no less than £9. 18s 6d (£9.92) per pound. Speirs had it woven into muslin, the first piece being sent to Queen Charlotte 'as the greatest curiosity of British manufacture'. This was the sort of publicity Owen himself would undoubtedly relish and, if he is to be believed, few could compete with him as a fine cotton spinner. His nearest rival 'in the ordinary numbers or fineness' was another Scot, Archibald Buchanan, who with his elder brother, John, established Deanston mill in Perthshire in 1785, the same year Dale began New Lanark. Owen went as far as to claim that his single-handed development of fine yarn led to an enormous expansion of muslin weaving in Paisley and adjoining parts of Renfrewshire. While this was clearly an exaggeration there can be little doubt that his increased expertise and slick marketing strategy had boosted his reputation not only in and around Manchester but also further afield among the merchants and cotton spinners of the Scottish Lowlands.[24]

Two other circumstances further enhanced Owen's knowledge of cotton spinning. Firstly, Drinkwater had been so pleased with the changes and improvements Owen had made in the Piccadilly factory that he asked him to reorganise the Northwich mill and keep it under regular supervision. The main activity at Northwich, which employed several hundred workers, was warp-spinning of relatively low counts on Arkwright-type water frames, the prime mover being water power.[25] An elderly manager had been in charge for some time and Owen felt it was 'an ungracious task for one so young' to go over his head. He did so nonetheless, riding over to the mill once a fortnight. This gave him first-hand experience of mechanised spinning and moreover of water-powered plant, modest though it was compared to New Lanark. Secondly, he was able to appreciate for himself the potential for further mechanisation of mule spinning. In 1790, the year the Piccadilly factory began, William Kelly, one of Dale's managers at New Lanark, applied water power to Crompton's hand mule and three years later John Kennedy, from whom Owen had obtained roving, successfully spun fine yarn of 100 hanks to the pound using an improved mule driven by steam power.[26] Kennedy recalled that:

> Mr Drinkwater was the most extensive fine spinner at the time of which I speak. He was one of the early water spinners and in possession of the most perfect system of roving making. His large mill in Piccadilly was filled with mules of 144 spindles, each of which was worked by men's hands. Mr Owen was then his manager and they came to see the new machine in 1793. They approved of it and thought it practical. Mr Humphries [sic] of Glasgow, who was a good mechanic, and succeeded Mr Owen as manager . . . got instructions to apply this system of power to his fine work produced by the mules in the Piccadilly mill; and to make its advantages available he coupled these spindle mules together.[27]

Not only was the mechanically minded Robert Humphreys to succeed Owen at Drinkwater's but later followed him to New Lanark to replace the inventive William Kelly, whose services were soon dispensed with after Owen's arrival. More immediately Owen gained useful first-hand knowledge of machine spinning using both water and steam power.

Apart from his autobiography, the reminiscences of a handful people who knew him, and the odd newspaper advertisement, detailed information about Owen at this period is scant. Only a few short letters and invoices written when he was Drinkwater's manager have survived, the earliest documents in his handwriting. Two, dated 4 and 14 March 1793 are addressed to Boulton and Watt in Birmingham placing an order for a new boiler for the mill engine. This was to be made at John Wilkinson's ironworks at Bersham near Wrexham and transported by sea from Chester to Runcorn and then brought up the Bridgewater Canal via Preston Brook to Manchester. The first invoice, dated 20 July, unsigned but most likely in Owen's handwriting, shows Drinkwater supplying his prospective son-in-law, Samuel Oldknow, with yarn of counts up to 160, presumably for fine muslin production. Another to Oldknow of 30 October adds a note:

> Mr Saml. Oldknow,
> Sir,
> The above were intended for the exact nos. which you wanted, but upon trial found them to vary two hanks; if they are not sufficiently near to your order, on returning them, in a few days you shall have the Nos. required.
> Remaining for
> Peter Drinkwater
> Your humble servant
> Robt. Owen

The last shows Oldknow ordering a larger batch of yarn and indicates that Owen's management did not necessarily extend to pricing policy, for he wrote, 'Mr D has not positively determined upon the price: when he does, I will send you the account'.[28]

While he was with Jones and then with Drinkwater few other activities apart from business took up Owen's time. He was certainly concerned about the banking crisis of 1793, which adversely affected the expansion of the cotton industry and caused a number of casualties known to him personally. More generally, even if he only read a newspaper occasionally or learned of such things from associates, he would surely have found it difficult to ignore the tumultuous events in France and the ripple effect of the revolution on the English side of the Channel. In politics, so far as they touched him, he was a loyal supporter of the status quo. Together with his prospective partner, Richard Moulson, he signed the declaration published by a large group of 'Protestant Dissenters, Inhabitants of the Towns of Manchester and Salford' in December 1792. The signatories affirmed that they were 'steadily and affectionately attached to the British Constitution, consisting of Kings, Lords, and Commons . . . fully confident that a Constitution, thus formed, will not fail to redress every real grievance, and effect every necessary improvement'.[29] Its aim was to disassociate moderate Dissenters from the more extreme Radicals and fellow travellers whose sympathies lay with the French republic. He recalled that at the time he had 'a high opinion of the attainments of the wealthy educated classes, and of all above them', and presumably both knew his place in the social hierarchy and supported its maintenance.[30] Although he could not have realised it at the time the subsequent war with France was to provide an apparently endless backcloth against which he would make his own fortune and fame, giving him the entree to the salons of the highest in the land. It seems that he was still religiously inclined, though we have no way of knowing whether his churchgoing arose from his faith or was kept up merely for appearance's sake. His views may well have changed since his days with the McGuffogs. As a young man of independent means rather than an apprentice having to fit in with his master's ways he would theoretically have had the option of ignoring formal religion, although the convention of the circle in which he moved could well have limited his actions. As it was he appears to have been a practising Unitarian, one of the strongest of the Dissenting sects in Manchester, which attracted considerable support from the merchant community.[31] With its appeals to reason and conscience as the standards for belief and action Unitarianism might have proved more attractive to Owen than either the Anglican or Methodist creeds to which he had been exposed in his boyhood and earlier youth, and might even have influenced the development of his own social philosophy. While the Unitarians were to provide some useful contacts, probably more important and formative was Owen's participation in that great manifestation of the Enlightenment in the north, the Manchester Literary and Philosophical Society, which he joined in the autumn of 1793. The links between enlightened ideas and Dissent were particularly strong in Manchester, and as we will see in the following chapter, Owen found himself in the company of some distinguished and influential individuals.

As to his personality at that time, we have to rely entirely on his autobiography, which in its self-deprecatory picture shows how he saw himself at that age and perhaps more to the point, wanted to be seen. In a series of revealing observations he tells how he regarded himself as 'a novice in general society', saying that he 'had known it only as customers in retail business, or as a junior dependent in the houses of my employers'. He was, he says, 'from ten years of age a stranger, as it were among strangers, known only as a youth of business, and consequently left in a great measure to my own communings and inexperienced observations'. Further, he maintained that:

> Absorbed in my attention to business, I knew little of the habits, customs and fashions of families having pretentious to some standing in society, and I now began strongly to feel this deficiency.

This had become more of a problem as he moved from day-to-day business acquaintances into a wider and better educated social circle. Afraid of his own defects he felt reluctant to accept invitations to social occasions from people who wanted to further their acquaintance with him. As far as women were concerned he says he 'knew nothing of the female sex, except as customers in business' and that this also caused problems in 'making family acquaintances'.[32] He therefore compared himself with others who had a more privileged background, were apparently better educated, better equipped, and had more experience. He remained the ill-educated, inarticulate, socially unskilled individual who would triumph over these shortcomings and succeed beyond his own expectations and those of others. Like Robinson Crusoe he had to do everything on his own starting from scratch. He was on his own, on his own island and with an island mentality. Like Crusoe he was self-sufficient and independent and although he had a succession of Man Fridays to help him, was sometimes reluctant to acknowledge their role. Then and in future he wanted to see himself as fighting against the odds rather than as a natural inheritor of power. So the portrait he painted of himself needs to be treated with caution because it is difficult to relate the personality of the shy retiring youth to the precocious individual who had already become a dynamic and successful businessman.

In young manhood, as far as we know, Owen kept his distance from his parents and hence from the place that had so evidently influenced him in boyhood. Quite why this should have been so is hard to determine because living in Manchester he was at least within easier travelling distance of mid-Wales than he had been in either Stamford or London. Travel was getting easier but was still expensive and maybe he felt, in any case, that his life had moved on to a higher level in a very different environment, which even if not aesthetically appealing was dynamic, challenging and beginning to provide him with a good living. Indeed, most of his time during his first few years in Manchester, as he himself said, seems to have been taken up with his career. He clearly kept in touch with his older brother who lent him the money to get started with Jones and presumably he repaid the loan as soon as he could. Someone from the past who did get in touch, as we saw, was his old master, James McGuffog, who might be regarded as a surrogate father, since he patently had Owen's interest at heart and so greatly influenced the direction of his career during youth and early manhood. Owen warmly acknowledged his debt to McGuffog and, indeed, the only other individual he ever described in such appreciative terms was David Dale, though even he did not escape criticism.

Another remarkably successful entrepreneur, Oldknow, was responsible for Owen leaving Drinkwater. Having established himself in his imposing mill at Stockport as the leading manufacturer of muslin, Oldknow harboured ambitions to become a 'cotton lord' by securing control of Drinkwater's spinning operations. The means to this end was marrying one of Drinkwater's daughters, either Margaret or Eliza (it is unclear which), but she was not enamoured of the idea because Oldknow was much older than another suitor. According to Owen the 'ambitious and obstinate' Drinkwater eventually overcame her resistance and sometime in 1794 the match was in the process of being arranged. However, Owen's promised partnership now stood in the way of Oldknow's plans for 'exclusive dealing with Mr Drinkwater's property', for which he evidently had 'extensive views and arrangements'. Rumours about what was afoot had already reached Owen and when he was duly summoned to an interview with Drinkwater at Irwell House he wisely put his copy of their earlier agreement in his pocket. Drinkwater explained the situation saying that if Owen cancelled the agreement about a partnership he could stay on and name his own salary as manager. 'In an act of feeling, and not of judgement' Owen replied by throwing his copy of the agreement on the fire and announcing his intention of resigning. Since good managers were hard to come by Drinkwater had a problem on his hands and tried to persuade Owen to change his mind. Eventually Owen relented, but only as far as agreeing to stay on temporarily until a successor 'equal to the duties' could be found.[33]

In the circumstances Owen had an axe to grind but he was perhaps less than honest about Drinkwater's role in the success of the Piccadilly Factory.[34] He certainly gave his employer little credit for taking the risk of employing him in the first place and giving him the opportunity to acquire such wide management experience in a rapidly changing and increasingly highly capitalised venture. Owen refers to Drinkwater as 'a good fustian manufacturer and a first-rate foreign merchant', perhaps deliberately playing down his success as an entrepreneur in cotton spinning, but acknowledging that because of his great wealth he easily rode out the commercial crisis of 1793 without much loss. In 1794 Drinkwater was certainly well enough off to buy the manor of Prestwich and Pendlebury, Lancashire, from its then owner, Thomas William Coke, adding to his existing town and country properties and hence like Arkwright before him joining the ranks of the landed gentry.[35] This is something to which Owen himself would aspire and ultimately achieve as erstwhile laird of New Lanark, his most famous island, and later as feudal overlord of another community, another island in another world, New Harmony.

## NOTES

1. W.H. Chaloner, 'Robert Owen, Peter Drinkwater and the Early Factory System in Manchester 1788–1800', *Bull. of John Rylands Library* vol. 37, 1954, on which the following is partly based.
2. J. Butt, 'Robert Owen as a Businessman' in Butt (ed.), p. 169.
3. *Life*, p. 23.
4. *Directory of Manchester* 1794; Chaloner, p. 79.
5. *Life*, p. 23.
6. Chaloner, pp. 81–2; Owen recalled the year as 1791 in *Revolution in Mind and Practice*, 1849, p. 9. He was less clear in *Life*.
7. *Life*, p. 24.
8. *Life*, p. 26.

9. On Drinkwater see Chaloner, pp. 83–9.
10. *Life*, p. 26.
11. Chaloner, p. 86.
12. On Phillips see J.T. Ward *Factory Movement*, pp. 25, 27, 29; PP1816 III Report . . . on Children Employed, pp. 355–6 on Lee's evidence.
13. *Life*, p. 27.
14. *Life*, pp. 27–8 gives his account of the interview, which is clearly partial. Chaloner gives the background, pp. 92–3.
15. *Life*, p. 31.
16. Boulton and Watt Papers, quoted in Chaloner, p. 91.
17. Drinkwater's concerns about factory conditions were well known; discussed by Chaloner, pp. 88–90.
18. *Life*, p. 29. Butt in Introduction to *Life*, ix–x.
19. *Life*, pp. 28,29,31. It is hard to credit what Owen says about Drinkwater's infrequent visits, but he later claims much the same of Dale at New Lanark. See, for example, *Life*, p. 59.
20. Owen's account is given in *Life*, pp. 31–2.
21. *Life*, p. 32. This marketing tactic was further refined at New Lanark.
22. Claeys, footnote to *Life*, p. 84.
23. *Jones' Glasgow Directory*, p. 8; Claeys, note to *Life*, p. 84. This was not apparently the James Craig who later managed the Stanley Cotton Mills and was the recipient of the Owen correspondence preserved in the Atholl Mss.
24. For Owen's version of this see *Life*, pp. 33–5.
25. Chaloner, p. 86 and Lee's evidence, footnote 12.
26. On Kelly see I. Donnachie and G. Hewitt, *New Lanark*, pp. 52–5; Claeys, footnote to *Life*, p. 105.
27. J. Kennedy, *A Brief Memoir of Samuel Crompton*, pp. 27–8, quoted in Chalmer, p. 94.
28. Quoted in Chaloner, pp. 95–6.
29. Quoted in Chaloner, p. 99.
30. He did not have purely 'conservative' views as the rubric of the 1792 declaration suggests. He also signed a petition in 1795 supporting peace with France. See Claeys, 'Introduction', xxii, who suggests a certain independence in these matters.
31. On church attendance, see *Life*, p. 48.
32. *Life*, p. 34.
33. His account of this incident is given in *Life*, pp. 40–42.
34. Butt in 'Introduction' to *Life*, x.
35. Chaloner, p. 85.

# FOUR

# Partner in Cotton Spinning

H aving given in his notice Owen was anxious to make a fresh
start. He recommended as his successor Robert Humphreys, an
experienced engineer who had 'done millwright and other mechanical
work' for plant Owen managed. It was 'many months' or 'nearly a year'
before Humphreys was available, but in his memoirs Owen could not
recall whether he left Drinkwater in 1794 or 1795.[1] Perhaps he worked
with Drinkwater for about two and a half years, rather than the four years
he claimed, or possibly stayed on well into 1795, devoting a proportion
of the time to prospective business ventures. His standing among the
Manchester cotton masters was such that when he did eventually leave
Drinkwater, in what Butt described as a 'justifiable pique', he had already
rejected one potentially remunerative partnership and joined another.[2]

The first overture apparently came as soon as news spread that he and
Drinkwater were parting company:

> Mr Samuel Marsland, who with others had purchased the Chorlton
> Estate, near Manchester, with a view of building a new town upon
> it, applied to me and said he was going to build extensive mills
> upon this property, and if I would join him in the partnership he
> would find the capital and give me one third of the profits.[3]

Marsland and his younger brother, Peter, were the sons of Henry
Marsland, a pioneering Stockport mill owner who had diversified into
real estate, buying a portion of the Chorlton estate which was being sold
off piecemeal by the last owner of Chorlton Hall, Barbara Mynshull, in the
1780s. On his father's death in 1795 Samuel decided to develop Chorlton,
while Peter, more technically minded, took over the Stockport enterprise
and made important innovations in power weaving.[4] 'Very respectable
people, of great property' was the confidential reference Peter Ewart gave
them when the father first dealt with Watt.[5] They were strong supporters
of the New College, the Manchester successor to the Warrington Academy,
which had been established to educate Unitarians and other Dissenters,
and with which Owen also maintained some connection. Samuel was
brother-in-law of Ralph Harrison, an eminent member of its staff and a
minister of Cross Street Unitarian Chapel, the wealthiest and most influential congregation of Dissenters in the town and even a centre of intellectual
life in late eighteenth-century Manchester. Marsland possibly met Owen
through Unitarian connections, hence the association that led to the offer of

partnership. As Owen said, Marsland made him 'a very liberal proposal', but having greater confidence in his own abilities than before, he declined. He maintains this was because he was offered only a third of the profits, but others have suggested that the real reason was that he would not have been able to exercise full control since Marsland would have been on the spot and also had a detailed knowledge of current developments in cotton spinning.[6] Marsland, however, does not seem to have held Owen's refusal against him and the two men maintained, if not friendship, then at least a close business relationship in the development of the mills at Chorlton.

Before Marsland's schemes Chorlton was already being developed by some of its new owners as an industrial suburb with its axis on a recently opened turnpike road, Oxford Road. Green's map of the town in 1794 clearly shows the projected new streets marked as a grid over what was then still green fields. Although the water of the Medlock was exploited by dyeworks the river did not provide sufficient power to drive machinery so the development of Chorlton would depend primarily on steam power. Understandably Boulton & Watt kept a close eye on the business opportunities this presented, and indeed some cotton mills had already been built to the east of Oxford Road. An important artery, the Rochdale Canal, was being promoted to run a few hundred yards to the north of the unnavigable Medlock. The hamlet of Chorlton Rows (the present All Saints) became a genteel quarter where mill masters lived until it too was overtaken by development. Owen himself stayed for a time in the old mansion of Chorlton Hall.[7]

Having turned down Marsland's offer, 'in opposition', he reflected, 'to sound judgement', Owen had to find new partners. These were Jonathan Scarth and Richard Moulson, according to Owen's description, 'two young men, inexperienced in the business, although they had capital'. Scarth, the first of many Quakers with whom Owen was associated, was born in Whitby in 1772 and moved to Manchester in 1792 or 1793. The capital Scarth brought with him derived from his father's successful whaling venture. Apart from signing the Dissenter's declaration in 1792, when he gave his address as Dolefield, not much is known about Moulson apart from the fact that he subsequently became a partner in Moulson and Fawcett, a muslin manufacturing enterprise in Blue Boar Court.[8]

'We were to build mills, and to divide the profits equally between us', said Owen, 'and I was to have the management of the whole concern, under the firm of 'Moulson, Scarth and Owen'. The partnership was to build cotton mills on land purchased from Marsland and Company.[9] Evidently Owen and his partners worked closely with Marsland, who was constructing his own mill next door. Indeed the two buildings in Cambridge Street, shown on a projected plan dating from October 1795, were originally intended to be virtually symmetrical and share the same steam engine. It has been suggested that Marsland may have picked the site partly for its water supply as there was a spring forming a pond just to the south, and Chester Street on which a line of mills fronted was laid along the line of a stony escarpment providing solid foundations. The total length of the buildings on the Cambridge Street axis was 270ft, the width being 107ft. The two mills were ranged round a courtyard with the preparation rooms opposite and the main entrance opening on to Chatham Street. Owen's mill was of six stories, but unfortunately we do not know either what it cost the partners to build and equip or how many spindles it housed.[10] The partnership was evidently well enough capitalised to join Marsland in purchasing a steam engine to drive the machinery in their adjoining mills. Marsland seems to have made the first approach to Boulton & Watt but Owen himself visited the Soho Works sometime in the latter half of 1795, agreeing to purchase a rotary steam engine for £1,492. This was confirmed by the following letter:

> Messrs. Boulton and Watt.
> Gentlemen,
> We have concluded to have an engine of 30 horses power and with the advice of Mr Lowe to fix it at the end of all the buildings, within side the factory; we intend soon to send you a ground plan with the elevation of the buildings and a plan of the Chorlton Lands. We shall be much obliged by having the engine forwarded as early in the spring as you possibly can.
> We are,
> Respectfully yours,
> Robt. Owen & Co.
>
> Chorlton Hall,
> Manchester. 27 Oct. '95.

The agreement, ante-dated 2 October, was duly signed by the three partners. Given that Marsland was to guarantee half the cost of the engine James Watt jun. wrote asking whether he wished his name to be added. However, it was explained that Marsland's relationship with Moulson, Scarth and Owen was 'of a private nature' and therefore his name was not included in the agreement. 'Of larger size than the common run of rotative engines', the unit Boulton & Watt supplied was fitted with a 31 inch cylinder cast and bored by John Wilkinson and described by the engineers as 'one of the most perfect that ever passed through our hands'. Quite apart from Marsland's role in selecting and ordering the engine, Owen had evidently learned a great deal about the potential of steam power at Drinkwater's cotton mill.[11]

Boulton & Watt's promise to deliver the engine by the spring may well have been fulfilled, but meantime the partnership with Moulson and Scarth had run into difficulties. These might have been personal as well as financial. Maybe the ill-defined role of Marsland, who had wider real estate interests, was a factor, but sometime in the middle of 1796 the partnership was dissolved. This must have been after February, when Boulton addressed a letter to the firm about the engine, but it is unclear exactly when the split came.[12] But certainly Owen did not exaggerate the significance of what then transpired when he wrote that, 'a new arrangement was made, which was destined to give another direction to my future life'.[13] The arrangement may have been brokered by Marsland, but such was Owen's reputation as a fine cotton spinner, it seems likely that he would not have had to wait long to find new associates. So it was that the Chorlton Twist Company, with its influential partners, larger capital and wider connections, came into being. The constituent partners included Messrs Barton, wholesale merchants and cotton manu-facturers in Manchester, and Borradaile and Atkinson, hat manufacturers in Salford and London. John Barton was a wholesale merchant and cotton manufacturer of 6 Phoenix Street, in partnership with his brother, Henry, who appears in local directories from 1788 to 1804. William Borradaile was in partnership in London with his brother, Richardson Borradaile. He and John Atkinson were merchants and hat manufacturers in Greengate, Salford and had London premises at 34 Fenchurch Street in 1790.[14] Both companies had long-established and extensive business connections, reaching as far afield as Scotland. Scarth and Moulson maintained some interest but it is unclear exactly what share they held in the new company. Owen was to be manager, assisted by Thomas Atkinson, John's brother. He does not record what the terms were, but presumably as good if not better than the arrangement he previously had with Drinkwater, making him by the standards of the time, and for his age, a rich man.[15]

While the engine was at least up and running the new partnership immediately faced difficulties caused by another financial crisis during the winter of 1796–7. The previous company, probably through Owen's earlier contacts, had found ready custom for its yarn among the fine cotton weavers in Scotland and Borradaile and Atkinson continued to exploit this market. But this seems to have caused the company problems, for, writing to Boulton and Watt on 15 October, Thomas Atkinson explained:

> We should have answered yours of the 22nd. ult had we not been in daily expectation of Mr Marsland paying us his proportion of the engine which he at present does not find convenient to do. From the great scarcity of money in Scotland we have been disappointed in getting bills discounted and even prolonging the credit to six months, which lays us under the unpleasing necessity of remitting you a bill at that period drawn on Wm and Rdn Borradaile and Co. for £1,527.10.8. We, however, hope you will not find much inconvenience in paying it away.[16]

Atkinson offered further explanation of the situation by assuring Boulton and Watt that 'nothing but the great scarcity of money in the commercial world would induce us to ask for longer credit', but since the great engineers usually insisted on payment within two months they cannot, in any case, have been overly concerned about the financial health of the Chorlton Twist Company. While these were troubled times in the world at large they seem to have affected the company only in the short-term. From the outset it was reckoned to be a highly successful enterprise, well-placed to capitalise on the continuing demand for yarn, and for fine yarn in particular. The company might have been seen by some to be in direct competition with Drinkwater, but Owen insisted that the contrary was the case since his former employer 'had always been kind and liberal, except in not being firm in maintaining his engagement' and so he did not want to 'injure him', as he put it. Nevertheless another company with the machines and skills to match the quality of yarns Owen claimed to have achieved at Drinkwater's certainly represented competition, even if it could not immediately match the scale of production at the Piccadilly factory.[17]

However much he may have wanted to get his own back on Drinkwater, it would not have been in his interest to do so. Although by his skill he had greatly increased Drinkwater's profits and his own financial status into the bargain, he may also have been indebted to his former employer for his enhanced social standing and entry to the Manchester elite. His achievements as a cotton spinner meant that he had become 'a person of public celebrity' and one whose name 'stood prominent before the Manchester public'.[18] While Drinkwater was no reformer at least he seems to have been concerned about the morals and condition of his workforce, and for whatever reason, this rubbed off on Owen. Nor is it surprising that the successful young factory manager with a nascent interest in social conditions and a questioning mind in the matter of religion should attract the attention of like-minded individuals who formed the intellectual core of the Manchester Literary and Philosophical Society.[19]

He attended his first meeting as a visitor on 4 October 1793, when the society was already twelve years old. It developed from weekly meetings, chiefly on literary topics, held at the home of Thomas Percival, the other co-founders being Thomas Barnes and Thomas Henry. These and other leading figures in the society, such as John Ferriar, president when Owen joined, and John Dalton, the chemist and natural philosopher, were in their different ways true sons of the Enlightenment. Percival, a key figure, was a physician and reformer. Debarred from entering an English university because of the need to subscribe to the Thirty-Nine Articles, he attended the Warrington Academy and then like many other Dissenters went north to study medicine at Edinburgh, where he associated with Scottish Enlightenment figures like Hume and Robertson.

While still a student he became a Fellow of the Royal Society and later completed his studies in Leyden. After practising in Warrington he moved to Manchester and took an interest in social conditions, publishing in 1773 his 'Observations on the State of the Population in Manchester', which stressed the high mortality rate in manufacturing centres. Percival was greatly concerned about the condition of the poor and in 1796 played an important role in establishing the Manchester Board of Health, to which Owen also belonged. It is possible that Owen first met Percival when he came to inspect the new sanitary arrangements in Drinkwater's factory. Barnes was another graduate of Warrington Academy and became a Unitarian minister, moving from Ainsworth near Bolton, where he apparently trebled the congregation, to the Cross Street Chapel in 1780. Apart from his association with the Board of Health and the House of Recovery he was also an educational reformer. He was involved in the establishment of a College of Arts and Sciences, lecturing on moral philosophy and commerce, and later became principal of the Manchester College. Interestingly Barnes was made an honorary D.D. by Edinburgh University in 1784, a rare distinction for an English Dissenter. Thomas 'Magnesia' Henry, an apothecary and magnesia manufacturer, was also an educationist who helped pioneer the teaching of science and medicine in Manchester. Although Dalton achieved greater fame, Ferriar was perhaps the most interesting of the leading figures in the society. A Scot, born at Oxnam near Jedburgh, he also studied medicine at Edinburgh. After a spell practising in Stockton-on-Tees he moved to Manchester becoming physician at the Infirmary in 1789. A fever epidemic led Ferriar to urge the authorities to pay more attention to sanitation, closing or cleansing insanitary dwellings, establishing baths, and restricting the hours of work of factory children. He too was involved in the Board of Health and his *Medical Histories and Reflections* (1792–98, with an American edition published in Philadelphia in 1816) clearly linked the spread of disease to social conditions. He was also interested in literature and anti-materialist philosophy, on which subjects he both read and published papers and books, including one on Sterne (whom, it will be recalled, Owen had evidently read in boyhood) published in 1798. If Owen was to learn more about social reform he could hardly have chosen better company.[20]

As the minute books reveal the papers read before the society covered a wide range of subjects, literary, philosophical, scientific, medical, and humanitarian. Within a few weeks of its founding it offered a medal worth 5 guineas (£5.25) for the best paper on 'the arts employed in the manufactures of Manchester' and throughout the years it took a great deal of interest in the town's staple industry. Indeed, Owen's introduction to the society was a paper on 'The Nature and Culture of Persian Cotton' by a Dr Guthrie. When it came to the discussion, Percival, from the chair, and much to Owen's embarrassment, announced:

'I see a young friend present, who I am sure can if he will give us some valuable information upon the subject. I mean Mr Owen, so well known for his knowledge in fine-cotton spinning.'[21]

At this Owen blushed and 'stammered out some few incoherent sentences', it being the first time he had ever spoken in public. He was particularly annoyed about his awkwardness because quite patently he knew more about the different kinds and qualities of cotton, and about the history of the material, than any of the others who joined in the discussion. Again his reflections on this highlight his awe of the distinguished and well-educated company in which he found himself, apologising not only for his lack of education but also for his shyness and diffidence. These defects contrast quite dramatically with the characteristics of the dynamic, thrusting and successful manager he had become by the age of 22. Despite what he says he was solicited to join and became a member on 1 November 1793. He was again precocious enough to turn the knowledge he possessed on the town's main industry to good account, writing a paper entitled 'Remarks on the Improvement of the Cotton Trade', which he read at the meeting on 29 November. This went well, generated some interesting discussion, Percival was encouraging, and complimented him on his paper. As a result he now found himself on equal terms not only with the distinguished luminaries, physicians and scientists, but also clergy, merchants and fellow manufacturers, certainly more inspiring company than 'the plodding men of business, with limited knowledge and limited ideas' he dealt with in his daily routine.[22]

Having proved to himself that he was perfectly capable of holding his own in such erudite company he seems to have become an enthusiastic and regular attender at the meetings of the society, recalling that:

The meetings became very pleasant and useful to me; making me familiar with the ideas, habits, and prejudices of a new class in society. I say prejudices, – for the literary man has, like all others, his strong educated prejudices.[23]

He delivered a second paper on 'The Utility of Learning' a month after the first. The title of the third, given on 6 March 1795 was 'Thoughts on the Connection between Universal Happiness and Practical Mechanics', the last, read on 13 January 1796 being 'On The Origin of Opinions, with a View to the Improvement of Social Virtues'. At least two and possibly three of these contributions had some relevance to his subsequent philosophy and social psychology, especially his emphasis on the influence of environment in shaping character. Unfortunately none of his papers were published which suggests that they were somewhat hackneyed.[24] At that time every member was supposed to give a paper each session and many must have been little more than short statements to

set the discussion going on a particular topic. But it is possible that Owen
carried some of the more important ideas he was then wrestling with
either to write his papers or to raise in discussion into his later work.

Opportunities certainly abounded to extend his education by listening
and debate. Contemporary with Robert Owen a John Owen (not the
later John Owens, a founder of the University of Manchester) was also
a member of the society and it is sometimes difficult to tell which Owen
the minutes refer to. But it seems that Robert Owen attended no fewer
than 37 and no more than 41 meetings during his spell in Manchester.
He was present to hear discussed, among others, topics on civilisation,
philosophy, politics, citizenship, public health, and the growing problem
of the poor, especially in an urban-industrial context. On 13 December
1793 he heard a paper by James Percival, Dr Percival's son, on 'A
Philosophic Enquiry into the Nature and Causes of Contagion', on 19
April 1794 Samuel Bardsley, another physician, who later gave evidence
in support of Peel's factory bill, spoke on 'Party Prejudice, Moral and
Political', and on 1 April 1796 Bardsley addressed himself to 'Cursory
Observations, Moral and Political, on the State of the Poor and Lower
Classes in Society', a subject of great concern to the authorities and one
under-pinning much of Owen's later views on society.[25]

Among others he heard was one given by Ferriar on 3 October 1794
on the subject of 'Genius and Modern Prophets' which tried to prove
that 'anyone . . . might become a genius, and that it only required
determination and industry for anyone to attain this quality in any
pursuit'. This was apparently very learned and was met with 'a profound
silence' despite the efforts of the president to generate discussion. Owen
was accompanied by Dalton and a friend, William Winstanley, another
Unitarian minister, and was disappointed that they were going to miss
any discussion. 'With a view to induce debate' he got to his feet and
said it was a most ingenious paper, but 'as it was read it occurred to
me that I have always had a great desire to become a genius, and have
always been very industrious in my application for the purpose, but I
could never succeed. I therefore am obliged to conclude that there must
be some error unexplained in our learned author's theory'. Ferriar went
red with anger or perhaps embarrassment and only managed to stammer
out a confused response before he was rescued by others joining in the
discussion. Not suprisingly Owen never found Ferriar as friendly as he
had been before, but despite this incident he must have made a good
impression generally because he was soon invited to join the committee.
Most of his fellow members on the committee were older than Owen, had
college or university educations, were non-conformists, and many had
interests extending into the community at large. So there was a significant
link between the ideas discussed at the society and practical applications
in Manchester and beyond. As far as he was concerned his presence in

such company probably further reinforced his sense of triumph over what he regarded as his own defects in terms of background and education.[26]

His membership of the Literary and Philosophical Society also opened doors and brought introductions into other circles.

Percival was widely connected with savants on the Continent and in the United States, many of whom, regardless of the war and their alien status beat a path to his door during visits to the British Isles. As one of the fastest growing industrial centres in England, Manchester tended to attract visiting scientists and physicians anxious to see what they could of the new technology and assess its impact on social conditions. Accordingly, Percival held open house, often for visitors and friends alike, and it is quite probable that Owen was part of this circle. He was evidently well regarded by Percival and it may have been at his behest that he became a member of the Manchester Board of Health when it was established in 1796.[27] This proved to be a highly influential body, which because of its interests in factory conditions and in particular child labour, ranged far beyond Manchester. Indeed, anticipating the campaign that ultimately led to 'Peel's Act', the first legislation dealing with factory conditions, in 1802, it began gathering evidence from masters about the treatment and condition of apprentices in their mills. The board obviously went to a great deal of trouble and solicited information on prevailing conditions from far and wide. Dale was among those who responded to the board's questionnaire. His replies were fulsome and it is an interesting speculation that Owen may well have learned for the first time about the regime at New Lanark when he scrutinised Dale's detailed responses to the questions about how apprentices were treated in his mill.[28] In any case, he almost certainly knew about the large water-powered mills that had been built in Scotland including several with which Dale was associated and may even have read about them in the early volumes of Sir John Sinclair's *Statistical Account*.[29]

A second circle, with over-lapping personnel, congregated around the Manchester College, where Barnes was principal, and Dalton and Winstanly, both 'intimate friends' of Owen, were assistants. Dalton, a Quaker, was to become an important figure in the world of science as a pioneer of magnetism and around the time Owen met him had already published *Meteorological Essays and Observations* (1793), which spelled out some of his early ideas. Winstanley, the Unitarian, studied under Barnes from 1793-5 and remained in Manchester until 1798 when he moved to Derby.[30] His brother-in-law, Dr John Hull, a botanist and physician at the Lying-in Hospital in Manchester, visited New Lanark in July 1797 accompanied by John Peschier, a physician from Geneva.[31] Owen and the others regularly met to discuss religion, morals, and the scientific discoveries of the day, and on one occasion Coleridge joined them, evidently to debate matters of religion with Owen. Coleridge, then at

Jesus College, Cambridge, was briefly a disciple of William Godwin (whom Owen would meet later in life), and would almost certainly have opposed Owen's growing scepticism. Coleridge was renowned for his verbosity, so it could very well be that Owen's claim to have won the argument by 'few words, directly to the point' can be sustained. However, it seems unlikely that they would have discussed the pantisocracy, or community in which all would have equal power, later projected by Coleridge, Southey and Lovell. When Coleridge read a copy of *A New View of Society* he was greatly impressed and told Owen that he could well profit from the plain and simple style in which it was written. He may well have changed his mind if he read some of Owen's later publications.[32]

Another interesting acquaintance and one of the circle of 'enquiring friends' was Robert Fulton, then a fellow boarder in lodgings at 8 Brazenose Street (an appropriate enough address for Owen since he had an extremely large and prominent nose). Fulton, an engineer and inventor who pioneered steamships in the United States, was living in Manchester and had been drawn into the same circle as Owen. Fulton seems to have been forever dreaming up new schemes, soliciting advances to get them off the ground and constantly in debt to friends and business associates alike when his various enterprises failed to come to fruition. In his autobiography Owen provides a detailed account of his dealings with Fulton including his joint partnership in an enterprise to develop an inclined plane for lifting canal barges from one level to the other (hence eliminating the need for locks) and what seems to have been, for its time, a highly innovative steam digger for excavating canals. Toward the end of 1794 Fulton had resolved to leave Manchester and head south to Gloucester where the ill-fated Gloucester & Berkeley Canal was under construction and he felt he might successfully apply to the commissioners to have his digging machine adopted on this project. Owen had agreed to make him an advance but judiciously had a partnership agreement drawn up before he did so. This was duly signed by the two parties on 17 December 1794. Owen agreed to advance up to £400 to help Fulton develop his inventions but, wisely in the event loaned him only £93. 8s (£93.40). In March of the following year this was converted into a debt with interest at 5 per cent, and at the same time Owen agreed to loan Fulton another £80. While it is unclear whether or not he did so he claims that Fulton used the advance not only to pursue the canal schemes but to visit Glasgow. There, on the Clyde, according to Owen, he saw Henry Bell's prototype steamboat, 'imperfect, and, as to profit, impotent', and quickly realised both its defects and potential. However, any connection between Fulton and either Bell or William Symington, another Scottish steamboat pioneer, is far from clear. That Fulton in July 1801 saw Symington's steamboat, the 'Charlotte Dundas I', sailing not on the Clyde but on the Forth & Clyde Canal, is an attractive idea, for he tried a boat of similar design on the Seine not long after. But at that time Fulton was in Brest, working with the French government and busy with experiments aimed at blowing up the British fleet, and was hardly likely to travel to Scotland and announce himself as 'Mr Fulton'. Fulton did visit England in May 1804, calling on Boulton & Watt, and it is possible he went to Scotland to see Symington's second boat 'Charlotte Dundas II' around that time.[33] Whatever transpired there is a measure of truth in Owen's story for Fulton crossed the Atlantic with the knowledge he had gained in Britain and on the Continent. Industrial espionage of this kind was also common in the cotton and iron industries, virtually impossible to police, and potentially profitable either on the Continent or in the United States. While, as Owen says, Fulton brought 'great advantage to his country and the world', through his pioneering steamboat which first sailed on the Hudson River in 1807, he made no profit from it and died in virtual poverty eight years later. But Owen at least got £60 of his loan back, and later may have had cause to reflect on the contribution he had personally made to Fulton's work during his numerous trips by steamboat up and down the rivers of the American interior.[34]

Business for the Chorlton Twist Company also brought social connections beyond Manchester and Owen tells an interesting story, to some extent against himself, which further highlights how he rose to and overcame a new challenge. Typically this was personified, as he set himself against another apparently more experienced individual. He made regular visits to Blackburn where the company had customers, among them Cardwell, Birley and Hornby, one of the largest and most successful enterprises in the town. Having ridden there on a hired hack, he was a bit taken aback to be asked by Hugh Birley, one of Birley Sr.'s sons, if he would join in the hunt the following morning. Owen explained that he had never hunted in his life, was not all that keen on the idea, and had no suitable mount. Birley replied, 'Oh! That need not prevent you, for I have a good hunter at your service'. Owen felt cornered but in the circumstances could hardly refuse since the Blackburn firm was one of his best customers. He takes up the story as follows:

> The hunter was sent to me the next morning, and I mounted it, being an inexperienced rider upon such horses for such purposes, with the impression that I should never return without broken limbs or even with life. I arrived on the ground just before the game was found, and at this critical moment I found myself by the side of the clergyman of the parish, who was extremely well mounted. He was young and was esteemed the most dashing rider who followed these hounds.

Owen and the parson were on the other side of what he thought was an 'impassable wall' when the fox was startled on the other side. 'Now for it', said the parson, turning his horse towards the wall and clearing it easily:

> My horse (which I discovered was a practised hunter, although I was not) immediately followed the Parson, and how I continued to keep my seat I know not, but so it was that I was safe in the saddle after a pretty good shake, and off went the Parson and I . . . and the sport was continued for some hours. I was a light weight, my horse was powerful, thorough bred, and a well taught hunter. I let him take his own way, and I soon found he knew much better than I did which was the best.

The two riders led the field until late in the day when Owen returned to his hotel invigorated by the experience and much to his surprise having greatly enjoyed himself. He could perfectly well appreciate that the fresh air, exercise and excitement he had experienced would induce others to spend a great deal of time following the hounds. It had proved an exhilarating experience and given him a good appetite into the bargain. Next day he received the plaudits of his friends for keeping up with the parson and all the other hard riders who led the field. He was conscious, he said, that he little deserved their praise, which should more appropriately have been directed at the horse.[35] The fact that during this experience he was able to match equally a man of the cloth is unlikely to have influenced his views on religion, but it highlights his pluck and determination to overcome challenges where the odds against success were longer than he would have liked. Just as important perhaps, it was yet another means of bolstering his self-image. Hugh Birley, incidentally, led the Manchester Yeomanry at the Peterloo Massacre in 1819.[36] A year later a similar disturbance in Scotland so alarmed local elites in and around Lanarkshire that they asked Owen to make suggestions for relieving social distress, from which his island of New Lanark seemed so mercifully free, and this led ultimately to the publication of his *Report to the County of Lanark*.

Owen's rising income and success in climbing the social ladder was reflected in the rapidity with which he changed his place of abode. He took lodgings with Woodroofe, apparently adjacent to the mill, in 1791–2, he was sharing with Fulton in Brazenose Street in 1794, and by 1797, according to John Scholes's *Manchester Directory*, he was living at 2 Cooper Street, very near Drinkwater's town house in Fountain Street. At some unspecified time thereafter we find him 'living as a bachelor' in the old Chorlton Hall, which despite rapidly encroaching development, was still complete with its gardens. All of his lodgings were within easy reach of the town centre, the chapel, the concert hall, the meeting rooms of the Literary and Philosophical Society, and the residences of friends and business acquaintances. His income was already substantial by the time he left Drinkwater and must have been even higher with the Chorlton Twist Company. A measure of this financial success was his move sometime in 1797 or early 1798 into part of Greenheys, a splendid residence erected at the cost of £5,000 by a wealthy merchant who unfortunately never lived long enough to occupy it. It was about two miles from Manchester, set in ornamental grounds, and had a large walled garden. The house itself was beautifully appointed with mahogany doors and windows, fitted as appropriate with plate glass. He and Matthew Marshall, briefly a partner in the Chorlton Twist Company, bought Greenheys between them and divided it up to make a family house for the Marshalls and 'very complete bachelor accommodations' for himself. He was well enough off to hire two elderly retainers to take care of the house, the garden and stable. He evidently still stuck to simple fare for he recalls:

> The old housekeeper came always after breakfast to know what I would have for dinner, my reply was 'an apple dumpling', which she made in great perfection, 'and anything else you like'; and this practice was uniform as long as I remained unmarried.

All his time, so he says, was devoted to 'business and study' and he could not be bothered to think about 'the details of eating and drinking'.[37]

If, in his memoirs, Owen gave an accurate account of his increasing scepticism about religion during his period in Manchester, there seems little doubt that at the same time he at least continued to attend church, most likely the Unitarian chapel in Cross Street, where many of the Literary and Philosophical Society and those associated with the college were members of the congregation. He says as much in his autobiography, but admits an ulterior motive, the opportunity of seeing a beautiful young woman, whom he does not name, but says he also saw at public concerts he occasionally attended. One of several sisters, her family were respected and wealthy, but 'so far in advance of any pretensions' Owen might have had, that getting to know her was apparently impossible. However one day when he was still staying at Chorlton Hall two ladies called asking to see the gardens, to which he readily agreed, conducting them round personally. He takes up the story:

> These visitors were the lady alluded to and her aunt. I was too timid and bashful to enter into conversation with them, and too unsuspecting to imagine any object other than the one mentioned – and with the utmost simplicity and deference allowed them to depart as they came, and certainly much disappointed with the result of their visit to one so stupid as I must have appeared, for there was not the slightest indication of gallantry in anything I said or did.

Inevitably, or at least so he says, he learned too late that the young woman was favourably impressed by him and preferred him 'to all the many suitors who were anxious to obtain her hand'. This might have been wishful thinking on Owen's part, but, as he recalled, 'circumstances were opposed to it, and another destiny was awaiting me'.[38]

Owen's principal responsibilities as one of the managing partners of the Chorlton Twist Company were the purchase of raw materials, overseeing production, and marketing. The last function took Owen round customers engaged in the production of cloth for printing and for muslin. Most were in Lancashire, but building on his earlier reputation Owen soon developed the firm's business in the west of Scotland, for 'having many customers in and around Glasgow, it became necessary for me to go to see them and to endeavour to enlarge our business connections'. There is some confusion surrounding the date of his first visit to Scotland, for it might have been in 1797 rather than 1798, the date of his first recorded visit to New Lanark. In his autobiography he certainly confused dates and got mixed up about various people he met and incidents that occurred during his visits to Glasgow on behalf of the company. He remembered the first journey, in the company of another manufacturer from Preston, who had no particular business to transact but just wanted to see the country, as something of a nightmare, taking 'two nights and three days incessantly travelling in coaches' over deplorable roads to get from Manchester to Glasgow. After a midnight crossing of what he referred to as 'Trickstone Bar', probably Errickstane Hill on the old road entering Upper Clydesdale (the then equivalent of Beattock Summit on Thomas Telford's later turnpike), and 'always passed in fear and trembling by the passengers', they arrived safely in Glasgow first thing in the morning. No one was up and about at their hotel and on such a fine summer's morning they decided to take a walk on Glasgow Green (coincidentally, if he did not already know, very near Dale's town house in Charlotte Street). Here they were treated to the remarkable sight of washerwomen tramping clothes in tubs outside their washhouses. Whether or not this was a peculiarly Scottish custom it was certainly new to the two men, and more to their surprise as they got closer they saw the women's naked legs and 'clothes held up much higher than decency required, or than appeared to us at all necessary'. This was, he recollected, 'a singular introduction into Scotland' and he never imagined that he would 'become so interested in this locality as he afterwards was', a reference to his future wife rather than the barelegged washerwomen.[39]

By the late 1790s Glasgow, formerly a small cathedral and university city on the lowest bridging point of the River Clyde, had become the Manchester of Scotland. Like its southern counterpart it had experienced dramatic growth, with the population increasing from 25,000 in 1755 to around 67,000 by 1791 and 77,000 at the time of the 1801 census. It achieved this first as an entrepot for the tobacco trade with the North American Colonies and then as a commercial centre of the textile industry. Like Manchester much of the initial expansion had been based on linen until the later switch into cotton turned Glasgow into a manufacturing as well as a commercial centre. Entrepreneurs who had formerly orchestrated linen and cotton spinning and weaving on the domestic system enthusiastically adopted the new spinning technology imported from the south during the 1770s and early 1780s, particularly Arkwright's water frame, which was installed in considerable numbers in new mills located on the larger rivers of the Scottish Lowlands. One of the leading entrepreneurs in the Scottish cotton trade was David Dale, a remarkably successful textile merchant, manufacturer, dyer and banker. He had joined forces with others, including briefly Arkwright himself, to build several country spinning mills, the largest being New Lanark, begun in 1785. There were few of the city's institutions, commercial or otherwise, with which Dale was not associated, so by dint of his own efforts he had become one of the leading citizens. But he had also made a very useful marriage to Anne Caroline Campbell, of the Campbells of Jura, a prominent Highland family. Her father was a director of the Royal Bank of Scotland, and through his influence Dale had become the agent of the bank in the city. Although by then a wealthy man, and living in considerable style with a fine town house in Charlotte Street and a country residence at Rosebank to the south of the city, Dale was far from ostentatious in himself. He was even widely credited with numerous acts of philanthropy both in the city and beyond. A man of strong religious conviction he had seceded from the Church of Scotland to form his own sect, the 'Old Independents', which derived much from the teaching of John Glas, a minister ordained in 1719. Dale was very much a family man, his wife having given him six children, but the only son died in 1789, followed by his wife two years later. The five surviving daughters, of whom the eldest was Ann Caroline, were thus potential inheritors of an extensive business empire and consequently a large fortune.[40]

By an interesting quirk of fate, Ann Spear, the sister of Robert Spear, the cotton broker with whom Owen had previously dealt, was visiting the Dale household at that time. One day when Owen was out walking near Glasgow Cross he happened to meet her and Caroline, to whom he was introduced. Learning that Owen was in the cotton business Caroline suggested that he should visit Lanark to see the Falls of Clyde and her father's mill. She offered to provide Owen and his travelling companion with an introduction to her uncle, James Dale, who was Dale's half-brother and joint manager of the plant. Owen and his friend took due advantage of this offer, and under James Dale's guidance inspected New Lanark, which, he recalled, 'consisted of a primitive manufacturing Scotch village and four mills for spinning cotton'.[41] Quite when this visit took place is hard to determine. The staff at New Lanark were assiduous in recording visitors to the mills and the earliest surviving Visitors' Book covering the years 1795–99 provides a detailed record of several thousand visitors. Most no doubt went that way to see the famous and romantically situated Falls of Clyde, upstream of Dale's works, but many called in to see the mills and village. Large factories were unusual, objects of curiosity, especially given the large numbers of children that worked in them, but also held mechanical secrets that the mill masters wanted to keep to themselves. Hence the care that was taken admitting and recording visitors. It seems unlikely that Owen and his friend could have visited without their names being recorded, even if they were special guests, so this would date his first visit to 9 March 1798. However, on that date there were only two other visitors, a Mr Donald from Carlisle and a Mr Findley from Glasgow, who could have been Kirkman Findlay, another cotton spinner. There is no mention of any visitor from Preston, so Owen's memory must have been defective on this as well. However on 31 July of the previous year there is an entry recording the visit of a Mr Wallace of Glasgow and two anonymous gentlemen, possibly Owen and his companion.[42] Another explanation is that Owen and his companion visited New Lanark unannounced and had a good look round as unobtrusively as they could. Whenever it was and whatever the circumstances, Owen, standing in front of the mills, allegedly turned to his friend and said, 'Of all the places I have yet seen, I should prefer this in which to try an experiment I have long contemplated and have wished to have an opportunity to put into practice'. This conversation and his supposition that there was hardly a 'distant chance that the wish would ever be gratified' could well be pure invention, but it is more than likely that the place made a strong impression on him.[43]

Owen's first inspection of New Lanark was certainly a significant milestone in his life. The journey with his companion up the Clyde valley from Glasgow to Lanark may well have brought back boyhood memories. The prospect along the way was similar to his native Severn valley, which he had not seen for many years. It was either spring or summer, hence the richness of countryside and orchards helped sharpen his memories. The old town of Lanark and the location of New Lanark deep in the valley below were all familiar, even if far removed from mid-Wales. Indeed the surroundings may have made him feel at home after a footloose existence for most of his youth and early adulthood. The visit to the mills and village showed to the keen business eye a well-established enterprise which with better management might have enormous potential for expansion and profit-taking. If, as he claimed, he had already formulated ideas about social betterment and engineering, a cursory look around the mills and village highlighted what might be done. Assuming he did not know at that stage that Dale might wish to sell, or, indeed his partners wish to purchase the place, he might at least have been thinking about the prospect of making a good marriage to Caroline Dale, whom he was almost bound to see again on future visits to Glasgow.

During his later years in Manchester the Crusoe-like Owen had faced many difficulties and challenges, grasping what came to hand, jumping effortlessly from island to island, and extending his domain with every leap. Many of the threats to his progress had been removed or short-circuited, including the apparently incompetent Jones, the skilled and competitive Lee, the sleeping partners Scarth and Moulson, and the intellectually challenging Ferriar, who had been disarmed by his questioning. Not only had he survived but also prospered and his claim to be 'the first fine cotton spinner in the world' (meaning the best) might well have been sustained by his peers. Now the wanderer had found another island where the threats and challenges to his progress were to prove even more daunting than any he had yet encountered, but the potential rewards greater than he could ever have imagined.

## NOTES

1. *Life*, p. 42.
2. Butt, 'Introduction' to *Life*, p. x.
3. *Life*, p. 42.
4. Chaloner, pp. 98–9; Claeys, notes to *Life*, p. 74; S. Clark, 'Chorlton Mills and their Neighbours', *Ind. Arch. Rev.* vol. II, 1978, from which the following section partly derives.
5. Quoted in Clark, p. 207.
6. *Life*, p. 42; Chaloner, p. 99.
7. Clark, p. 207 describes these developments.
8. Claeys, notes in *Life*, p. 94.
9. *Life*, p. 42.
10. Clark, p. 208.
11. Chaloner, p. 99–100.
12. Quoted in Chaloner, p. 100.
13. Quoted in Chaloner, p. 100.
14. Claeys, notes to *Life*, pp. 94–5.
15. *Life*, pp. 42–3.
16. Quoted in Chaloner, p. 101.
17. *Life*.p. 42.
18. *Life* p. 35.
19. E.M. Fraser, 'Robert Owen in Manchester, 1787–1800', vol 1 xxxii, 1937–8, provides some details on Owen's activities at the society.
20. On Percival, Barnes, Henry, Hull, Ferrier and Dalton see *DNB*; notes by Claeys in *Life*, pp. 87–9; and W.H. Brindley, *The Soul of Manchester*, Manchester, 1929, pp. 44–7.

21. *Life*, p. 37.
22. Fraser, p. 37.
23. *Life*, p. 38.
24. Butt, 'Introduction' to *Life*, xxiv.
25. Fraser, p. 39.
26. This tale is recounted in *Life*, pp. 37–8.
27. Claeys, footnote to *Life*, p. 87.
28. Donnachie & Hewitt, pp. 42–3. This was one of several favourable accounts given by Dale of the regime at New Lanark, corroborated by many independent observers.
29. Sir J. Sinclair (ed.), *Statistical Account of Scotland*, Edinburgh, 1795, vol.xv, pp. 460–67, where the description closely resembles Dale's responses to the questionnaire.
30. On Dalton see *DNB* and A. Raistrick, *Quakers in Science and Industry*, Newton Abbott, 1968, pp. 270–1; on Winstanley and Hull, Claeys, notes to *Life*, pp. 87–8.
31. Gourock Mss., Visitors' Book, 10 July 1797.
32. *Life*, p. 36.
33. W.S. Harvey and G. Downs-Rose, *William Symington. Inventor and Engine Builder*, London, 1980, p. 139.
34. Owen's account of his relationship with Fulton is in *Life*, pp. 64–70.
35. See *Life*, pp. 43–4.
36. On Birley see Claeys, note to *Life*, p. 95.
37. *Life*, p. 49.
38. *Life*, p. 48.
39. The first visit to Glasgow is described in *Life*, pp. 44–5.
40. On Dale see D.J.McLaren, *David Dale*, Glasgow, 1983.
41. *Life*, p. 46.
42. Gourock Mss. Visitors' Book, dates cited.
43. *Life*, p. 46.

# FIVE

# Entrepreneurial Heir

W hen Owen got to Glasgow he discovered that his name had gone
before him and that it was already known to many of his customers
from the bundles of yarn sent out from Drinkwater's factory.[1] Hence
raising new business for the Chorlton Twist Company was less of a
problem than he imagined. Indeed his visit to the centre of the Scottish
cotton industry may well have been a pretext for a fact-finding mission.
His partners may have sent him to find out about the state of the spinning
industry north of the border, particularly any developments that had been
made in fine spinning and muslin weaving. Even at that stage he and his
partners could well have heard from business acquaintances that Dale was
in declining health and wanted to decommit from some of his activities.
On a personal level, the astute and ambitious Owen, having himself heard
about New Lanark, Dale, and his daughters, might have had other motives.
He says as much of his second visit which evidently created 'other feelings
than those of mere business'.[2] At any rate after the visit to New Lanark
Owen called on Caroline to thank her for the introduction and to say how
much he had enjoyed the scenery near the Falls of Clyde and the site of
the mills. Caroline was just going out for a walk with her sisters along
the banks of the river so he accompanied them. This outing was repeated
several times and before he left she said she would be pleased to see him
again when he came back to Glasgow.

The business trip obviously brought results because the orders for
'Chorlton Cotton Twist' from Scottish customers, mainly in Glasgow
and Paisley, gradually increased. Fortuitously for Owen, his partners
thought it would enhance business still further if he could personally call
on customers every six months. He had also been in touch with Ann Spear
who told him a great deal about Caroline, including the encouraging news
that although there had been plenty of men anxious to become her suitor,
none so far had proved particularly attractive. She also seemed to feel that
the majority were just after her money.[3] Quite how Owen reacted to this
last assertion is impossible to determine but he had the useful pretext of
delivering a letter from Ann to Caroline on his next visit to Glasgow. This
was probably in May 1798, which meant the trip occurred sooner than he
or his partners anticipated. Certainly Owen, in the company of one of his
partners, John Barton, and Heatley Whittle, another Manchester merchant,
revisited New Lanark on the 16th of the month.[4] This suggests that even
at this early stage the other partners of the Chorlton Twist Company

were already taking more than a passing interest in Dale's enterprise. At the same time Owen, despite his apparent backwardness with women, had several more opportunities to meet Caroline before he returned to Manchester.

Ann Spear now played the role of go-between and confidant, telling Owen that Caroline had been greatly impressed by him and since they met had even turned down several offers of marriage. Armed with this useful information and another letter Owen determined to 'look decidedly to Scotland for a wife'. He recognised that it would be more than a matter of winning Caroline's heart because he would need to obtain the approval of her father, a man of high religious and moral principles, of high social standing, who, in any case, he had never even met. Undaunted he set out for Glasgow and in the course of further meetings and walks with Caroline and her sisters learned that Dale was anxious to retire and wanted to sell New Lanark 'finding it not managed with the success that he had expected'. This revelation may well have inspired Owen to push his case with Caroline harder than he had previously but he was delighted to find that she would agree to marry him if he could obtain her father's consent. It presented something of a problem but plucking up his courage he resolved to go and introduce himself to Dale. He got a cool reception, which turned to suspicion when Owen inquired about the rumour going about Glasgow that Dale wanted to dispose of the mills. To this Dale said, 'You cannot want to purchase them – you are too young for such a task'. But replied Owen, 'I am connected in partnership with older heads, and with men having large capitals, and we are already largely in the cotton trade in Manchester'. Dale asked if he had seen New Lanark to which Owen replied that he had seen something of it but not in detail. 'Go and examine it', said Dale, suggesting that afterwards he went straight to Manchester to report to his partners. If they wanted to buy he would be willing to negotiate. Owen left with the feeling that he had not been taken seriously but nevertheless had broken the ice and obtained Dale's authority to give New Lanark a thorough inspection. He rushed from Glasgow to Lanark, apparently without any small change, for he had nothing but guineas or half-guineas in his pocket. No fewer than three toll keepers, suspicious of anything other than Scottish bank notes, allowed him to pass without paying, leading him to conclude that he had 'come into a very primitive district'.[5]

Before leaving Glasgow for Manchester he told Caroline what had transpired and the pair resolved to correspond. On the basis of his report, his partners, to his surprise (or at least so he says), were enthusiastic about purchasing the mills. Together with Atkinson and Barton, he immediately returned north and the three duly visited New Lanark on 22 July 1799.[6] Since he and Barton were already familiar with the place only Atkinson remained to be convinced. All of them were evidently 'much pleased with their situation and the general outline of the establishment'. However, on the personal front, Caroline's report of her conversation with her father about Owen was far from optimistic. He wanted no 'land louper' from England but 'an honest Scotchman' to marry his daughter and succeed him.[7] She could not contemplate marrying Owen without her father's permission and it was going to be difficult to get him to change his mind. The partners met Dale who was pleased to hear that they wanted to buy the mills. He knew the high reputation of their respective firms but nevertheless duly made enquiries about their financial standing. The following day Dale announced, 'I am now satisfied of your respectability and I am willing to treat with you for the land, village, and mills at New Lanark, with everything as the establishment now stands'.

When it came to the question of a price, Dale responded, 'Mr Owen knows better than I do the value of such property at this period, and I wish that he would name what he would consider a fair price between honest buyers and sellers'. He later claimed that he himself took the decision, which seems unlikely in the circumstances, but replied, 'It appears to me that sixty thousand pounds, payable at the rate of three thousand a year for twenty years, would be an equitable price between both parties'. Dale accepted and arrangements were immediately made to sell the mills to the New Lanark Twist Company.[8]

Atkinson and Barton returned south leaving Owen to take charge of the transfer. He installed himself in the Clydedale Inn in Lanark because one of the two managers' houses in the village was occupied for the summer by the Dale sisters and their retinue, and it had been agreed that they should stay on for another six weeks. This gave Owen and Caroline further opportunities to meet, walking and talking with her sisters by the banks of the Clyde. Apart from familiarising himself with the mill Owen had to visit Dale frequently on business either connected with the transfer or with parish and county affairs likely to affect it. Gradually Dale seemed to warm to him, a process evidently assisted by two allies, another of the Royal Bank's Glasgow agents, Robert Scott Moncrieff, and his wife.[9] They had a soft spot for Caroline, befriended Owen, and eventually talked Dale into blessing their marriage. The story of Owen's courtship further confirms his great capacity for dealing successfully with others, especially since Dale was clearly so sceptical at the outset.[10]

Owen and Caroline were married at Dale's house in Charlotte Street on 30 September 1799. The brief ceremony followed the rights of the Church of Scotland and was conducted by Dale's near neighbour, the Rev Robert Balfour, minister of St Paul's Outer High Kirk.[11] Balfour was duly presented by Dale with a full suit of clothes, 'hat and all', of such fine quality that it lasted the rest of his life. Immediately the wedding breakfast was concluded the couple and Caroline's servant left for the journey south, Dale's carriage taking them to the first stage and thereafter they posted over very bad roads to Manchester. As they at last passed through Chorlton, Owen, showing some evidence of humour, pointed out a vinegar factory as their future home, to the obvious chagrin of both his wife and her servant. However, the situation was retrieved when the carriage drove into the opulent setting of Greenheys, with which Caroline was 'uncommonly well pleased'. There they spent their honeymoon.[12]

While this is not the place to go into the complexities of Owen's subsequent finances there is no denying that his marriage was very propitious. By then he had accumulated a capital of £3,000 and Dale offered him an equivalent sum as a dowry, on the condition that he settled £300 per annum on Caroline and any children of the marriage in event of his death. Apart from doubling his personal wealth, Owen's marriage provided him with access to substantial trading capital, for Dale was worth over £100,000 and had access to further funds through his position with the Royal Bank. Dale's connections through marriage and business with the powerful and wealthy Campbell clan gave Owen further financial advantages, direct and indirect, should he ever have cause to exploit them. Owen and his partners paid Dale £60,000 for New Lanark, his personal share being one ninth of the capital. Even allowing for the £6,000 he was worth after his marriage, his shareholding was financed partly by the generous terms on which Dale transferred ownership. According to the agreement between Dale and the new partners the purchase price was to be paid over twenty years at £3,000 per annum with five per cent interest. Owen and his partners were effectively given an extended bridging loan, all the more favourable in that Dale could not reasonably be expected to live until 1820, and in the circumstances Owen himself was likely to be a trustee on his estate. More to the point the loan was secured by the property at New Lanark and with good trade the partners might well repay Dale from the profits. Owen's salary as managing partner was £1,000 a year, a huge sum, equivalent to the income of a prosperous laird or merchant. He undoubtedly came to New Lanark as the entrepreneurial heir of David Dale.[13]

In its short existence the Chorlton Twist Company had undergone several changes in its partnership structure. In January 1798 Moulson had withdrawn entirely from the concern, which then consisted of Owen, Atkinson and Scarth. Later in the year Marshall, Owen's neighbour, had become a partner in the firm, but he and Scarth withdrew on 9 August 1798, leaving Owen and Atkinson as the sole remaining partners in the concern.[14] Quite what Barton's role was by that time is impossible to determine, but he had clearly played an important part in the groundwork for the acquisition of New Lanark. Affairs there had been left in the hands of Dale's managers, Owen having 'arranged all matters as well as [he] could' before leaving for the south. According to Owen things at New Lanark did not go according to plan, James Dale and Kelly did not see eye to eye, and were 'little capable of conducting such a concern in the manner we wished and expected'.[15] Whether this was true or not the partners clearly thought their investment needed personal supervision. Chorlton mill seems to have been capably managed by Thomas Atkinson; in 1801, excluding buildings, it was insured for £16,200. Yet the business of the much more highly capitalised enterprise was clearly a priority. The company's Scottish market could be supplied from nearer at hand and thus safeguard it, or it could complement its supply of fine yarns with the medium and low counts produced at New Lanark. It would be possible to play off the yarn market in Scotland against those in England, and, given the return of peace, trade effectively via Glasgow and the Forth and Clyde canal with the Baltic, particularly with Russia, a developing market for medium quality yarns.[16] Thus within a few months, and by mutual agreement, Owen and his wife returned to Scotland, staying initially with Dale in Glasgow. Owen, as he put it, duly 'entered into the government of New Lanark' on 1 January 1800, when 'the groundwork on which to try an experiment long wished for' could begin.[17]

What Owen failed to make explicit in his memoirs, like much else, was the fact that New Lanark already had a history before he could either make it or invent it. It had been established fifteen years earlier and been operational for fourteen. Alongside the original mill others had been built and further back from the river rows of tenement houses provided shelter for the community's rising population, which had already reached 1,334 by 1793. The labour force had been recruited from far and wide, some even from the Highlands, but a large proportion were orphan or pauper apprentices drawn either from institutions or recruited from parish authorities in Glasgow and Edinburgh. There were other spinning mill communities in the Scottish Lowlands but the sheer size of New Lanark, the fact that it housed and usefully employed large numbers of youngsters, and its location near the romantic Falls of Clyde meant that from the outset it attracted considerable attention. While Dale, as in his other varied enterprises, had profit first and foremost in mind, he early established a reputation as a humanitarian employer, an attribute widely recognised both in his native country and beyond. Indeed the earliest detailed account of the mills and village which appeared in the *Statistical Account of Scotland* in 1793 was the first of many that highlighted the beneficial effects of Dale's paternalism and the regime on the inmates of the community. His son-in-law was later to paint a very different picture.[18]

All the evidence indicates that during much of the first partnership Owen was almost totally absorbed either in business activities or in attempting to establish his credo with Dale and among the Glasgow merchant community. Apart from the New Lanark business to which he had to attend, Dale was ailing and came to rely increasingly on him for financial and management advice. Copies of Owen's correspondence preserved in the archive of Blair Castle, which apart from some business and legal papers, represent the most extensive cache of material from this period, give clues to a frantic timetable. He travelled frequently, generally on horseback and sometimes by coach, between Glasgow and the mills. He made a number of trips to Manchester, where the company continued to be based, travelling on to Wales on at least one occasion. He undertook regular visits of inspection to another spinning mill in which Dale had an interest at Stanley in Perthshire, often travelling there via Edinburgh, and sometimes combining the visit with sight seeing trips to Dunkeld, the Trossachs and Loch Lomond. He also toured the Highlands, venturing as far north as Sutherland, to inspect yet another mill with which his father-in-law was associated.[19]

Owen must have realised that his management of the enterprise at New Lanark would give him considerable power and freedom of movement with his partners at such a distance in Manchester. It seems that he started his reforms almost at once, although it is not known for certain when some of the more radical innovations, either in the community generally or on the factory floor, were actually introduced. Nor do we know exactly when the services of Dale's former managers were dispensed with, possibly (but by no means certainly) soon after he arrived back at the mills as resident managing partner. According to Owen, Dale 'knew little about cotton spinning' and visited New Lanark as infrequently as every two or three months, so these two individuals had therefore been largely responsible for the mills and community for much of their existence. James Dale, born in 1753, was Dale's half-brother, their father having married for a second time, Martha Dunlop. Remarkably little is known about him, apart from the fact that after he left New Lanark he set himself up as an agent and broker in Glasgow, dying in 1819.[20] The likelihood is that James Dale attended to the books and also had responsibility for recruiting and supervising the large and diverse workforce, no easy tasks, given the aversion to 'indoor labour', especially in cotton mills, which evidently prevailed among workers throughout the Scottish Lowlands. Kelly was certainly much the more mechanically minded, having started out as a clockmaker, thus acquiring skills which became highly marketable in the cotton industry. He was also an inventive genius and claimed to be the 'first to turn the mule by water power' in 1790. His most important innovation, patented in 1792, was the self-acting mule, in which the need for a skilled adult spinner, usually male, was eliminated. However, it was not widely adopted because the mules rapidly increased in size to 300 spindles and upwards, so 'the idea of saving by spinning with boys and girls was superseded'. Kelly, while in Dale's employment, also devised more efficient means of 'erecting the great gear' in cotton mills. He contacted the Board of Trustees in 1793, claiming it would result in significant savings in water power, not to mention 'the benevolent tendency of preserving the lives of children and others that may be entangled by the drums or shafts'. Heating the mills, always a problem because of the fire risk and high insurance premiums, was successfully tackled by Kelly when in 1796 he constructed a stove with a series of hot air ducts, which, he declared, 'was sufficient to warm a mill of 150 feet by 30 or upwards'.[21] Kelly also used his skill to design a unique clock, still to be seen in the foyer of the Visitor Centre at New Lanark. It caught the attention of John Aspinwall, an American who visited the village in 1795, and duly recorded that:

> This manufactory of cotton yarn employs 1,300 people. There are about 12,000 spindles going in these mills. There is a remarkable clock with a face something larger than a common clock. It has five dials, one for the hours and minutes and seconds; one for the weeks; one for the months; one for the years; one for the ten years . . . and by which they regulate the mill as the same wheel turns the clock and the mill.

While Owen may not have been impressed by their performance, Dale and Kelly, under the paternal guidance of their employer, had probably achieved a great deal more in one of the largest enterprises of the early industrial era than he was later prepared to admit.[22]

In a recurrent pattern of behaviour already evidenced in earlier relationships in Manchester it could be that Owen saw James Dale and William Kelly as some sort of threat, individuals who could reasonably claim much of the credit for what had been put in place in terms of social provision under Dale's aegis. While there was apparently much that could be criticised both in the efficiency of the plant and in the morality and domestic economy of the village, there was also a great deal that elicited favourable comment, indeed, praise from visitors or investigators. However, as far as Owen was concerned Dale and Kelly 'were incompetent to comprehend my views or to assist me in my plans' and he therefore dismissed them. It is difficult to know how his father-in-law reacted to this, even if he had been convinced by Owen of their inefficiency. But he may already have been too ill to care. Moreover, 'for new measures it was necessary to have new men' and Owen soon initiated a general reorganisation of the rest of the supervisory staff in the mills.[23] Sometime during or after 1803 (though it may have been as late as 1805) he recruited Robert Humphreys from Drinkwater's mill as under-manager on a twenty-year contract at a salary of £350 per annum and 2.5 per cent of the profits. (Humphreys was definitely at New Lanark by 1803, although he may just have been visiting).[24] In the light of their subsequent relationship this certainly represented a strong expression of Owen's belief in Humphreys' ability to be his understudy.[25]

While 'the changes were to be made gradually, and to be effected by the profits of the establishment', there is firm evidence of his Manchester experience being almost immediately applied on the factory floor and to environmental and social control in the village. As early as September 1800, John Marshall, the Leeds flax spinner, visited the Falls of Clyde, passing by New Lanark, and noticed:

> The cotton works late Mr Dales – 4 large mills 6 stories high abt. 50 yds. long each – 2 for twist and 2 for mule spinning. A number of houses are built for the workmen, & 400 or 500 apprentices are lodged in a half of one of the mills which has not yet been worked. They give them 1½ hour's schooling each night after the usual mill hours 7oclock. The present proprietors it is said wished to give that up, but could not because it was contracted for in the indentures. Mr Dale not only taught the children reading & writing but the polite accomplishments he had singing masters & one year actually employed 2 dancing masters to teach the factory girls to dance. They weave some muslin, & employ in the whole abt 2000 hands.

'They are said', continued Marshall, 'to be under better discipline and to do more work with fewer hands than in Mr Dale's time'.[26] These changes had evidently come about partly through a tightening up of working practices on the factory floor, and partly in consequence of a new set of rules and regulations issued by Owen earlier that year.[27]

There were good reasons for a strict regime in country spinning mills, especially on the scale of New Lanark. The community was set low in the valley of the Clyde only a mile from Old Lanark, separated from the little burgh but not remote from it, and reached by a steep and winding road. The entry way was guarded by two symmetrical gatehouses and where the river or the steep valley sides did not intervene between the mill lands and the outside world, adjoining gentlemen's estates were walled against trespass. Among these were the policies of Braxfield, property of the notorious and recently deceased Robert Macqueen, Lord Braxfield, judge in the trial of the 'Scottish Martyrs', which was later to become Owen's family home. Into this community was crammed a mainly youthful population, many young women and a large number of children, among whom the need for discipline and morality required constant vigilance. In the crowded tenements, where the typical dwelling was mainly the traditional Scottish one-roomed 'single-end', or on the floors of the mill reserved as boarding houses or dormitories for the apprentices, health could be jeopardised by insanitary conditions and infection speedily spread among the populace. After the long working hours there was nowhere for folk to go apart from their dwellings and therein apart from each other's company, resort might be made for solace to the bottle. The resulting drunkenness arising from the consumption of alcohol obtained from the village grog shops or imported from Old Lanark posed yet another threat to morality and good order, apart from any absenteeism and inefficiency in the workplace that might arise in consequence. Between the tenements and the factory ran the mill lade, like the river beyond, an ever present danger of drowning for young children.[28] In the mills themselves, cotton dust choked the lungs, open machinery threatened life and limb, and, since so much of it was constructed of timber, and candles or lamps were needed morning and night, there was a constant risk of fire. Finally, pilfering was widespread in the early factory system and evidently rife at New Lanark. It was 'carried on to an enormous and ruinous extent', with the result that Dale's property 'had been plundered in all directions, and had almost been considered public property'.[29] Social and environmental controls, it must have seemed to Owen, were therefore necessary not only for improved business efficiency, but also for the maintenance of good order.

On the factory floor Owen exercised control through under-managers and overseers or 'superintendents' who assessed the behaviour and performance of every worker and duly recorded it in 'books of character'. The evidence could be seen by all, displayed publicly by means of a 'silent monitor' or 'telegraph', an idea almost certainly borrowed from Joseph Lancaster, the Quaker educationist. Although we do not know exactly when he introduced it, Owen, in his memoirs, described the device as follows:

> This consisted of a four-sided piece of wood, about two inches long and one broad, each side coloured – one side black, another blue, the third yellow, and the fourth white, tapered at the top, and finished with wire eyes, to hang upon a hook with either side to the front. One of these was suspended in a conspicuous place near to each of the persons employed, and the colour at the front told the conduct of the individual during the preceding day, to four degrees of comparison. Bad, denoted by black and No. 4, – indifferent by blue, and No. 3, – good by yellow, and No. 2 – and excellent by white and No. 1.

> 'Then', he continued, 'books of character were provided for each department, in which the name of each one employed in it was inserted in the front of succeeding columns, which sufficed to mark by the number the daily conduct, day by day, for two months; and these books were changed six times a year, and were preserved; by which arrangement I had the conduct of each registered to four degrees of comparison during every day of the week, Sundays excepted, for every year they remained in my employment'.

There was a degree of equality, regardless of status, and also a means of appeal:

> The superintendent of each department had the placing daily of these silent monitors, and the master of the mill regulated those

of the superintendents in each mill. If any one thought that the superintendent did not do justice, he or she had a right to complain to me, or, in my absence, to the master of the mill, before the number denoting the character was entered in the register. But such complaints very rarely occurred. The act of setting down the number in the book of character, never to be blotted out, might be likened to the supposed recording angel marking the good and bad deeds of poor human nature.[30]

In his *Improvements in Education*, first published in 1803, Lancaster described a similar arrangement of 'leather tickets, gilt and lettered differently, expressive of the various degrees of merit they were intended to distinguish . . . as a badge of approbation' used in his schools. Masters issued paper tickets for scholarship (the results being duly recorded in a book by monitors) and when a fixed quota of tickets had been obtained successful pupils were issued with the badge (and given small prizes), which could be worn unless forfeited by bad behaviour. 'The system of encouragement', Lancaster claimed, 'proves serviceable as a preventive of punishment, the attainment of the tickets being an award; the forfeiture of them the reverse'.[31] Apart from the likelihood that Owen borrowed this idea from Lancaster there were other instances of similar methods of managerial control elsewhere. What does appear to have been a more genuine innovation was the right which the workers possessed to appeal to Owen regarding the assessments made of them by the superintendents.

Apart from the books of character and the silent monitor there is further evidence that Owen rigidly enforced discipline in the mills. Whether the statement of Duncan McKinlay to the Factory Commissioners in 1833 that 'a constant system of beatings took place, not a day without someone suffering' is reliable or not, there are other grounds for believing that Owen operated a strict regime at New Lanark.[32] Besides random searches of workers to reduce the thieving which had become widespread by the time of his takeover, regular notes were taken of any errors made by employees. Others were summarily dismissed for being absent without permission or indulging in what was described in one instance as 'a fraudulent transaction altering lines'. According to Owen's eldest son, Robert Dale, when his father visited the mills, which he did most mornings when in residence, he made certain that everything was punctiliously kept. As he progressed through the spinning rooms Owen picked up the smallest flocks of cotton from the floor, handing them to some child nearby to be put in the waste bag. 'Papa', said the young Owen one day, 'what *does* it signify, such a little speck of cotton?'. 'The value of the cotton', replied Owen, 'is nothing, but the example is much. It is very important that these people should acquire habits of order and economy'.[33]

Beyond the factory compound the rules and regulations issued by Owen in 1800 certainly derived much from those set out by Percival and his associates on the Manchester Board of Health, and presumably similar to those adopted in Drinkwater's mills. They instructed the inhabitants of the village to observe proper cleanliness, order and good behaviour. Every house was to be cleaned once a week and whitewashed at least once a year by its tenant. The tenants, in rotation, were to undertake to clean the common stairs and sweep the roadway in front of their dwellings. It was forbidden to throw ashes and dirty water into the streets, or, perhaps reflecting how close many of the village folk were to their rural roots, to keep cattle, swine, poultry or dogs in the houses. There were provisions for the prevention of trespass and damage to the company's fences and other property, both evidently on-going problems. In the winter months all doors were to be closed at 10.30 pm, an effective curfew, since no one was to be abroad without permission after that hour. Public order by what were described as Owen's 'military police' was to be as important in the community as environmental controls. The minimum age that a child could work in the mill was fixed at ten (a much publicised requirement of later factory legislation), and from five to ten children could attend free of charge the school provided by the company. Temperance in the use of alcohol was ordered. Religious toleration was recommended as 'a means of uniting the inhabitants of the village into one family' and, finally, every inhabitant, 'consistent with their duty to God and society' was to endeavour both by word and deed 'to make every one happy with whom they have any intercourse'. This last instruction was, as far as we know, Owen's first statement on the vexed question of religion. It might also provide evidence of his earliest thoughts on social philosophy, although his interpretation of 'happiness' was something very different from that of the later Utilitarians.[34]

These rules and regulations show that as well as strict working practices Owen was equally concerned about the social conditions and behaviour of a labour force which, by his account, had been 'collected hastily from any place from whence they could be induced to come, and the great majority of them were idle, intemperate, dishonest, devoid of truth and pretenders to religion which they supposed would cover and excuse their shortcomings and immoral proceedings'.[35] While an earlier biographer judiciously remarked that 'no man is an impractical witness to his own cause', Owen does seem to have had some grounds for concern about the standards prevailing at New Lanark on his takeover.[36] Drunkenness, for instance, was one problem. Thus, to combat the habits of workers, such as the brother of one of his under-managers who apparently went on a regular 'spree', he instigated the evening patrols around the village streets. Those workers, including apparently some errant apprentices, who were reported to Owen, would subsequently be fined and if they persisted in getting drunk were ultimately dismissed. Owen's tactics proved reasonably effective although the celebrations on New Year's Day, the King's Birthday, and the local ceremony of Riding the Marches in Old Lanark remained something of a problem despite the offer of a day's holiday in the summer to those prepared to work on those occasions.

Another reform, the object of much favourable comment by later visitors, was the introduction of a factory store. Located at the far end of the New Buildings, Owen's only recorded architectural contribution before 1816, it was partly designed to counter the rapacious activities of the retail traders in the village. Its prices were approximately 25% lower than its rivals, but it was still able to make an annual profit of around £700 which was eventually used to support the school. Adjacent to the store, at one end of Caithness Row, was the counting house where earnings were paid out in cash or in the form of a wages ticket. Hence the 'Ticket for Wages', an interesting forerunner of the labour note, whereby a worker either presented the ticket and received goods at the store or exchanged it for money from the cashier in the counting house. Employees who ran short of cash, which many apparently did, since they were only paid monthly, could obtain credit through a system of tin tokens. Twelve of these were equivalent to one shilling and the amount borrowed was deducted from their next wages. Counter-marked foreign currency, such as Spanish dollars, was also sometimes used as had prevailed under Dale's regime.

While Owen also introduced a sick fund to which his workers contributed one sixtieth of their pay, as well as a savings bank which by 1818 had deposits amounting to £3000, his most contentious measure was undoubtedly his campaign to improve housing and sanitation in the village. On arriving he had encountered a depressing state of affairs; dirty unswept streets and every house with rubbish heaps and dunghills outside it. The dwellings themselves were in a bad state of repair and Owen initiated a long-term programme of renovations, linked to the immediate adoption of his regulations. Undoubtedly these were far from popular as one eye witness, a former teacher, recorded. Writing in 1839 he remembered that Owen advised the villagers to 'appoint a committee from amongst themselves, every week, to inspect the houses in the village and to insert in a book, to be given for that purpose, a faithful report of the state of each house as they might happen to find it'. 'This recommendation,' the author continued, 'was upon the whole acceded to by the male part of the population but the rage and opposition it met from the women was unbounded'.[37] The upshot was that the female occupants refused to open their doors to what they derisively termed the 'Bug Hunters'. But the tenants had reluctantly to conform and agree to be supervised by Owen's 'military police'. Failure to do so would lead to banishment to an insalubrious part of the village, known, appropriately, as 'Botany Bay'.[38]

A highly significant development, although not immediately obvious from the statistics gathered for the censuses in 1801 and 1811, was the gradual disappearance of the pauper apprentices.[39] Owen, on his arrival, had declared himself committed to ending this system and, as evidenced by his rules and regulations, to having no employees under the age of ten. Advertising for families in the *Glasgow Courier* of 5 June 1806, Owen specifically stated that only children over ten would be employed. He was probably well on the way to eliminating the practice by 1807 when John Marshall paid his second visit to New Lanark. Marshall, on his first trip in 1800, calculated that there were between 400 to 500 such apprentices. By 1802 there are known to have been 264 'boarders' living in No 4 mill, about two thirds of them, it has been estimated, orphans or paupers indentured by David Dale, such as those he obtained from Corstorphine, near Edinburgh, in 1796 and 1799.[40] However, when Marshall returned in 1807 he noticed that Owen 'was nearly giving up the plan of having parish apprentices'.[41] This made a great deal of sense since they cost money to feed and clothe and also took up potentially productive space on the mill floors. So, in the words of one local observer, 'in the course of time the system of bondage was abandoned and freedom was restored to all'.[42] However, Owen, like the Scottish coal and salt masters, was astute enough to realise that by discontinuing the indentures he would be freed from obligations to the apprentices, a situation likely to work more in his favour than theirs.

The discipline and order brought about by Owen's reforms mirrored the sort of regime he had established at Drinkwater's factory and (he says) prevailed in the other mills he later managed in Manchester. As early as 1804 he was writing to James Craig, the managing partner at Stanely, to say that he hoped 'to show a greater improvement in our Mills than you saw when the last time you visited them'.[43] By insisting on consistently high standards the mills and village were in a constant state of readiness for the frequent visits of inspection by his partners. He may have been able to exercise a great deal of power as manager, but despite his access to substantial funds, he was still a junior partner. Most of the initial reforms were designed to cut out waste, improve efficiency and workflows, increase output, and above all, enhance profits.

The company continued to maintain its headquarters in Manchester and during the lifetime of the Lanark Twist Company Owen made several journeys there to appraise his partners of developments. At the end of February and beginning of March 1802 he spent a few weeks there, and reported his visit to 'one of the best spinning works in this country', evidently a steam powered mule mill:

> The average number spun at these works is 46, the spinning in
> general runs from 40 to 70. The mules contain 120 spindles each.
> One boy or girl works two of them without any pain. For the last 12
> months they have produced 12 hanks per spindle per week, average
> as before mentioned, 46, and for which they receive 6 shillings for
> 2,000 hanks, coarse or fine numbers, that is 50 lbs of number 40,
> 40 lbs no. 50, 33 1/3 lbs no 60 for 6 shillings. This is the cheapest
> spinning I ever saw and this is done within 7 miles of Manchester
> where living is very expensive.
>
>   These children, [he continued,] after they have been some time
> in practice, produce 3,000 hanks per week and some of them will
> exceed that quantity in summer when they have long days without
> candle light. [And the tenuous peace with France, quite likely a topic
> of conversation with both his partners and fellow cotton spinners,
> put him in reflective mood, for as he wrote,] We shall have much
> to contend with in this country, but perseverance and attention will
> still, I think, put the advantage in our favour.[44]

At the same time as occasionally travelling to Manchester, attending
to routine maintenance, installing new machinery, such as a cast-iron
water-wheel and some improved shuttles, enforcing new rules and
regulations at New Lanark, or overseeing the stock and books in the
company's warehouse at St Andrew's Square in Glasgow, Owen was
also increasingly drawn into management of his father-in-law's extensive
business empire.[45] Dale himself seems to have suffered poor health
from 1800 so Owen undertook many of his commitments, particularly
those associated with the Royal Bank and with the settlement of Dale's
outstanding capital accounts in the mills at Catrine, Newton Douglas
and Spinningdale. He also kept an eye on the business at Stanley, which
another James Craig (not apparently the same one Owen dealt with while in
Manchester) and James Mair, both manufacturers and merchants, bought
in 1801 with financial assistance from Dale. Scott Moncrieff, Dale's partner
and fellow agent of the Royal Bank, evidently found Owen congenial
company for within eighteen months of his arrival he noted: '22nd June
1801: In comes Mr Owen to tell me the honest man [Dale] is arrived
back from Lanark and is to be with me at 7. He is a clever lad, far from
being sanguine or speculative'. Indeed, Owen's relationship with both his
bankers was evidently so intimate that any request for funds was likely
to be looked upon sympathetically. As in Manchester his business ability
was soon recognised to such an extent that John Marshall could observe
that Owen had 'the management of the Bank of Scotland at Glasgow
where he spends half his time'. Marshall may have been confusing the

banks, but nevertheless it is an interesting comment on Owen's activities at the time.[46]

If Dale was so anxious to disengage from his numerous commitments, which he did on Owen's advice at Catrine and Newton Douglas, his investment in Stanley may well have been an aberration, though his friendship with Craig cannot be ruled out as the principal motivation. Stanley was bought at a knock down price of £4,600, as against the original asking price of £6,500, so speculation may have been uppermost in mind. Dale paid the third instalment of the purchase price in 1803 and although he and Craig never entered a formal partnership kept the enterprise supplied with working capital to the tune of £24,270 until his death in 1806.[47] However it was not a particularly propitious time to restart a mill that had already experienced problems, the year 1803 in particular being relatively depressed and causing Owen to observe that 'the spinning trade both in England and in Scotland was never perhaps worse than at this moment and many are sacrificing a great deal of money in this business'. [48]

In May 1802 Dale had agreed to act as a cautioner for Craig for a cash account with the Perth Bank, at which point Owen told Craig that 'the old gentleman is in tolerable good spirits about your concern at present and I hope things will now go well'.[49] Owen visited Stanley regularly and advised Craig about every aspect of the business, including later that year a proposed new mill:

I have been thinking a good deal about the plans for the Newmill which you left with me, the result of which is that whenever sufficient funds can be provided something much better and more complete may be executed and which I think will be the most superior work of this kind yet built or perhaps thought of.[50]

Owen's initial relationship with Craig at that stage seems to have been congenial, with the latter making a regular dispatch of Tay salmon to the Dale-Owen household ('quite fresh when it came and most excellent in flavour', wrote Owen in acknowledging one). But Dale was clearly worried and by May 1803 was asking for a full account of 'the cotton yarn, machinery, and all other stock' as well as a full set of balance sheets.[51] By December that year Owen reported that Dale was still ill and wanted to know 'what probability there is of him being relieved from the concern'. According to Owen, Dale 'blames himself and me very much for having anything to do with the Stanley property as it has again involved him in business and locked up a large capital which he says he has great occasion for and which I have reason to think is true'. Dale evidently regretted becoming involved in Stanley and thus Owen told Craig that 'unless you advance in equal capital with him that he will not enter into a contract of partnership nor will he advance any more capital into the business; and this appears to be his firm determination'.[52]

However, Dale, perhaps contrary to Owen's advice, continued to advance working capital for Stanley. Owen himself kept up a regular correspondence with Craig and visited the Perthshire mill several times annually. When he could not go he sent Humphreys. His letters provide practical guidance as well as business intelligence to someone who was clearly very much out of his depth. In May 1804 he told Craig that 'a clever person to manage the spinning would be a great advantage to you' but not until December of that year was one that might be suitable found.[53] The bulk of the correspondence in the period before Dale's demise concerns raw cotton supplies, yarn qualities and prices, and the state of the markets.[54] The only obvious mention of the workforce is Owen's advice to Craig to 'find candles for the spinners' as 'there is not anything lost by a fair encouragement of work people'.[55] Despite the shrewd advice on this and other matters Craig received, he experienced continuing financial and technical difficulties at Stanley. Craig's predicament was to remain an acute concern of David Dale's trustees and of Owen personally for many years to come.

Dale was evidently worried about increasing competition in the cotton trade, particularly from plant with more modern equipment, and there can be little doubt that apart from its distance from the Glasgow market that was the biggest problem posed by Stanley. Dale's other interests included a share of a small mill, built to an almost identical design as No 1 Mill in New Lanark, at Spinningdale on the Dornoch Firth, one of the few developments of its kind anywhere in the Highlands. Dale's partners in this unlikely venture were George Macintosh and George Dempster of Skibo, near whose seat in east Sutherland the mill was erected. Macintosh, like Dale, was a successful Glasgow merchant, whose family originated in Easter Ross. He had earlier joined Dale in setting up the first turkey-red dye works in Britain and was the father of Charles Macintosh, inventor of the water-proofing process which bears his name. Dempster, an advocate, the MP successively for Forfar and for Fife Burghs, and a director of the East India Company, was active in the promotion of fisheries and agrarian improvement. Before Spinningdale was sold off, Owen, accompanied by Macintosh, set off on a trip to the Highlands, probably in the summer or autumn of 1801 or 1802, calling in at Stanley and then proceeding north over General Wade's roads and bridges to inspect the most remote outpost of the British cotton industry.[56]

This 'formidable undertaking', which took him up and down the straths and over the Grampian mountains, seems to have rekindled his enthusiasm for nature and many years later he recalled how exhilarated he felt about the scenery and fresh air and how much he enjoyed Macintosh's company. Thanks no doubt to the latter's foresight, word of their journey had preceeded them and when they arrived in Inverness they were received with considerable pomp by the authorities and given a splendid reception in the Town House at which they were both presented with the freedom of the burgh. Such 'entertainments in favour of the burgh' were held at regular intervals, but unfortunately not all the names of those honoured on each occasion were recorded. The reception on 20 September 1802 can be taken as typical. It must have been a riotous affair, because the burgh treasurer recorded outgoings of £10 4s 6d on no fewer than 3 dozen bottles of best port, 2 bottles of superior sherry, 3 pots of anchovies, 6 lbs of raisins, 4 lbs of almonds, 3 bottles of olives, 4 lbs of hard biscuits, 2 lbs of English cheese, 4 lbs of wax candles and a dozen extra wine glasses. Similarly lavish provision had been made at events the previous July and in July and September of 1801, any of which Owen might well have attended.[57] He was surprised both by the conviviality of the proceedings, something he was to witness again when he sought to become a member of parliament for Linlithgow Burghs, and by the 'great purity' of the English spoken by the inhabitants. He does not say whether or not he was able to understand any of the native Gaelic they heard spoken on their journey north, though Macintosh certainly spoke the language. Thereafter they pressed on by packet boat across the Moray Firth to reach Spinningdale where Owen found the works were 'not extensive . . . and in ordinary condition'. They only stayed long enough for Owen to assess what improvements could be made, for in his opinion, 'the locality was unfavourable, for extension or for a permanent establishment'.[58]

For Owen, the expedition to Sutherland apparently gave him his first opportunity to put forward some of his earliest notions about reform to 'the several respectable highland families' with whom he and Macintosh lodged. Among their number, according to Owen's memoirs, was the Rev James Grant of Laggan (Owen calls him Grant of Logan, clearly a misprint or miss-spelling), suggesting that the pair retraced their steps rather than travelling south via the Great Glen. Assuming he was referring to James Grant, whose patron was Alexander, Duke of Gordon, it places the journey in 1801, for Grant died in December of that year. He would be unlikely to forget him because Grant was known for his 'accomplished mind', cultivated tastes and geniality, and not only that, his wife, Anne, afterwards became the famous authoress of *Letters from the Mountains* (some of which were written to her friend Mary, Macintosh's wife), published in 1806, *Memoirs of an American Lady* (1808) and most notably, *Essays on the Superstitions of the Highlands* (1811). [59]

Owen kept a journal of this tour but unfortunately later mislaid it. By the time he wrote his autobiography he could not remember exactly who he and Macintosh stayed with or those with whom he discussed his ideas. On the other hand, it also enabled him to make the welcome discovery that 'such was the keenness and purity of the air, with all the exercise we took, that contrary to my former habit, I could take the spirit manufactured there so pure in the Highlands without suffering any inconvenience but which practice I never could adopt in the Lowlands'.[60] On return Owen recommended that Dale dispose of his interest in Spinningdale and that Mackintosh do likewise. This turned out to be sound advice. Although staffed with cheap labour provided by victims of early clearances in the upper straths of Sutherland, there was little prospect of the venture paying much in the way of profit and more to the point the mill was gutted by fire in 1809.[61]

For obvious reasons Owen does not seem to have been so active in the social and cultural life of Glasgow as he had been in Manchester. But since his family lived with Dale for much of this period, and he himself was the son-in-law of one of the city's most distinguished citizens and a major figure in the Scottish cotton industry, Owen wasted little time in making his presence felt among the merchant community. Hence at a meeting on 2 February 1803 of the Committee of Management of the Board of the Cotton Trade in Glasgow, which included Archibald Campbell of Jura and Kirkman Finlay, he presented a short paper entitled 'Observations on the Cotton Trade of Great Britain'.[62] This contained a useful survey of the progress of cotton spinning up to that point, his estimates of its contribution to the national income, the deleterious effects of the duty on raw cotton imposed by parliament the previous year, and some remarkably prophetic statements about the potential danger from rivals on the Continent who were not only free of taxation on their raw materials, but could also benefit from ideas pirated from British inventors (something that was already evident in the United States). This was evidently well received by his fellow cotton masters and merchants and shortly afterwards he announced to Craig that he could not go to Stanley as expected because 'public business of the first importance to cotton spinners and manufacturers' would detain him the best part of a week, possibly the preparation of his observations for the press, approved at the meeting.[63] Apart from the threat of foreign competition the cotton masters had cause to be worried because 1803 was a bad year. In May 1803 trade was 'dull', news of trade from England was 'very bad', and it was well after the summer that Owen could report that 'commercial affairs are beginning to look better in Glasgow, where I hope they have been at the worst'.[64]

Shortly after Dale's death Owen's endeavours on behalf of the cotton trade and the Glasgow Chamber of Commerce were duly acknowledged when, on 2 June 1806, he was admitted as a burgess and to the guild brethren of the city.[65] No doubt his relationship to Dale helped ('as married Anne Caroline, daughter of David Dale, merchant', the citation recorded) but such recognition was equally a measure of his position as effective heir to the great Dale and the speed with which he became established among the city's business elite.

Surprisingly little is known of his family life, but fortunately we have some interesting glimpses. He seems to have made Dale's town house in Glasgow the main family home, travelling to New Lanark and further afield as business dictated. Owen's extended family, including, when not at boarding school in Edinburgh, Caroline's younger sisters and their retinue, spent much of the summer and sometimes the early autumn either in Dale's country house, Rosebank, near Glasgow or in the Owen house at New Lanark.[66] Dale himself joined them for some of the time and was thus able to observe the changes that Owen had initiated, causing him to tell the workfolk (or at least so Owen says) that 'if the mills had been managed as they are now, and you had worked for me as you are now working for Mr Owen, I would not have sold the establishment to strangers'.[67] Caroline had a son, David Dale, born 21 July 1800, but sadly he did not survive. On 7 November 1801 Robert Dale was born, followed in 1802 by William, probably named after Owen and his brother.[68] Although described as 'doing well' after William's birth Caroline seems to have experienced recurrent spells of ill-health, possibly the result of a weak constitution due, no doubt, to the number of pregnancies she had had.[69] Whether or not this sharpened Owen's subsequent interest in birth control for himself and the workers is impossible to tell, but it may well have done so. The Owens subsequently added two more sons, David Dale and Richard, and three daughters, Anne Caroline, Jane Dale, and Mary to their family.

It is not generally known that Owen paid a visit to Wales sometime in late April or early May 1803, when his mother was seriously ill. He travelled south to Newtown via Manchester, where he presumably stayed for a while, seeing his partners and giving them the latest news from New Lanark.[70] His mother died on 13 July, but there is no record of his actual movements at that date or whether or not he attended the funeral. Owen's father, Robert, subsequently died on 14 March 1804 and the evidence in the correspondence which survives from that period suggests that Owen was in Scotland, though he may well have made another unrecorded visit to mid-Wales before then.

While the sale of his interests in Catrine, Newton Douglas and Spinningdale 'released Mr Dale from much anxiety and allowed him to pass the remainder of his life more quietly and much more to his satisfaction', he unfortunately did not enjoy good health.[71] In December 1803, according to Owen, he 'still continued indisposed and thinks himself seriously ill'. The following January he was still confined to his room, and in May that year his health was precarious and he had been complaining a good deal since Owen left Glasgow for New Lanark.[72] He continued to decline in health and died in January of 1806. His death was apparently met with universal regret throughout Glasgow and the West of Scotland. During the 'interminable' funeral procession Owen walked just behind the hearse, hand in hand with the five-year-old Robert Dale, who recalled that crowds of mourners were to be seen 'along every street'.[73]

Owen's father-in-law's obvious virtue and humanity could readily be appreciated in a splendid obituary notice which appeared in the *Scots Magazine* shortly after his death:

At Glasgow, in the 67th year of his age, David Dale, Esq. formerly proprietor of the Lanark Cotton Mills, and one of the Magistrates of Glasgow – generally known and admired for a noble spirit of philanthropy – in whose character were strikingly combined, successful commercial enterprise with piety, active benevolence, and public spirit. Here, if ever, a tribute of respect and admiration is due to departed worth. Originally in a low station of life, by prosperous adventures in trade, he was raised to a state of affluence, which he directed on grand scale, to the encouragement and relief of the distressed. In a romantic den on the banks of the Clyde, the lofty mills of Lanark arose, under his eye and fostering hand; surprised and delighted the traveller, as with a scene of enchantment; and exhibited a pleasing picture of industry walking hand in hand with instruction and comfort. Thither were transplanted, and trained to virtuous habits, numerous orphans and outcasts of the streets who had been a prey to vice and misery. And there many 'hapless sons of Caledonia', who were emigrating to a foreign land, found a comfortable asylum. For many years he discharged, with distinguished reputation, the office of Pastor to the Independent Congregation in Glasgow, for which he was peculiarly fitted, by a thorough knowledge of the Hebrew and Greek languages. His discourses bespoke a cultivated understanding, and liberality of sentiment. A steady friend to civil and religious liberty, he embraced men of every persuasion. Possessed of a disposition kind, hospitable and benevolent, of a heart generous, sincere, and truly philanthropic, his charities, public and private, were probably not surpassed by any individual in Scotland. As a Magistrate, he tempered justice with mercy; and, on trying occasions, he displayed a spirit of resolution, scarcely expected by those who were familiar with his unassuming manners in private society. In private life he was very affectionate to his relatives and intimate friends; sometimes in a musing contemplative frame, and sometimes endearing by a peculiar vein of cheerful pleasantry. Hence they bewail the loss of a kind father, friend and faithful monitor. The poor will feel the want of a bountiful benefactor. Glasgow is deprived of an illustrious citizen. Public institutions have lost him who was looked up to, as the general patron of every generous and laudable undertaking. Humanity has lost a warm and steady friend.[74]

Given this accolade, whoever followed Dale in his role as philanthropic employer at New Lanark, had much to live up to. Anyone who tried to decry it certainly risked public disapprobation.

Despite Dale's high standing at his death it is not too fanciful to see him in the role of Man Friday to Owen's Robinson Crusoe, providing the platform for the self-sufficient hero, the entrepreneurial heir to Dale's island at New Lanark.

## NOTES

1. *Life*, p. 46.
2. *Life*, p. 47.
3. *Life*, p. 47.
4. Gourock Mss. Visitors' Book 16 May 1798.
5. The encounter with Dale is described in *Life*, pp. 51–2.
6. Gourock Mss. Visitors' Book 22 July 1799.
7. *Life*, p. 52. Owen clearly saw himself as a 'successor' to Dale as well as marrying his daughter.
8. *Life*, p. 53.
9. *Jones' Directory*, p. 8.
10. Butt in 'Introduction', x.
11. *James' Directory*, p. 9.
12. *Life*, pp. 55–6.
13. Butt in 'Introduction', x.
14. Chalmer, p. 101.
15. *Life*, p. 56.
16. Butt, 'Owen as Businessman', p. 171.
17. *Life*, p. 57.
18. See reference 29, ch. 4.
19. Atholl Mss, Correspondence of Robert Owen, reveal the schedules he maintained.
20. Mclaren, p. 7; Claeys, note to *Life*, p. 99.
21. Donnachie and Hewitt, pp. 52–5.
22. Ibid, p. 55.
23. *Life*, p. 59.
24. Atholl Mss. Owen to Craig 28 Sept.1803.
25. Butt in 'Introduction', xix; Butt, 'Owen as Businessman' pp. 183–4.
26. Tour Book of J. Marshall, quoted in Butt, p. 188.
27. On the rules, see subsequent discussion and reference.
28. See Anne Taylor *Visions of Harmony*, Oxford, 1987, pp. 61–2 on the physical dangers and threats to children; on discipline, Butt, pp. 188–95.
29. *Life*, p. 57; I. Donnachie 'The Darker side': A Speculative Survey of Scottish Crime During the First Half of the Nineteenth Century', *Scottish Econ. and Social Hist.*, vol. 15, pp. 12–13 on theft in factories.

30. The silent monitor is described in *Life*, pp. 80–81.
31. J. Lancaster, *Improvements in Education*; London, 1803, pp. 47–51.
32. PP1833, XX, 74.
33. R.D. Owen, *Threading My Way*, London, 1874, p. 73.
34. Owen, *New Existence*, pt. V, 1854, appendix, reproduces the rules and regulations.
35. *Life*, p. 57.
36. The following section is derived from Donnachie & Hewitt, pp. 70–71.
37. One formerly a teacher at New Lanark, Manchester, 1839, pp. 4–5.
38. H.G. McNab, *The New Views of Mr Owen of Lanark Impartially Examined*, London, 1819, p. 126.
39. Gourock Mss. Census Data 1801 and 1811.
40. Corstorphine orphans apprenticed 1796–99. Corstorphine Kirk Session Records, 5 April 1796; 5 May 1797.
41. Tour Book of J. Marshall, quoted in Butt, p. 191.
42. W. Davidson, *History of Lanark*, Lanark, 1828, pp. 166–78.
43. Atholl Mss. Owen to Craig 21 September 1804.
44. Ibid, Owen to Craig 2 March 1802.
45. Ibid, Owen to Craig 10 June 1802.
46. Tour Book of J.Marshall, quoted in Butt, p. 173; Donnachie and Hewitt, p. 63.
47. A. Cooke, 'Robert Owen and the Stanley Mills', *Business Hist*. Vol. 21, 1979, provides a detailed account of the relationship between Dale and Craig.
48. Atholl Mss. Owen to Craig 19 December, 1803.
49. Ibid, Owen to Craig 13 May 1802.
50. Ibid, Owen to Craig 12 September 1802.
51. Ibid, Owen to Craig 24 May 1803.
52. Ibid, Owen to Craig 19 December 1803.
53. Ibid, Owen to Craig 17 May, 21 September; 11 December 1804.
54. Cooke, 'Robert Owen', p. 107.
55. Atholl Mss. Owen to Craig 31 August 1802.
56. On Dempster see McLaren, pp. 17, 30, 34, 77; on Macintosh, ibid, p. 30.
57. Highland Council Archive, Inverness Burgh Records, Treasurer's Accounts, dated cited.
58. *Life*, p. 75.
59. *Stat. Account* vol. III, pp. 145–52; *Fasti of the Church of Scotland*; DNB on Anne Grant.
60. *Life*, p. 74.
61. (Second) *New Statistical Account*, vol.xx, p. 20.
62. Printed for private circulation, Glasgow 1803. Reproduced in Claeys (ed.) *Selected Works* vol. 1, pp. 1–6.
63. Atholl Mss. Owen to Craig, 13 February 1803.
64. Ibid, Owen to Craig 30 May, 28 September 1803.
65. J.R. Anderson (ed.) *Burgess and Guild Brethren of Glasgow*, Edinburgh, 1935, p. 240.
66. Atholl Mss. Owen to Craig 24 October 1803.
67. *Life* p. 78.
68. Old Parish Registers, Lanark, 21 July 1800 (David Dale), 7 Nov. 1801 (Robert Dale), 17 December 1802 (William), all born at Glasgow.
69. Atholl Mss. Owen to Craig 11 February and 23 December 1802.

70. Ibid, Owen to Craig 23 April and 24 May 1803.
71. *Life*, p. 78.
72. Atholl Mss. Owen to Craig 19 December 1803, 25 January and 17 May 1804.
73. R.D. Owen *Threading My Way*, pp. 18–19.
74. *Scots Magazine*, January 1806; and quoting Donnachie and Hewitt, pp. 56–8.

# SIX

# Prince of Cotton Spinners

Throughout most of the years before the breakdown of the third partnership in which he was involved Owen was kept busy at New Lanark, attending to the affairs of his father-in-law's trust, or wrestling with the problems at Stanley. But at the same time, having begun to play some sort of role in the mercantile affairs of Glasgow, progressively developing an interest in factory conditions, and education in particular, he began to assume a higher public profile. In these spheres and others his island at New Lanark came increasingly to be a test bed not only for practical means of educating the poor, ameliorating social conditions and at the same time ensuring appropriate levels of social control, but also the basis on which to develop first a social psychology and then a social policy. The seeds of both can be discerned before 1812, culminating in his first publication of any significance, *A Statement Regarding the New Lanark Establishment*.[1] On first reading this seemed to be a rather descriptive business plan written in the manner of the time, but on closer examination promised potential investors greatly enhanced profits if his strategy for social betterment was implemented in the community. Nevertheless it exuded strong philanthropic overtones which Owen knew were likely to appeal to other reformers.[2]

Quite how far Owen had taken his reforms of what in his statement he was to describe as the 'living machinery' at New Lanark before Dale's demise is impossible to tell, either from his autobiography or other sources. While, for perfectly sound business reasons, such as the employment of child apprentices taken into the mills under the previous regime, things could not be changed overnight, all the evidence indicates that the pace of reform was stepped up after Dale's death. When John Marshall, the Leeds flax spinner, visited New Lanark in 1800, he noted that the 2,000 or so 'hands' were said 'to be under better discipline and to do more work with fewer hands than in Mr Dales time'. Returning in 1807, Marshall saw that the concern was being extended. 'They have built more houses and are nearly giving up the plan of having parish apprentices . . . Mr Owen is said to be very strict and is not popular in the neighbourhood'.[3] This was hardly surprising given that Owen's prime concern, as earlier, was maintaining business efficiency and improving productivity at a time when the exigencies of the prolonged war with France continued to generate economic uncertainty.

Hence the 'dead machinery' was as important as the living and harnessing the two effectively required close supervision. So despite

Humphrey's presence as under-manager Owen was directly involved in the day-to-day operations of what was then one of the largest enterprises of its kind in world. His correspondence with Craig reveals much greater involvement with engineering and production difficulties than has previously been realised. For example, early in the New Year of 1808 he wrote to Craig saying that 'for some weeks past I have been continually occupied from early and late with several heavy repairs which while they were doing kept between 3 and 400 people idle that I had not ever time to attend to many pressing matters belonging to the Lanark concern'.[4] This was almost certainly work on a water-wheel, for as Owen reminded Craig several years later, 'the first moving power is of so much importance in a cotton mill that no pains should be spared to have it in all respects perfect and complete'.[5] It is not known for certain if the lay-off Owen described coincided with the cotton embargo of that year, but it demonstrates the problems of continuous working in large water powered spinning mills.

Attention to detail, evident in his earlier management of Drinkwater's mills, was therefore vital. Output, labour costs, hours of work, stocks of yarn, types of cotton and their origin as well as every other aspect of factory production were rigorously supervised, as the superbly kept 'Produce' and 'Report Books' amply illustrate. Owen's 'Produce Books' contain a fortnightly abstract which provides a wealth of data for every room in the mills. There he itemised the number of spindles in use, the species of cotton and the quantity used, the time taken to spin the yarn with a note of any delays which occurred, the precise weight and number of hanks produced as well as the wages of all the workers. Thus from early on in his management between 31 December 1802 and 14 January 1803, using cotton imported from such diverse sources as Georgia, New Orleans, Trinidad, Jamaica, Granada and Guadeloupe, Mill No 1, with its 6556 spindles worked for 137 hours 30 minutes with 12½ hours lost during the period. 7225lbs or 159,394 hanks of cotton yarn were spun in this interval while the wages of the workforce were £153.10.6d. Owen meticulously maintained his records so that at any time he could present an extremely accurate figure for the annual output of the whole factory as well as the total production costs for each year. For example his annual report, submitted on 25 December 1806, provided his partners with a detailed statement of produce and costs in each of the mills, which he summarised thus:

| | RAW COTTON | YARN |
|---|---|---|
| Mill No 1 | 415046lbs | 397223lbs |
| Mill No 2 | 37715lbs | 364495lbs |
| Mill No 3 | 294891lbs | 285635lbs |

| EXPENSES | MILL NO 1 | MILL NO 2 | MILL NO 3 |
|----------|-----------|-----------|-----------|
| Picking | £ 602 | 562 | 279 |
| Preparing | £2823 | 2205 | 2391 |
| Spinning | £3104 | 2793 | 1747 |
| Reeling etc. | £ 799 | 713 | 717 |
| Store | £1436 | 1203 | 1108 |
| Extras | £ 128 | 123 | 126 |
| Repairs | £2519 | 1692 | 2160 |
| Total | £11411 | £9296 | £8528[6] |

Looked at in the long run from 1801 until 1812, when in a disagreement with his partners over financial and other affairs he was temporarily relieved of management, the surviving accounts prove that he was remarkably successful in cutting out waste and raising productivity. Yarn output rose from an estimated 514,750lbs weight in 1801 to 736,925lbs in 1805. By dispensing with child labour and bringing most of No 3 Mill into full production he managed to boost output to 1,146,842lbs in 1809 and more than 1.6 million lbs in 1812.[7] The increased costs of substituting adult for child labour were partly offset by the fact that Owen, like most country mill masters, was able to pay lower wages than those in the towns (partly compensated for by cheap rents and other social provisions, such as the school and store). Nonetheless the enormous increase in production was a remarkable achievement and was further reflected in the general profitability of the enterprise. On this score alone his partners ought to have been pleased with his performance on their behalf.

As for other expenses incurred in the store, repairs or extras, Owen, in a policy likely to keep himself in favour with fellow merchants, was careful either to purchase locally or nearby in central Scotland. Thus, such things as glue, candles, coal, whale oil, soap, flour, nails, locks, hinges and tacks were all provided by Lanarkshire merchants. Fifteen trees were bought from the Braxfield estate in March 1805 (Owen did not lease Braxfield House himself until 1807) but timber was normally purchased from R. and A. Sheriff and Company, Leith. Among the huge range of other materials needed for the maintenance of the mills were iron frames and wheels from the Omoa foundry, bar iron from the Muirkirk iron works, while two Glasgow firms, H. and R. Baird and Robert Gray and Sons supplied iron castings, tin lamps and glasses.[8]

This, as Owen frequently observed to Craig, was a tricky time for cotton spinners as the constantly changing political situation made it as difficult to get the yarn to foreign buyers as to maintain raw cotton supplies. Although he had little success Owen evidently tried to keep Craig on the straight and narrow as far as managing a cotton mill was concerned and also kept him up-to-date on business intelligence, some good and some bad. Around the time of Dale's death he was writing from Glasgow to say that 'matters of business here are worse and worse' and that 'yarns continue low in price, particularly the middle and fine numbers of mule'.[9] And among the first letters from Braxfield House while thanking Craig for another salmon and asking him to send it when he had company (quite how Craig was meant to know is unclear), he tells him that he could not manage to visit Stanley that month as one of his partners mentioned coming from Manchester in a few weeks time. There was a good demand for yarns in Lancashire, he had heard, but 'unlooked for political events' either on the Continent or across the Atlantic could change all that.[10] Almost every letter to Craig reflected on the current state of the war and its influence on markets, such as the occasion when, writing from Glasgow, he observed that 'The continental politics remain in a very uncertain state though it is generally expected that Austria will declare against France and strong hopes are entertained that Russia and Prussia will join her'.[11] Owen was right and, unlike Craig, was astute enough to seize every window of opportunity, even if it involved considerable risk.

The cotton yarn produced and methodically checked by Owen and his staff at New Lanark was destined for both overseas and home consumption. Although a few consignments were regularly destined for outlets in Trieste and Smyrna the main foreign exports were to St Petersburg. There, especially after the defeat of Napoleon in 1812–13, Owen, assisted by his agents Allan Stewart and Company, cornered a major share of the trade in yarn. Subsequently, he commissioned John Winning, one of the art teachers in the school, to design a label with an illustration of the village on it for sticking on these consignments. They became known to the Russians as 'Picture Yarn'. In the home market Owen had contacts all over Britain but undoubtedly Glasgow firms like James Finlay and John Bartholomew were among some of his best customers. However, as the Sales Book reveals he was selling yarn to manufacturers over the length and breadth of Scotland, from Aberdeen to Wigtown and from Kilbirnie to Kirkcaldy. Moreover, his prompt resort to litigation to recover debts outstanding to the Lanark Twist Company, for instance against a business in Dysart in February 1808 and another in Langholm three months later, emphasises his hard-headed approach to business management.[12]

Owen was well aware that many of the changes he had instigated both on the factory floor and in the community, not to mention what effectively amounted to another hour on the working day, were widely disliked in New Lanark. However, in his autobiography he claims that the turning point in his relations with the workforce came in 1808 following his generous behaviour during a major crisis in the cotton industry. This resulted from the United States government's act of 22 December 1807 placing an embargo on cotton exports to Britain, American retaliation for the British government's Orders in Council restricting trade. The latter banned all trade with France, including by neutrals like the United States, who could only do so if they were selling British goods or if their vessels first touched at a British port, declared, unloaded and reloaded their congress, and paid a duty. While the Embargo Act eventually backfired the consequence of this economic warfare was, as Owen stated, that 'the prices of all kinds of cotton immediately advanced so rapidly and so high that the manufacturers of the article were placed in a dilemma'. Owen's solution was to halt production temporarily but meanwhile to continue paying wages to his workers for a period of up to four months at one point, an action very much in the tradition of his late father-in-law when he acted similarly following the fire in 1788 which had destroyed Mill No. 1.[13] The highly unpopular embargo, which had badly hit American merchants, expired on 15 March 1809, after which Owen anticipated a flood of raw cotton into British ports.[14]

Owen's benevolence in 1808 probably converted many of his workers and evidence of their loyalty to him was seen in a dispute which arose shortly afterwards between him and one of his neighbours. These were the Edmondstones of Corehouse, sisters who owned the estate on the opposite bank of the Clyde. In 1804 they had reached an agreement with the Lanark Twist Company regarding the construction of a dam across the river which would give the factory a greater supply of water, especially during dry spells. Under the terms of the contract there were various safeguards to placate the Edmondstones. The dam, for example, would be made as 'impassable' as possible in order to prevent workers crossing it 'during the hours they are unemployed' while the sluices would be closed at eight p.m. and would not be opened until five a.m. 'unless when it was necessary to keep the works going during any part of the night'. By 1809 relations between Owen and the Edmondstones had deteriorated badly and both sides became involved in legal action against each other. Owen, in his defence, stressed the fact that 'the undertaking was encouraged by the approbation of all the neighbouring proprietors'. Furthermore it occurred to them that the projected cotton mills would not only be productive of general utility but would lead to 'the increase of the value of all properties in the neighbourhood.' Lord Braxfield himself, he reminded his neighbours, had feued the ground to Dale because 'he had a quick and comprehensive view of all these advantages'. The sisters were not impressed. Miss Anne Edmondstone observed in reply that 'A boll of oats or potatoes sells no higher in Lanark than it does at Hamilton nor are greater rents paid for an estate than for lands of the same quality at

50 miles distant'. In any case as far as she was concerned the mills were a nuisance 'for the people employed there, notwithstanding the vigilance of the manager, are perpetually committing trespasses on her garden and her woods to a very great extent'. And she added a personal attack, observing that 'Mr Owen, a man of the greatest acuteness and ability, may affect when it serves his purpose an ignorance of the law which would disgrace the meanest and stupidest of his spinners'.[15]

Owen told Craig the following October that he was still 'plagued by our opposite neighbour regarding the right of water between us' but expected 'some understanding of the business will take place between us in a few days'.[16] The quarrel was therefore settled by the company agreeing to pay the Edmondstones a new annual water rent of £200. Meanwhile during the whole altercation Owen's workers had manifested, to quote again the former New Lanark teacher, 'a general feeling of sympathy'. Indeed the whole episode was quite a lively affair, given what was at stake for the company and its workers. On one occasion, for example, when a party of the Edmondstones' estate workers were on the opposite side of the river a disabled worker apparently still on the mill pay-roll had suggested that the sluice gates should be raised in order to swamp those on the other bank. Owen, however, sternly rebuked him declaring, 'If the workers of New Lanark could not be saved without the loss of life, to let them go'. On another occasion, in similar circumstances, a party from Corehouse was pelted with missiles by the irate inhabitants of the village.[17]

Owen's problems with his neighbours were as nothing compared to other difficulties that had to be faced at that time. While his reform programme had been concerned with improving arrangements on the factory floor and cleaning up the community it could be seen to contribute to improved efficiency and better order. But by this time he felt he was in a position to push on with his plan 'to clear the foundation for the infant and other schools, to form the new character of the rising population'. He also suggested other radical ideas – including the public kitchen, which featured in his *Statement* and later caught the imagination of John Griscom, one of many prominent American visitors.[18] However, Owen's suggestions, not surprisingly, received an unenthusiastic response from some of his partners when they came north to study his proposals.

Although Owen was presented with an engraved silver salver, the partnership was clearly under some strain. The precise date of its actual dissolution is uncertain but in May 1810 Owen wrote warning Craig that 'in consequence of new arrangements forming between the partners in the Lanark Twist Company, none of your bills can be renewed' and that he would have to pay them himself when they fell due.[19] This was a clear reference to Owen's efforts to involve another group of capitalists in the venture while safeguarding his own position. Discussions continued over the summer and ultimately the contract of co-partner for the new business, purchasing the assets of the New Lanark Company for £80,000, was signed on 5 October 1810. All of this, according to Owen, had been very time-consuming and kept him away from home a great deal but now everything had been resolved and he had been joined in partnership by a fresh group of associates with stronger Scottish connections.[20]

In fact, John Atkinson, one of Owen's original partners in the Chorlton Twist Company and by far the most influential of his Manchester associates, remained with him. This suggests that relations between them were still amicable and that Owen's subsequent criticism of Atkinson as ambitious and driven by profit motive alone arose from subsequent disagreements over Owen's handling of the firm's finances rather than his philanthropic schemes. Owen was also joined by Robert Dennistoun and Alexander Campbell of Hallyards, sons-in-law of Campbell of Jura and prominent Glasgow merchants, while the final member was Colin Campbell, a business colleague, but no relation, of Alexander Campbell. Such was the financial appeal of New Lanark as 'one of the most lucrative concerns in the Kingdom' that another capitalist, Colin Campbell of Jura, Archibald's son, intended joining but was too late in intimating to Owen his wish to be included.

While the new partnership paid £80,000 for the property and machinery, the capital stock was set far higher at £182,000. Of the 26 shares, Owen took ten (with a paid-up value of £70,000), Atkinson six (£42,000), Dennistoun four (£28,000) Campbell of Hallyards three (£21,000), and Colin Campbell three (£21,000). Of the total capital £30,000 was to be paid up by January 1811 and another £30,000 the following year. In addition, to meet the purchase price the partners were to pay £8,000 annually for ten years. The remaining £42,000 was to be paid when the majority vote of the partners decided. The likelihood was that profits would cover the annual advances and the partners cautiously agreed not to distribute any profits until the capital had been fully subscribed. Owen 'from motives of friendship and attachment among the partners' undertook management without salary but received £1,000 annually for his expenses. Decisions were to be settled by majority vote, Owen and Atkinson having three each, and the other partners two each. Where the votes were equal the number of partners determined the outcome. This meant that Owen in alliance with Atkinson could not defeat the Glasgow partners and if Owen could not get hold of Atkinson's votes or those of two of the Glasgow partners, his position was prejudiced and he could lose control.[21]

The partnership, according to Owen, operated amicably enough at first but, like the previous one, as soon as he became involved in his school building projects he sensed 'a strong spirit of dissatisfaction in the two sons-in-law of Campbell of Jura'. This animosity, so Owen would have us believe, was entirely based on his partners' conviction that 'they were commercial men carrying on business for profit and had nothing to do with educating children; nobody did it in the manufactories: and they set their faces against it and against all my measures for the improvement of the condition of the work people'. While there is every likelihood that Owen's colleagues disapproved of his enlightened plans for New Lanark, they had other reasons for opposing him which he largely ignored in his version of events. Thus in his *Life*, where he refers to a sum of £20,000 lent to him by Campbell of Jura and that this transaction caused his sons-in-law 'to have been filled with the spark of undying revenge', Owen fails to mention some of the other aspects of this financial arrangement.[22]

The complex details of Owen's business activities have been meticulously unravelled by John Butt and others, but what follows is essentially what happened. Shortly before Dale's death Owen assumed responsibility for Campbell of Jura's investments on the understanding that this money would be transferred to the New Lanark Company. However, Owen failed to do this and, instead, retained Campbell's money for the next six years in his own partnership account. By 1812 Owen owed Campbell of Jura over £25,000, a fact which began to give the latter increasing cause for concern since the war with France and the quarrel that year with the United States had plunged the cotton industry into deep recession. Consequently, in July, Campbell endeavoured to recover £6,000 from Owen and at the same time tried to obtain some form of guarantee about the remainder of his money. He was assisted in his efforts by his two sons-in-law. The latter, although they might also have been discomfited, as Owen alleges, over their father-in-law's clandestine dealings with him, were more likely to have been seriously concerned about the relatively low profit figures for 1811–12 (mainly caused by the war with the United States) and Owen's inability to repay such a large lump sum. Accordingly, for the next twelve months a legal battle took place between the two sides with Owen finally being rescued from bankruptcy proceedings by the intervention of Dale's daughters, led by Jane Maxwell Dale. Thus, by a settlement reached on 15 July 1813 with the Misses Dale as guarantors, it was agreed that commencing from November 1818 the capital sum owing to Campbell of Jura would be repaid in five equal instalments of £4,000.[23]

As it transpired, Owen's worries about the Campbell debt were only temporarily allayed by this arrangement since in September 1816 investigations were begun into the affairs of John More, Dale's successor at the Royal Bank. These enquiries had almost immediate repercussions particularly when it was revealed that the Dale trustees not only owed the Royal Bank over £33,000 plus interest but, since the bills concerned related to the Stanley Mills between 1806 and 1813, that Owen was also deeply implicated. Such revelations prompted Campbell of Jura to consider further action and by 10 October 1816 he was writing to one of his sons:

> It having lately come to my knowledge that the affairs of Mr More of the Royal Bank are in a deranged state, and that it is given out, that the Trustees appointed by the late David Dale owe a good deal of money to the Royal Bank, I desire therefore that you will lose no time in enquiring into this matter, as I am at a loss to conceive how it can be . . .

While this might suggest that Owen's financial affairs were precarious he survived this crisis and others, thanks to the large capital gain he made when the mills were sold to his third partnership in 1813 and the substantial profits returned by the enterprise during and after 1813. He also had the advantage of access to funds from Dale's trust, diminished though it was by More's problems and the losses incurred at Stanley before it was sold off. Such was Owen's wealth that he could easily have paid off his debt to Campbell of Jura but it was ultimately discharged in November 1822, a date which in retrospect may well have had some influence on his ultimate decision to abandon New Lanark.[24]

Meanwhile, during the course of 1812 Owen's differences with his partners led to the disintegration of the partnership. On 30 June of that year he knew that he would lose his post as manager of the mills when his partners dismissed him with effect from August. Their motive was his secret dealings with Humphreys, the under-manager, with whom, contrary to the co-partnering agreement, Owen had arranged a deal whereby he took Humphreys' share of the profits and the latter received instead an additional £350 per annum on top of his annual salary of £350. Although his partners did not know it at that stage Owen had also borrowed money from his under-manager, a situation which was ultimately to cause friction and lead to a parting of the ways between the two men. His partners' action in dismissing him (and promoting Humphreys as manager at £700 per annum) was followed six months later by a proposal from Atkinson supported by the others that New Lanark should be put up for sale.

Owen, however, had taken good care to prepare himself for such an eventuality and meantime had drafted, and then engaged an Edinburgh printer, John Moir, to publish *A Statement Regarding the New Lanark Establishment*. This pamphlet has aptly been described as a 'refined company prospectus' containing, as it does, the information that Owen 'had resigned the management' and that 'the other proprietors are willing to dispose of it on the same terms as they purchased about two years ago'. Moreover, as he went on to explain, by ensuring that the profits had been ploughed back into the business and by following enlightened management principles there had been created an establishment which was more like 'a national benevolent institution than a manufacturing works founded by an individual'. Consequently, Owen concluded, the opportunities presented at New Lanark were immense 'and so soon as peace shall again take place very abundant profits may be reasonably expected'.[25]

Despite circulating his *Statement* 'among the best circles of the wealthy benevolent, and of those who desired with sincerity to commence active measures for the improvement of the condition of the poor and working classes', Owen's initial attempts at recruiting new partners were unsuccessful. Moreover, at a meeting with the old ones in February 1813 the dispute became more rancorous when he accused them of undervaluing the partnership shares for their own benefit. This may well have been the case since his partners probably feared that Owen would be declared bankrupt at any moment and that under the terms of the partnership they would be legally bound to buy him out. At the same time, it was also normal commercial practice to act in this fashion in such a situation in order to make allowance for the unpredictability of the markets.[26]

Owen, when not engaged in committing his thoughts to paper, spent much of 1813 making strenuous efforts to find other capitalists willing to form a new partnership and buy New Lanark. On this occasion he went armed not only with his *Statement* but with the first of his *Essays on the Formation of Character*, written in 1812, published early in 1813, and eventually part of *A New View of Society*. This time he was successful, forming a partnership which has been fittingly described as 'a mixture of pietistic philanthropy and shrewd, rational calculating Quaker acquisitiveness'.[27] The justification for this description was the presence of four leading members of the Society of Friends, John Walker, Joseph Fox, Joseph Foster and William Allen. Of the first three, Walker, a rich and cultivated individual, was to become closest to Owen. Allen was undoubtedly the most prominent member of the group being the owner of a large chemical works, a Fellow of the Royal Society, a part-time lecturer at Guy's Hospital and a religious zealot who was ultimately to become disenchanted with what he regarded as Owen's 'infidelity'.[28] Of the others, Michael Gibbs subsequently became Lord Mayor of London, but by far the most renowned was the final member, Jeremy Bentham. At this stage in a long career the utilitarian philosopher had recently become converted to political radicalism, largely through the influence of another notable political theorist, James Mill. Moreover, it was he who played a major role in arousing Bentham's interest in New Lanark as the following correspondence between the two of them clearly indicates:-

Newington Green 3d. Decr. 1813

Yesterday I complied with an entreaty of Wm. Allen to dine at his
house, <u>in order to meet with Owen,</u> who has just come up from the
Lanark Mills.

I took occasion to put to Mr Allen the questions respecting the
mines which you had directed me to put, and the answer was such
as, I think, I had better send you. As soon as the questions were
out of my mouth, he began – 'Do entreat Friend Bentham, to have
nothing to do with mines' – he added, 'or at any rate to wait till I can
write to Cornwall, where I have friends upon the spot, and can get
him accurate information.' He said that he himself had embarked
several years ago about £700 in a Cornwall mine, and that it had
never produced any thing. He said, that as far as his information
or experience went, more had been lost by the Cornwall mines than
had been gained.

Hearing all this, Owen then spoke, and said, <u>if Mr Bentham
wants to lay out a sum of money, to greater advantage, than on
any opportunity that almost ever occurs, he should buy a share of
the Lanark Mills, which are to be sold at the end of this month.</u>
<u>The price Owen says, will not exceed £100,000 for the whole</u> – and
that he himself will buy one half – that the raw produce, and the
good which they have on hand, with the materials of the buildings,
would sell for nearly the whole sum which the concern is likely
to fetch – that he has now brought the manufactory to so great
perfection particularly the rational machinery, that even last year,
when other manufactories of the sort could make little or nothing,
they have cleared 20 percent upon their whole capital, and that now
(viz. the continent open) they will clear a great deal more – that in
short he knows not of any occasion within his memory, when so
profitable a speculation can be made. An obvious question was,
why then on the present profile, so willing to get out of it? To this
the answer was, that they had in general got soured with him on
account of his perseverance in his endeavours (to which they were
averse) to improve the population of the mills; and that even now,
though they felt the advantage of his proceedings, they would not
acknowledge them – that they were also in some measure bound by
their repeated declarations to him, of a readiness to quit the concern,
upon even the purchase money of their shares being made good to
them – and that it was now his earnest desire to get such partners,
as would go along with him, in his efforts to show what can be done
to make a manufacturing population, virtuous, and happy, and far
more productive than they have yet been.[29]

The scene was now set for a dramatic showdown between Owen and his former partners. In the interval they had acquired a replacement for him, namely Colin Campbell of Jura, and they had also persuaded Humphreys to take over Owen's position as manager at New Lanark. Accordingly, the 'well known and extensive cotton mills beautifully and advantageously situated on the river Clyde' were advertised for sale with Owen's rivals obviously convinced they could purchase them for a knock-down price. However, Owen, strengthened by the support of his new partners, three of whom, Allen, Foster and Gibbs, accompanied him to Glasgow, undoubtedly had other ideas. He encouraged his former partners to think he was the sole bidder and kept the identity of the new ones secret by closeting them in a local hotel. Thus, the auction of the New Lanark mills held at the Tontine Rooms, Glasgow on 31 December 1813 demonstrated his business shrewdness and resulted in a triumphant victory over his opponents.

At first, his old partners suggested an upset price of £40,000 but when they rejected a private offer of £60,000 by Owen he persisted on this figure being the starting price. Meanwhile he had given instructions to his lawyer, Alexander Macgregor, 'never to bid at any time more than one hundred pounds and to follow up the bidding to one hundred and twenty thousand pounds'. The bidding rose to £84,000 at which point his ex-partners paused for further consultations with each other. It resumed once more rising to £110,000 before there was another delay. At this point, at least according to Owen, Kirkman Finlay, one of Glasgow's leading merchants, a customer of Owen's and a prominent figure in the city, was heard to forecast that Owen would triumph. If he did, he was certainly correct with his prophecy since, when the bidding reached £114,000 and Macgregor topped it with another £100, his ex-partners conceded defeat. 'Confound that Owen', Atkinson reputedly said to Finlay 'He has bought it, and twenty thousand pounds too cheap!'[30]

Owen's financial manoeuvres had undoubtedly got him in trouble but they need to be seen against the background of a booming if volatile industry and his astute management practices. Even his old partners stood in good stead when they were finally beaten at £114,000 because this represented a capital gain of £34,000 on the 1810 price. After a relatively unsuccessful year in 1812 large profits amounting to over £52,000 had been made in 1813 under Humphreys and without Owen's aid or management. Owen himself gained most, since the value of his paid up capital rose to £44,000, a gain of 50 per cent on a valuation of 1812. The new partners, who had earlier agreed to bid up to £120,000 without even seeing New Lanark, had to invest cash direct, but Owen could transfer his old shareholding at a higher cash value. So his five shares of £10,000 each were readily paid for and his share of the undistributed profits from the old partnership, amounting to something in the region of £42,000, would make him a rich man.[31]

Owen returned immediately from Glasgow to New Lanark where he
and his party were given a rapturous welcome by the inhabitants. A
letter to the *Glasgow Herald* published on the 10 January 1814 gave a
graphic description of the reception which they received:

> There were great rejoicings here yesterday on account of Mr Owen's
> return, after his purchase of New Lanark. The Society of Free Masons
> at this place, with colours flying and a band of music, accompanied
> by almost the whole of the inhabitants, met Mr Owen, immediately
> before his entrance into the burgh of Lanark, and hailed him with
> the loudest acclamations of joy; his people took the horses from his
> carriage and, a flag being placed in front, drew him and his friends
> along, amid the plaudits of the surrounding multitudes, until they
> reached Braxfield, where his Lady and two of her sisters being
> prevailed upon to enter the carriage, which was then uncovered, the
> people with the most rapturous exultation proceeded to draw them
> through all the streets of New Lanark, where all were eager to testify
> their joy at his return. On being set down at his own house, Mr Owen,
> in a very appropriate speech, expressed his acknowledgements to
> his people for warmth of their attachment, when the air was again
> rent with the most enthusiastic bursts of applause. Mr Owen is so
> justly beloved by all the inhabitants employed at New Lanark, and
> by people of all ranks in the neighbourhood, that a general happiness
> has been felt since the news arrived of his continuing a proprietor of
> the mills. The houses were all illuminated at New Lanark on Friday
> night when the news came, and all has been jubilee and animation
> with them ever since.[32]

Unquestionably New Year's Day 1814 was a significant watershed in
Owen's career. From the day he had taken over New Lanark in January
1800 until that date he had been struggling to persuade his employees
to put his principles into practice. Whether or not they agreed with him
his popularity had certainly soared. At the same time he had also been
fighting a losing battle with his partners regarding their acceptance of his
farsighted plans for the village and its workers, notably in the treatment
of children and their education.

Owen's interest in education – apart from his personal experience – was
probably aroused in Manchester, where, it will be recalled, he presented
at least one paper on the subject to the Literary and Philosophical Society.
At New Lanark, despite his partners' attempts to dispense with it, he
inherited Dale's school, where according to Marshall, in one and a half
hour's schooling after the usual mill hours and beginning at 7 o'clock at
night, children were not only taught reading and writing, but also 'the
polite accomplishments'. Dale evidently employed singing masters and
dancing masters to teach the factory girls and boys to dance. Apart from

instituting day schools to accommodate the children under ten who were no longer to be employed in the mills, quite what other changes were made to this regime before 1814 is not known. But Owen, already thinking about how his ideas could be more widely applied, must certainly have known of the activities of reformers interested in promoting working class education, including an old associate of Dale's, Patrick Colquhoun, long removed from Glasgow to London, and Sir Thomas Bernard.[33] Prominent among them, however, was Lancaster, whose badge system Owen adapted for use as the silent monitor on the mill floor. Lancaster's *Improvements in Education as it Effects the Industrious Classes* was published in 1803. Therein was described a monitorial system which allowed the instruction of large numbers of children at once, using specially selected older pupils sufficiently trained in the three Rs to pass on the knowledge to their juniors. While Lancaster had no monopoly on this system it had made some progress in London and elsewhere thanks to the practical and financial support offered by the Quakers and other dissenters.

Lancaster's system was explained at some length to incredulous readers of the *Glasgow Herald* in an article carried in its edition of 20 November 1807:

> Paradoxical though it may appear above one thousand children may be taught and governed by one Master only, at an expense now reduced to *five shillings per annum, each child*; and supposed still capable of further reduction. The average time for instruction, in Reading, Writing and Arithmetic, is twelve months.

'Among many other advantages which distinguish this system', the article continued, 'is a new method of teaching to Read and Spell, whereby one Book worth Seven Shillings, will serve to teach Five Hundred Boys, who, in the usual method would require Five Hundred Books, worth above Twenty-five Pounds'. And, it concluded, 'any boy who can read can teach Arithmetic with the certainty of any mathematician, although he knows nothing about it himself'.[34] While the system was unlikely to attract favourable comment from publishers of school text books, on the grounds of costs alone it must have had an instant appeal to those engaged in popular education. Interestingly, the same paper in 1810 reported the opening in Glasgow of two schools on the Lancasterian system.[35] Owen is known to have provided financial support to Lancaster and the originator of the other system, Bell, but whether this was at that time or later is not made clear in his autobiography. He stipulated that he would prefer a non-denominational approach and was prepared to give £1,000 if this was adopted, though only £500 if guarantees could not be given to this effect. Lancaster did so and Bell did not. So the likelihood is that his direct backing for Lancaster refers to a later period when Owen had begun his campaign against religious sectarianism.[36]

He was certainly instrumental in encouraging Lancaster to visit Scotland in 1812 which the reformer duly did following five months of travelling in Ireland 'for the purpose of introducing his system into that country'. In a frenzy of activity, mirroring Owen's timetable from then on, Lancaster lectured in Ayr and Kilmarnock before visiting Paisley, Greenock and Edinburgh, returning to Glasgow to give a lecture and demonstration in the theatre there. According to the report the youth who accompanied him, one of his apprentices from London, though only 14 years old, had already organised several schools on the system.[37] At a public dinner held at the Black Bull honouring Lancaster the chair was taken by Owen, supported on one side by two university professors from the Glasgow College and on the other by a minister of the Kirk. His reply to Lancaster's address provides an insight into the way his own ideas on education were developing. Given a rational education, said Owen, 'all those in the lower walks of life, and the character of the whole community, will rise many degrees . . . and while none will suffer, all must be essentially benefited'. Further, those exposed to the system 'must learn the habits of obedience, order, regularity, industry' which were as important as learning to read, write and account, vital though these skills undoubtedly were. In an oblique reference to future plans for New Lanark he suggested the schools which 'contain the younger children in the day time, will likewise serve for evening and Sunday schools, at which times those who may be past the proper age for the first, and strangers who may come amongst us, may be instructed'.[38] The last could well be a reference to New Lanark's Gaelic population or the more modest numbers of Irish migrants finding their way to the mill gates. But if any of these ideas were to become reality Owen had to have the support of like-minded individuals. Possibly Lancaster provided him with introductions to his Quaker supporters, notably William Allen, who with other philanthropists was also heavily involved in efforts to educate the children of the poor. Certainly, given the presence of these enthusiasts the nexus of this activity was the metropolis, so if Owen was to make any headway it was there.

Children also featured prominently in Owen's life beyond the mills, the counting house and the public arena he had just entered. His growing family and status necessitated a move from the modest village house with its tidy little garden overlooking the mills to the grander and more spacious surroundings of nearby Braxfield House, leased in 1807 from the MacQueen family.[39] Braxfield was to become not only the family home but also an important base for his future propaganda campaigns. The Dale sisters were also part of his extended family and with Caroline are occasionally mentioned in the correspondence that survives from this period. Whatever the physical or personal attributes of Owen's older sisters-in-law, their wealth made them desirable catches. John Wright, who was Dale's and then Owen's clerk at the Glasgow counting house, had his eye on one of them, although Owen thought he had no chance, maybe even actively discouraging his employee in his suit. On the other hand he seems to have encouraged a possible match between Craig and another of Caroline's sisters but despite at least one family visit to Perthshire this never materialised. This may have been all to the good because of the debt the hapless Craig had already accumulated at Stanley.

In contrast to Owen, Craig as Crusoe could hardly have survived for long on his island. As it was Owen had used what materials, living or dead, had come to hand, not only proving himself to be a survivor but also prospering greatly. By the standards of the time he was already rich and his wealth gave him power, opening doors well beyond the merchant communities of Glasgow and Manchester, where he had an established reputation as an astute, indeed sharp, businessman. Despite the various financial and partnership difficulties, the majority of which had been resolved by this time, he remained a 'prince of cotton spinners'. His progressive ideas may have offended some, especially his fellow factory masters, but none could decry the increased profits they generated both for Owen and those associated with him. If the methods practised at New Lanark brought order and enhanced profitability, they might even be improved upon to greater effect. And more to the point they could well have universal application at a time when threats to order were manifest beyond the shores of New Lanark.

## NOTES

1. R. Owen, *A Statement Regarding the New Lanark Establishment*, Edinburgh, 1812 reprinted 1973, and also in Claeys (ed.) *Selected Works*, pp. 13–21.
2. Butt, 'Owen as Businessman', p. 186.
3. J. Marshall quoted in Butt, p. 191.
4. Atholl Mss. Owen to Craig 20 January 1808.
5. Ibid, Owen to Craig 8 January 1811.
6. Gourock Mss. Produce Book 1803–05; Report Book, 1803–08.
7. Ibid and Co-operative Union. Owen Correspondence, Statement of wages and produce, 1822; data in Butt, p. 209.
8. Gourock Mss. General Ledger 1804–08; Donnachie and Hewitt, pp. 66–7.
9. Atholl Mss. Owen to Craig 10 and 24 January 1806.
10. Ibid, Owen to Craig 9 March 1807.
11. Ibid, Owen to Craig 21 March 1809.
12. Gourock Mss. Sales Book 1814–15; Butt, p. 197.
13. *Life*, p. 63.
14. Atholl Mss. Owen to Craig 18 April 1809.

15. National Archives of Scotland, Court of Session, Lanark Twist Co. Edmonstoun, 1810.
16. Atholl Mss. Owen to Craig 17 October 1810.
17. One Formerly a teacher, pp. 6–7.
18. *Statement* (in Claeys vol. 1) pp. 17–18; J. Griscom, *A Year in Europe*, New York, 1823, vol. II, pp. 383–4. In 1819, when Griscom visited, Owen thought he could save £4–5000 per annum, 'besides the superior training and improved habits it will produce'.
19. Atholl Mss Owen to Craig 14 May 1810.
20. Ibid, Owen to Craig 17 October 1810; in *Life* p. 86 he mentions the sum as £84,000 but the contract in NAS, Campbell of Jura Muniments, 5 October 1810, gives the lower sum.
21. Butt, 'Owen as Businessman', pp. 82–3.
22. *Life*, pp. 86–7.
23. *Life*, p. 87; Butt, pp. 173–9; on the details of these financial transactions see also A.J. Robertson 'Robert Owen and the Campbell Debt 1810–22', *Business Hist.*, vol. 11, 1969, pp. 23–30.
24. Butt, pp. 179–82.
25. Owen in *Statement*, p. 16.
26. *Life*, pp. 88–9; Butt, p. 177–83 explains the complexities of Owen's position in detail.
27. Butt in 'Introduction' to *Life*, xv.
28. On these individuals see Friends' Library, Quaker Biographies; Allen's *Life*; DNB
29. Bentham Corr.
30. Owen's version of the famous auction is given in *Life*, pp. 89–93.
31. Butt, pp. 187, 200.
32. *Glasgow Herald* 10 January 1814; Life, pp. 92–3, 97–8.
33. See for example, P. Colquhoun, *A New and Appropriate System of Education for the Labouring Poor*, London, 1806 and T. Bernard, *Of the Education of the Poor*, London, 1806,
34. *Glasgow Herald*, 20 November 1807.
35. Ibid, 8 October and 5 November 1810.
36. *Life*, pp. 106–7.
37. *Glasgow Herald* 20 April 1812.
38. 'Mr Owen's Speech' reproduced in Claeys *Selected Works*, vol 1, pp. 7–10.
39. Atholl Mss. Owen to Craig 17 February 1807.

# SEVEN

# Social Theorist and Factory Reformer

New Lanark came to play a vital role in Owen's ambitious plans for a New System of Society and had a significant impact on later community experiments and Owenite activities. The influence that New Lanark exercised on both Owen the man and the movement he inspired was of such significance that even a separate chapter here can hardly do justice to the full story. After 1812, when his public career really began, a narrative history of the mills and community under his management figured prominently in practically all Owen's pamphlets, books, periodicals, speeches and evidence to parliamentary enquiries. His interest in reform gradually broadened from children's employment and working conditions in factories, to education and poor relief, leading ultimately to the wider social and economic concerns addressed in his collected essays published as *A New View of Society* and later writings, most critically his *Report to the County of Lanark*. As far back as Dale's time New Lanark had been an object of curiosity, for as we saw earlier, large factories of this kind were unusual. Hence the community attracted many visitors and was a place of note for tourists en route to the Falls of Clyde. But Owen – a skilled publicist with the means to sustain a long-term propaganda campaign – made it even more famous. Although he was temporarily no longer master and was about to travel far beyond its shores New Lanark remained his own personal island and rather like Crusoe he had set about writing its history, indeed inventing it if reality did not fit the public image he wanted to present. New Lanark therefore became his role-model for other communities and even more ambitiously, the future organisation of society.[1]

While the pamphlet of 1812 describing his early management of New Lanark and articulating his aspirations for the future gave some indication of the way his thoughts were developing, we have no idea how many copies he circulated, apart from those that ended up in the hands of potential partners. It is certainly possible that the pamphlet found its way into political circles, where anyone reading it would have been impressed by the idea that New Lanark under Owen's management 'might be a model and example to the manufacturing community, which without some essential change in the formation of their characters, threatened, and now still more threatens, to revolutionise and ruin the empire'. The idea that the character of the labouring class could be suitably moulded by these modest proposals, including whatever educational provision was required to make it more efficient (and thereby boost profits), was likely to have had considerable appeal in the increasingly volatile atmosphere of the time. Political radicalism in all its various forms was an anathema to the government of the day, but machine breaking by gangs of Luddites represented a direct physical threat to mill masters – and worse, perhaps the government itself.[2]

Owen's precise movements after dismissal by his disgruntled partners cannot be ascertained. But the likelihood is that he set out for London during the autumn or early winter of 1812, apparently in some haste, leaving Caroline to borrow £100 for household expenses from Humphreys.[3] It was to be the first of many such journeys from Scotland to the south undertaken in the cause of reform. Travel by mail coach remained a hazardous business despite the many improved turnpike roads that had been built since Owen first travelled from Manchester to Glasgow on behalf of the Chorlton Twist Company. The journey time had been much reduced but still involved virtually perpetual motion including overnight travel, the only alternative being by sea from Leith to the Thames. Despite its risks Owen enjoyed travel and when he reached London, which he does not appear to have visited since his youth, had the great advantage of knowing his way around. Although he was rich enough to take rooms in a hotel he probably stayed with his brother before finding his own lodgings. He certainly knew plenty of fellow merchants, gentry and MPs from Scotland, and no doubt carried in his pocket introductions to others. Whoever else he knew was certainly able to open doors on his behalf, even suggesting a Masonic connection, but this he vehemently denies in his autobiography.[4]

He arrived in the metropolis to find it seething with news of momentous events on the Continent, especially Wellington's victories in the Peninsula and Napoleon's retreat from Moscow, of the course of the war in the United States, and closer to home, of a series of political crises made more acute by the growing unrest in the country. While the international situation remained perilous and world events were to exercise a growing influence on Owen's later life, it was the prevailing politics and personalities with whom he associated which affected his reception. Intelligence of his management at New Lanark and of his views had almost certainly reached the government of Lord Liverpool, who headed a Tory administration appointed by the Prince Regent following the assassination of the previous Prime Minister, Spencer Percival, and had resumed office in June following a dramatic vote of no confidence in May. Liverpool, who had been present at the fall of the Bastille, was no great enthusiast for parliamentary reform.[5] The essentially reactionary regime that prevailed during the first eight years of his government was to be counter-balanced by Liverpool's pragmatic approach to political events and new developments in the economic sphere. The latter embraced the landed, commercial and manufacturing interests, all of which to a lesser or greater degree were now represented in parliament, and any one of which the government ignored at its peril.[6]

There is some evidence that as early as 1810 Owen had been in touch with Liverpool, then Secretary for War, about a proposed 'Bill for the Formation of Character Among the Poor and Working Classes' aimed at establishing a national system of education.[7] This object was a logical extension of Owen's experience among the workers at New Lanark married to the possibilities of mass education under the monitorial system and both figured prominently in *A New View of Society*. Liverpool, understandably, had other things on his mind at the time and nothing came of the proposal. Owen may have been disappointed, concluding that his proposal needed further refinement if it was to prove worthy of parliamentary time. But even in its wording it provided the idea central to his essays on the formation of character.

The story of the background to Owen's writing of the four essays in the series that made up *A New View of Society* shows how he set the concept of character formation into a larger frame, drawing extensively on the ideas and help of others. When Owen arrived in London ostensibly seeking new partners he naturally sought out the company of those likely to be sympathetic to his cause or rich enough to invest in the New Lanark concern when it came on the market. Quite who he sought out in the first instance we do not know, but Lancaster and his supporters, Quaker or otherwise, must have been high on his list. At a dinner given for him in January 1813 by a Scot, Daniel Stuart, a supporter of the Tory government and proprietor of a newspaper, the *Courier*, he met William Godwin, the prominent social philosopher and author of *An Enquiry Concerning Political Justice*, which had been published in 1793. Godwin's work was a skilful summary of ideas generated during the Enlightenment and argued for a new social order stressing justice, freedom and equality for the individual. Education, private and public, figured prominently in Godwin's thinking, as did character formation and happiness. The entries in Godwin's diary prove that during the spring of the year, as Owen worked on the second, third and fourth essays, he was frequently at Godwin's house for breakfast, tea or dinner. Between January and May Owen met Godwin at least twice a week.[8] Godwin later recorded that on one occasion he converted Owen from 'self-love' to 'benevolence', although the next time they met Owen claimed that he had been too hasty in altering his opinion.[9] However, his attempt to derive benevolence from a desire from happiness was not very different from Godwin's. Of course this does not prove that Owen's work owed much to Godwin's but it probably exercised a great deal of influence, especially when allied to the ideas Owen himself had already picked up either from his reading, through his association with enlightened thinkers in Manchester, Glasgow, and Edinburgh, or from discussions with visitors to New Lanark.

Owen was to list Godwin among his main literary companions and Podmore rightly described the philosopher as his master.[10] Owen certainly never acknowledged a direct debt to *Political Justice*, perhaps because he never properly read it.[11] Yet many of the fundamental ideas and sometimes the actual phrasing of Owen's works resemble the doctrines of *Political Justice*. Like Godwin, Owen constructed his theory of progress on the premises that characters are formed by their circumstances, that vice is ignorance, and that truth will ultimately prevail over error. Both individuals equated happiness with knowledge and spoke in the language of utility. Other features in common were the moral regeneration of mankind and the importance of economic reform in advance of political reform. They argued that the best way of eradicating the evils that beset society at the time was not the system of punishments and rewards advocated by Bentham, but by rational education and universal enlightenment. Both condemned political agitation but favoured instead a voluntary redistribution of wealth, which Owen later hoped would be achieved through co-operation. Their ultimate social ideal, as Marshall put it, was that of a decentralised society of small self-governing communities of the kind that Owen was to propose in his villages scheme.[12] Since Godwin had fallen out of fashion Owen could be seen as his replacement for the new century.

Moreover, Godwin introduced Owen to the great Radical, Francis Place, in whose shop and library at Charing Cross he also seems to have spent time. Owen, Place recalled, was 'a man of kind manners and good intentions, of an imperturbable temper, and an enthusiastic desire to promote the happiness of mankind'. 'A few interviews made us friends', said Place, 'and he told me he possessed the means, and was resolved to produce a great change in the manners and habits of the whole of the people, from the exalted to the most depressed.' This could be an early reference to birth control, but at that stage it seems unlikely. Owen told him that most of the existing institutions prejudiced welfare and happiness but that his proposals were so simple and so obviously beneficial that any thinking person could understand them. Owen evidently presented Place with a manuscript asking if he would read and correct it for him, but whether this consisted of the first two essays or all four is unclear. Friendship apart, Place was incredulous that Owen believed he was the first to observe that 'man was a creature of circumstances' and that 'on this supposed discovery he founded his system'.[13]

Among other savants with whom Owen also kept company during 1813–14 was James Mill, the political economist and close associate of his then prospective partner, Bentham. Although Owen never acknowledged the fact, it was probably Place and Mill who edited *A New View of Society* and gave the essays the clarity that is missing from most of his later works. Even his supporters thought much of his writing was very 'woolly'.[14] Place was greatly offended not only by the second comprehensive edition of the essays, published in 1816, which contained material he had earlier read and rejected, but also by Owen's apparent arrogance in the face of reasoned criticism. Moreover, as far as Place was concerned, practical politics were clearly not Owen's strong point.[15] Owen steered well clear of suggesting, far less articulating, an agenda for political as opposed to social reform. Perhaps he did not want to prejudice his immediate plans, realising that the authorities were unlikely to look with much favour on anything that remotely whiffed of Radicalism. Pragmatism, as in his financial and business affairs, was the watchword.

The earliest essay, 'by one of His Majesty's Justices of the Peace for the County of Lanark' and entitled 'On the Formation of Character', was dedicated in its first edition to William Wilberforce, the evangelical Christian MP and humanitarian. Wilberforce had long fought for the abolition of slavery, from which indirectly Owen had built up his fortune, though he never acknowledged it. It was prefixed by the oft quoted statement, central to the 'New View', that 'Any general character, from the best to the worst, from the most ignorant to the most enlightened, may be given to any community, even to the world at large, by the application of proper means; which means are to a great extent at the command and under the control of those who have influence in the affairs of men'.[16] In Owen's view environmental planning and education held the key to the formation of character – and thus suitably moulded characters could produce a pacific and harmonious working class. The excesses of industrialisation and the Factory System must be corrected otherwise 'general disorder must ensue'. 'Happiness' could even be equated with 'pecuniary profits' – as he himself would presently demonstrate.

Little of this, as Place observed, was really new. The influences of environment on individuals and society came from Rousseau and other thinkers of the Enlightenment era, whose ideas Owen had probably first read as a member of the Manchester Literary and Philosophical Society.[17] According to Owen the fundamental precept that character and environment were mutually related could readily be applied in an industrial context. There paternalistic methods might produce a humanitarian regime and generate greater productivity and profit, in which, theoretically all could share. Unity and mutual co-operation were concepts for the future. At this time too Owen's thoughts on education were probably still being formulated, but expanding his earlier statement of 1812, he duly acknowledged his debt to Lancaster and to Bell, the other reformer who had pioneered the simultaneous instruction of large numbers of children. This was likely to appeal in the first instance to other educational reformers, including his Quaker associates who were anxious to encourage the development of schools applying Lancaster's principles.[18]

The second essay, also written and published in 1813, described the progress he had made at New Lanark since assuming management. As we have seen, he certainly exaggerated the poor state of the population before he went there, even if he told the truth about the hours worked by the child apprentices. He provided a glowing picture of the numerous improvements, environmental, moral and social, which his paternalistic methods had effected – showing the 'incalculable advantages' brought to both workers and proprietors. Inevitably considerable attention was again devoted to the role of education and training, which had proved vital in removing 'unfavourable circumstances'. Owen was also able to claim that because there was constant communication between Old Lanark on the hill and New Lanark in the valley below his experiment had not occurred in isolation and that if expanded his ideas could have unlimited potential nationally and internationally.[19]

This was the underlying theme of Owen's third essay, mixed with a general attack on human error and how truth could be made to prevail over it. There was further exemplification of his principles with reference to New Lanark, though more about its future rather than its past and present. He described the central educational role to be played by his 'New Institution', also highlighting the importance of relaxation to his workforce. In this context he attacked the Scots Sabbath as being a day of extremes – on the one hand 'superstitious gloom and tyranny over the mind', on the other 'of the most destructive intemperance and licentiousness'.[20] Written in 1813 and at first circulated privately the essay and its successor in the series were not actually published until July 1816. Nevertheless this first public attack on religion set a dangerous precedent for the future, prejudicing his relationship with his partners and the Scottish clergy, particularly the local presbytery back in Lanark. Quite why Owen maintained his subsequent campaign against religion is hard to determine, because his wife and family were highly religious and he clearly tolerated and even encouraged church attendance, probably as another means of promoting order and morality. Indeed he even made special arrangements for the Gaelic-speaking population by engaging preachers in the language. For many years the summer communion at Lanark parish church was celebrated – on the invitation of Owen's neighbour, Lady Mary Ross – by Dr John Macdonald, the famous 'Apostle of the North' and the most popular Gaelic preacher in the Highlands. On these occasions tables were set apart for New Lanark's Highland population and Macdonald 'gave the addresses in their own native Gaelic'.[21] Owen's views on religion were not what they seemed and he was not only misunderstood but also much maligned in consequence.

Again generalising from his experience at New Lanark and possibly influenced by the views of one of his new partners, Jeremy Bentham, Owen argued in his fourth essay for government intervention to develop a national system of education, to counter increasing problems of poverty and unemployment, and generate greater 'happiness'.[22] This was a return to the earlier proposals he may have submitted to Liverpool. There was also a logical link between Owen's practical experience in Manchester and at New Lanark and his interest in three major concerns of the day – the social impact of the Factory System, poor law reform and popular education. He was not alone in realising how closely all three were related and that New Lanark might provide lessons for universal problems, the central theme of the fourth essay. He took up these issues at a crucial time. Certainly the suppression of a dangerous, poverty-stricken, under-class and the creation of a conforming and profitable workforce had an obvious appeal to the governing elite, regardless of party. Indeed for a while Owen could count on as much sympathy from the governing Tories as from the opposition Whigs and he took every opportunity to use his connections in high places to advance his ideas.[23] But were the authorities prepared to act? John Quincy Adams, then US minister in London, who became acquainted with Owen and read the essays, did not think so. He was scathing of the government's attitude noting in a letter to his father, the former president, that 'the distressed state of the country is treated with virtual contempt by the authorities'. 'They will feed as many as they can by subscription', he continued, 'let the rest starve, and keep soldiers to shoot down the rioters'. Continuing disturbance, in Adams's opinion, certainly gave 'a new spur to benevolence, by bringing motives of charity closer to home', but this seemed unlikely to have much impact on official policy.[24]

To whom then were Owen's *New Views* directed in the period between their writing and publication for sale? Given the rigours of censorship then prevailing Owen wisely resisted immediate publication and had the essays printed and circulated privately. Some survive in pamphlet form, others as broadsheets, but we have no record of the exact number in total he had run off the press, nor do we know in detail to whom they were sent. There is also some doubt about when they were circulated for the first time, though the first two had been seen by carefully chosen recipients before the autumn of 1813. He says that the 'heads of administration and the churches' were most anxious to see them prior to publication and that at first his main communications were with 'leading members both in church and state'. One of the earliest recipients of the first two essays, and, presumably the request of an audience, was Charles Manners-Sutton, the Archbishop of Canterbury. After Owen had finished the remainder in manuscript he met the archbishop at Lambeth to discuss progress, reading him essays three and four in one sitting. Manners-Sutton was interested but cautious, though Owen claims that at the archbishop's request they established a long-standing and friendly correspondence.[25] Another early recipient of the first two essays was Liverpool, by this time Prime Minister. Owen later had an interview with Liverpool and his wife, who was said to have read the essays with interest. 'I am very desirous to induce the ladies to take into their consideration the cause which I advocate', Owen told his hosts, 'and especially the subject of education, now becoming so useful, and so important to all of the female sex'.[26] Both Liverpool and his wife apparently approved of his ideas, the latter in particular being anxious 'to ameliorate the condition of the working classes and to raise their characters'. As he left he was introduced to Robert Peel, son of Sir Robert Peel MP, a fellow textile magnate, who had helped engineer the bill to protect factory apprentices. Peel Sr. was to figure prominently in the revived campaign for legislation to protect working children with which Owen subsequently became involved and the two men were to become close associates in the cause of factory reform.

At this juncture, however, Owen's most important contact with the authorities was undoubtedly Henry Addington, Lord Sidmouth, Home Secretary in Liverpool's administration. Consistent in his conservative views, Sidmouth was responsible for the surveillance and suppression of radical activities and other threats to social order in those troubled times. The ultimate censor, Sidmouth had to be convinced that the essays posed no threat and, as Owen hoped, might help implement his ideas for popular education. To this end Owen sought an interview with Sidmouth probably sometime in early 1813, presumably taking with him the two essays which had already been circulated and perhaps drafts of the others. He apparently kept Sidmouth informed of the progress of his scheme for reform. Certainly in September he was telling Sidmouth that the basis of his further proposals he had promised to submit for 'a systematic plan for the gradual improvement of the British Empire' was to be 'wholly founded' on the principles set out in the two essays which Sidmouth, the Prime Minister and other members of the administration had already seen.[27] Possibly at the same or a later meeting Owen promised to draw up proposals for a bill on the lines of the one that he had earlier suggested to Liverpool, its object being 'improving the character and ameliorating the condition of the poor'. This he duly did, the undated printed proof being headed 'For the General Amelioration of the Poor and Lower Orders through Their Education'. He enclosed with it an estimate of the outlay needed to get his scheme going, ranging from £10,000 in the first year to £40,000 in the fourth and subsequent years. In a letter to Sidmouth he said that he had spoken to Nicholas Vansittart, Chancellor of the Exchequer, who 'obligingly offered to attend a meeting on the subject any time his lordship should name' – a very neat piece of side-stepping on the part of Vansittart.[28]

In his memoirs Owen presents a very confused account about the status of the essays. He evidently suggested to Sidmouth at some point that 200 copies of the essays be prepared 'bound with alternate blank leaves' which would be dispatched to the leading governments on the Continent and America, to the most learned universities, and to those whom the Home Secretary thought 'best calculated to form a sound judgement upon them'. Sidmouth duly sent off the essays, not all 200 it has to be said, as several in this odd format still survive. According to Owen a substantial number were returned and the comments, while generally favourable to his ideas, were mainly concerned with details of people the writers thought most likely to object to minor points in Owen's thesis. Whether or not it was his intention to incorporate the feedback in revisions of the essays is unclear, but he says that he and Sidmouth looked over the copies that were returned. When this occurred is uncertain, though it may well have been later.[29] Wary of censorship, which had even got some of the Scottish clergy in trouble, Owen was clearly desperate to avoid alienating anyone who might help promote his ideas. This was the most powerful reason for deliberately understating the political message that Place and the other Radicals would have liked to read. However, the polite attentions of Sidmouth and others in high places for politically neutral proposals that on the surface could do little harm were far from being commitments to act.

Even before the four essays were published as a single volume Owen's ideas provoked considerable reaction. Crucially back in Scotland, where by the beginning of 1814 he was reinstated as manager at the New Lanark, those who had grudges against him wasted little time in condemning the 'New View'. In the *Glasgow Courier* 'Gracchus' and others rounded on Owen for saying that an individual's character was formed for him, rather than that 'each individual forms his own character'. Owen's reply was characteristically forceful, maintaining that if individuals did form their own characters then poverty, crime and misery would be inevitable, whereas under his system 'mankind will become one heart and one mind'. More dangerous in the longer term was Owen's criticism of the prevailing regime before he took over, in particular the 'strong sectarian influence'. This was much improved, thanks to the new system. But he recognised that he had 'considered the possible dire consequences to himself' that might result from any interference in matters of religion, a danger he was to encounter sooner than he perhaps realised.[30] The likelihood is that these early attacks came from disgruntled factory masters or members of the established Kirk because clergy in other Scottish sects, such as the Associate Kirk, the Secessionists and the Congregationalists, were for the moment more tolerant.

At that point it was not the 'New View' that brought Owen onto a national stage, but rather his attempts to ameliorate factory conditions through parliamentary legislation. His participation in the movement for factory reform is universally acknowledged and has been the subject of several detailed studies.[31] Although mainly concentrated in the period 1815–19 it had really begun in 1803 with his paper on the cotton trade addressed to the Glasgow cotton masters. This showed his renewed concern, first evidenced in Manchester, about the impact of the Factory System on society – a theme to which he consistently returned.[32] Many years later he was to reflect on his attitude at the time:

> As employer and master manufacturer in Lancashire and Lanark-shire, I had done all I could to lighten the evils of those whom I employed; yet with all I could do under our most irrational system for creating wealth, forming character, and conduct in all human affairs, I could only to a limited extent alleviate the wretchedness of their condition, while I knew that society, even at that period, possessed the most ample means to educate, employ, place, and govern the whole population of the British Empire, so as to make all into full-formed, highly intelligent, united, and permanently prosperous and happy men and women, superior in all physical and mental qualities.[33]

However, he added, superstitions and mistaken self-interest prevailed to such an extent that he realised one of the most effective ways to make a start was protective legislation, particularly for the thousands of children set to work in textile mills. His personal record on the employment of children at New Lanark could certainly be held up as an example of good practice for the cotton trade, which in Owen's words was invariably 'destructive of health, morals, and social comforts of the mass of the people engaged in it'.

His campaign for improved conditions began in Glasgow on 25 January 1815 at another meeting of fellow cotton barons, which he later claimed to have called, presided over by the prominent merchant and then Lord Provost, Henry Monteith. In his speech Owen claimed that despite high levels of taxation the cotton trade was worth £35 million and supported 3 million workers whose condition, though certainly better than those in agriculture, was worse than the slaves in the West Indies. He then called for industrial reform on the grounds that 'the main pillar and prop of the political greatness and prosperity of our country' was trade which degraded its workers. The cotton industry, he said, had driven children into mills which in some instances had become 'receptacles for living human skeletons, almost disrobed of intellect, where, as the business is often now conducted, they linger out a few years of miserable existence, acquiring every bad habit, which they disseminate throughout society'. According to his thinking, mechanisation had actually made things worse because, 'It is only since the introduction of this trade, that children, even grown people, were required to labour more than twelve hours a day, including the time allotted for meals'. Not only had hours greatly increased, morals had degenerated, to such an extent, he maintained, 'that the sole recreation of the labourer is to be found in the pot-house or gin-shop'. Worse still, he concluded, 'it is only since the introduction of this baneful trade, that poverty, crime, and misery, have made rapid and fearful strides throughout the community'. If anything was to goad them into action it must have been this last statement, but while his fellow employers were enthusiastic about asking for remission of the tax on imported cotton 'not one would second my motion for the relief of those whom they employed'.

While Owen again neglected to mention the large rewards he and his partners had derived from the trade, he perhaps felt his humanitarian approach and his proposed reforms spoke for themselves and justified his position. At least he was prepared to act, even if independently, by publishing the address in the newspapers, getting up a draft bill, and taking things further in the country.[34]

The substance of the Glasgow oration was soon elaborated into a pamphlet, *Observations on the Effects of the Manufacturing System*, which, at considerable cost, he distributed from New Lanark to every MP and peer. This, he claimed, 'made me yet better known to the government, and was afterwards a passport for me to all the members of both Houses of Parliament, and created a considerable sensation among the upper classes and manufacturing interest over the kingdom'.[35] His pamphlet, while stressing the need for factory reform, also provided its readers with an intelligent manufacturer's view of the social and economic implications of industrialisation. The rapid progress in industry and technology had brought 'accompanying evils', notably adverse 'political and moral effects'. Industry, he said, was bringing about 'an essential change in the general character of the people', and 'ere long the comparatively happy simplicity of the agricultural peasant would be wholly lost'. 'The lower orders' had been driven by the need to acquire wealth and by competition 'to a point of real oppression, reducing them . . . to a state more wretched than can be imagined by those who have not attentively observed the changes as they have gradually occurred'. He reiterated the view that workers were more degraded and miserable than they had been before the introduction of factories 'upon which the success of their bare subsistence now depends'.[36]

Owen further reflected on the wider implications manufacturing had on the economy. Exports, previously useful, were now essential 'to support the additional population which this increased demand for labour had produced'. But Owen thought that the country's export trade would gradually diminish, partly because of the impact of the new Corn Law, which had just reached the statute book. Echoing some of the ideas

presented in *A New View of Society* he maintained that economic liberalism
had destroyed what he called 'that open, honest sincerity, without which
man cannot make others happy, nor enjoy happiness himself' and that
this had particularly harmed the working classes. In Owen's opinion it
was only in the last thirty years that parents had allowed children under
fourteen to work regularly and that twelve hours per day, including
rest and meal times, had been regarded as enough for 'the most robust
adult'. Moreover, and perhaps anticipating his later village scheme, he
thought that in the rural context workers were generally led by the
example of the landed proprietor 'in such habits as created a mutual
interest between the parties'. This meant that even 'the lowest peasant'
was generally considered 'as belonging to, and forming somewhat of a
member of, a respectable family'. The idyllic rural community of perhaps
only a generation before was thus in marked contrast to those in which
the majority of factory operatives now found themselves. Their children
toiled for fourteen hours for a bare subsistence. Even on the grounds of
efficiency this made little sense for experience had taught him that 'in
a national view, the labour which is exerted twelve hours a day will
be obtained more economically than if stretched to a longer period'.
To 'effect amelioration and avert danger' he proposed the draft of a
parliamentary bill calling for a limit on regular hours of labour to
twelve per day including one and a half hours for meals; preventing
the employment of children under ten and limiting the hours of those
under twelve to six hours per day; and providing basic education for
children so employed.[37]

Around about the time Owen was working on the pamphlet on the
evils of the manufacturing system he also wrote to Sidmouth about
a related and highly contentious issue, the Corn Law. A Corn Law,
designed to protect agricultural prices, was first introduced in 1804.
However, the continuing French wars forced up prices, encouraging
agricultural investment, so that by 1814 there was fear of post-war
collapse. That year a government committee recommended that foreign
corn should be imported free of duty only when the price of wheat had
reached 80 shillings per quarter. Obviously the landed interest, who
dominated parliament, were likely to welcome the protection of prices
the law offered; conversely industrialists, concerned about the impact
rocketing wage costs might have on profits, were generally opposed.
The more astute on both sides would also recognise the potential for
disorder high food prices might well generate. In his letter Owen said
some of the Corn Bill's supporters expected it to steady prices, some that
it would 'maintain the present rents', and others that it would 'render
unnecessary a foreign supply of grain and make us more independent of
other countries'. He did not think so. On the contrary, he said, it would
reduce the value of our currency, gradually reduce foreign trade (as he

said in his pamphlet), and 'create general discontent which will keep the country in a perpetual ferment and prepare the way for the loss of that proportion of our political power which depends on our foreign commerce'. There followed a lengthy statement on the impact of the war, increased taxes and currency restrictions on the economy, especially land and labour. 'This forced state of matters', Owen told Sidmouth, 'could be supported only while we were deprived of intercourse with other countries . . . and if we do not return as speedily as possible to our formal natural currency we shall give our hard-earned advantages to strangers'. He thought that 'to force an unnatural result' was impolitic and that rather than the landed interest benefiting by the measure 'they would ere long suffer equally with all other classes in the country'. He denied any 'partiality for the manufacturing interests', saying that the evils of the system had made him anxious 'to see it gradually diminished'. He felt this would happen in any case, without the Corn Bill, but it would be better to have a 'temporary protecting duty' to 'give more time for matters to find their just and natural level'. While there was some confusion in his mind about the operation of the laws of supply and demand, this communication provides an interesting insight into how his economic ideas were developing. It did not, however, persuade the Home Secretary or the administration to change their minds about the Corn Law.[38]

Predictably the landed interest triumphed in this instance, so it is therefore odd that Owen later gave a mistaken explanation of his difficulty with his children's bill as the strength in the House of Commons of the industrial interest, and hence its influence on MPs 'whose election was much under its control'. After considerable lobbying, apparently including discussions with Vansittart about both the cotton tax and the children's bill, Owen succeeded in persuading some members of both Houses that a bill on the lines he proposed should be introduced. Viscount Lascelles, a Tory member from Yorkshire, helped him organise a series of meetings at the King's Arms Hotel in New Palace Yard. As a result the draft bill was amended and it was decided that Sir Robert Peel would act as sponsor.[39] Peel was an appropriate choice because of his background as a textile manufacturer and his long-term interest in the welfare of young workers in the Factory System.

Owen's bill of June 1815, as amended during discussions with the parliamentarians, was to apply to all 'Cotton, Woollen, Flax, and other Mills, Manufactories, or Buildings, in which Twenty or more Persons shall be employed under the age of Eighteen years'. No child under ten should be employed and none under eighteen should work over 10½ hours (excluding an hour and a half for meals and half an hour for instruction). To prevent night work this labour should be performed between 5 a.m. and 9 p.m. Teachers were to report annually to the local Clerk of the Peace, who, with a Justice of the Peace and a clergyman of the established church would carry out regular inspections. As in the bill of 1802 measures would be taken to maintain health and prevent the spread of disease, physicians being consulted as required. Half of any fine, not exceeding £10 and not less than £5 for contravention of the act was to be set aside by the justices for poor relief. This last proposal, invariably overlooked, showed Owen's awakening concern about the problem of the poor.[40]

Peel wasted no time introducing the bill on 6 June 1815. *Hansard* reported Peel's provision for 12½ hours, of which ten were for work and 2½ for meals and instruction, a modification of what Owen had proposed. But in any case with the intervention of Waterloo and the end of the parliamentary session the bill was deferred. Owen was highly critical of the delay and particularly unfair to Peel, who succumbed to illness later that year. Peel was subsequently put under pressure to agree to an enquiry and on 3 April 1816 he moved for the appointment of a Select Committee to take evidence. While this could be seen as a delaying tactic Owen could speak optimistically about the intentions of the country's rulers in his address during the opening of the New Institute at New Lanark a few months earlier on 1 January of that year.[41]

At some point between Peel's introduction of the bill and the meeting of the committee Owen and his eldest son, Robert Dale, then just fourteen, set off on a tour of inspection in Scotland and England to gather evidence. Robert Dale Owen says the journey was undertaken in the summer of 1815, but according to Owen Sr.'s evidence they also visited a number of premises in northern England a few weeks prior to Owen's appearances before the committee. They were certainly in Carlisle, Skipton, Leeds, Stockport, and possibly Manchester before posting south to London.[42] Sixty years later Robert Dale was to describe the conditions they found in many mills as 'utterly disgraceful to a civilised nation'. Although biased, both father and son were outraged by the conditions they claimed to have seen in the mills belonging to some of their rivals. Children of ten years old worked 14 hours a day, with half an hour for a mid-day meal eaten in the mill. The working environment was hot, dusty and polluted with cotton fibres. 'In some cases', wrote the young Owen, 'we found that greed had impelled the mill owners to still greater extremes of inhumanity. Their mills were run fifteen, and in exceptional cases sixteen hours a day, with a single set of hands; and they did not hesitate to employ children of both sexes from the age of 8'. They even found some below that age and that corporal punishment was common. 'Most of the overseers openly carried stout leather thongs', Robert Dale recalled, 'and we frequently saw even the youngest severely beaten'. While this seems unlikely, punishment was certainly pretty universal, even, it was rumoured, at New Lanark. The Owens quizzed surgeons and found stories of brutal abuse, deformed children crippled by excessive toil, and severe illness 'often ending in death'. 'These stories haunted my dreams', Robert Dale remembered all those years later.[43]

Tactically the journey was probably a mistake for what really amounted to spying missions further upset already alienated mill masters.[44] Visitors were not particularly encouraged in these places and by Owen's admission they got very few straight answers, which was hardly surprising in the circumstances. Interestingly in detailed evidence to the committee about employment and working conditions in the Scottish cotton industry, Henry Houldsworth, the Glasgow mill master, was able to cite data for every mill in Scotland *except* New Lanark, a fact which at least suggests a measure of secrecy on Owen's part.[45] Consequently Owen and his son seem to have gathered many impressions but few hard facts and under questioning before the committee Owen was sometimes forced on the defensive. He was also understandably reticent about naming names, which he was forced to do on several occasions, causing consternation among fellow industrialists on the committee and greatly annoying those he cited, whether or not they were guilty of exploiting the labour of children. Something, of course, that was never mentioned was the fact that, good or bad, philanthropic or otherwise, they all made their money out of slavery and other forms of exploitation at various stages in the production process, so the whole thing was hypocritical. But not in Owen's eyes or those of his contemporaries.

The Select Committee under Peel's chairmanship sat from 25 April, hearing 47 witnesses, including 29 mill masters, before closing its investigations on 18 June. Owen himself made no fewer than five appearances, on 26 and 29 April and 6, 7 and 10 May. On at least one other occasion he handed in data on the New Lanark schools. He was thus the most important witness and his evidence took up 24 pages of the report. What Owen had earlier said about the issue of children's employment and the need for legislation to improve matters made sound sense and his evidence on both counts would have been convincing. However, during the appearances before the committee, apart from one extended session on what had been enacted at New Lanark, Owen was closely questioned on what he and Robert Dale had seen on their tour. Regarding his own mill, he explained that his reduction of factory hours and other reforms were partly humanitarian and partly on the grounds of improved efficiency. He thought the changes had not increased costs or reduced family income. He was able to produce school registers which indicated increased attendance as a result of shorter working hours, though only since January of that year. All this was fair enough, but when it came to his observations on conditions in other places he found himself exposed to some critical questioning.[46]

He soon felt the heat, literally, because he was asked to compare the temperatures in the spinning rooms at New Lanark with those of a mill he had visited in Carlisle and could only give an impression since he had seen no thermometers in either place. There followed further questions about the appearance of children, the attitudes of parents to children working long hours, and what children would be doing if not set to work in factories. Inevitably some of his answers were subjective, or based on hearsay. He made a great many allegations, which opened him to further criticism. He was also asked about illegitimacy at New Lanark and was able to say that it had declined dramatically since Dale's time especially since his introduction of fines payable by both parties to a village poor's fund he had set up. At one point he was closely quizzed by one of several mill owners from his former Manchester days who now sat before him as members of the committee. This was George Philips, whose personal attack, partly on the religious issue, was so vicious that it was later expunged from the record on the motion of Henry Brougham, the advocate and Whig MP, who supported this and other reforms and later played some part in trying to advance Owen's ideas.

The arguments of the other mill masters, supported in some cases by medical evidence, sought to prove that the measures were unnecessary because they were already being implemented, that cotton mills were perfectly healthy places, and that children would be better put to work than becoming a burden on the parish or taking to a life of crime. Among those called to give evidence was another old associate of Owen's, Lee, by then a mill master in Manchester. He thought parliamentary legislation could not secure cleanliness and good management, which would only be produced by example. Whether Lee could claim to have done so or not at least Owen had attempted it at New Lanark, his reforms covering all clauses of the proposed legislation. But, according to the evidence of Adam Bogle, partner with Henry Monteith in a large Glasgow enterprise, some of Owen's other reforms had not gone down well and many operatives had left the village to work in his firm. He cited the evidence of one woman who stated that 'they had got a number of dancing-masters, a fiddler, a band of music; that there were drills and exercises, and that they were dancing together till they were more fatigued than if they were working'.[47]

But there is no doubt that as a large manufacturer supporting the bill Owen faced some particular hazards which added up to more than just personal attacks. In his autobiography Owen relates the story of Houldsworth: of how the hostile cotton masters sent Henry Houldsworth and another of their associates 'on a mission of scandal hunting' to New Lanark. At Lanark they bent the ear of the parish minister, the Rev. William Menzies, who felt slighted by Owen's patronage of dissenting clergy and thought his address at the opening of the Institute to be 'of the most treasonable character against church and state'. This was just what they wanted to hear as a charge of sedition brought against

Owen by the Lord Advocate could prove embarrassing and ultimately damning. The masters persuaded Menzies to communicate this directly to Sidmouth, but on doing so he was forced to admit that he had not actually heard the speech and was merely recounting his wife's report. Whatever the true nature of Owen's relationship with Sidmouth the accusation was dismissed 'as most frivolous and uncalled for'. Sidmouth apparently crushed the idea that Owen's speech was in any way seditious, telling the mill masters that 'the government has been six months in possession of a copy of that discourse, which it would do any of you credit to have delivered, if you had the power to conceive it'.[48] This attempted vilification was to prove the first of many, particularly over Owen's increasingly public views on organised religion and religious sectarianism.

The likelihood is that Owen exaggerated his role at that time. 'After attending the committee every day of its sitting during two long sessions' he later wrote, 'I took less interest in a measure now so mutilated, and so unlike the bill when introduced from me: and I seldom attended the committee, or took any active part in its further progress'. The committee completed its work and the 383 pages of evidence were ordered to be printed on 28 May and 19 June. For all the errors and surprising vagueness abut the results of reduced hours at New Lanark and the other places father and son had visited, Owen's evidence did have some long term importance. He spoke of employing children in relays, something that was picked up later in 1833 as a means of maintaining the long working hours of adults. He also envisioned a half-time system for child workers, under which they would be instructed half the day and work in the mills for the other, with two sets of children being employed during working hours. This was suggested by Sir James Graham, a later factory reformer, and incorporated in the Factory Act of 1844. The productivity issue might even be solved, Owen believed, by workers' gratitude arising from their wish 'to make up for any supposed or probable loss that the proprietors might sustain in consequence of giving this amelioration to the workpeople'. 'Such conduct', he said, 'is most likely to make them conscientious.' It has to be said, though, that the valiant role Owen retrospectively recorded for himself scarcely radiates from the committee's evidence in the Blue Books.[49]

The evidence collected by Peel's committee was inconclusive and this was the main cause of parliamentary delay in taking any further action. During 1816 and 1817 there was continuing agitation for change in which Owen played some part, but by that time his main interest was the application of the New View to poor relief and his village scheme. When Peel introduced a very much weakened measure on 19 February 1818 it was to apply only to children employed in cotton mills. Even this caused reaction among the mill masters, including Owen's associate, Kirkman

Finlay of Glasgow, who said that excepting one instance in Lancashire where 17 girls locked in for a nightshift had been burned to death 'there was no proof of the existence of any evils which could justify legislative interference'. Nevertheless, Peel's bill continued its progress through the House of Commons.

Owen issued two further statements on the employment of children, the first dated 20 March addressed directly to Lord Liverpool, the second ten days later 'to the British Master Manufacturers'. In these he reiterated his policy that 'no child should be employed within doors in any manufacture until he is twelve years of age'. Children of ten might perhaps be employed for five or six hours daily in order to learn manual dexterity, but Owen believed that 'any advantage thus procured could be obtained only by tenfold sacrifices on the part of the children, their parents, and their country'. He appealed to the humanity of his fellow masters, saying that if they simply heeded the facts they 'must instantly be aware of the injustice and useless cruelty, which we thus inflict upon the most helpless beings in our society'. Personally, he added, he was 'almost ashamed to address any human being on such a subject'.[50]

Owen's pleas, coming on top of the flurry of propaganda generated by the New View during 1817, may well have had some impact on the legislators. Peel's modified bill passed through the Commons, the second reading being carried by a vote of 91 to 26. The bill was then taken up in the Lords by Lord Kenyon. It ran into some problems there, particularly from a Scottish peer, the Earl of Lauderdale, one of Owen's critics. However, Kenyon obtained a committee of peers which sat from 20 May to 5 June taking more evidence. Another troop of medical practitioners sent by the factory masters provided further testimony on the excellent conditions prevailing in the mills and the danger of reform. There was further delay until Kenyon secured another committee which in 1819 took evidence from workers, one of the first to do so. The bill ultimately reached the statute book on 2 July 1819, by which time Owen thought it had 'finally spoilt' his original proposal of 1815. Owen had evidently sat through the Lords' debates in utter frustration as the bill was 'strongly opposed, and often by the most unfair means, by almost all the cotton spinners and manufacturers in the kingdom, except Messrs Arkwright, the Strutts and the Fieldens'.[51] The resulting act was to apply to cotton mills only, specifying that no children under nine be employed and that children under 16 should not work more than 12 hours (excluding meal breaks) with no night work. Although Owen regarded it as pretty much of a dead letter it nevertheless owed much to his determination and was slowly improved upon by subsequent acts in 1825 and 1833. Indeed, the first Factory Inspectors to visit New Lanark after the Act of 1833 came into force could report that it was still a model establishment of its kind.[52]

There is no doubt that a fundamental humanity and desire to see the injustice of children's employment righted strongly influenced Owen's participation in the movement for factory reform. It was a campaign with a clear focus and a specific objective which stood a good chance of being realised. Since it suited the factory masters the evidence collected may well have been contradictory, but in the end no one could deny that exploitation of child workers could only be taken so far in what purported to be a humane society. In fairness to Owen, the confusions and contradictions that arose over the issues of education and religion, either in his evidence or his propaganda had little bearing on the outcome. But his wider campaign for the 'relief of the poor and the emancipation of mankind' was a different matter.

## NOTES

1. On the Crusoe theme and its influence see *Life*, p. 3. and Taylor pp. 61, 148.
2. Owen talked incessantly of New Lanark as a 'model' or 'experiment', see, for example *Life*, pp. 80–81.
3. Signet Library, Session Papers, Humphreys v. Owen 1815, Butt, p. 184.
4. The search for a Masonic connection has proved negative at least in the Scottish records.
5. On Liverpool see N. Gash, *Lord Liverpool*, London, 1984.
6. J.E. Cookson, *Lord Liverpool's Administration*, Edinburgh, 1975.
7. British Library, Liverpool Papers, Ms 38, 361 ff. 47–51; Claeys, 'Introduction', xxi.
8. Bodleian Library, Abinger Papers, Wm. Godwin's Diary 8 January 1813; subsequent dates January–May 1813 and April–May 1814.
9. P.H. Marshall, *William Godwin*, New Haven/London, 1984, p. 310.
10. Podmore discusses this pp. 119–121, 647.
11. D. Locke, *A fantasy of reason. The Life and Thought of William Godwin*, London, p. 262.
12. Marshall, pp. 310–11.
13. British Library, Place Papers, Add.27, 791, ff. 262–8, see also Podmore, pp. 121–4.
14. Taylor, p. 65.
15. Place Papers, Add. 35, 152, f.218.
16. R. Owen, *A New View of Society* Everymans' Library ed., London, 1972, pp. 5–6, 14.
17. See Fraser previously cited; Butt in 'Introduction', xxiv.
18. Owen *New View*, pp. 18–19.
19. Ibid, 29–35 on improvements at New Lanark.
20. Ibid, 42–3.
21. See below on the status of the essays. The 2nd ed. was published in 1816. MacNab and Davidson have many references to religious activity in the community.
22. Owen, *New View*, pp. 74–7.

23. See, for example, *Life*, pp. 103, 211–2.
24. Adams Corr. Vol VI, pp. 123–5, letters of 3 and 12 December 1816.
25. *Life*, pp. 107–8; Devon Record Office, Sidmouth Papers, Owen to Canterbury 6 May 1818.
26. *Life*, p. 109.
27. Sidmouth Papers, Owen to Sidmouth 1 September 1813.
28. Ibid, Estimated bill; Owen to Sidmouth 23 March 1813.
29. *Life*, pp. 109–10.
30. *Glasgow Courier*, 7 March 1815.
31. Notably J.T. Ward, 'Owen as Factory Reformer' in Butt (ed.), pp. 99–134, on which the following is partly based.
32. *Life*, pp. 115–26.
33. Ibid p. 113.
34. *Glasgow Courier* 31 January 1815; R. Owen, *Observations on the Cotton Trade*, Glasgow 1815 reprinted in Claeys (ed.) vol 1, pp. 101–107.
35. *Life*, p. 114.
36. R. Owen, *Observations on the Effects of the Manufacturing System*, London, 1815 reprinted in Claeys (ed.) vol 1, pp. 109–119.
37. Ibid, pp. 113–114; Ward, pp. 103–105.
38. Sidmouth Papers, Owen to Sidmouth, 16 March 1815.
39. *Life*, p. 115.
40. *Life*, IA, Appendix G, pp. 23–6.
41. Ward, pp. 105–6; R. Owen, *Address Delivered to the Inhabitants of New Lanark*, London, 1816, reprinted in Claeys (ed), vol 1, pp. 120–142.
42. Itinerary from evidence to Select Committee, cited below.
43. R.D. Owen, *Threading My Way*, p. 101.
44. Podmore, p. 193.
45. PP 1816 III, p. 236.
46. Ibid, pp. 20–8, 36–40, 86–8, 89–95, 113.
47. Ibid, p. 167.
48. *Life*, pp. 119–20.
49. PP 1816 III, pp. 93–4; Ward, pp. 111–112.
50. R. Owen, *On the Employment of Children in Manufactories* and *To the British Master Manufacturers* both London, 1818.
51. *Life*, pp. 225–6.
52. PP1833 XX and 1837–38 XXXIII provide testimony to this effect.

# EIGHT

# Propagandist

While his involvement in the campaign for factory reform had made his name familiar in parliamentary and manufacturing circles, the publication in its entirety of the second edition of *A New View of Society* in 1816 brought Owen widespread celebrity and greatly raised his profile. The appearance of the essays also raised the stakes in his efforts to have his proposals implemented. At that stage these were modest enough in that they linked his current concerns about the nature of manufacturing industry, the condition of workers, the state of the poor, and the need for national educational reform, with the central tenet of the essays, character formation and moral regeneration. He was soon to take things a stage further, the main driving force being the improvement of the poor, though the appeal went beyond them to members of every class willing to aid him in this task. Considering how much interest was taken in the problem of the poor by the government and others far more prominent than Owen, how did he come to be the arch pundit on the matter? The answer lies in the power of a simple message and the scale and extent of the propaganda which a rich man like him could deploy.

Owen's views on the problem of poverty were directly influenced by his personal experience at New Lanark and had particular relevance to the difficult era that opened up after the Napoleonic Wars. Economic depression exacerbated growing problems of poverty and unemployment and the Liverpool government struggled against a rising tide of disorder, which was manifest in protests and riots. The administration of the Poor Law, which had been a problem before, became a nightmare. From a purely personal point of view Owen could see that the contribution he and other property owners had to make was becoming intolerable. He again canvassed his views widely in letters and pamphlets, mostly published in the wake of the second edition of *A New View of Society*, which caused Place offence because Owen had apparently not incorporated some of the changes he had suggested. But, as we saw, Owen probably had good reason to be cautious on the issue of political reform and like many in his position probably actually feared it. Social amelioration seemed like a safer alternative, especially if it produced conforming characters. This Owen emphasised again in 1816 during his evidence to another parliamentary select committee, this time on the education of the lower orders in the metropolis, to which we will return.

That the condition and burden of the poor were causing widespread alarm among the elites is evidenced in the establishment in the summer of 1816 of an organisation calling itself the Association for the Relief of the Manufacturing and Labouring Poor. One of the Prince Regent's brothers, the Duke of York, would act as president and its remit was to consider measures for the relief of the prevalent distress. The meeting appointed a committee, to be chaired by the Archbishop of Canterbury, which would recommend practical measures for poor relief, one of the members being Owen. When the committee met there was a heated debate among the 'prominent political economists' present, including Colquhoun and possibly Torrens and Ricardo, which Owen regarded as 'verbiage'. His reticence of speaking in public was again somehow overcome and he gave an explanation of the current situation as he saw it. There were two main causes. The immediate cause of distress was the sudden cessation of the extraordinary demand for goods and services created by the war, or in his own telling words, 'on the day on which peace was signed the great customer of the producers died'. The second longer term cause was the 'displacement' of human labour by machinery. He shocked Colquhoun and others on the committee when he told them that 2,000 young persons and adults at New Lanark completed as much work as the whole population of Scotland might have managed sixty years earlier.[1]

Sutton then asked him what his remedy for the existing distress was. Perhaps wisely at that juncture Owen was unwilling to say, but he did agree to prepare a report on the subject for an adjourned meeting of the committee. Just as he was completing his appraisal parliament set up a Select Committee under Sturges Bourne, to collect evidence on the operation of the Poor Laws, and this it duly began in February 1817. Owen presented his findings to Sutton's committee which seemed taken aback by 'a report so extensive in its recommendations, so new in principle and practice, and involving great national changes'. After consulting Liverpool's supporters on the committee Sutton, presumably alarmed by the radical nature of the recommendations and in a neat sidestep, suggested that Owen present his report to the select committee. This had among its forty members the ubiquitous Brougham, whom Owen then approached offering to give evidence. He was apparently called but after keeping him waiting for nearly two days the committee announced that it had decided by a small majority not to question him. When told so by Brougham, Owen exclaimed, 'It is indeed strange and most extraordinary, as the members know how much I have studied these subjects, and how much extensive experience I have had with the working classes. But it is of little consequence. I will find means to enable the public to learn my views on this subject'.[2]

Owen's *Report to the Committee for the Relief of the Manufacturing Poor*, with a covering letter to the chairman of the committee on the Poor Laws dated 12 March, was duly published in the newspapers on 9 April and around the same time in the *Philanthropist*, a periodical owned by his partner, Allen. In the report Owen first proposed his village scheme – the famous Plan – that obviously drew quite specifically on arrangements at New Lanark. But unlike it the physical appearance of the proposed villages had a symmetry that more resembled military barracks built around a square located in plots of between 1,000 and 1,500 acres, which with careful husbandry would result in self-sufficiency. However, the new communities could combine both agriculture and industry so they might be said to have something in common with the numerous planned estate villages which by this time dotted the Scottish Lowlands and must have been familiar to Owen. The population was to be similar to that of New Lanark, 1,200 to 1,500 persons, who would be educated and employed according to their abilities and skills – and at a potential profit once the capital cost of building had been recovered. The reader could be excused for thinking that this much resembled a workhouse, though this was not Owen's intention. And the emphasis on the communities as projects likely to generate a reasonable return on capital might make them attractive to investors.[3]

Francis Place was offended by the fact that Owen included in the second edition of the *New View* a passage which expressed contempt for electoral reform and the common people, whom the radicals wished to see enfranchised. He complained to Owen about his 'want of candour, honesty and falsehood in these passages . . . faults which you of all men should have been the last to commit. You have done the people an injustice and if the Essays could be widely distributed you would have made man an enemy to man'. The people, said Place, were not responsible for electoral and other disturbances which so alarmed Owen, it was the fault of repressive government, especially Sidmouth and other ministers, 'the very persons whom you laud to the skies'.[4] Despite these misgivings the two men maintained close contact for Owen evidently discussed his ideas about the village plan with Place shortly after its inception. Place asked him how the scheme was to be financed to which Owen replied that he would mortgage the Poor Rate to buy the land and then:

> With another part of the money build an oblong square . . . and on each of its largest sides build a row of huts, or houses, each containing two rooms . . . in the space between these two rows a public kitchen, dining room, store houses, a school and a nursery . . . from 800 to 1,000 paupers are to be put in them . . . they are to cultivate the land and as they are for some time to be fed and clothed at the cheapest rate they are to produce at once much more than they consume and the surplus is to be sold to pay the interest of the money.

Eventually, Place noted, when both the interest and the capital had been paid off, the land would become the property of the community, though everything would continue to be governed by strict regulations. Writing to Mill, Place conveyed a good sense of the ideas racing through Owen's mind, to such an extent that:

> No objection can be taken, they (the paupers) are not to become as it were a rabbit warren, the population is to be regulated, there are to be no squabbles as to who the first occupiers shall be, they must be the paupers . . . No objections from those now interested, none from prejudice or custom, no paupers to be made after first removal, no poverty, no crime, a true millennium, not for a thousand years but to eternity.[5]

Here Place mentioned a conundrum that much perplexed social thinkers of the day and was made fashionable in the writings of the Rev. Thomas Malthus: the population problem. And how was the population to be regulated, if not by the means that was never spoken, birth control? Owen gave the first hint of this in one of the letters explaining his scheme.[6] He also later admitted in evidence to another select committee that there would be heavy fines during the first five years 'by way of punishment for any infringement of the rules' but he did not elaborate on the question of promiscuity. The very shape of the villages was crucial. Why had the villagers to live in squares? Could the people not live in separate dwellings? No, Owen retorted, the arrangement was essential 'to place the conduct of the people at all times before the eye of the community'.[7] As Place and others were to realise Owen kept to himself much else about life in the proposed villages.

There is some evidence that Owen had already publicised the village scheme before 1817. Replying to a letter from Owen, which may well have mentioned the scheme, Sir Robert Liston, the distinguished Scottish diplomat, told him that while he considered man 'as a religious animal . . . what I long beyond expression to see is the practical effects of your establishments, from which, in consequence of what I have observed of the success of others, though instituted and conducted by very inferior men, I am inclined to augur a great deal of good'.[8] The other experiments to which Liston refers may well have been the pauper colonies being set up at Fredericksoord in Holland and the House of Industry established at Munich in Bavaria by Benjamin, Count Rumford, both of which were known to British philanthropists, and later alluded to by Owen in his letters to David Ricardo. Some at least took a positive view of Owen's proposals. While few in Britain would see the poor as 'children of the state' as they did in Holland, especially under the Batavian Republic, it was far from clear how the proposals might be implemented in the prevailing economic climate even if the government could be persuaded to act.

So in the summer and thanks to his energy for self-promotion and a massively expensive propaganda campaign using press, pamphlets and public meetings, 'Mr Owen's Plan' received widespread publicity. On 29 May the *Times* published a letter from Owen vindicating his proposals. He even mentioned the fact that the poet, Robert Southey, whom Owen knew personally, had criticised the plan as lacking any religious foundation. Owen told readers that 'he understands true religion to be devoid of all sectarian notions' and that in the proposed establishments there would be full liberty of worship. An encouraging editorial in the same newspaper pointed out to readers that 'Mr Owen is not a theorist only, but a man long and practically familiarised to the management of the poor: we are most desirous that a trial should be made of his plan in at least one instance'.[9] On 24 July at a meeting of merchants and others summoned by special invitation to the 'George & Vulture', a City tavern, Owen expounded his plans for the poor and unemployed. The inevitable committee was formed to consider the scheme and collect subscriptions.[10]

Almost immediately Owen published on 25 July and 9 August two letters containing further thoughts on his plan. The first consisted of the evidence Owen might well have given to the Select Committee on the Poor Laws had he been given the opportunity. Therein a ghostly inquisitor puts questions to Owen who replies at length about his credentials, his views on land and labour, the causes of distress and unemployment, and how these ills can be alleviated by the new establishments.[11] While believing that he had a well conceived plan he acknowledged John Bellers, whose pamphlet of 1696 proposing a College of Industry he had been given by Place.[12] This was subsequently reprinted in 1818 accompanying an account of the Shaker communities in the United States and further notions on *A New View of Society*. The account of the Shakers mentioned a community in Indiana but not by name. However, Harmonie was soon to be well known to those who took an interest in Mr Owen's activities. As the propaganda expanded so also did his expectations. While in the letters he protested that: 'I merely ask to be permitted to relieve the poor and working classes from their present distress' he was already talking of 'combinations' and 'communities of mutual and combined interests'.[13] Quite how these equated with a return to venture capitalists of five per cent annually was not immediately obvious.

In this sustained campaign he used his influence in places of power and wealth to advantage, especially among government ministers, members of the Lords and Commons, and wealthy individuals known to be of a humanitarian disposition, like his Quaker partners and their Utilitarian friends. Among the Whigs, Tories and others of no party there were many of philanthropic disposition. Up to a point Liverpool seems to have been sympathetic and as far as we know even Sidmouth and Vansittart were prepared to listen to these more specific proposals. The fact that Owen now moved in such circles encouraged others to look favourably on his ideas. Indeed, at that time his views even attracted a measure of support from the upper levels of the British aristocracy, most notably two other Royal dukes, the Duke of Kent, father of the future Queen Victoria, and the Duke of Sussex. Owen's autobiography is crammed with the great and good who he says identified with his ideas. It has to be said that Owen naively took the politeness of many of the British elite with whom he now associated as a commitment to act, when they were simply prepared to listen to a rich man who had some interesting solutions to the daunting social problems that threatened the established order and their own class.[14] One early recipient of Owen's plan and a visit from its author was John Quincy Adams, then U.S. Minister to Britain. Adams, like others no doubt, kept their opinions to themselves, but privately he was suspicious, describing Owen in his memoirs as 'crafty crazy . . . a speculative, scheming, mischievous man'.[15] Nevertheless Adams listened politely and as far as his diplomatic status would allow, promised to help him with his plan.

According to Owen, reports of the plan and the two letters were widely published by the London and provincial newspapers. The *Stamford Mercury*, for one, reported with some pride Owen's plans and activities including the forthcoming public meetings, reflecting on his origins, his early association with the town and evident success as a businessman and philanthropist.[16] He says that he personally purchased 30,000 copies of newspapers containing summaries of his proposals and dispatched them all over the country to every parish minister, every member of both Houses of Parliament, every chief magistrate and banker, and 'one to each of the leading persons in all classes'. Whether this was before or after the meetings is unclear. Certainly the *Times*, the *Morning Post* and most of the other major papers carried with reports of the plan an advertisement to the following effect:

> A Public Meeting will be held at the City of London Tavern, on Thursday, 14th August next, when those interested in the subject will consider a Plan to relieve the Country from its present Distress, to remoralise the Lower Orders, reduce the Poor's-rate, and gradually abolish Pauperism, with all its degrading and injurious consequences.[17]

Expectations were thus raised to fever pitch and the general flurry of activity 'created universal excitement'. The 'millennialist moment', as Oliver described it, had arrived.[18]

Robert Owen, according to Taylor, believed he had been 'chosen and endowed' for his colossal task by some supernatural force as powerful as that which had driven the God-fearing Harmonists from their native Germany to establish communities in Pennsylvania and later in Indiana.[19] Such was the strength of this conviction, that Owen may well have been blinded by it. So rational was the plan, so convinced were those in high places with whom he had spoken, so extensive the publicity machine he had set in motion, that he lost sight of reality. He certainly annoyed some of his supporters with the increasingly superior manner of a philosopher-reformer, one of Bentham's friends observing that Owen 'nodded to me as if crowned with laurels'.[20] Nevertheless, on 14 August the City of London Tavern was 'crammed to its utmost' by a large audience including some political economists and many of the leading London radicals. Owen expounded at length on his plan and as he spoke there was 'a silence of riveted attention'.[21] Everything went well enough until he neared the end of his speech when 'the violent and most ignorant of the democracy endeavoured to excite a tumult . . . and create disorder'. Most of the radicals, including Henry Hunt and William Cobbett, were plainly hostile to Owen's paternalistic and oppressive plan 'to turn the country into a workhouse' or 'rear up a community of slaves', particularly when there was not one mention of either parliamentary reform or reduced taxation. The economists, led by Robert Torrens, already sceptical, were given further ammunition for their attack on a scheme which contradicted most of the prevailing theories of the day. From Owen's point of view, as Claeys observed, this was a somewhat unfortunate alliance between two groups who otherwise rarely saw eye to eye.[22] In the end the meeting was adjourned in good order.

The next day all the papers carried reports of the meeting and Owen says that this was one of the occasions when he ordered 30,000 copies with his name printed on the wrapper and sent them out to every corner of the land.[23] Apparently to save postage Owen was assisted by a squad of MPs, including Lascelles, who franked the papers prior to dispatch, then a common abuse of parliamentary privilege.[24] The post office was so overwhelmed that every mail coach leaving London was delayed by twenty minutes. More worrying was the alarm all the publicity caused in government circles because most of the papers in London and the provinces took Owen's side making him, he says, the most popular man of the day. But to keep himself in the clear he asked to see Liverpool and assured him that his only concern was helping the poor, rather than inciting disorder. What he really wanted from Liverpool was an assurance that he would allow his name, those of the cabinet and members of the opposition, to appear on the committee of investigation he would propose at the next meeting. Liverpool agreed but warned Owen that he must not implicate the government directly.[25]

The following day 21 August Owen addressed another monster meeting. He started by tackling the radicals, arguing that reduced government expenditure would only create further unemployment by throwing out of work those whose jobs depended directly or indirectly on state spending, a view supported by most political economists of the day. He renewed his attack on mechanisation: a great blessing on humanity but also a curse for with every passing day 'a very large portion of human beings are thrown idle against their will'. The only answer was employment on the land. Owen then condemned rival plans for poor relief, particularly those on 'the separate individualised cottage system', though at the same time he suggested that communities of the wealthy could well employ the poor and working classes. In the proposed villages, however, the entire labour of the country 'would be directed under all the advantages that science and experience could give'.[26]

But, showing an amazing lack of tact in the circumstances, he then complicated his campaign by declaring openly against religion, or rather against religious sectarianism. A few clergyman let out some low hisses but these were immediately drowned out by wild applause from the rest of the audience. Owen turned to a couple of his philanthropic supporters, Thomas Rowcroft and William Carter, telling them, 'The victory is gained. Truth openly stated is omnipotent'.[27] This was not new but, whether or not he realised it at the time, going public was a move which in the longer-term was likely to alienate him from some potentially useful allies. William Allen, for one, was greatly disturbed when he heard of the outburst for not only was he himself a pious individual but he also saw Owen's outburst posing a threat to the British and Foreign School Society, with which he was closely associated.

Owen concluded his speech and a lively debate ensued in which an alliance of political economists and radicals tried to defeat Owen's resolution that a committee be formed to investigate his plans for the relief of the poor. According to his recollections the more respectable members of the audience had been tired out and wisely gone for their dinner, and as more workers on their way home packed the meeting, chaos ensued. In the end Owen says there was a majority in his favour, and such was the general disorder that 'to terminate the meeting peaceably' he moved against the motion, no doubt hoping this would clear the air.[28] The reality was that Owen's proposals were rejected by a vote at the end of the meeting and the audience dispersed.[29]

Owen claimed in a letter to *The Times* that the public campaign had produced a more favourable response than he could have anticipated, a view violently disputed by Torrens, one of the political economists present. According to Torrens, Owen's report of the proceedings was 'the most barefaced and impudent thing which ever appeared in print' and he found it difficult to decide whether Owen was a knave or 'an interesting enthusiast in whose brain a copulation between vanity and benevolence has engendered madness'.[30] The radicals were even more critical. Cobbett for one scathingly denounced the proposed villages as 'parallelograms of paupers'. Owen, he said:

is for establishing innumerable *communities* of paupers. Each is to be resident in an *enclosure*, somewhat resembling a barrack establishment, only more extensive. I do not clearly understand whether the sisterhoods and brotherhoods are to form distinct communities, like the nuns and friars, or whether they are to mix together promiscuously; but I perceive that they are all to be under a very *regular* discipline; and that wonderful peace, happiness, and national benefit are to be the result.[31]

This was a penetrating assessment echoing his earlier critique of life in the Harmonist community, though he had only read about it and certainly if he had visited he would have found it hard to detect much in the way of promiscuity. But this sort of aside could still be potentially damaging.

Another critique appeared as a leading article in the *Reformist's Register* edited by the political satirist, William Hone. With the splendid by-line 'Let Us Alone, Mr Owen' readers were told that:

Robert Owen, Esq, a benevolent cotton spinner, and one of His Majesty's Justices of the Peace for the county of Lanark, having seen the world, and afterwards cast his eye over his very well regulated manufactory in the said county imagines he has taken a New View of Society, and conceives that all human beings are so many plants, which have been out of the earth for a few thousand years and require to be reset. He accordingly determines to dibble them in squares after a new fashion; and to make due provision for removing the offsets. I do not know a gentleman in England better satisfied with himself than Mr Robert Owen. Everybody, I believe, is convinced of Mr Owen's benevolence, and that he purposes to do us much good. I ask him to *leave us alone*, lest he do us much mischief.[32]

Like Cobbett, Hone concluded that Owen's scheme aimed to turn the country into a giant workhouse.

Altogether more sinister was the assessment given by Jonathon Wooler, editor of the ultra-radical paper, the *Black Dwarf*. Wooler accused the government of secretly financing Owen's propaganda machine, not only as a means of controlling the poor, but also of stifling legitimate opposition to its oppressive regime and to reform.[33] There may well have been some truth in this for Vansittart had evidently said the he was prepared to ask parliament for £20,000 from the public purse to establish a prototype village should private initiatives or subscriptions fail to raise the capital. This came to nothing nor did public appeals prove more successful in the short term.[34] Wooler's insinuations, for that it is all they were, could nonetheless prove potentially damaging, especially if they alienated the artisans that might be attracted to the new communities.

For someone who protested his reticence and humility Owen in reality presented a very different picture in public. The man may not have been what he seemed, but as Hazlitt observed in a scathing piece about men with one idea, the message was consistent, even unrelenting:

> Mr Owen is a man remarkable for one idea. It is that of himself and the Lanark cotton-mill. He carried this idea backwards and forwards with him from Glasgow to London without allowing anything for attrition, and expects to find it in the same state of purity and perfection in the latter place as at the former. He acquires a wonderful velocity and impenetrability in his undaunted transit. Resistance to him is vain, while the whirling motion of the mail-coach remains in his head.

And, Hazlitt continued:

> He even got possession, in the suddenness of his onset, of the steam-engine of the Times Newspaper, and struck off ten thousand wood-cuts of the Projected Villages, which afforded an ocular dem-onstration to all who saw them of the practicability of Mr Owen's whole scheme. He comes into a room with one of these documents in his hand, with the air of a schoolmaster and a quack doctor mixed, asks very kindly how you do, and on hearing you are still in indifferent health owing to bad digestion, instantly turns round, and observes, that 'That all that will be remedied in his plan: that he thinks too much attention has been paid to the mind, and not enough to the body; that in his system, which he has now perfected, and which will shortly be generally adopted, he has provided effectually for both . . .' And having said this, this expert and sweeping orator takes up his hat and walks downstairs after reading his lecture of truisms like a play-bill or an apothecary's advertisement; and should you stop at the door to say by way of putting in a word in common . . . he looks at you with a smile of pity at the futility of all opposition and the idleness of all encouragement.[35]

Although he disclaimed it there was also a certain arrogance in Owen's manner especially to those beneath him on the social scale. At one of the monster meetings called to discuss the village scheme an artisan had got to his feet and presented an informed and sensible critique of the plan. This Owen had evidently rejected with derision. Torrens heard this rebuttal and reported to Place, 'All my respect and kindness for Owen, as a benevolent man, could not retrain some movements of indignation at his daring arrogance in charging with brutal ignorance and stupidity a people from amongst the labouring classes of which such admirable displays of intellect are daily breaking forth'.[36] There was an arrogance too in his dismissal of criticism from the likes of Torrens, who could certainly not be regarded as 'ill-trained and uninformed . . . until instructed in better habits, and made rationally intelligent'.

By September of the same year an even more millennialist tone expressed in the language of religion had begun to creep into the propaganda and the communities proposed by Mr Owen's Plan had been transformed into 'Villages of Unity and Mutual Co-operation'. They were now to include all classes, not just paupers. However, he was careful to emphasise that equality could not immediately prevail and that social class (in four divisions), sectarian or religious affiliation and appropriate skills would be important criteria in the selection of personnel. He even appended a fantastic table showing all the possible combinations of religious and political sects to which future villagers might conceivably adhere. The pamphlet entitled *Relief of the Poor* contained this famous table of classes, an item bound to generate controversy, though perhaps he did not realise quite how much. The version dated 6 September and issued from 49 Charlotte Street, Portland Place, announced that offices would be speedily opened in London and other places where those wishing to become what he called 'members of the New State of Society' could enrol under the class, sect and party of their choice. 'By aid of the table', wrote Owen, 'this may be done without trouble or loss of time'. Since he was so opposed to sectarianism in religion it seems odd that he should have opted for such divisions, but perhaps he was showing more realism than earlier. As soon as 500 'associates' had signed up 'the operations for one of the establishments' might begin and 'others may follow in rotation'. A footnote suggested where people could enrol in person, appropriately at six bookshops, including Hatchards of Piccadilly and Longmans of Paternoster Row. He also advised those who wished to write to him personally to do so by post-paid letter addressed to him at 'New Lanark, North Britain'.[37]

A subsequent address on 'Measures for the Immediate Relief of the Poor', dated 19 September, said that he had been deluged with enquiries and felt a progress report was required. Therein he recognised 'the full distress' of the present situation but had to guard against panic measures. Hence the first village had to be in every sense a model for others all over the country, indeed, all over the world. He thought it unlikely that arrangements could be made to begin 'the foundation of Villages' before the spring of the following year. Meantime he proposed that a paper, the *Mirror of Truth* would keep people informed of progress and serve as an organ for supporters of both the Old and New Systems to voice their opinions. The New State of Society Enrolment Office, Temple Chamber, Fleet Street, could be approached directly and there a Dr James Wilkes would attend to enquiries.[38] Subsequently two numbers of the paper appeared in October-November, but the fate of the proposed office remains a mystery.[39]

After these exertions Owen seems to have retreated once more to his island at New Lanark. Since his partners had seen and heard so much of him in the metropolis they must have been more than a little concerned about the management of their investment north of the border. Allen certainly had strong opinions about Owen's campaign and was always complaining that he was not kept adequately informed about the financial and other decisions Owen took on his and the other partner's behalf at New Lanark. Perhaps on a personal level Owen was glad for a time to be back with his family and absorb himself in the day-to-day activities of running the cotton mills, supervising the curricular developments in the schools, overseeing innovations in the community at large, and acting as host to the growing numbers of visitors the place attracted thanks to the massive publicity since the appearance of *A New View of Society*. Some of the coverage was positive, but he could not relax for long as the critics took up their pens to pass judgement on his views: on education, moral reform, the village scheme, and inevitably, religion. One of the first to do so and to comment about the totality of Owen's views, including the role New Lanark had played in his schemes, was the Rev. John Brown.

Brown's critique was perceptive, and while prepared to give Owen credit, made a number of accusations that might in the longer term prove potentially damaging. Brown was a dissenting clergyman in a nearby parish at Biggar where he was minister of the Associated Congregation, and hence not tarred with quite the same brush as his colleagues in the established Kirk. While this gave him a certain detachment on theological matters it was the local knowledge and astute observation of Owen and his activities that made his assessment especially important. Originally published in an Edinburgh periodical called the *Christian Repository*, it appeared as a pamphlet late in 1817.

Apart from the mill masters who gave evidence to the select committee on children's employment, Brown was the first to latch on to Owen's exaggerated claims about his achievements at New Lanark. He doubted Owen's description of the difficulties he had encountered. 'A change to the better has taken place, though we have reason to doubt whether that be quite so great as it is represented'. Owen, he claimed, 'represented the state of society at New Lanark as considerably worse than it really was when he came to it, and its present state as somewhat better than it really is'. Certainly theft was unknown, intoxication not evident in *public*, but 'illicit commerce of the sexes' had greatly increased.[40]

While starting out as a new community with a varied population it had gradually become much more homogenous, but the changes had been less to do with improved education and more the result of the 'bonds of relationship and neighbourhood'. So it already was when Owen found it. However Brown thought that Owen's 'attention to the education of children and the wise measures of police' were praiseworthy. All this was made possible at New Lanark by the large capital the proprietors had invested and the 'wise and prudent conduct of its manager'. The enterprise, Brown thought, had 'been distinguished by an almost unparalleled degree of steady operation' giving it many advantages over other industrial communities which had suffered recession.[41]

The reverend author clearly knew Owen and his observations are especially interesting coming from someone who had followed his progress closely:

> Affluent fortune, and extensive influence, are in him connected with considerable acuteness in devising plans, and singular perseverance in carrying them into execution; and even were we strangers to the princely munificence with which he contributes to every scheme calculated to promote general improvement, there is evidence enough in the works before us, that he is sincerely anxious to turn all his talents to the best account in the service of his brethren.

However, because of 'a radical error respecting the source of human misery and the means of removing it' Brown thought that Owen's efforts were likely to do little good and might even prove 'positively mischievous'.[42]

Owen's books and speeches, said Brown, were 'distinguished by an over-bearing tone' which he thought unjustified. 'A man never writes with so much certainty, as when he writes unintelligibly. There are cases, and we rather think the present one of them, where to state all that we believe to be true, is not advisable'. For all that, Brown felt a sincere respect for Owen despite the fact that he had evidently 'entangled himself so deeply in the mazes of error'. He was particularly scathing of the table which had appeared in the latest version of the Plan, describing it as utterly absurd.[43] Another thing Brown noticed was that 'the principles of the new system have never been brought to bear directly on the sentiments and habits of the inhabitants of New Lanark'. And, Brown added, 'the truth is, Mr Owen admits it'.[44] This contradiction between fiction and reality was to have profound implications for the Village Scheme and future communities. Again, like much else, Owen kept this to himself.

At the end of the conflict with Napoleon the floodgates of tourism opened once more for British visitors to the Continent. Starved of their foreign pleasures they flocked back to Paris and on to the Alpine or Mediterranean resorts even if they did not undertake the Grand Tour to Italy and Austria in its entirety. But it was a two-way process for many foreigners returned again to England, visiting the metropolis, and then if they were not interested in taking the waters at places like Bath or Cheltenham, the more adventurous travelled north to see the romantic surroundings of the Yorkshire Dales or the Lake District. Some even found their way to Scotland, where Edinburgh, Stirling and the Trossachs were

favourite places of resort. Tourists also went out of their way to visit the
Falls of Clyde, invariably calling in at New Lanark to inspect the schools.
Owen's publicity undoubtedly attracted many more, including members
of the intelligentsia and reformers from all over Europe. These were what
we might call philanthropic tourists, and many were themselves engaged
in similar causes to Owen's. Hundreds came every year anxious to see
what his reforms had achieved.[45]

Among their number was Marc-Auguste Pictet-Turretini, a Swiss
physician and naturalist who explored the rocks of Mont Blanc and
the glacial formations of the Alps. He and his brother, Charles Pictet de
Rochemont, a statesman and diplomat, came from a distinguished family,
prominent in the cultural life of Geneva.[46] There was also a cousin, Albert
Gallatin, brought up by their aunt, who emigrated to the United States.
He became secretary of the Treasury under Jefferson and Madison, and,
as a diplomat, helped negotiate the Treaty of Ghent ending the war of
1812. Gallatin subsequently became US minister to France from 1816 to
1823, before moving to London in 1826–27, succeeding Owen's friend,
Richard Rush.[47] Pictet, from bases in both Geneva and Paris, was one
of several Swiss reformers who was in regular touch with counterparts
in England including inevitably, Owen's partner, William Allen, whom
he met in 1801 during the brief truce between Britain and France.[48]

Owen probably met Pictet in 1817 during a visit to London and
invited him to New Lanark. The two obviously struck up a friendship,
based apparently on mutual respect, suggesting that Owen had by that
time overcome his feelings of humility in the presence of someone
more formally educated than himself. In fact the celebrated Pictet, 'one
of the best and most learned men of his age', was an enlightened
individual typical of those to whom Owen was drawn during his stays
in Manchester and Glasgow. Pictet stayed at New Lanark for some time,
showing particular interest in the schools, for he had previously been a
Commissioner of Education in France. They obviously spoke at length
about education. Pictet told Owen about schools in his own country,
perhaps even suggesting that Owen send his sons to one of them, a rather
unusual establishment near Bern run by Emanuel von Fellenberg. Owen
followed this up and Robert Dale and William were duly dispatched to
Switzerland sometime in the spring of 1818.[49] As we will see Owen was
generous in his hospitality and no doubt out of courtesy many of his
guests extended invitations to him in return. Pictet invited him to Paris
and Switzerland where he assured Owen 'a kind and warm reception
from the first men of the day in France, Switzerland and Germany'.

At that stage there was no immediate prospect of the Plan being taken
up officially and the children's employment bill was grinding its way
through committees over which Owen exercised little influence, so he
probably felt he could afford the time to take up the invitation. There was

1. Watercolour by Mary Ann Knight, about 1800, the first known likeness of Owen. Possibly done for his engagement or marriage, but it may be later as the title suggests he was already at Lanark. Owen is shown as a dashing if shrewd-looking individual. The portrait may exaggerate his good looks but also catches his vitality and dynamism on arrival from Manchester as managing partner at New Lanark.

1. Owen's future father-in-law, David Dale, as depicted in James Tassie's medallion portrait of 1791, six years after the foundation of New Lanark.

3. New Lanark from the north-west by John Winning, about 1818, showing mills, housing and Institute, behind the tower of Mill One. Also shown, opposite the bow-fronted Counting House, are the New Buildings, constructed by Owen. He could well be one of the figures in the foreground, taking a party round the village.

4. Schoolroom scene, probably in the upper apartments of the Institute, by G. Hunt, about 1825. Visitors look on as village girls, wearing uniform dresses, dance to music provided by a trio. The famous visual aids show exotic beasts and a large map of Europe. The figures looking on from the lower right may well be Owen and his son, Robert Dale Owen, who wrote a detailed description of the schools in 1824.

*Bent on Love, or Love's last Shift.*

London, Published by J.J. March, 1819, at 48 Strand.

5. 'Bent on Love, or Love's Last Shift', published 1819. Owen, dressed as a dandy, but resembling a hunchback, walks with a tall, elegantly dressed woman, said to be Miss Beaumont, an actress at Covent Garden. The title of this amusing, if bitter, caricature, to which Owen certainly laid himself open, may refer to a revival of Colley Cibber's 'Love's Last Shift' (or 'The Fool in Fashion'), but the inferences are hard to determine. He was often in female company, so this may be an oblique and salacious reference to his views on birth control as part of the social reform agenda.

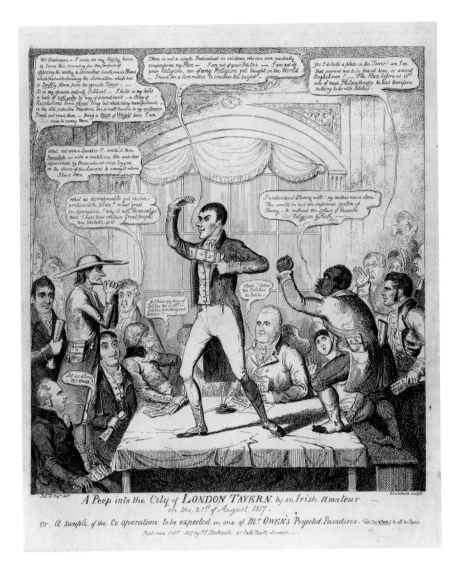

6. George Cruikshank's satire of the scene in the City of London Tavern during one of the famous meetings called to discuss Owen's plan, 21 August 1817, published in October of the same year. Cruikshank suggests that it shows 'a sample of the Cooperation to be expected in one of Mr Owen's Projected Paradises'. Owen, standing on a table, rails against his critics. Those present include the Radicals, William Hone and Jonathan Wooler.

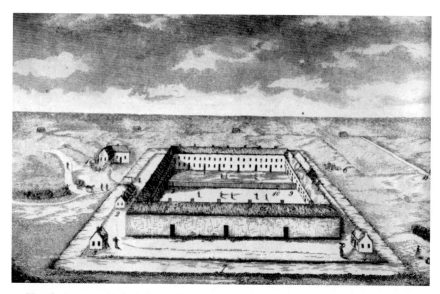

7. Veenhuisen agricultural workhouse, as it appeared when visited by Robert Dale Owen in 1825. It was one of several in the Netherlands built by a Society of Benevolence, itself founded in 1818. The barrack-like building bears some resemblance to the earliest designs for Robert Owen's proposed village, though this was later much embellished by Steadman Whitwell, the Owenite architect, who also constructed the famous model displayed publicly in Britain and the United States.

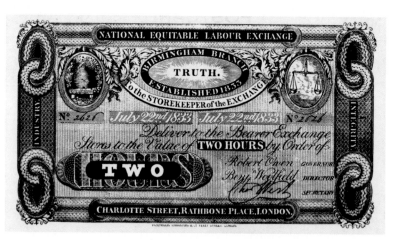

8. A labour note issued by the Owenite National Equitable Labour Exchange, 22 July 1833. Owen proclaimed that the natural standard of value was labour and in his *Report to the County of Lanark* of 1820 first described how he thought labour notes would work. They were clearly based on the Tickets for Wages he issued for exchange at the New Lanark store. Not evidently used at New Harmony, they were adopted by the Owenite, Josiah Warren, for his 'Time Store' in Cincinnati, 1827, one of several experiments linked to early consumer co-operation.

# THE CRISIS,

## OR THE CHANGE FROM ERROR AND MISERY, TO TRUTH AND HAPPINESS.

## 1832.

IF WE CANNOT YET ... RECONCILE ALL OPINIONS,

LET US ENDEAVOUR ... TO UNITE ALL HEARTS.

IT IS OF ALL TRUTHS THE MOST IMPORTANT, THAT THE CHARACTER OF MAN IS FORMED FOR—NOT BY HIMSELF.

Design of a Community of 2,000 Persons, founded upon a principle, commended by Plato, Lord Bacon, Sir T. More, & R. Owen.

### EDITED BY
## ROBERT OWEN AND ROBERT DALE OWEN.

### London:
PRINTED AND PUBLISHED BY J. EAMONSON, 15, CHICHESTER PLACE,
GRAY'S INN ROAD.
STRANGE, PATERNOSTER ROW, PURKISS, OLD COMPTON STREET,
AND MAY BE HAD OF ALL BOOKSELLERS.
1833.

9. Frontispiece of *The Crisis*, volume of 1832. A genial Owen, surrounded by appropriate Owenite homilies, is pictured above an engraving of Stedman Whitwell's design for a community. Although embarking on his most radical phase, Owen has not lost sight of the ideal community as the basis of social reform.

10. *Philantropist* was stuck in the ice at Safe Harbor, eight miles from Beaver, but after four weeks was released by cutting a channel to open water. Lesueur's drawing shows the progress that had been made by 8 January 1826.

11. *Philantropist* in open water and approaching Captina Island, south of Wheeling, 10 January 1826.

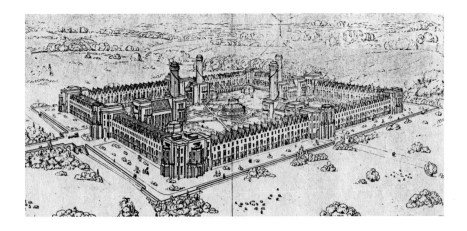

12. New Harmony imagined in a drawing by Owen's architect, Whitwell. Much reproduced, this version appears to be contemporary with the phalanstery planned near New Harmony, 1825–26, but soon abandoned.

13. New Harmony as it was, in a view from behind the Hall, showing Harmonist dwellings, set in their yards and gardens, and where, presumably, individualism prevailed. The original layout and many buildings survive from the Harmonist and Owen eras.

14. New Harmony, May 1826, showing, in the foreground, the Harmonist Frame Church, and in the background the Brick Church, called the Hall by the Owen Community. To the left is the tavern, where Owen himself evidently stayed for much of the time while in residence.

15. Another street scene showing typical Harmonist brick and timber-frame buildings as they appeared in the Owen era, 1825–28. Lesueur is in the square, east of the Frame Church, and his view takes in (from left to right) the houses of the shoemaker, the tailor, the warehouse, and store. The piles of wood may well be for the tavern.

16. A scene during the notorious Owen-Campbell debate in Cincinatti, 13–21 April 1829, described in Fanny Trollope's *Domestic Manners of the Americans*. Owen, on his feet, holds forth. Rev. Alexander Campbell is on his left, a scribe to his right, while from the pulpit a ghostly figure, said to be Campbell's father, oversees the proceedings.

17. Joyful workers haul Robert Owen to his home on his return to New Lanark, seen in this imaginative reconstruction of the event.

18. Robert Owen in 1834, by Ebenezer Morley.

also the possibility that during the journey he could visit Aix-la-Chapelle where in the autumn monarchs and statesmen from all over Europe would assemble to discuss the continent's ills. He might use the opportunity to publicise his ideas. But how far Owen was motivated to take the tour by a desire to spread the gospel of the New View to Europe and present memorials to the assembled monarchs at Aix is difficult to tell. The likelihood is that his prime motive was to visit his sons, to inspect some of the Swiss and German experimental schools which Pictet had described, and that the visit to the congress was an afterthought. According to his autobiography the European tour, regardless either of its propaganda implications or any attempt to measure its success in promoting his views, was clearly one of the highpoints of his life.[50]

So that summer, abandoning his family once more, Owen and Pictet set out for London. There he briefed his disciples on the conduct of the campaign during his absence before setting out with Pictet and his associate, Georges Cuvier, the French zoologist and statesman, who with his wife and daughter had come over to meet them. Owen was clearly worried that he could not speak French but Pictet assured him that he need not worry because if required he would act as interpreter. Pictet personally knew most of the leading thinkers they were likely to meet so this would put Owen at his ease. Cuvier was on some diplomatic mission so Owen and the party crossed the Channel in a French frigate, which landed them at Calais. They travelled on by coach to Paris, where Owen and Pictet duly settled in for a stay of some weeks.

Owen was preceded, of course, by the two hundred or so 'imperially bound' copies of A New View of Society, which Sidmouth had sent to the governments, universities and leading savants on the Continent inviting their comments. In his memoirs he claimed that even the great Napoleon, while exiled on Elba, had studiously read the essays and if given the opportunity would have devoted the rest of his life to implementing the New System. Owen does not say if any of the Bourbons ever read his essays, but it seems most unlikely. However, he carried with him letters of introduction, including one from the Duke of Kent to the Duc d'Orleans (later Louis Philippe), which helped smooth his way into the salons of Paris. His first call was on Louis Philippe, who had just returned from exile in England. In what Owen says was a 'most private' interview Louis confided in English that the reigning family were jealous of him. He told Owen, 'They are afraid of my liberal principles. I am watched, and I feel it necessary to be guarded in my private and public conduct. I therefore live very quietly and take no active part in any of the movements of the day. But I observe all that takes place, and the day may come when I have more liberty to act according to my views'.[51] He warned Owen that his ideas were too well known for him to openly support them and that despite Pictet's presence he was likely to be watched closely all the

time he was in France. Like Vansittart's and others' this could be seen as
a clever manoeuvre to avoid either comment or commitment. Whatever
the truth of the matter, Owen later had the satisfaction of being back in
France for the momentous events of 1848 when revolution swept Louis
Philippe and his July monarchy from power.

The following day he had an interview with Richelieu, the French
prime minister, who also expressed interest in his views. Pictet had
accompanied him as translator and both men were struck by the courtesy
with which they were received. The discussion lasted much longer than
Owen expected and even continued as the minister showed them out
through no fewer than three ante-chambers. Pictet told him that this was
a singular honour, since ministers rarely saw their visitors beyond the first
ante-chamber. Like so many of Owen's stories this can be interpreted in
several ways, but it shows that the regime was anxious to extend him the
utmost courtesy and that individuals at the highest level were willing to
listen to what he had to say.

This was perfectly understandable in the circle to which Cuvier and
Pictet afterwards introduced him. It included two of the most noted
scientists of the day, Pierre-Simon La Place, the mathematician, astronomer and physicist, and Alexander von Humboldt, the explorer and
writer. Owen was warmly received by them and clearly relished the
opportunity to discuss his ideas about 'human nature and the science of
society' with such distinguished individuals. He was greatly impressed
by Humboldt's 'quiet unobtrusive simplicity' which he felt came over
strongly in their discussions. Other prominent individuals he met included
Francoise Antoine, Count de Boissy d'Anglas, politician and writer,
Camille Jordan, revolutionary politician, and the Duc de Rochefoucauld,
an educator and reformer. The last, 'from patriotic motives', had built
a cotton spinning mill on his country estate, which Owen proceeded to
inspect, concluding that it only managed to stay in business because of
the high duty imposed by the government on British imports.[52] As he
pointed out most of the people he met had survived the revolution and
the various post-revolutionary regimes so, he concluded, they had strong
instincts of self-preservation as well as powerful intellects. The highlight
of his sojourn was an introduction by Cuvier to a sitting of the French
Academy. Here, as everywhere, so he claims, he was at a loss 'to account
for the extraordinary deference and attention which was paid to me by
all parties'.

Before leaving Paris Owen was joined by his sisters-in-law who had
crossed from England to make the Grand Tour to Italy. Thereafter the
party set off through the French countryside towards Geneva, a journey
which enthralled Owen, especially as they crossed the Jura, where they
walked much of the way in front of their carriage. His first view of Mont
Blanc made a deep and lasting impression: even Pictet, who had seen it

many times, said he had never seen it to greater advantage. So he and the party arrived in Switzerland, where the magnificent scenery served as a reminder of the beauties of nature, rather than the genius of Enlightened man to which he had been exposed during the previous six weeks.

Throughout all the upheavals of the French Revolution and Napoleonic era Geneva had remained a place of resort, though temporarily closed to most British travellers. It also continued to be something of an intellectual centre, where the influence of Voltaire still touched the lives of the many savants who lived or gathered there. The most famous, of course, was Anne-Louise-Germaine Necker, otherwise Madame de Stael, the writer. Owen, when not sightseeing with his sisters-in-law, soon found himself caught up in another hectic round of social engagements orchestrated by Pictet and his brother. Among those he met was Albertine-Adrienne Necker, widow of Jacques Necker, finance minister under Louis XVI, Albertine de Stael, Madame's daughter, and the political economist, Jean-Charles-Leonard Simonde de Sismondi, with whom Owen had a long discussion about the New View. Owen also ran into some old friends. Further along the shore of Lake Geneva a fellow cotton master, Joseph Strutt, was holidaying with his two daughters, while John Walker and his family had taken a villa on Lake Lucerne. Owen duly visited his partner after taking leave of the Dale sisters, who having seen as much of Switzerland as they wished, set out for Italy.[53]

Further introductions provided by the far-travelled Allen and arrangements made by the obliging Pictet gave Owen the opportunity to inspect several experimental schools, notably those run by Father Giraud at Fribourg, Johann Heinrich Pestalozzi at Yverdon, and, of course, Philipp Emanuel von Fellenberg at Hofwyl. Giraud's was a charitable school for poor children, much like those being encouraged by the British and Foreign Schools Society, but 'according to the old mode of teaching'. When the arrangements and curriculum at New Lanark were explained by Pictet the cleric was surprised to hear about Owen's views on infant education, the use of punishment, books and rewards. Although impressed by this earnest and devoted individual who was doing the best he could, Owen concluded that his efforts brought limited results. They next visited Pestalozzi, by far the most famous of the three educators on whom Owen called during the tour. He followed in the footsteps of Allen, Bell and Brougham, who had all been to Yverdun the year before. Pestalozzi, by that time an old man, subsequently gave his name to educational methods, which, like Owen's, were far ahead of their time. There was a similar emphasis on early education in a child, the need to call on the personal sensory experience of children in helping them to develop ideas, and to use their surroundings in teaching them to synthesise experience. Owen thought this theory very good and condescendingly observed that Pestalozzi was 'one step beyond the usual routine', hence attracting the same attention as the schools at New Lanark. But the latter, he thought, could claim greater attention to 'dispositions and habits' and 'real utility by which to earn a living'.[54]

Owen attached much greater importance to his last visit, the schools run by a disciple of Pestalozzi, von Fellenberg, because it was to him he had sent his two sons. At Hofwyl, a place name that looks more Welsh than Swiss, he and Pictet spent a convivial three days enjoying von Fellenberg's hospitality, seeing Robert Dale and William, and inspecting the boarding schools which their host had established to serve both rich and poor. This was certainly a unique arrangement though the schools were separate. All students followed much the same curriculum and were expected to work in the fields of the surrounding estate, much as Owen's communitarians were supposed to embrace what became fashionably known as spade husbandry. The aim was to elevate the lower and train the higher orders, hopefully bringing them closer than previously possible. Owen was impressed by von Fellenberg's liberal principles and with Pictet again acting as translator the two men had a detailed discussion of the New Views and how Hofwyl might be adapted to promote them. So impressed was Owen with von Fellenberg's school that, although it would be expensive, he arranged for his other sons to be sent over from Scotland to pursue their studies at some point in the future.[55]

Several of the Swiss reformers Owen met on his travels subsequently visited New Lanark, so there can be no doubting the interest taken in the schools if not the larger vision articulated in *A New View of Society*. At least one of Pestalozzi's assistants, Joseph Neef, who set up his own Pestalozzian school in Paris, crossed Owen's path again on the other side of the Atlantic. Neef in 1806 had been offered a post in Philadelphia by another educational pioneer, William Maclure, Owen's future associate at New Harmony, thus becoming the first Pestalozzian teacher in the United States.[56] Von Fellenburg's assistant, Vehrli or his son, Jacob Vehrli, may well have assisted Owen at a later date. The Swiss schools certainly attracted a lot of attention, because apart from Maclure, another American reformer, the New York Quaker and scientist, John Griscom, a friend of Allen's, followed much the same road in Switzerland before his visit to New Lanark the following March.[57]

There followed what proved to be another momentous event in his life, the visit to Aix-la-Chapelle, where the monarchs of Europe were due to deliberate in October. Believing that he might be able to influence the congress to declare in favour of his schemes he had evidently discussed with both Pictet and Walker a proposal to travel to Frankfurt and then on to Aix where he would present the assembled dignitaries with two memorials on behalf of the working classes. The desire to present his memorials in person could well have been one of the main motives for the tour. After reluctantly leaving Pictet, and agreeing to see him on the return journey, he joined Walker, who was to accompany him to Germany and act as interpreter. On or about 27 August they set out from Lucerne and travelled immediately to Frankfurt, where sometime at the beginning of September, he wrote the memorials and had them printed at his own expense in English, French and German under one cover.[58] Publication had to await the approval of the Prussian censors, who according to one report, hesitated for some time before granting permission.[59] They were reprinted in Aix the following month and later in Paris, as well as appearing in instalments in the *Times*.

Owen's objective was to present 'the most important truths for man to know' in order that nations might be peacefully reformed and united under the new system. He obviously thought deeply about how this might be achieved and apparently wrote at length to Caroline, in correspondence now lost, explaining his feelings. The 'truths' revealed by the memorials were certainly more temperate than his utterances in London the previous year: there were no attacks on religion, priests, marriage, private property, or lawyers, and no direct mention of the village scheme. His starting point, as before, was the overwhelming effect of the new mechanical power which would soon create such riches that the wants and desires of every human being might be more than satisfied. But under the existing system of distribution the increased production would benefit only one person in a thousand, a situation bound to generate evil passions and social unrest. Such a system, he thought, could no longer continue and a better one would have to supersede it. Because character is formed for man and not by him, society can banish social ills through proper education in a favourable environment. Such training ought to be provided by governments which should use a proportion of the increased wealth of society for this purpose. So that the practicalities could be further explored Owen suggested congress appoint a commission to examine his proposal and visit New Lanark to see for themselves and hear him explain how the condition of the working classes might be ameliorated.[60]

At Frankfurt the German Diet was in session attended by representatives from Prussia, Austria and the lesser German states. But at the same time the city also played host to the Prussian delegation on its way to the congress and to a distinguished assembly of politicians, diplomats, noblemen and bankers either bound for Aix or anxious to make their views known to delegates. The politicians and diplomats needed the great Jewish international bankers who were likely to finance the French indemnity and extend loans to Austria and Prussia, among them the Rothschilds. The congress really began at Frankfurt where a succession of dinners, receptions and conferences offered numerous opportunities to delegates to become acquainted with one another and discuss informally the subjects on the agenda. Early participants included Metternich, Hardenberg, Capo d'Istria, and as well as Rothschild, the bankers Parish and Bethman. Orchestrating much of the interchange was the ambitious and reactionary Friedrich von Gentz, secretary of the congress and author of its protocols. Owen met Gentz on 7 September at a sumptuous dinner given by Bethman and took the opportunity to explain the substance of his memorials. Gentz, who spoke English, replied to Owen's arguments, 'Yes, we know that very well; but we do not want the mass to become wealthy and independent of us. How could we govern them if they were?'. Owen says he was somewhat taken aback and realised that he had a long way to go if he was to succeed in convincing 'the governments and the governed of the gross ignorance under which they were contending against each other'.[61] A few days later at another dinner Owen and Gentz met again, the latter recording in his diary, 'Diskussion mit dem langweiligen Owen' ('Discussion with the boring Owen').[62] While other diplomats were more supportive, his attempts to secure an interview with Emperor Alexander, thought by many to support at least limited reform, were unsuccessful. Owen felt particularly aggrieved by this since the Emperor's brother, Grand Duke Nicholas, had only recently visited New Lanark and been the family's guest at Braxfield. He had also explained his views to Alexander's sister, the Grand Duchess of Oldenburg, when she visited London. On the other hand the delegates to Aix were overwhelmed with petitions and memorials on every issue of the day.

Having earlier parted company with Walker, Owen left Frankfurt, arriving at Aix about 4 October. The city streets were crowded and the hotels and inns so packed that even diplomats found it difficult to get lodgings. There he had the memorials reprinted and gave copies to Castlereagh who had promised to present them to congress. This promise was evidently fulfilled but Owen was disappointed not to be asked to explain them in person. Unfortunately for him other memorials advocating reform secured more attention, notably those of Thomas Clarkson, pleading for Negro slaves, and the Rev. Lewis Way, asking governments to extend equal civil, social and educational rights to the Jews. Moreover, both Clarkson and Way secured interviews with Emperor Alexander. So far as they were considered at all, Owen's comparatively visionary schemes were characterised by one French diplomat as being similar to the Jesuit establishments in Paraguay. The *Times* correspondent at Aix wrote that Owen intended to ask the sovereigns and ministers 'to go down to Scotland, to examine their justice, in the experiment of his cotton-spinning establishment at New Lanark' and that, in his opinion, 'Mr Owen will not succeed better at Aix in proselytising their Majesties, than the Quaker did who went to Rome to convert the Pope'. Nonetheless Owen was respected as a celebrated and benevolent reformer who had done a great deal of good at New Lanark.[63] Probably sensing that he was unlikely to make much more progress, Owen stayed less than three weeks at Aix-la-Chapelle. About 23 October he left to return to Paris.

As Owen so rightly observed, a prophet has no honour in his own country, and there is no doubt that he proved this again during his tour of 1818.[64] His discussion with many leading figures on the international stage confirmed what he probably knew already: that to make any progress with his schemes in Britain under the prevailing regime was likely to prove very difficult. On the other hand much that was positive emerged from the propaganda campaign in Britain and the same could be said for his activities during the tour. He had raised his profile enormously and confirmed himself as a benevolent reformer and philanthropist, which even the likes of Gentz could hardly gainsay. Indeed his reception among like-minded reformers had been overwhelmingly positive, especially in Switzerland. The company of Pictet and other members of the Academy of Natural Sciences was stimulating, and his discussions had been pursued in an atmosphere of 'unbroken harmony'. But he had been away a long time, business in England was pressing, and the long journey north to Scotland lay ahead.

Back in Paris, he was probably with Pictet at the Académie des Sciences, where on 26 October his companion gave a report on the New View of Society. Owen again had the Aix memorials reprinted. He says that a French minister there told him his memorials were considered by members of the congress, but none of the protocols issued from Aix even mentions them. Retrospectively Owen attributed greater influence to the memorials than they were likely to have with the reactionaries assembled at the congress, though there is little doubting their importance not only in the development of his own ideas, but also their longer-term influence on Owenism, as it moved closer to the working class after 1830. The memorials themselves were reprinted many times, for example, incorporated in the 1818 edition of *A New View of Society*, and later in the United States printed in the *New Harmony Gazette* in July 1826. They also provided the ideas for his memorial to the Mexican republic of 1828 and the address to the governments of Europe and America issued by the Co-operative Congress in 1832. So despite their rejection by the congress at Aix in 1818 they had much longer term significance in the sense that his ideas continued to influence liberal and radical reformers in both Europe and the United States for several generations to come. However the immediate problem remained: how to make progress with the village scheme. If anything was to be achieved it would have to draw heavily on the reality of his island of New Lanark rather than some fantastical parallelogram created at random from Old Society.

## NOTES

1. *Life*, pp. 124–5; Podmore, pp. 215–16.
2. *Life*, pp. 132–3.

3. Reproduced in Claeys (ed.) vol. I, pp. 143–155.
4. Place Papers, Add.35, 152, f.218.
5. Ibid, f.222.
6. Taylor, p. 173; Owen, *Life*, IA, pp. 74–5 may be an allusion.
7. PP 1823 VI, p. 90.
8. National Library of Scotland, Liston Papers 5660, f.52, 26 November 1816.
9. *Times*, 29 May 1817.
10. Ibid, 25 July 1817.
11. Both reproduced in *Life*, IA, pp. 65–92.
12. On Bellers and his proposals see G. Clarke (ed.) *John Bellers*, London/New York, 1987.
13. As 11 above, First Letter, p. 77; Second Letter, p. 83.
14. Donnachie & Hewitt, p. 123.
15. Quoted in Taylor, p. 55.
16. *Stamford Mercury*, 1 August 1817.
17. *Life*, IA, P.92.
18. W.H. Oliver, 'Owen in 1817: the Millennialist Moment' in S. Pollard and J. Salt (eds.), *Robert Owen*, London, 1971, pp. 166–87.
19. Taylor, p. 41.
20. Place Papers, Add.35, 153, f.14.
21. *Life*, p. 157.
22. G. Claeys, *Machinery, Money and the Millennium*, Princeton, 1987, pp. 40–1; Claeys, notes to *Life*, p. 215.
23. *Life*, p. 157.
24. Claeys, note to *Life*, p. 211.
25. *Life*, p. 159.
26. *Life*, IA, p. 113; Claeys, *Machinery*, p. 41.
27. *Life*, p. 162.
28. Ibid, p. 162.
29. Claeys, note to *Life*, p. 217.
30. British Library, Place Papers, Add.37, 949, f. 50.
31. *Political Register*, 2 August 1817.
32. *Reformist Register*, 23 and 30 August 1817; see also the cartoon of the same period.
33. *Black Dwarf*, 20 August 1817.
34. *The Economist*, 28 April 1821 refers back to the offer in the context of the Lanark Report; Taylor p. 50.
35. *Complete Works of William Hazlitt*, vol. 8, pp. 66–7.
36. Place Papers, Add.37, 949, f.50.
37. See Goldsmith's Library copy of *Relief of the Poor*.
38. *Life*, IA, PP.138–141.
39. Claeys, notes to *Selected Works*, vol. 1, p. 235.
40. J. Brown, *Remarks on the Plans and Publications of Robert Owen*, Edinburgh 1817, pp. 42–43.
41. Ibid, p. 43.
42. Ibid, p. 4.
43. Ibid, pp. 57,60.
44. Ibid, p. 44.
45. Testimony to this are the unique Visitors' Books in the Gourock Mss, from 1795 onwards, but with many gaps.

46. On the Pictets see *Dictionaire Historque et Biographique de la Suisse*, vol. 5, pp. 287–91.
47. On Gallatin and Rush see *Dictionary of American Biography*.
48. W. Allen, *Life*, vol I, pp. 56–7.
49. Burgerbliothek, Bern, Owen-Fellenberg Correspondence, Owen to Fellenberg, 17 January 1818.
50. The European Tour is recounted in *Life*, pp. 166–88.
51. *Life*, p. 167.
52. Ibid, pp. 169–70.
53. Ibid, pp. 173–4.
54. Ibid, p. 177; on Pestalozzi, see K. Silber, *Pestallozzi*, London, 1960.
55. *Life*, pp. 177–9.
56. Silber, p. 307.
57. For his itinerary see *A Year in Europe* and his life *DAB*, Vol VIII.
58. Owen-Fellenberg Corr, Owen to Fellenberg 26 August 1818.
59. *Life*, p. 182; *Times*, 23 October 1818; reproduced in Claeys (ed.) Vol I, pp. 251–67.
60. Owen, *Two Memorials*; A.T.Volwiler, 'Robert Owen and the Congress of Aix-la-Chapelle', *Scot. Hist. Rev.* vol XIX, 1921–22, pp. 96–7.
61. *Life*, pp. 183–4.
62. M. Weiner, *The Sovereign Remedy*, London, 1971, p. 95, Volwiler, p. 99.
63. *Times*, 9, 23, 26 October and 6 November 1818; Volwiler, p. 103.
64. *Life*, p. 163.

# NINE

# Laird of New Lanark

O wen returned from his European tour with mixed feelings. On the one hand he was elated at the reception he had received among the liberal minded thinkers of Paris and Geneva, on the other he was clearly disappointed that his ideas had not been given greater prominence in the discussions of the mighty at the congress of Aix-la-Chapelle. So once more he retreated to his island at New Lanark, where he knew he was in almost complete control of events, could assess what his campaign had achieved to date, and work on strategies for the future direction it might take. He says that pressing business awaited him in both England and Scotland, the first item on the agenda being to reassure his anxious partners about the safety of their investment and that the community and schools were being conducted according to their agreement.[1]

It was a different homecoming from that four years earlier when the sale of the mills and village at the close of 1813 undoubtedly represented a major turning point in his development of New Lanark as a test-bed for his social psychology and economic philosophy. Reinstated as manager of New Lanark and supported in capital and ideals by his philanthropic sleeping partners, who were safely located far away in London and thus unlikely to interfere much in day-to-day management, he had at last been able to pursue his goals. At that moment Owen had entered what was undoubtedly the most dynamic and productive phase of his life. His continued success in business at New Lanark coincided with, and indeed made possible, his rise to national and international prominence as a social reformer and philanthropic savant following the publication of his essays on *A New View of Society*. There is no doubt that New Lanark played a vital role in his propaganda campaign for improved social conditions and the re-ordering of society. The further reforms and innovations he introduced after 1814 built on what had been achieved and showed how his community ideals could be applied to Old Society. As Owen made clear, the prime vehicle for social reform was education, which it will be remembered, figured prominently in *A Statement Regarding the New Lanark Establishment*, the prospectus Owen had drawn up in 1812 to attract potentially sympathetic partners. Education remained the key element of on-going reform at New Lanark, and like the enterprise itself the schools took on their own momentum. They were also the centres of attention as far as the majority of visitors were concerned.[2]

Although Owen was effectively an absentee landlord during the time he was away sowing the seeds of the New System, he certainly relished the role of Laird of New Lanark. As the mills and village were increasingly bathed in publicity and becoming an essential place of resort for curious middle and upper class visitors from home and abroad, Owen, when in residence, delighted in showing them the well-ordered and productive industrial colony. But during his many absences day-to-day supervision of the well-oiled machine and the improvement of those tending it fell to others, including the young Robert Dale Owen. Indeed most visitors, even the critics, remarked on the regularity and good order maintained by New Lanark's management – with or without Owen's presence.

Central to Owen's success at New Lanark during 1814–24 was the fact that the mills remained a well-capitalised, professionally managed, highly profitable enterprise. By contemporary standards the place was a large production unit, generating substantial economies of scale and probably with lower overheads than similar places of its size. Owen's efforts to boost output and profits represented a considerable achievement in the turbulent years which coincided with the closing stages of the Napoleonic War and its immediate aftermath. Some of his business and legal records have survived as testimony to his skills. Moreover, because a visit to New Lanark was high on the agenda of most luminaries of the day, we can also draw upon their travel and personal diaries for detailed and sometimes perceptive accounts of what they saw during their tours of the factory and village. While there was some truth in the observation of the Swedish traveller Eric Svedenstierna, visiting New Lanark in 1802, that 'a tourist cannot expect straight answers to improper questions', the remarks of visitors provide a useful gloss on the evidence of the business records and Owen's reports and writings.[3]

In 1814 New Lanark was one of the largest cotton spinning mills in the country, having by Owen's estimate a capital cost of around £200,000, the equivalent of its turnover, and in consequence a huge enterprise for its time. He had effectively solved the problem of capital provision by creating the new partnership but to maintain its momentum and profitability, as well as subsidise more ambitious plans for further social and educational reform, he insisted on greater labour efficiency and the elimination of indiscipline in the plant and its surroundings. Production problems inevitably continued and had to be minimised on a routine basis. Education was to play an important role in the furtherance of these objectives. As Owen knew only too well the cotton business was always volatile so success and profitability also necessitated close attention to raw material prices and supplies as well as vigorous marketing of yarns in an increasingly competitive environment.[4]

While the waters of the Clyde were vital, Owen's prime resource was labour, hence the attention devoted to its control and improvement under the new partnership. According to the data collected periodically by

Owen's staff the total workforce stood at 1,480 by 1815, having fallen
from 1,562 four years earlier. This endorses Owen's evidence in 1816
that the number actually employed in the mills varied between 1,500
and 1,600. Two-thirds of the total were women, reflecting the trend
towards an increase in the female component of the labour force, but
shedding relatively more expensive male operatives. The latter could
certainly be expected to be more mobile, especially the mechanics who
numbered 58, assisted by 22 labourers. The various production processes
in the plant were carried out by 244 pickers, 481 carders, 512 spinners,
and 129 reelers and sorters – all under the supervision of seven under-
managers. Additionally two schoolmistresses provided instruction and
eight storekeepers had charge of the company and mill stores.[5]

Given the large number of people involved, labour problems were
constantly present and Owen vigorously enforced his regulations, particularly in relation to punctuality and conscientious performance, both
being closely supervised by the under-managers or overseers. As far
as we can tell his 'Silent Monitor' or 'Telegraph' continued to be used
as a check on performance. Good order and discipline were generally
remarked upon by visitors, but it seems probable that most either
took away a superficial impression or were dazzled by the novelty of
such a regimented industrial colony, with its well-conducted workers,
school-children and infants. If the entries in what is described in the
Gourock Ropework papers as 'Robert Owen's Diary', but more like a
rough note-book kept periodically by himself and his under-managers,
are anything to go by, indiscipline in both the mills and village was still
something of a problem. Stoppage through human error, absence without
leave (in some cases to engage in casual harvest work, which may well
have been better paid), quarrelsome behaviour and even theft in the
factory were not uncommon, while drunkenness, vandalism, trespass
and swearing did not go unreported in the village at various times during
the period 1813–22. Overseers had even to go through the spinning rooms
after meals 'to prevent any running about the stairs' and general disorder
among the youthful workfolk.[6]

Efficiency as well as morality can be perceived in Owen's directive
of 1819 relating to the employment of pregnant women. The all-male
management was to enforce the rule that 'No young women who are in
a state of pregnancy can be allowed to stop in the works when unable to
perform their usual quantity or keep up with their work as usual' and that
'those who are unfortunate cannot be admitted until they have satisfied the
church where (they) keep session' as to the origin of their condition. This
was perhaps another modest effort to placate both his anxious partners and
the increasingly suspicious local clergy on matters of sexual morality and
religion. The Kirk certainly continued to act as a moral police, so what
happened at New Lanark was in any case quite usual.[7]

Though described as 'a very temperate body of people' and drinking as 'a fault the villagers are very seldom guilty of', inebriation certainly occurred – especially on festive occasions like New Year's Day, Lanimer Day and St James' Fair. Also in line with Owen's aim of character formation were the directives of 1820 requesting village boys 'to give up play at the shinty or clubs and throwing stones, as they are by the first practice destroying the woods and by the latter breaking windows and sometimes hurting persons', and cautioning against the use of foul language to local estate and farm workers. Trespass seems to have been a common problem, villagers crossing the river to Corehouse by the dam or entering the adjacent Bonnington and Braxfield estates. Indeed, Owen specifically ordered that people be excluded from his estate of Braxfield, partly because they were said to be 'conveying away waste wood' and taking saplings. For all his pretensions to the contrary it seems Owen still regarded his operatives with some suspicion and even fear, members of a potentially dangerous under-class that needed to be closely policed if its character could not be immediately moulded to his requirements. Significantly one of New Lanark's most perceptive visitors noted that Owen's staff were effectively operating as police officers and 'moral schoolmasters' of the colony. Another observer, John Griscom, the American chemist and reformer, while recognising that 'humanity to the labourers' was the prevailing ethos of the place, said the community was nonetheless 'subjected to a strict discipline'.[8]

The labour-intensive nature of cotton spinning at New Lanark clearly created management problems that could only be solved by resort to a mixture of strong discipline and incentive. Technical and production problems were perhaps easier to anticipate, but could just as readily affect the smooth operation of the mills. Machinery breakdown, water supply difficulties, poor lighting, shortages of raw material, transport, and the omnipresent danger of fire all had to be coped with to mini-mise disruption. Cotton spinning being essentially a flow process, the breakdown of any one piece of machinery could be highly disruptive, so routine maintenance was vital. Another difficulty faced by the mechanics was power supply which had been a major source of acrimony between Owen and the Edmonstone sisters across the Clyde at Corehouse. Even the settlement of 1813 had imposed constraints on working: under normal circumstances the sluice had to be closed at 8pm and not raised till 5am; and Owen had also to agree to 'keep the said sluices down during the whole of each Sabbath day'. Being dependent wholly on water power, a dry summer or a cold winter could severely affect work in the mills. For example, in June 1814 intermittent night work was introduced to compensate for lost production due to water shortages and the following winter of 1814–15 severe frost periodically stopped the mills. In January and February the clock was altered by 20 minutes to maximise light and

in March 1816, following the introduction of a shorter working day the
previous January, the dinner hour was cut by ten minutes for a similar
reason. Generally, as in 1818, the clocks were put on half-an-hour in
summertime – and then put back in October. The relative isolation of
New Lanark meant that raw material supply and transport difficulties
invariably went hand in hand. High prices might cause short-term
problems, but the bad roads in winter presented a constant problem
every year.[9]

Fire was a constant danger and on the night of 26 November 1819 No 3
Mill, devoted to mule spinning, was burned to the ground 'except a few
stretching frames and mules saved from the west end'. This occurred during
one of Owen's frequent sojourns in London and before leaving for New
Lanark he penned a note to Jeremy Bentham as follows:

1 Decr 1819
My Dear Sir
   I regret to inform you that I have received intelligence from
Lanark that one of the large Mills and attendant buildings have
been destroyed by fire. The loss of actual property is chiefly I hope
indeed altogether covered, but the inconvenience and derangement
arising from such an event cannot be insured.
   I will endeavour to see you in a few days, that is, before I return
to Scotland to give you more particulars, which I expect to receive
in reply to letters I have forwarded to Scotland.
With great esteem
I remain
My dear Sir
yours sincerely
Robt Owen.

Owen lost no time introducing 24-hour working in No 4 Mill from 6
December and re-deploying the workforce accordingly – an arrangement
maintained throughout 1820–21. A week later fire precautions were
tightened by a directive from Owen who 'told all first masters and
many seconds that no person would get to inside of gates till last Bell
rings in morning and all masters must be in their places 10 minutes
before six am, 4, 5 or 6 minutes before home time at breakfast and
dinner'. Moreover, he continued, 'A master must always be along with
the person who lights Lamps or Candles, none of Little stoves shall be
lighted till after the workers come in'.[10]

A high degree of labour efficiency and the minimising of production
problems gave Owen a sound basis for profit-making at New Lanark,
although many other factors had to be taken into account. Both the
cotton-wool and yarn markets were very volatile, and transport and
wage costs were other significant variables. Following the disruption

caused to American and West Indian cotton supplies by the war of 1812, the trade quickly recovered. Indeed such was the increase in raw cotton cultivation and export from the plantations that prices fell continuously after 1814 and for most of the period to the mid-1820s. For example, in 1819 Owen could obtain New Orleans cotton for a third of what he paid in 1814, while Georgia, Grenada, Pernambuco and Demerara cottons also fell in price. Such price falls benefited the British industry generally but Owen had the advantage of flexibility in concentrating on low-to-medium quality yarns, mainly 20–30 hanks per lb on a scale from 9 to 46. He could sell the finer mule yarns to domestic buyers while the lower counts were primarily directed at European markets, although again he had room for manoeuvre depending on the circumstances. The bulk of his home sales were done through the Glasgow yarn market, although the company made sales throughout Britain to places as far apart as Dublin and Norwich. European sales, especially to Holland, the Baltic and Russia, were of great importance, the majority being made through his agents in Amsterdam, Elberfeld and St Petersburg. Owen's obvious business skills are clearly apparent in the way he could rapidly change production in the mills to suit demand and in the sharp marketing policies he adopted. He saw to it that each 10lb bundle of yarn had a label showing a print of the mills – and as a result the product was often recognised by foreign buyers as 'Picture Yarn'. This incidentally helped create what we would describe as a 'corporate image' not just aimed at his customers but giving his labour force pride in their work and community.[11]

New Lanark was not very accessible and accordingly transport was always a significant problem. It was partly overcome by co-ordinating raw material supplies and yarn deliveries to the company's Glasgow warehouse, where Owen habitually kept a close eye on stocks. Foreign trade – generally via Glasgow or Leith – was also fraught with difficulties and delays, especially shipping in stormy or winter weather, customs regulations and the need to afford long-term credit to customers, which made it a very risky business. Hence Owen's use of known and reliable agents wherever possible.

Owen's wage costs were apparently less of a difficulty for it was widely recognised that New Lanark, in common with other Scottish country spinning mills, paid lower wages than their urban counterparts, and which in turn were lower than those prevailing in England. The deputation sent to New Lanark in 1819 by the Guardians of the Poor in Leeds noted specifically that 'high wages it is quite manifest are not the cause of the comfort which prevails here. Amongst us their earnings would be thought low'. At that time male operatives under 18 were paid 4s 3d per week for day work or 5s 4d for piece work; females got 3s 5d and 4s 7d respectively. Average weekly wages of those over 18 were 9s 11d for men and 6s for women for day work; and 14s 10d and 8s for piece work. Moreover, average labour costs declined marginally after 1816, despite shorter working hours and improved yarn quality. This is confirmed by data on New Lanark's output, together with the average count of hanks per lb. and corresponding labour costs which have been identified from surviving business records. The figures show that during 1814–21 production averaged 1.4 million lbs per annum, and that yarn counts gradually increased despite falling labour costs. Clearly Owen was able to effect savings on wages by other inducements, such as cheap supplies, housing, schooling and other social provisions. Even these were not enough to prevent protests in 1824 as trouble spread throughout the Scottish cotton industry. Owen's relationship with his partners may have been sticky when it came to the school curriculum, but they could hardly complain about his ability to return profits. Between 1814–25 Robert Owen & Company made a total profit of nearly £193,000, another vast sum for its time. While this was not universally known, philanthropy could nevertheless be seen to pay handsome profits at New Lanark. Owen could claim that these justified the investment in social welfare designed to promote wellbeing and happiness, by which he really meant docility.[12]

The development of the mills and village under Owen had brought about an increase in population which rose, partly by migration and partly by natural increase, from 1,793 in 1806 to 2,177 at the national census in 1811 and thereafter to its probable peak of about 2,300 in 1819. For the first five years after 1818, when more detailed records began, Owen's clerk provided a recapitulation of events, showing that in 1818 there were 29 marriages (the average age of men being 29, that of women 25), 48 births (16 male and 35 female), and 53 deaths. The population that year he estimated at 2,500, including nearby Bankhead and Kingsonsknowe on the hill above the village, giving a mortality rate of one in 47. Of the 48 births that year nearly two-thirds occurred in the spring and summer months (almost 40 per cent being in the third quarter), statistics which at face value suggest a higher level of sexual activity during the preceding autumn and winter months than at other times of the year. For all Owen's boasts to the contrary it seems New Lanark was no more moral than elsewhere for an average of one in eight births was out of wedlock. The presence in Lanark between 1810–14 of French prisoners of war, one of whom taught the Owen children, had apparently contributed to the number of illegitimacies at New Lanark.

While we have no way of knowing for certain, it seems likely that young female spinners were discouraged from early marriage by potential loss of earning power; and Owen's policy on the employment of younger children may also have encouraged later and smaller families since there was no longer an immediate outlet for the labour of small hands. Sadly, despite both Owen's supposed environmental improvements and the efforts of the surgeon, infant and child mortality was high with 13 infants under two and six children under ten dying during the year. Roughly the same pattern was repeated until 1822.

There is little evidence to indicate Owen's advocacy of birth-control at New Lanark, though this was rumoured to be so. At that time there was a continuing debate about the ideas of Malthus concerning population growth and the natural checks he thought would regulate it even in an industrial society, and Owen was one of many who contributed to it. If he did not know already, and he evidently did not practice it, he may have gained some knowledge of birth control from Place, who later became an advocate. During his tour of 1818 he might have learned of the rudimentary methods of contraception, such as the vaginal sponge, that had been used in France and elsewhere since the previous century. He certainly hinted at it in the later stages of his campaign but he never actually mentioned it by name. Birth control was almost certainly seen by him as one means of eliminating poverty, but how far he was prepared to take such an argument is unknown.[13]

To accommodate a growing population Owen continued his earlier improvements to the housing and other facilities, but the most radical innovations occurred in education. According to his autobiography he had begun 'to clear the foundation for the infant and other schools, to form the new character of the rising population' in 1809, though it is possible that his memory was defective and that work did not start until much later. Certainly *A Statement Regarding the New Lanark Establishment* described the planned 'New Institution', and provided a detailed account of his ideas for its development at that point. When New Lanark was advertised for sale in the *Glasgow Herald* of 24 December 1813, a building 145 ft long by 45 ft broad 'at present unoccupied' was described as having been 'planned to admit of an extensive Store Cellar, a Public Kitchen, Eating and Exercise Room, a School, Lecture Room and Church'. Quite likely this was what ultimately became the Institute and was said by Owen in his statement to have been erected at a cost of £3,000. The articles of the new partnership, by which Owen was bound, called for the establishment of a school run on Lancasterian lines. Teaching aids would be provided by the British and Foreign School Society, the brain-child of Owen's partners, among others, and religious instruction was to be non-sectarian, with the Bible being used only as an aid to reading. Now that Owen was in effective control of the mills and village, the long-planned building to be entirely devoted to education could be fitted out to his specifications at the cost of another £3,000. Some uncertainty surrounds the date of the building ranging with the mills which was also used as a school. It was marked as 'Public Kitchen' on a plan of 1809 but if built by then was certainly never used as a school at that time. When Griscom visited New Lanark ten years later he noted that this building was 'nearly completed' and had been designed as 'a kitchen for the whole village'. At that point Owen thought this refectory could save £4–5,000 a year, 'besides the superior training and improved habits it will produce', but it never became a reality. Unfortunately most of the descriptions leave us somewhat confused about which activities were pursued in the Institute and which in the School. They were probably interchangeable as far as the instruction of the children went. William Davidson, writing in 1828 long after Owen's departure, observed dancing being taught in the school, which was also used for lectures given in rooms which still housed the 'historical maps and paintings' as well as a terrestrial globe 19ft in circumference.[14]

As it was, the new Institute for the Formation of Character did not open officially until New Year's Day 1816. In a lengthy 'Address to the Inhabitants of New Lanark', mercifully punctuated by a musical recital, Owen expounded his educational aims and explained to an audience of 1,200 villagers the main objects of the Institute. The basis of his speech was a reiteration of the central thesis underpinning *A New View of Society* in which he articulated his unfailing belief in some sort of material determinism 'that the character of man is without a single exception, always formed for him'. He stressed the importance of a proper education from early years saying that 'it must be evident to those who have been in the practice of observing children with attention, that much of good or evil is taught to or acquired by a child at a very early period of its life; that much of temper or disposition is correctly or incorrectly formed before he attains his second year; and that many durable impressions are made at the termination of the first 12 or even 6 months of his existence'. Owen probably got much of this from his own experience. But a critique of Pestalozzi's methods was published in Paris as early as 1805 and it is possible he may have known of this and had it translated by his boys' tutor.[15] In essence his theory of character formation and general education involved the belief that social training ought to begin from the very moment a child 'can walk alone'.[16]

The Institute for the Formation of Character with its school was considered by many who visited New Lanark to be 'one of the greatest modern wonders' and Owen, revelling in the role of paternalist Laird, took great pride in showing it off. Many descriptions of the Institute's arrangements survive, but the most helpful is that furnished by the young Robert Dale Owen, who following his return from Switzerland occupied himself in teaching and writing a book about the school and its curriculum, published in 1824. According to the younger Owen:

> The principal school-room is fitted up with desks and forms on the
> Lancastrian plan, having a free passage down the centre of the
> room. It is surrounded, except at one end where a pulpit stands,
> with galleries, which are convenient when this room is used, as it
> frequently is, either as a lecture-room or place of worship.
>
> The other and smaller apartment on the second floor has the walls
> hung round with representations of the most striking zoological
> and mineralogical specimens, including quadrupeds, birds, fishes,
> reptiles, insects, shells, minerals etc. At one end there is a gallery,
> adapted for the purpose of an orchestra, and at the other end
> are hung very large representations of the two hemispheres; each
> separate country, as well as the various seas, islands etc. being
> differently coloured, but without any names attached to them.
> This room is used as a lecture- and ball-room, and it is here that
> the dancing and singing lessons are daily given. It is likewise
> occasionally used as a reading-room for some of the classes.
>
> The lower storey is divided into three apartments, of nearly equal
> dimensions, 12 ft high, and supported by hollow iron pillars, serving
> at the same time as conductors in winter for heated air, which issues
> through the floor of the upper storey, and by which means the whole
> building may, with care, be kept at any required temperature. It is in
> these three apartments that the younger classes are taught reading,
> natural history, and geography'.[17]

Robert Dale Owen's *Outline* is perhaps the fullest description of the New
Lanark schools, and is of particular value when set alongside the elder
Owen's memories of the infant school in *The New Existence* and his later
autobiography. According to Owen, the school was attended by 'every
child above one year old', although some observers thought the youngest
were probably two or three years old. During the first few months of the
nursery schools Owen 'daily watched and superintended . . . knowing
that if the foundation were not truly laid, it would be in vain to expect
a satisfactory structure'. With his usual finesse in matters of human
relations he 'acquired the most sincere affections of all the children' and
apparently also won over the parents 'who were highly delighted with
the improved conduct, extraordinary progress, and continually increasing
happiness of their children'.

Owen was cautious about the selection of teachers in the 'new rational
infant school', for 'it was in vain to look to any old teachers upon the
old system of instruction by books'. He says he had very little belief
in books, which is strange given his own enthusiasm for reading as a
boy. At any rate Owen evidently parted with the old dominie at New
Lanark and selected from the villagers 'two persons who had a great

love for and unlimited patience with infants'. His unlikely choice was a
former handloom weaver, James Buchanan, condescendingly described
as a 'simple-minded, kind-hearted individual who could hardly read
or write himself', but who was willing to do exactly what Owen told
him. Buchanan's assistant was to be Molly Young, a seventeen year old
village girl.

Owen's instructions to his new infant master and assistant were
simple:

> They were on no account ever to beat any one of the children or
> to threaten them in any word or action or to use abusive terms;
> but were always to speak to them with a pleasant voice and in a
> kind manner. They should tell the infants and children (for they
> had all from 1 to 6 years old under their charge) that they must on
> all occasions do all they could to make their playfellows happy – and
> that the older ones, from 4 to 6 years of age, should take especial care
> of younger ones, and should assist to teach them to make each other
> happy.

Much of this came indirectly from Pestalozzi, who also emphasised the
importance of kindness and common sense in his teaching. It was all
apparently very Utopian, echoing the views of Bentham, Owen's partner,
regarding the greatest happiness of the greatest number. But by 'happy'
Owen meant 'docile', an adjective that recurs in much of his writing at
the time.

The nursery school occupied the playground in front of the Institute
in fine weather, and on wet days the three main rooms on the ground
floor. The principle on which the school was run we would call the play
principle, no child being forced in any way, not even to mid-morning rest,
although 'when an infant felt inclined to sleep it should be quietly allowed
to do so'. Toys were rarely seen, for to Owen's mind 'thirty or fifty infants,
when left to themselves, will always amuse each other without useless
childish toys'. When they became bored or distracted 'a young active
teacher will easily find and provide something they will be interested in
seeing and hearing explained'. Owen's lengthy description of the infants'
actual instruction is worth quoting in part:

> The children were not to be annoyed with books; but were to be
> taught the uses and nature or qualities of the common things around
> them, by familiar conversation when the children's curiosity was
> excited so as to induce them to ask questions respecting them.
> The schoolroom for the infants' instruction was furnished with
> paintings, chiefly of animals, with maps, and often supplied with
> natural objects from the gardens, fields and woods – the examina-
> tion and explanation of which always excited their curiosity and

created an animated conversation between the children and their instructors.

The children at four and above that age showed an eager desire to understand the use of maps of the four quarters of the world upon a large scale purposely hung in the room to attract their attention. Buchanan their master, was first taught their use and then how to instruct the children for their amusement – for with these infants everything was made to be amusement.

It was most encouraging and delightful to see the progress which these infants and children made in real knowledge, without the use of books. And when the best means of instruction or forming character shall be known I doubt whether books will be ever used before children attain their thirteenth year.[18]

Again the emphasis on observation and experience was borrowed from Pestalozzi. But the infants at New Lanark were, in Owen's opinion, completely unlike others of their age, indeed, he said 'unlike the children of any class of society'. Griscom took a more pragmatic view, probably shared by Owen, when he observed that 'this baby school is of great consequence to the establishment, for it enables mothers to shut up their houses in security, and to attend to their duties in the factory, without concern for their families'.[19] As Owen showed his visitors around, children would come forward to be patted.[20]

In addition to this elementary instruction, those over two were given dancing lessons and those four and upwards taught singing. Military-style exercises were also a major feature of both schools, and the sight of youthful marches led by fife and drum was frequently remarked upon by contemporaries, especially the upper-class dignitaries who much approved of such discipline. Conformity in the children was further reinforced by a 'beautiful dress of tartan cloth, fashioned in its make after the form of a Roman toga'. However, like the kilt and plaid worn by older boys this was thought by some of Owen's partners to encourage sexual promiscuity. According to Captain Donald Macdonald of the Royal Engineers, who like the Laird, Archibald Hamilton of Dalzell, had become a convert to the New System and who accompanied Owen on the visit of inspection to Harmonie in 1824–25, the New Lanark dresses and plaids were part of the baggage. Owen showed them to fellow passengers and apparently had them copied in New York to be displayed there and in Washington along with his plans and models of the Village Scheme. The dress code for the new communities was another subject about which Owen said little unless pressed to do so.[21]

Robert Dale Owen also left a detailed report of the school for the older children of the community. At the time of writing the Institute had been functioning for nearly eight years, and although it was in some respects a biased account, Dale Owen's *Outline*, did make some attempt to assess his father's experiment. The age group concerned was that from about five to ten or twelve, the majority of youngsters being removed from school at ten by their parents to begin a full day's work in the mills. Most working children, however, continued their education at evening classes in the Institute. Attendance at the school for all ages was practically free – the payment being only 3d per month for each child, hardly sufficient, said Owen, 'to pay for the consumption of books, ink and paper'.

Owen gave details of attendance at day and evening classes in the Institute during 1816 to the Select Committee on Education of that year. It is interesting to note that prior to his reduction of working hours average attendance at evening schools was often less than 100 per night. After the opening of the Institute and reduction of the working day to ten and three-quarter hours (less meal-breaks) attendance rose rapidly. In January 1816 the average was 380, rising to 396 in March. According to Owen's evidence this upward trend continued giving an average of 485 per evening session. The annual cost of running the schools in 1816 was said to be £700, £550 being for the salaries of a headmaster and ten assistants, and £150 for materials, lighting and heating.[22]

In the preparatory classes all the children learned to read, write and cipher. Owen adopted in part the methods of Lancaster, whereby certain boys and girls chosen to be monitors passed on lessons learned by rote to other children, in a sense the factory system applied to education. Great difficulty was experienced in finding suitable books for the pupils. Tales of adventure, voyages and travel were popular, and, though much misrepresented on the fact, Owen consented to the use of the Bible and catechism. Children were questioned on all they read, and encouraged to look upon books as a means to an end. In writing, copy-books were abandoned as soon as possible, and the children encouraged to develop their own style. Arithmetic was at first taught 'on the plan generally adopted at that time in Scotland', but soon after Pestalozzi's system of mental arithmetic was introduced.

Alongside these elementary studies, and forming perhaps the most notable feature of Owen's educational system in the Institute, was instruction by lecture, discussion and debate, in geography, natural science, ancient and modern history, and what we might well call civics or contemporary studies, all subjects much favoured by Pestalozzi. These lectures were a feature of both day and evening schools, and would be attended by 40–50 children, though possibly over 100 on some occasions. As far as the subject matter allowed the lecture would be illustrated with maps, pictures and diagrams, aids always much favoured by Owen. The talk was usually short, so as not to lose the attention of the young listeners and time would be allowed for questions. Owen also loved plans and models and contemporary prints show the extensive use made of visual

material for all age groups. Outstanding in this respect were geography
and history, which both had an important place in the curriculum at
New Lanark. The history time-charts or 'Streams of Time', as well as
other visual aids were painted by a teacher, Catherine Whitwell. A
sister of the Owenite architect, Stedman Whitwell, who produced designs
for a community and accompanied Owen on the second journey to New
Harmony, she was said to be an advocate of free love. Following her
dismissal from New Lanark by Owen's partners she later taught at the
Orbiston Community. Her teaching aids were certainly as novel for the
time as her ideas about sexual relations:

> Seven large maps or tables, laid out on the principle of the Stream
> of Time, are hung round the spacious room. These being made of
> canvass, may be rolled up at pleasure. On the Streams, each of
> which is differently coloured, and represents a nation, are painted
> the principal events which occur in the history of those nations. Each
> century is closed by a horizontal line, drawn across the map. By
> means of these maps, the children are taught the outlines of Ancient
> and Modern History, with ease to themselves, and without being
> liable to confound different events, or different nations. On hearing
> of any two events, the child has but to recollect the situation on the
> tables of the paintings, by which those are represented, in order to
> be furnished at once with their chronological relation to each other.
> If the events are contemporary, he will instantly perceive it.[23]

Both Owen and his son were at pains to stress how everything was made
relevant for the children, that they should understand what they were
learning and why, and that they should enjoy what they were doing.
Geography lessons played a prominent part in the education of children
at New Lanark, and seem to have been practical as well as relevant.
Geography also had a strong moral undertone, for the children were often
reminded that but for an accident of birth they might have been born into
a different society with values totally unlike those of their own. They were
taught to respect other people's ideas and way of life and never to be
uncharitable or intolerant. Field studies were important, and youngsters
were encouraged to go out into the woods and fields surrounding the
village, through which Owen cut paths and walks, collecting specimens
and making observations. Owen himself painted a fascinating picture of
a geography lesson during which something like 150 children vied with
each other in pointing out places on large wall-maps:

> This by degrees became most amusing to the children, who soon
> learned to ask for the least-thought-of districts and places, that they
> might puzzle the holder of the wand, and obtain it from him. This
> was at once a good lesson for 150 – keeping attention of all alive

during the lesson. The lookers-on were as much amused, and many as much instructed as the children, who thus at an early age became so efficient, that one of our Admirals, who had sailed round the world, said he could not answer many of the questions which some of these children not 6 years old readily replied to, giving the places most correctly.[24]

Owen aimed at giving children a good basic education, fitting the village youth for the world of work in the mills, but at the same time not educating them enough to pose a threat to the existing order of society.

The curriculum apart, what most impressed the 20,000-odd visitors who came to gape at New Lanark between 1815 and 1825, was the importance of dancing, music and military exercise in the school curriculum. Dancing lessons were begun at two years of age and visitors were astonished to see how 'these children, standing up 70 couples at a time in the dancing room, and often surrounded by many strangers, would with the uttermost ease and natural grace go through all the dances of Europe, with so little direction from their master, that the strangers would be unconscious that there was a dancing-master in the room'. Dancing lessons were also given in the evening and Griscom saw 50 or 60 young people thus engaged. 'Owen', he noted, 'has discovered that dancing is one means of reforming vicious habits. He thinks it effects this by promoting cheerfulness and contentment, and thus diverting attention from things that are vile and degrading'. The children were also taught to sing in harmony in choirs of 200 or more, performing settings of Scottish and other traditional songs, to the delight of Owen and his visitors. Before the close of the evening school all the pupils would gather in one room and sing a hymn, presumably religious rather than secular. It is not without its interest that singing and music later featured prominently in the social life of New Harmony, and that much of the New Lanark repertoire was carried across the Atlantic by William Owen and others, including Joseph Applegarth, another ardent Owenite who taught at New Lanark and participated in the organisation of the schools at New Harmony and Orbiston. In addition both boys and girls were regularly drilled in the playground in front of the Institute 'with precision equal, as many officers stated, to some regiments of the line.' Contemporary accounts described these military exercises in glowing detail, though in the context of the time this was probably quite understandable and was less sinister than it might have appeared. Owen nevertheless expounded on their value in several of his writings.[25]

Owen was not without his critics, but few could quarrel with his system of education at New Lanark. He seems to have evolved a system based on a mixed bag of contemporary social and educational thought linked to benevolent paternalism, deriving from earlier experience in Manchester and of running New Lanark. His basic assumption that character could be formed under favourable conditions seemed to work in that context, and if we are not to discount the multitude of evidence about the New Lanark schools, he succeeded in creating a system which was able to produce conforming and apparently happy (or docile) children equipped with basic literacy and numeracy. Owen's community was certainly not unique in this regard for Archibald Buchanan in 1816 reported a thirst for knowledge and a high level of literacy among the cotton spinners of Catrine and other mills under his management. In many other industrial districts throughout Scotland the same observations could no doubt have been made. However, New Lanark was different, at least according to Dr Henry Macnab, who in 1819 had been sent to report on the place by Owen's most regal supporter, the Duke of Kent. 'The children and youth in this delightful colony', wrote Macnab, 'are superior in point of conduct and character to all the children and youth I have ever seen. I shall not attempt to give a faithful description of the beautiful fruits of the social affections displayed in the young, innocent and fascinating countenances of these happy children'.[26] Owen's educational venture at New Lanark certainly helped to pioneer infant schools and the claims he made for his achievements were not far removed from reality. Yet education was only a single facet of a more powerful social gospel which already preached community building on the New Lanark model as a solution to contemporary evils in the wider world.

Also much publicised and famous in the annals of consumer co-operation, was the store, which Owen built to improve the retailing arrangements set up under Dale's regime. Its actual date of foundation is difficult to establish. The detailed advertisement which appeared in the *Glasgow Herald* when the mills were up for sale in December 1813 does not mention it, though it was almost certainly in existence by that date. Located directly opposite the Institute, it was a three storey building with slightly bowed display windows on the ground floor, which has subsequently had an almost continuous existence as the village store or shop. The upper floors (now dwellings) were used for storage of goods, while butcher meat was supplied from a slaughter house at the back. A bakehouse was added sometime after Owen quit. From the outset the store provided milk and fresh produce (much of it from the company farm in season) and bulk buying 'of the best quality' made possible cheaper prices than previously prevailed, to such an extent it was said that people from Old Lanark travelled down to avail themselves of its facilities.

During his tour of inspection Dr Macnab noticed 'a large store-house in the very centre of the colony, in which were furnished all the necessaries of life, and also those which labouring men regard as the luxuries of the poor' (an oblique reference to meat, tea, and alcohol, among other items). He estimated that the prices were 25 per cent cheaper than elsewhere, but apparently this did not encourage over-indulgence. According to Macnab 'one of the chief directors of the works is constantly in attendance, and recollecting that the luxuries of life could not be had without being known publicly, our reformer was well aware, that the publicity of vice thus effected in individuals, would be one of the most powerful causes of reformation'. As in the mills Owen could exercise considerable moral pressure to produce conforming characters.[27]

Owen paid his workers in both the coin of the realm and by the remarkably simple device of the cheque. The former was often in short supply, hence the widespread use of counter-marked Spanish dollars and privately circulated copper tokens; while the latter, known as the 'Ticket for Wages' (in various denominations) was a highly practical alternative in the closed community of New Lanark. Interestingly it also provided Owen with a model for the 'Labour Note' introduced by his later National Equitable Labour Exchange and also exchangeable for goods. Indeed, from the employer's point of view the 'Ticket for Wages' can be seen as a useful device to avoid payment in cash, enforce the procurement of goods at the store and hence maximise its profits. This, after all, was common practice elsewhere, though much criticised. It could also, incidentally, be regarded as a useful device to prevent over-expenditure on drink, but at least the profits of the store (which, as far as we know, did not sell alcohol) were used to defray the expenses of the school.

Whatever the situation of the average worker at New Lanark, Owen's personal income could now be measured in thousands. By judicious business management and astute financial dealings, using his own and other people's money, he had made himself a rich man, a millionaire by modern standards. Robert Dale Owen, who took prime responsibility for the family's financial affairs after Owen finally returned to Britain from the United States, reckoned his father was worth more than a quarter of a million dollars (about £50,000 sterling) in 1817 by which time he had already spent substantial sums on his propaganda campaign. Despite this continuing outlay and other expenses, such as hospitality, school fees, electoral entertainment, and travel, on which he spent liberally, he was probably never worth less than this sum and probably a great deal more until he ceased to be manager in 1825. Although he maintained that he was personally far from ostentatious he had a lifestyle to which many a Laird could never aspire.[28]

While a frugal lifestyle may have accorded better with the ideological position he wished to project the reality was that Owen had well-developed aristocratic pretensions. He had long been known as 'Robert Owen of New Lanark' or 'Mr Owen of Lanark', much in the fashion and style of address traditionally adopted by Scottish lairds. As early as 1799 or 1800 the engagement or marriage portrait he had painted by Mary Ann Knight (presumably as a present to Caroline) was inscribed 'Mr Owen of Lanark', and this before he even moved into the place. He invariably told people who might wish to correspond with him that he could be contacted by such an appellation, as if he really was a Laird: 'A letter addressed to me as Mr Owen of New Lanark, N.B. (North Britain, a much earlier Hanovarian usage, irksome to most Scots, but continuing even into the twentieth century) will readily reach me', he told the Harmonist leader, Father George Rapp, and no doubt others.[29] Whether this was an arrogance arising either from his undeniable wealth and position or from his high public profile is impossible to tell, but it served to emphasise another odd aspect of his personality that some noticed, even friends and allies.

Braxfield House, though rented from the MacQueens, was a fashionable if unpretentious country house set in magnificent park and orchard lands stretching along the banks of the Clyde and well removed from the town of Old Lanark and the factory village of New Lanark. Owen himself noted that it was near enough the mills for convenience but far enough away not to be annoyed by them. Robert Dale Owen, as a child, once walked with his father some distance downstream of the village, and turning, looked back at Braxfield. So splendid did it appear surrounded by its neat paddocks and greenery that he could not believe it was the same house where he and his family lived.[30] It was big enough to house not only Owen's large family and other relations, but also to accommodate the numerous parties of visitors including royalty, government ministers, ambassadors, social reformers and many other important persons from home and overseas.[31]

The Owens also had well-connected landed gentry, some even in the lower levels of the aristocracy, as neighbours. Prominent among them were the Ross family of Bonnington, the adjoining estate, through whose property ran the River Clyde as it plunged over the famous Falls of Clyde. Apart from his business and social connections in both Glasgow and Edinburgh it was probably the Rosses that introduced Owen to the local gentry and the many visitors they themselves received.[32] Robert Dale, who with his brother, William, rode to hounds, remembered many of these people as 'a good natured rollicking set'.[33] Owen, of course, had extensive dealings with all the local gentry who constituted the Commissioners of Supply for the county, a body which later sought his views on poor relief. And, having become a Justice of the Peace he was also well acquainted with the local judiciary. Incidentally the Rosses had useful connections with the Irish aristocracy since Lady Ross's son, Sir Charles Ross, had married a sister of the Duke of Leinster. A cousin of the Dale sisters, Sir Guy Campbell, subsequently married Pamela Fitzgerald, daughter of Lord Edward Fitzgerald, the Irish rebel, and Madame de Genlis, on which occasion at Bonnington Owen gave away the bride.[34]

Owen had a personal staff, his clerical and secretarial aide John Wright, who looked after the books and ran the Glasgow office, a personal man-servant, butler, coachman, and footman. Other domestic staff appropriate to the Owens' standing included the housekeeper, a nurserymaid, a governess for the children and a retinue of servants and houseboys. There was even a mailman (who doubled as an odd-job man) with a post-bag emblazoned with Owen's arms to carry the mail to and from Old Lanark. Owen acquired other manifestations of his increasing status. His signet ring and seal bore the crest of a double-headed eagle, which he most probably copied from the arms of the burgh of Lanark. These arms also featured on the dinner service and cutlery at Braxfield. Such trappings were probably no different from those sought by the majority of successful merchants and businessmen, Arkwright and Strutt being comparable examples from the same industry who set themselves up as gentry. And certainly at home Owen himself was careful to lead a modest lifestyle, characteristic of his father-in-law, an important side of the private Owen, much in contrast to the public figure.[35]

The education of the children was very different from that of others in Owen's class. He evidently made clear to his sons, especially the eldest boys, Robert Dale and William, that they had been born into an unusual family, that Owen himself had a mission in life that they would continue. It was this, he told von Fellenberg, that their upbringing and education must prepare them for.[36] In part fulfilment of this training for their future roles both Robert Dale and William were sent in 1818 to von Fellenberg's institution in Switzerland, where they spent three years. Caroline retained her religious faith and saw to it that all her children were brought up with a sense of Christian duty. Indeed many visitors remarked that they found Braxfield to be a religious household, so whatever Owen's personal views might have been he was careful not to force them on his wife and children.

The children were taught by governesses or teachers from the New Lanark schools, though it is not entirely clear whether or not any of them actually attended Owen's schools, either in infancy or childhood. One thing certain is that they were taught French by Levasseur, one of several French army officers, prisoners of war billeted out on parole in Old Lanark, a place considered sufficiently far inland to prevent escape, should they feel thus motivated (but judging by the enthusiasm with which they were received by the local ladies, they had little cause to contemplate it). Another private tutor, Manson, taught Robert Dale and William Latin and Greek, and one of the village dancing masters came twice a week to give the children lessons.[37] Dancing and music were favourite family recreations, as they were among the workers and their families at New Lanark.

While books do not seem to have featured greatly in some of the classrooms at New Lanark there was, Robert Dale recalled, a 'pretty extensive' library at Braxfield. Its contents reflected the interests of a widely read social scientist, and when Robert Dale first remembered him his father read a great deal. Latterly Owen just glanced over books, except those containing statistics, with some curt remark like 'the radical errors shared by all men make books of comparatively little value'. One of his favourite books was evidently Colquhoun's *Resources of the British Empire*. Owen rarely took notes and although he continued to read a great deal it was mainly newspapers and other periodicals. Whatever he thought about the use of books in the New Lanark schools his own children were encouraged in their reading. Whether Owen exercised any choice in the matter he does not record but Robert Dale Owen's first book had been *Robinson Crusoe*. This, he says, 'was poured over with implicit faith'.[38]

After the opening of the Institute Owen made the community with its schools and dancing children into a showpiece. Its advantageous situation relative to the Falls of Clyde meant that visitors to this natural wonder would also stop to inspect the village and the schools, which the majority did. Unfortunately the visitors' book for this period has not survived so we do not know exactly how many people came to see what was already a major tourist attraction. It was probably around a thousand a year, the great majority, some even on foot, travelling out from Edinburgh or Glasgow.[39] But there was already a growing number from further afield, including many who had read the *New View* and were curious to see if what it claimed was true, or others whom Owen had met in London or elsewhere and invited to visit him. All of this must have imposed some strain on Owen's staff, especially on a busy day, when upwards of twenty visitors or more might be expected. Of course the routine visitor would have seen little of the actual works, perhaps one spinning room, and then be whisked off to the schools. Industrial espionage remained a problem, so Owen must have had to strike a fine balance in showing off the mills and the various social facilities, especially to foreign visitors.

The most elevated personage in this last category was Grand Duke Nicholas, brother of Emperor Alexander, who had been sent west in the autumn of 1816 to complete his education, travelling not as a royal military officer but as far as possible as an ordinary person.[40] The emperor, while not utterly resistant to reform, wanted his younger brother to observe the constitutional state of England to reinforce its limited applicability in Russia. Alexander need not have feared that Nicholas might be enamoured of British institutions, for though he enjoyed his visits to the nobility at places like Chatsworth, he was nonplussed by the prevailing social and political unrest reported to him on his travels. Sidmouth's spies tracked him every mile of the way, reporting that despite the wintry weather the Grand Duke travelled habitually with 'great good humour' in an open carriage. He was expected in Edinburgh about a week before Christmas and would later travel on to

Glasgow.[41] It was there that Owen probably invited him to inspect New Lanark, though he says in his memoirs that the Grand Duke had specific instructions from his mother to do so.[42]

The visit passed off without incident, the Grand Duke and his party viewing the falls and then being shown over the mills and schools by Owen in person. The future despot was particularly taken by the military drill. The party spent two nights at Braxfield, where Nicholas found the family so charming that he requested that Owen's sons, Robert Dale and William, return with him to Russia, where under his patronage they would finish their education. He even suggested that if Owen cared to bring two million people with him he would 'provide for you all in similar manufacturing communities'. Robert Dale Owen remembered that the Grand Duke noticed the crest on the tableware and cutlery much resembled those of Russia and that his father had suggested making a gift of some of it to him. However, Caroline's good sense prevailed and Nicholas left without his tableware. But the Grand Duke was evidently impressed and his visit was widely reported, as Owen, in another neat piece of public relations, must well have realised.[43]

Many a Scottish Laird, far less the English nobility, or the European and American reformers who visited New Lanark during and after the first great wave of publicity surrounding the launch of Owen's scheme, would have envied what he saw in the community by the Clyde. Here was a substantial enterprise, well managed, and evidently highly productive and profitable. The workers were well regulated and apparently happy. The children were being educated in surroundings to rival any in the country. Good order prevailed, while beyond the gates, disorder threatened. All of this was testified to by respectable and reliable witnesses, who despite some misgivings about Owen's theories, judged the New Lanark experiment a success. Whether it was appropriate or not, it continued to serve as a testbed for the New System and to give Owen the model he thought he needed in resuming his campaign for a trial of the village scheme.

## NOTES

1. *Life*, p. 187; the following section is largely derived from Donnachie and Hewitt, pp. 86–99, 101–108.
2. Especially women, a point picked up by William Maclure, see below.
3. M.W.Flinn (ed.) *Svedenstierna's Tour of Great Britain 1802–3*, Newton Abbot, 1973, p. 146. On New Lanark see pp. 148–9.
4. Owen, *Statement* in Claeys (ed.) vol. 1, pp. 18–20; Butt, 195–9.
5. Gourock Mss, Census Statistics.
6. Ibid, Notebook 1813–22.

7. Ibid.
8. Macnab, p. 126; Griscom, vol. II, p. 376.
9. Gourock Mss, Legal Papers of New Lanark Co, Agreement of 1813; Notebook 1813–22.
10. Bentham Corr. Owen to Bentham, 1 December 1819; Notebook 1813–22.
11. Butt, pp. 195–9, 209–10.
12. Leeds Deputation's Report in *Life*, IA, p. 256 Co-operative Union, Owen Corr. Wright to Owen, 10 January 1853; Butt, pp. 199–200, 212.
13. Gourock Mss. Census data for New Lanark; Place Papers, Add. 35, 152, f.222; Taylor, p. 173. On birth control generally at the time see A. McLaren, *A History of Contraception*, Oxford, 1990.
14. Owen, *Statement* on both Kitchen & Schools; the plan is in Signet Library, Session Papers, Lanark Trust Co V Miss A. Edmonstonn, 1809; Griscom, Vol. II, pp. 383–4; Davidson, pp. 181–2.
15. Robert Owen Memorial Museum, Item 312.
16. Owen, 'Address' in *New View* (Everyman's ed. 1972), pp. 93–119; ibid, Third Essay, p. 40.
17. R.D. Owen, *Outline of the System of Education at New Lanark*, Glasgow, 1824, p. 28.
18. *Life*, pp. 138–42.
19. Griscom, Vol. II, pp. 385–6.
20. Sidmouth Papers, Mary Townsend's Letters from Scotland, 10 October 1821.
21. Macdonald Diaries, p. 169.
22. PP.1816 III, pp. 91–2 on Owen's evidence; PP.1816 IV, pp. 238-4. There was also a Sunday school paid for by the Company, see PP.1819 IX, Report . . . on the Education of the Poor (1818), p. 1389.
23. R.D. Owen, *Outline*, p. 30.
24. *Life*, p. 144.
25. Owen on Dancing *Life*, 141–2; Griscom, vol. II, 378 and most other accounts cited here. Much of the music turned up at New Harmony, see C.K. Studer, 'Music in the Overnite Experiment at 'New Harmony', *Pros. of the International Communal Studies Assoc.*, 1988.
26. Macnab, pp. 136–7.
27. Ibid, pp. 132–4.
28. R.D. Owen, *Threading My Way*, p. 165.
29. Owen to Rapp, 4 August 1820, quoted in Arndt, *Indiana Decade*, pp. 89–90.
30. R.D. Owen, *Threading my Way*, 44–50.
31. *Life*, pp. 145–151.
32. Ibid, p. 82.
33. R.D. Owen, *Threading My Way*, p. 96.
34. *Life*, p. 82.
35. R.D. Owen, *Threading My Way*, pp. 36–7, 39–40, 119–120.
36. Owen-Fellenberg Corr. Owen to Fellenberg 17 January 1818.
37. R.D. Owen, *Threading My Way*, pp. 64, 88, 92.
38. Ibid, pp. 50, 67.
39. *Life*, pp. 147–8.
40. M.B. Lincoln, *Nicholas I*, London, 1978, pp. 65–6.
41. Sidmouth Papers, Sir W. Congreve to Sidmouth, 12 December 1816.
42. *Life*, p. 145; the *Times* gives a detailed itinerary.
43. *Life*, p. 146; R.D. Owen, *Threading My Way*, pp. 115–119.

# TEN

# Propagandist Once More

Despite his declaration against sectarian religion Owen's reputation as a philanthropist stood high, and after returning from his Continental tour and taking direct charge of affairs at New Lanark again, he could devote his attention to his schemes for reform. Owen, as Hazlitt said, seemed to be obsessed with one idea but the New System now embraced character formation, popular education, poor relief, and the community plan, all of which were increasingly seen in national and international, rather than local terms.[1] He was friendly with many of the country's leaders and was assured of a respectful hearing for his plans of social betterment, and thanks to his wealth could continue to use a variety of platforms to advance his proposals. In 1819, a year of further discontent and protest in the country, he renewed the campaign, concentrating on efforts to get a trial of the village plan and trying to counter the attacks of critics, including the political economists.

In a pamphlet comprising three letters on his proposed arrangements addressed to the political economist, David Ricardo, who had earlier expressed interest in the *New View*, and participated in the 1817 meetings, he gave one of his clearest statements about the relationship he saw between population growth, poverty, education and the community scheme. At the outset he claims to have an extensive knowledge of political economy and human nature, but does not regard himself as a visionary.[2] He argues that his scheme is consistent with Malthus's views and the possibility of increasing the 'means of support and comfort of the population'. Famine, crime and misery, he says, can be repressed by increasing the means of subsistence. He then sets out the main principles on which the village scheme is based. First, they will provide self support for the unemployed and industrious poor. Second, they will employ capital to advantage. Third, they will provide moral training and useful education. Fourth, they will lead to a 'gradual increase of the comforts of the poor as the proposed societies advance in intelligence'. Fifth, that they offer the opportunity 'to take up any number of the industrious poor' and in few years limit parochial aid 'to those only for whom it was originally instituted, namely, the infirm and diseased'. Lastly, that they provide the only means which offers a check on population 'without the introduction of crime and misery, when such a check may be found absolutely necessary'.[3]

After reverting to a long description of the New Lanark experience, the 'one rational attempt to remove the evident causes of these unhappy effects', the 'check' of birth control reappears, but is not mentioned directly. 'Superior benevolence inculcated by Christianity', he claims, 'acts as a moral check to population', as does 'a tolerable share of prudence and foresight alone'. But there are limits beyond which he is not prepared to venture, for the accounts of Harmonie which he cites 'disclosed prohibition or discouragement of marriage and scarcely any infants in the settlement'. To this, he wrote emphatically, 'Mr Owen decidedly objects'.[4] Summarising the benefits of his scheme, he says that at the very least the industrious unemployed would find work and 'some risk might reasonably be encountered to get rid of the overwhelming burden of the poor-rates and allay the irritation and suffering of the lower orders'. His success at New Lanark 'in the face of the greatest opposition' might encourage the hope that 'his benevolent views will be seconded by every enlightened economist and opulent proprietor'.[5]

Owen emphasised here the link between capital and labour, and the notion that the villages were to be seen as investments capable of producing returns for venture capitalists. Apart from his description of the high morals prevailing in the place, he was able to use Harmonie as an example of successful and profitable community organisation. He reiterated this aspect of the proposed communities again and again, for example, later in the year he used the columns of the *Glasgow Journal* to report further details of the German Settlement he had in correspondence from George Courtauld and Thomas Hulme, who had both visited the Harmonists, the latter publishing an account of his travels in the American west.[6]

Another pamphlet returned to these ideas, this time directed not at the theorists but the workers. In his *Address to the Working Classes* he hammered home the message that social conditions could be changed by rational behaviour rather than revolutionary action. This had been a central theme of the memorials written earlier for the congress, and while likely to appeal to despots and many of his middle- and upper-class supporters was certainly not calculated to inspire the radicals either to join his cause or sign up for membership of the proposed communities.[7] But again he spoke not only of new 'notions and arrangements' but also of the 'means' by which the suffering and degradation of the working class could be banished. All that was needed was 'the knowledge of how to direct these means', almost certainly another reference to birth control.[8]

If the workers proved reluctant to embrace Owenism at that stage, he was more successful in his efforts to persuade some of his middle- and upper-class followers to take up the cause. So on 26 June a 'select meeting' of notables under the presidency of the Duke of Kent was held at Freemasons' Hall in London. The duke, like his brother, Sussex, had embraced good causes, but whether he was there out of altruism or self-interest is unknown, since he was indebted to Owen for financial guidance and a loan. However, Kent gave a good account of Owen's proposals, saying that decisive measures were needed to counter the prevailing distress, that reports from all sides testified to his success at New Lanark, and that contrary to the rumours that had circulated for the past two years Owen gave 'every facility to the performance of religious duties'.[9] Owen then presented his proposals concluding with a prospectus of the proposed community. Several motions were afterwards adopted, strongly commending Owen's scheme and proposing that a committee of the 'most respectable and intelligent public characters of all parties' be appointed to consider the next step. Those proposed included the royal dukes, Kent and Sussex, the archbishop of Canterbury, four bishops, nine lords, and six MPs, including Ricardo, Wilberforce, and Sir William de Crespigny, who was to prove one of Owen's most loyal supporters.[10] Many of those approached evidently declined but at a public meeting in the City of London Tavern on 26 July, a committee was announced. This was headed by Kent and his brother, a number of reforming clergy and surgeons, some political economists including Torrens, and a clutch of MPs, prominent being Sir Robert Peel, Ricardo, and de Crespigny. There was clearly still some confusion in Owen's mind about the economic principles that were to prevail in the proposed villages. Torrens actually asked, 'Are the commodities produced to be consumed in the villages, or sent to market?', and Owen replied, 'It is so arranged it may be one or the other'.[11] However, the committee duly published an advertisement on 11 August calling for subscriptions of £100,000 to try an experimental community primarily devoted to agricultural labour.[12]

As a result of all this publicity New Lanark that year attracted even more attention than before. Among the visitors in August were representatives of the Leeds Poor Law Guardians, who were greatly impressed by what they saw. A highly moral atmosphere prevailed, working people conducted themselves with decorum and were more interested in their children's education than in drinking and brawling. Kent's personal physician, Dr Henry Grey Macnab, was sent by the London committee to undertake a thorough investigation. Macnab subsequently published a very favourable report on the moral condition of the inhabitants and the provision for their welfare, apart from Owen's one of the most detailed appraisals of the system at New Lanark. Not only did Macnab's royal connections seem to put the highest seal of approval on Owen's establishment, but the good doctor also wrote positively about religious observance both in the community and in the Owen household at Braxfield.[13]

One of Sidmouth's right hand men, John Beckett, formerly under secretary of state of state for Home affairs but by then judge advocate general and MP for Cockermouth, also made his way to New Lanark about the time of Peterloo, probably to report directly to his superior on the community which apparently so interested one of the royal dukes. Beckett was delighted with Edinburgh and Glasgow though he noted a strong contrast between 'the cultivation of Law, Physic and Divinity at the one and the spinning of cotton twist at the other'. 'I returned through Lanark', he told Sidmouth, 'and visited Mr Owen's establishment for spinning Morals and Manufactures'. 'He is quite an enthusiast', Beckett reported, 'and begins by laying it down as an indisputable Proposition that the world nowadays must be governed by Intelligence and not by Ignorance. I took for granted that he was the former personified and as the present Governors did not encourage *Him* to the utmost that they were the representatives of the other'.[14]

Whatever Beckett's personal opinion, the prevailing unrest meant Owen's ideas for well conducted colonies still had some appeal: in October Beckett was sending Sidmouth alarmist reports from Leeds about the demoralised gentry of the West Riding, who felt abandoned by the government in their attempts to quell radicalism.[15] Moreover the unrest was widespread, almost reaching the gates of New Lanark itself.[16]

Another visitor was the poet, Robert Southey, a close acquaintance of Wordsworth and Coleridge, third of the 'Lake Poets' and Poet Laureate. While few of the Romantic poets or writers of the day were particularly sympathetic to the march of industry, Southey's description of the community is very perceptive. Southey apparently liked Owen but thought he was somewhat misguided. The diary entry highlighted what Southey regarded as the manipulation of the workforce in a remarkably efficient and productive enterprise, and indicated to his readers some of the fundamental weaknesses in Owen's social philosophy. Southey likened the buildings of New Lanark to 'a large convent', built in 'such a dingle' and reached by such a steep descent that 'you might throw a stone down the chimneys'. The rows of houses he thought were 'cleaner than the common streets of a Scotch town, and yet not quite so clean as they ought to be', giving, to his eyes, the general appearance of what might be expected 'in a Moravaian settlement'.

Southey had been forewarned of Owen's flowing enthusiasm and had consequently decided to devote only a day to his tour. Nevertheless Owen 'made as full an exhibition' as time allowed, conducting Southey and his party through both the mills and Institute. The former, thought Southey, were 'perfect in their kind, according to the present state of mechanical science' and apparently well managed. Like many visitors he noted the cleanliness (essential in textile mills because of the fire risk to wooden machinery and from waste materials), the attention to ventilation (vital for the control of temperature and humidity) and the lack of any 'unpleasant smell'. According to Southey maintenance costs were £8,000 a year, a figure that must have come from Owen himself.

Southey's account of the Institute, 'a large building just completed, with ball and concert and lecture rooms, all for "the formation of character"', is highly revealing, both of Owen's paternalism and the regimentation of his system. The party were shown a 'plan', most likely one of the 'Streams of Time', which, as they were designed to do, clearly caught the eye of the youngsters in the party. Then followed the customary exhibition of children's marching and dancing. Southey thought the youngsters' 'puppet-like motions' might have been produced by the water wheel and compared them to Dutch cows whose tails, tied to a common string, wagged in unison. He was better pleased with the infant school, whose inmates 'made a glorious noise, worth all the concerts of New Lanark and London to boot'. Owen's paternalism was vividly displayed as he took genuine pleasure in his role of father-figure to his infant charges, also noticed by Lady Sidmouth.

Kind looks and kind words were all very well but 'Owen in reality deceives himself', wrote Southey. Owen might as well be director of a plantation. Though the workers were white and could quit his service at any time they were under the same 'absolute management as so many negro-slaves'. Driven by a variety of motives, Owen would make his 'human machines' as happy as he could and 'make a display of their happiness'. In all this, said Southey, Owen was jumping to the 'monstrous conclusion' that because he could manipulate 2,210 mill workers to do his will the whole of mankind could be 'governed with the same facility'. But man is not a machine and Owen was wrong to presume that what worked in his cotton mills had universal application 'to the whole empire'. Then comes a statement which on the evidence of history proved remarkably prophetic, for Southey observed that Owen 'keeps out of sight from others, and perhaps from himself, that his system, instead of aiming at perfect freedom, can only be kept in play by absolute power'. Owen's problem was that he never looked beyond one of his 'ideal square villages' – or indeed New Lanark itself – to work out the implications of his system for the rest of humanity. Rather than forming character, Owen's institutions would lead to its destruction, with the result that 'the power of human society, and the grace, would both be annihilated'. Despite Southey's misgivings, however, the New Lanark experiment was regarded by most onlookers as a success. It continued to give Owen both the means and the model he needed in his campaign for a trial of the village scheme.[17]

Southey was right about Owen's obsession with the symmetrical communities peopled by the differing classes. Owen loved drawings and models, and just as these figured prominently as visual aids in the school at New Lanark so he deployed them to great effect before his audiences. Apart from drawings, models of the new village, possibly the work of either John Winning, who taught art in the schools and to Owen's children, or of Stedman Whitwell, the architect, and various tables produced to show the likely social structure there was another appeal to the visual senses of Owen's listeners in the famous cubes. Based on a table in Colquhoun's *Resources of the British Empire*, nine cubes represented volumetrically eight classes of society, while the ninth represented the total population. The largest was almost four inches square, while that representing royalty, the lords and bishops was just a quarter of an inch square.[18] The two royal dukes were fascinated by the model and the cubes, which, should this have been necessary, vividly demonstrated their position in society relative to the working and pauper classes.[19]

On 23 August Kent's committee published another assessment of Owen's proposals. This was clearly designed to reassure those who might have been persuaded by critics that Owen was at best a deluded philanthropist with more money than sense and at worst a dangerous egalitarian secularist. Whether or not Owen himself had a hand in preparing this address, it certainly provided a well-reasoned set of replies to the critics. New Lanark was a model establishment, it claimed, especially remarkable being the schools, where 'the health, cheerfulness, intelligence, and excellent dispositions of the children have struck everyone who has visited the place with pleasure and surprise'. The proposed new community would combine agriculture and manufacturing, but agriculture would be its basis, and because it was beginning *de novo* would be superior even to New Lanark. Owen had always been tolerant of religious worship, had made provision in this regard for the Gaelic speakers of the community, his home was one of daily prayer, and his own conduct 'free from reproach'. There was a strong denial that a 'community of goods' would prevail in the new village or that there would be a 'tendency to the equalisation of ranks'(both inevitably divisive issues at New Harmony, Orbiston and other Owenite communities). The existing law of property would be respected and Owen pledged that any capital invested would return an adequate profit. This was not a scheme for perpetuating the poor laws, said the address, nor would it destroy the independence of the peasantry. Thus the co-operation of everyone interested in the welfare of society, especially the labouring classes, was 'earnestly solicited'.[20]

Sadly the address did not produce the necessary subscriptions, which by the time of the final meeting of Kent's committee on 1 December amounted to only £8,000. With regret the committee demitted office, publishing another address which pointed out that the present system of poor relief could not be sustained in its present form. The government must encourage and support further consolidation of parish relief, and as had already occurred in Suffolk and the Isle of Wight, construct workhouses to cope with the growing problem of local and itinerant poor. Crown land could be made available in selected districts where the villages could be tried, subject to 'proper restrictions' and with minimum inconvenience.

Two weeks later on 16 December de Crespigy moved a motion in the Commons for a select committee to investigate Owen's proposals for improving the condition of the lower orders. The motion was seconded by Lord Archibald Hamilton, MP for the county of Lanark, and supported by Ricardo, Brougham, and two others. All the speakers paid tribute to Owen's high character and to his achievements at New Lanark. The opposition arose less from the economics of the scheme than on religious grounds. An extract from the address of 21 August 1817 in which Owen had attacked religious sectarianism was read out and it was maintained that all that was good about New Lanark was due less to Owen's wise government than to 'the good old system of Christianity'. In the division, Ricardo, though he disagreed with Owen's views, was one of only 18 MPs to vote in favour, 143 being against. Despite royal patronage, another important opportunity for government support had been lost.[21]

While this must have been a major disappointment, Owen meantime exploited his local prestige to advance his ever-widening schemes by fighting a parliamentary by-election for Linlithgow Burghs, a seat that combined the burghs of Lanark, Selkirk, Peebles and Linlithgow. He had apparently contemplated this before, since his neighbours, the Ross family, exercised considerable influence in the selection of candidates. The vacancy arose through the death of Sir John Riddell on 21 April 1819. Riddell had reforming sympathies, supporting Catholic relief and criminal law reform and had been chosen for the Poor Law committee, to which he had given evidence from Scotland.[22] In his election address, dated 24 April 1819, Owen explained that the distress of the working classes arose from 'the rapid and extensive introduction of Machinery and other Scientific Power' which had destroyed the equilibrium between production and consumption. This could be corrected and all could derive benefit if 'new internal arrangements' were effected in the state of society. Owen claimed that the 'coming crisis' was near at hand but could readily be met by his plans.[23] His autobiography is confused about the sequence of events but it seems that he withdrew from the contest only to return to the fray at the General Election following the death of George III in February 1820. On that occasion, the voters in both Lanark and Linlithgow seemed willing to support Owen and such was his confidence that he told Robert Dundas, Viscount Melville, First Lord of the Admiralty and the government's Scottish manager, that he thought his return was secure. He was even able to cite the

unlikely support of a highly influential spirit, the ghost of Melville's
father, the great Henry Dundas. Writing to say that Linlithgow had
declared in his favour by 19 to 6 and that he needed only four more
votes to secure his election, he recalled the fact that Dundas, when
on a visit to Lady Ross of Bonnington, had promised 'to aid him in
his attempts to improve the condition of the lower orders'.[24] Although
Selkirk and Peebles declared for Henry Monteith, Owen's opponent
and neighbour, he claimed he could still have won had not four of
the Lanark voters, on whom he had depended not been bribed 'by
being feasted, [and] kept intoxicated' by the other candidate.[25] His
memory must have been defective because at Lanark he appears to
have lost to Monteith by 13 votes to 6, but amid considerable mayhem
and allegations of bribery from those who voted for him.[26] Although
he lost, his local prestige was greatly enhanced. He had himself been
entertained at a public dinner held at the hustings in Lanark which
celebrated his perseverance 'in his designs for public welfare and his
character in private life'. He later sent £100 to be distributed to the
needy.[27]

Politics apart, for much of the time Owen was still wrestling with
the problem of the poor which he thought could readily be solved
by the village scheme. To this end he met anther prominent reformer,
Rev Thomas Chalmers, already a public figure, who could reasonably
claim to have as much experience of the rural and urban poor as
himself. What passed between them during their meeting at St John's
in Glasgow is unrecorded, but it was seemingly a wide-ranging discussion embracing poverty, religion and the re-organisation of society.
'Either you are right and I am in error', Owen wrote to Chalmers, from
New Lanark on 24 April, 'or I am right and you are in error, or we
both misunderstand each other.' Since they were both convinced of
their respective views on how to improve society, Owen repeated a
proposal he had evidently made at their meeting for a 'great discussion
. . . to detect the error wherever it may lie'. At the same time he
invited Chalmers to New Lanark: 'Come and see what *is* done here
as a preliminary step toward the more important improvements which
with your aid and help a remedy may be immediately assured for our
suffering fellow creatures'. Chalmers sent his associate, William Collins,
to have a look at New Lanark and visited the place himself four years
later, but he did not follow up Owen's suggested collaboration and
the 'great discussion' never took place. Had it done so it would have
gone down in history as altogether more important that the famous
Owen-Campbell debate on religion held in Cincinnati some years later.
Still, as Brown observes, the two great communitarian thinkers of early
nineteenth-century Scotland had met and discussed their positions at
some length.[28]

Not long after Owen produced his most famous economic thesis, the *Report to the County of Lanark*, which further refined his plan for self-supporting communities, addressed some of the doubts raised by Torrens and others, and seemed to present another opportunity for a full-scale experiment. Again it came at an appropriate time. Echoing the concerns of the authorities in the West Riding, it was a combination of local poverty, social distress and the powder-keg of radicalism that provoked the landed gentry of Lanark into seeking Owen's help. New Lanark, after all, showed that philanthropy could produce docile workers and pay handsome profits into the bargain. For his part, Owen grasped the opportunity presented by those gentry who constituted the Commissioners of Supply for the County of Lanark in the hope that it might lead to an early experiment in community building. By this time Owen had embraced spade husbandry, an intensive agriculture which was receiving a wide press thanks to the flair for publicity of its alleged originator, William Falla of Gateshead. Even the provincial press, such as the *Leeds Mercury*, had devoted space to correspondence between him and Benjamin Wills, a member of Kent's committee, on its merits.[29] Falla's methods, which would clearly keep large numbers busy tilling the fields, figured prominently in the report laid before a meeting of the commissioners on 1 May 1820. Owen's presentation was received with some interest and a further explanation concluded with an enthusiastic account of his achievements at New Lanark, which 'instead of involving any pecuniary sacrifice [sic], are found to operate beneficially in a commercial point of view'.[30] At a later meeting of the commissioners held at Hamilton on 16 November 'a respectable gentleman of the County', Archibald James Hamilton of Dalzell, a young, disillusioned army officer on half pay who had met Owen some years before and become a disciple, expressed himself willing to grant a lease of land 'sufficient for the purpose of making a trial of the Plan' and 'being assisted by the Author, to superintend the whole, without charge to the County'. This development, claimed Hamilton, would obviate the need for a new Bridewell or prison, neither of which were exactly what Owen contemplated.[31] Hamilton in a letter of 5 December proposed to let 60 acres at nominal rent and 600 more at a rent of two-fifths of the produce. He also promised a subscription of £1,000. Subsequently, the first edition of the *Report*, published in 1821, incorporated a more detailed description and a map showing the proposed community by the banks of the River Calder near Motherwell.[32]

Persuading the authorities to act was no easy task. At another meeting called by the gentry of Lanark and comprising the commissioners, Justices of the Peace, freeholders and clergy, and held at Hamilton on 9 April 1821, Owen, armed with a set of plans and drawings, spelled out in detail the arrangements of his proposed village. These showed a community for 1,200 persons surrounded by gardens and set in 600 acres of land, to be cultivated by spade husbandry. He had also taken the precaution of preparing estimates of capital cost, which he reckoned at £40,000, and of income and expenditure, which, he said, proved the viability of the enterprise. 'A well devised association' would readily harness the labour of the community to 'supply a comfortable subsistence', including education for its inhabitants. Twenty years experience, ten of them spent implementing his New System, had convinced him this was the way forward. In asking the county to seek government support of his plan, he explained, probably exaggerating somewhat, that he had spent £50,000 'in various measures to prepare the public to take this subject fairly'. Although there was some dissension, John Maxwell, MP for Renfrewshire, reassured the doubters by recalling that Vansittart had told him of the government's willingness to make the grant of £20,000 in aid of the scheme. Maxwell then agreed to act as sponsor for a petition calling on parliament to consider Owen's measures.[33]

Owen then proceeded south with the petition, calling at Newcastle, Leeds and Derby. There he could report that 'a favourable disposition to his views [was] rapidly increasing among the most intelligent classes' and that in Newcastle a co-operative society, led by a number of Quakers, had just been set up. Owen arrived in London on or about 19 May. Thereafter those wishing to append their signatures to the petition were invited to do so at the office of *The Economist*, an Owenite periodical edited by George Mudie, which had begun publication earlier that year. Its edition of 19 May carried the full text.[34] Maxwell then presented the petition to the Commons and on 26 June, supported by de Crespigny and others, proposed a motion calling for a select committee to investigate New Lanark and the village scheme. The debate focused on two main objections to Owen's plan: religion and personal freedom in the proposed communities. Wilberforce, supported by Canning, president of the Board of Control, and Stephen Lushington, MP for Canterbury and a joint secretary to the treasury, expressed concern on the religious issue, while Londonderry (Castlereagh having succeeded his father as 2nd marquis on 6 April) led the objectors on the question of discipline and freedom. 'The state of discipline recommended by Mr Owen might be applicable enough to poor-houses', remarked Londonderry, 'but it is by no means agreeable to the feelings of a free nation'. Joseph Hume, a friend of James Mill and then MP for Aberdeen Burghs, was more prosaic, telling the house that 'If Mr Owen's system produced so much happiness with so little care, the adoption of it would make us a race of beings little removed from the brutes, only ranging the four corners of a parallelogram, instead of the mazes of a forest'. Other MPs joined in ridiculing Owen's 'quadrangular paradises' and at the end of the debate Maxwell's motion was negatived without a division.[35]

The Commissioners of Supply for Lanark also turned the scheme down but undaunted Owen and Hamilton got together and resolved to try a model community on the Dalzell estate at Motherwell. Even although official support was lacking there was still a great deal of goodwill towards Owen locally. One newspaper pointed out that his scheme was unlikely to 'introduce a new aspect on the affairs of the world' or to transform cities and towns, but nonetheless, it concluded, 'Mr Owen's villages will always be useful'.[36] Owen actually purchased 660 acres from Hamilton's father, General Hamilton, paying over £14,000 for the land. Capital to set up the community was to be raised by 2,000 shares of £25 each and as soon as 1,500 had been subscribed operations were to begin. Owen and Hamilton would oversee a Committee of management, but eventually, when initial capital had been repaid, the worker-members of the community would have full management of their own affairs. Arrangements for the 'New Village at Motherwell' would be completed during the winter and building would begin the following spring.[37] Further evidence of the effectiveness of Owen's propaganda campaign in Scotland is to be found in the setting up in Edinburgh of the Practical Society, one of its prime objectives being the education of poor children.[38] This society, with which both Hamilton and Combe were associated, might even form the nucleus of the new community.[39]

Meantime visitors flocked to New Lanark and indeed that year saw a huge surge in numbers that continued until Owen's departure for the United States. Among them were many Irish clergy and gentry, including Sir Edward O'Brien, MP, one of many useful contacts Owen had already established in Ireland.[40] Some important Americans arrived, notably William Lawrence, a young New York lawyer who attended the Sorbonne and later became secretary of the US legation in London during Albert Gallatin's mission to settle boundary disputes with the British. Gallatin had recommended Rush's appointment as US minister in London.[41] Another was the industrialist turned philanthropist, Peter Cooper, who had business interests in both New York and Baltimore.

One of the aristocratic visitors was the Hon Mrs Mary Townsend, a widow, accompanied by her father, Lord Stowell, a lawyer and judge.[42] Her uncle was de Crespigny, Owen's supporter. She was soon to become the second wife of Sidmouth to whom she sent an account of Owen, describing him as his 'intimate friend'. Stowell was obviously in a hurry to return south and had been warned to ask for a foreman to show them round but Owen, seeing their card, rushed out to greet them:

> He said it was impossible to see all at once, & that we must dine with him and attend in the Evening again. Consent was given & we entered the courtyard where all the Babes came round to have their heads *patted*. I was amused to see my Father engaged in the

imposition of hands to such an extent. We then passed through
some of the Schools, Apartments, saw the Shops etc and went to
B[raxfield] to dinner. I lamented to hear Mr O talk in so visionary
or I may add, insane a style as to his views and expectations. I had
feared there must be something very unsound in his plan from that
conceited shallow coxcomb my Uncle, Sir Wm de Cresp'y, having
advocated his cause, but I was most distressed that a person acting
on such benevolent principles as I *really* believe guide Mr O to be
such a victim to his own folly and irrationality. I think it is quite
of a piece with the Laputan extracting sunbeams from cucumbers
or any other of Swift's absurdities for him to suppose all the world
in the dark up to the present time, and that *he* alone can hold up
a Lanthorn to Mankind, and as asserted, 'this wisdom was derived
from causes over which he had no control'. I really think my dear
Friend you (as an intimate of his) should *try* to stop the torrent of
Absurdity that so blinds him – a hard task I doubt not!

Dinner also proved revealing, the party consisting of Owen, Caroline
('a very good sort of *steady headed* woman and of good manners'), some of
the Owen children, Catherine Whitwell, the teacher, and the Owenites,
Captain Donald MacDonald, (whom, it transpired she had met before
at her friends), and another teacher, Joseph Applegarth and his family.
Nothing was talked of but Owen's 'wild schemes for the formation of
human character', but he was evidently caught off guard when Stowell
asked 'if the birch was never called in?'. After a tasty meal of trout and
roast beef, the ladies and children withdrew whereupon Miss Whitwell
produced a phrenological head. Later the young Owens were seen 'feeling
their pater to ascertain if bumps, adhesives and Philo nonsense prevailed'.
After another visit to the school, where a hymn was sung at dismissal,
Mrs Townsend and her father escaped to the Clydesdale Inn at Lanark.
They both wrote notes declining a further visit, but nevertheless both
Owen and MacDonald appeared the following morning. Owen seemed
concerned about mistaking Stowell's identity and condemning lawyers
but could not persuade him to return to the mills. Owen then pressed
'a heap of his tracts and works respecting the cause' on them as their
carriage prepared to depart. 'Altogether I regret the visit', Mrs Townsend
told Sidmouth. 'I fear it will excite hopes of support and countenance
which I am sure ought not to be given to any plan so Chimerical'.[43]
Her account needs to be treated with caution but it highlighted again
Owen's misreading of the generally polite attentions paid to him. The
habit made him dangerous, said Taylor, so much so that people began
to distance themselves from him.[44]

Although funds were not immediately forthcoming Owen's scheme
still proved bold enough to attract some powerful support. This led to

the establishment of potentially the most influential body likely to effect progress, the British and Foreign Philanthropic Society for the Permanent Relief of the Labouring Classes. Its first meeting in London on 1 June 1822, with John Galt, the Tory novelist and parliamentary lobbyist, as honorary secretary, witnessed another assemblage of the great and the good to discuss 'the great distress prevailing over the country'. The audience comprised a number of lords temporal and spiritual, MPs, political economists, social reformers of varying shades of opinion, some of whom had been long-term supporters of popular education, poor law reform and similar causes.

Lord Torrington as chairman provided his own testimonial for the scheme, telling the audience that 'no language can do justice to the excellence of the arrangements' at New Lanark. 'To *see* it', he said, 'is to be delighted with the order and regularity that prevail there'. During a visit he had attended an evening meeting of over a thousand people, 800 of them from 16 to 20 years old, 'all uniting in friendly conversation, accompanied with some instrumental music'. He left the meeting early to see if any 'irregularity' occurred among so many young people, but 'their conduct was that of friendship and brotherly regard; and in ten minutes every individual was in his house, with order and regularity'. 'In my walks about the establishment', concluded Torrington, 'I requested Mr Owen not to attend me, that I might judge for myself; and I am convinced that whoever has seen *what I have seen* can have no doubt as to the excellency of the plan'.

This must have convinced any doubters and a large list of individuals promising loans and donations was drawn up. It included some prominent Owenites and other sympathetic figures like Elizabeth Fry and Henry Brougham. Another of the subscribers was his old ally, de Crespigny, who had previously embraced a variety of social reforms and helped him promote parliamentary support for his schemes. Whether these and other supporters' enthusiasm would be backed with cash was another question.[45] In December Owen told William Wilson, secretary of the Edinburgh Practical Society, which had been set up on the New System as an educational cum co-operative society, that he had 'not for a moment lost sight of Motherwell'. It was his intention to begin there as soon as possible, he hoped the following spring.[46] Two years later, as Owen left in haste for Harmonie, Hamilton, tired of waiting, joined forces with another ardent Owenite, the wealthy Edinburgh tanner and another key player in the Practical Society, Abram Combe, to revive the Motherwell scheme as the Orbiston Community.[47] We might just note in passing that Combe's brother, George, the famous phrenologist, actually examined Owen's head and pronounced himself amazed by the size of his 'bump of benevolence'.

Owen afterwards carried the lessons of New Lanark to Ireland, which

according to his recollections was then 'in a state bordering on bar-
barism . . . derived from religious hatreds and conflicts'. The visit to
Ireland, never before investigated by scholars, represented another important effort to attract government support for the plan, as he had probably
been informed that a select committee would soon be set up to investigate
the prevailing distress. He must have thought he might be called to give
evidence, and, as he did earlier in his investigative tour of textile factories,
set about familiarising himself with Ireland. He spent some months touring
places hit by famine and food riots and saw the miserable condition of
the poor and unemployed.[48] This he combined with a major propaganda
campaign, using every opportunity to discuss his plan with local elites and
expound on it on public platforms. In his later evidence Owen claimed to
have spent seven or eight months in Ireland but newspaper reports and
such correspondence as survives do not clarify whether or not he was
away the whole time or either went home or to London periodically. He
may well have been away from October to May.

Owen, accompanied by Macdonald, and possibly at the start of the visit
by Hamilton, crossed from Portpatrick to Donaghadee towards the end
of October and after calling briefly at Belfast 'passed hastily through the
north part of Ireland' heading south to Dublin.[49] From there he wrote to
Caroline saying that he had seen the Lord Lieutenant, Marquis Wellesley,
and had spoken to him for an hour and a quarter. 'I had a very favourable
hearing', he said, 'he has the plan now under consideration, and I am to
see him again'. Wellesley was a powerful figure, having been ambassa-
dor to Spain before becoming Foreign Secretary from 1809–12. Henry
Goulbourn, his Chief Secretary, had been an under secretary for war as
well as a peace commissioner with the United States in 1814. So Goulbourn
and Owen must have had many mutual acquaintances. For Wellesley
and his secretary the governance of Ireland was an enormously sensitive
and difficult issue and it is quite likely that Owen's investigations and
proposals may have caused anxiety in official circles. Apart from the
disturbances associated with near famine conditions in some parts there
was the omni-present question of Catholic emancipation. These and other
problems were the subjects of extensive correspondence with the Home
Office during much of the early 1820s, and especially during the period
of Owen's visit.

Always a great name dropper, Owen, in his letter to Caroline, also
mentions dining on successive nights with the Bishop of Down and the
Lord Mayor, and visits to Lord Cloncurry, another old ally, and to the
Duke of Leinster and the Bishop of Ossory.[50] All of this suggests that
his reception by the elite, especially the clergy, was amicable, as indeed
it appears to have been throughout his stay in Ireland. At some point,
whether while passing through Dublin on his way to the south and west
or on his return to the city in the spring, he also addressed Catholic divines

at St Patrick's College, Maynooth, which had been set up as a seminary for educating the priesthood in 1795. Apart from its religious objective it was a place designed to prevent the clergy's resort to the continent where the influence of revolutionary ideas might prove subversive. The Catholic bishops became converts to constitutionalism and exercised their influence against revolution fairly consistently. Endowments were made available to Maynooth from 1808 and by the time of Owen's visit the hierarchy was pragmatically supportive of the status quo, so quite what he expected to gain from his briefing of the divines is difficult to determine. Presumably he avoided all references to his views on the evils of sectarianism in religion.[51]

Accompanied for some of the time by William Falla, the agriculturist, he then proceeded to the south-west and by November was in Co Kilkenny before moving on in December to Co Cork.[52] He, and presumably Macdonald, stayed throughout the trip with local gentry and MPs, some of whom had either visited him at New Lanark or to whom he had been given letters of introduction. As he travelled around there were also many invitations to stay – and someone offered the loan of a carriage and another to forward mail gratis. He wrote to Combe and Wilson in effusive terms about his reception and the willingness of people to listen to his ideas. How much attention he actually paid to what he saw in the Irish countryside is difficult to assess from his correspondence, which, as usual, tended to concentrate on his own activities and the people he met.[53] By the middle of January he was in Limerick. There on 19 January he held a public meeting to explain his intentions. He pointed out that in Ireland there was on the one hand 'an abundance of agricultural and manufactured produce' and on the other much poverty and distress. He proposed the village scheme as the main remedy and exhibited a large drawing of 'the new establishment at Motherwell near Hamilton in Scotland', which he said 'is to commence in the course of this year'. He faced some critical questions on how the villages would actually operate in practice.[54] Nevertheless he was clearly in an optimistic frame of mind for he wrote enthusiastically to Hamilton saying that the evil intentions of Old Society could be turned to the advantage of the New System 'to accomplish the most valuable purposes'. The movement that had been set against him in Scotland, mainly on the grounds of his religious views, could readily be countered and the clergy there would soon see their influence vanish. 'I am prepared now to meet them on their own ground', he told Hamilton. He could with some justice argue that he had strong support among the Irish clergy with whom he may even have discussed the religious controversy that had arisen in Lanark. The Church of Ireland clergy might well have held more liberal notions than their Scottish Presbyterian counterparts, but then again he was hardly challenging them on their doorsteps as he was the Lanark presbytery at home.[55]

After this he went with Sir Edward O'Brien, MP for Clare and a consistent supporter of Catholic claims, to a session of the courts of Clare at Ennis where the local gentry heard him explain his plan. He continued his progression of the west with visits to Tipperary and Kerry, before returning east to inspect the counties there, notably Co Meath, which was one he later specifically cited to the select committee as the basis for his evidence of prevailing conditions in Ireland.[56] As he went round he rather foolishly declared that he would soon divulge a 'secret' that would put all to rights. Quite what he meant is unclear, but it may have been birth control, rather than the more obvious community scheme. Expectations were further heightened by a series of advertisements that began to appear in the newspapers from the beginning of April advertising various of Owen's publications including his arrangements for the distressed working classes, a report of the British and Foreign Philanthropic Society, and an Irish edition of *A New View of Society*.[57]

But at the first of several meetings held in Dublin on 12 April he showed little sympathy with the plight of Ireland and apart from a long exposition about character formation, all he could come up with to save the country was the village plan. Whether or not he intended to speak about alternative strategies to solve the press of population and poverty, including birth control, is far from clear. He might well have been a bit confused because he was suffering from a bad bout of influenza and was quite overwhelmed by the turnout. Nonetheless he caused a sensation, and the *Freeman's Journal* excitedly reported a meeting where 'an assemblage of rank, talent, fashion at the Rotunda [heard] the benevolent Mr Owen develop his plans for bettering the condition of Ireland's miserable peasantry'. 'The Great Round Room was thronged to excess, yet hundreds of the most respectable persons were unable to secure admission', the report continued, and the place was so crowded all the windows had to be thrown open as several ladies in the audience were overcome by the heat.[58] The large painting, said to be of New Lanark, but more likely his proposed community, 'excited general admiration'. Due to his indisposition Owen was evidently drained by the three hour exposition, which left little time for audience reaction. Dr Charles Orpen agreed to read out the rules and regulations for a community. While passing a few brief observations of his own about the 'anti-christian tendencies' of some of the principles he did not elaborate, as he later said, wisely realising it would 'only excite a tumult' among the audience.[59]

Clearly the response caused Owen to think twice about the next meeting, which was re-scheduled from the Wednesday to the following Saturday. Evidently much recovered, he was able to finish his statement about the community scheme, leaving time for discussion. Unfortunately although many spoke up in support, there were a number in the audience out to cause trouble, mainly on the grounds that Owen's system was said to subvert Christianity. After this even the great O'Connell, who presumably would have supported Owen in principle, failed through 'indecent rudeness' to gain a hearing. When order was restored Owen got to his feet and told the audience that his sole purpose in coming to Ireland was 'to promote peace and comfort amongst all, and remove the wretchedness and misery of the most neglected and suffering peasantry in the world'.[60] While he could readily conclude his visit by meeting only supporters he invited both friends and opponents to a more select meeting the following Thursday to discuss an experiment of a single village. He reiterated that religious opposition could be discounted because as he had repeatedly said there was no intention to interfere with the religious beliefs of the village inhabitants who would be provided with churches, chapels and meeting houses. General Browne of Co Wexford offered to lease 1,000 acres of the best arable land and to advance £1,000 towards the total capital. At this juncture the meeting broke up, apparently without further disruption.

People may have been unrealistic in their expectations but this did not prevent Owen being criticised openly as the papers and pamphleteers continued the debate. An anonymous freeman of St Andrews parish in Dublin supported Owen saying that 'the middle classes will aid this plan if the great and wealthy refuse to cooperate', a prophetic observation as it proved.[61] The critics were also ready with a series of rapid responses. He was attacked in print by an anonymous letter writer who criticised his 'delusive system' for improving the condition of the Irish people.[62] Another anonymous pamphleteer was evidently well informed about conditions in New Lanark where, he claimed, the 'morality of the factory' was less due to Owen's system and more to the fact that 'by his own admission he dwells in the midst of the most religious people in the world'. The author did not believe that Owen's ideas had stood the test of experience at New Lanark and that the 'exemplary character of the Scottish peasantry' provided the explanation for the ordered community there.[63]

Nothing daunted, Owen on 24 April went ahead with a fourth meeting, arranged mainly by invitation, and thus dominated by his supporters. Among their number were Cloncurry, Browne and a number of other gentry, who all favoured the scheme. Owen and his supporters followed this up by calling the first meeting of the Hibernian Philanthropic Society, its aim being identical to the British parent (already in financial trouble, as Owen must have realised), a trial of the village plan. Cloncurry seems to have played a key role and apart from Browne was joined by a number of other distinguished individuals, including Sir Frederick Flood, Sir William Brabazon, Sir Capel Molyneux and the Hon. Mr Dawson. A clergyman, Rev E. Groves, acted as joint secretary. A lengthy subscription list was drawn up and according to one newspaper report the table was 'literally covered with banknotes'. Cloncurry chaired the meeting at which Owen gave another long speech, at one point producing the cubes to explain how they showed the existing divisions of society.[64] All of this seemed promising enough but although his visit had a longer term impact on other Irish Owenites, who later established the community at Ralahine, the immediate impetus seems to have been lost after Owen returned to Scotland. Many Irish visitors subsequently came to New Lanark but nothing more was heard of the Hibernian Philanthropic Society which, like the British society, soon foundered.

His account of events, as earlier in 1817, presented a much more positive outcome. A pamphlet describing the proceedings in Dublin reprinted his statements and gave a rather over-optimistic account of his reception both in the city and the country.[65] Again he seems to have mistaken polite interest for commitment to action, even if he had the support of some of the elite. Whatever the truth of the matter, he was right in his assumption that some of his parliamentary supporters were still prepared to give him the benefit of the doubt. Thus he was called to London to give evidence before a select committee investigating the employment of the Irish poor in June and July 1823. Although the committee's remit was confined to Ireland it ranged over the general causes of rural crisis, the reform of poor relief and the education of the lower classes. It also looked as if it would need to give due consideration to his village scheme, since another petition seeking support then lay before parliament. This, he must have realised, might be a final opportunity to obtain government support for his plan.

Apart from handing in a detailed report on his findings he gave the most important parts of evidence on 25 and 26 June, providing detailed responses to questioning about what he had seen and how the problems might be tackled. Unfortunately things did not quite go his way. The committee, which had among its number Ricardo, were quite prepared to credit him with remarkable achievements at New Lanark, and he could claim, reasonably enough, that it proved that the villages *must* work. But there was a great deal more to it and the committee quizzed him closely on the fact that the villages were meant to be self-supporting and engender complete equality amongst the participants. His answers were not convincing. Surely the commercial success of his villages would be disruptive of existing settlements and how could equality, in moral as well as social terms, be justified? How would industry and skill be rewarded? And surely the examples of successful community organisation in the United States, like the Moravians, the Shakers and the Harmomists, were based on sound religious principles? He could only answer that the character of the new villagers would be reformed by becoming members of radically different communities than any that had preceded them.

He reiterated the well-worn account of how he had found New Lanark
when he assumed management. 'The very dregs of the Highlands' had
been raised to a higher station by 'the withdrawal of unfavourable
circumstances'. It was at this point that Owen, possibly realising that he
was again cornered, launched into yet another of his savage attacks, this
time on the law and lawyers. At New Lanark he had abolished recourse
to the law and for many years no disputes had come before the local
magistrates, because he himself had taken charge and levied fines on
recalcitrants, much as he intended in the new villages. Like the earlier
attack on religion this aside did little to improve his case, especially with
those of his supporters and their friends who happened to be members of
the legal fraternity.[66]

Owen's high public profile and pronouncements on religion had meanwhile caused some of his partners considerable disquiet and they could
also claim with some justification that his numerous absences resulted in
neglect of the business at New Lanark. The problem over religion, Owen
might reasonably claim, could be seen as part of the conflict between Old
and New Society and manifested itself in a long-running campaign by a
few members of the Lanark presbytery against his opinions and actions.
Inevitably this became internalised in an extended debate between Owen
and some of his partners concerning the role that religious instruction
should play in the school at New Lanark. Although the smear campaign
against him dated back to the publication of A New View of Society, it
was not until 1816, when he gave evidence to the select committee on
children's employment, that daggers were really drawn in earnest. Yet
the bulk of the evidence indicates that Owen was basically tolerant of
his workers' beliefs, which were 'complied with and aided to the utmost
extent' by the provision of facilities for worship and continuing to pay a
minister 'for performing divine service in the Gaelic tongue to Highland
workmen'. By Macnab's account, as we saw, religious observance was the
rule and Owen's own house at Braxfield one of daily prayers observed by
a large and moral family.[67]

There was a long running and highly public battle over the schools,
with claims and counter claims by Owen and other interested parties
dating from at least the summer of 1823. Replying to a letter from a Miss
Howell, Thomas Davidson denied her misquotation of his experiences as
a teacher at New Lanark. This seemed to focus on the vexed question of
books. Writing in 1817 he told an enquirer that all the school books he
had seen actually 'destroyed . . . human intellects', but he was forced to
use the 'usual scotch parochial school books' until he could commission
new ones that would be in 'undeviating union' with his principles.[68] Now
he went further and was said to regard school books as useless and that
music had a higher priority in the curriculum than reading. But the major
issues were always religious observation and instruction, both of which

generated a huge furore during 1823–24.

It was the recurring charges of atheism that caused Owen's partners, notably the 'busy, bustling, meddling' Allen, to investigate both the spiritual life of the community and the moral and religious content of the school curriculum. Allen at first opined that Owen's views referred wholly to worldly character, not the religious, but later became increasingly alarmed by his outbursts against religion. In company with Foster and Gibbs, Allen had first visited New Lanark after the new partnership had bought the mills in 1814, and, according to Owen, the three had returned home to London 'delighted with their mission'. Subsequent reports about increasing secularisation upset the Quakers who hardly shared the admiration of other distinguished visitors for the sight of four or five hundred children manoeuvring with military precision in kilts and singing secular songs. Allen and his companions returned on several occasions and during the visit of inspection in 1818 insisted on addressing the community on the importance of religion and the wickedness of elevating reason above the teachings of scripture. This time Owen was ready for them and had the villagers primed up with an address of welcome extolling the praises of the New Lanark establishment and the social and educational arrangements made for themselves and their children. Allen was clearly forced to back off and while admitting that there were those in the outside world who were 'watching for evil' concluded that 'in point of moral and religious feeling, as well as in temporal comfort, no manufacturing population of equal extent can compare with New Lanark'. Allen records that he and Foster afterwards spoke to two of the ministers in Lanark and were given a good account of morals in the village. One of the ministers was urged to visit the school, keep an eye on what was taught there, and report anything 'contrary to revealed religion'.[69]

It was another injudicious move on Owen's part that again showed his lack of tact and finally brought about an impasse with the Quakers. In 1823 he suggested to the school teachers that instead of reading the Bible the senior classes would derive 'more real benefit' from studying geography. When news of this reached Menzies he called an emergency meeting of the presbytery, which immediately and without proof condemned Owen for banning the Bible at New Lanark. A delegation from the presbytery made little headway and subsequently a vitriolic campaign in the columns of the *Glasgow Chronicle* and other papers that picked up the story gave the affair the sort of publicity it could well have done without. The consciences of Allen and his associates were re-awoken and, determined to have their way, the Quakers drew up an agreement for new arrangements in the school. The existing schoolmaster was to be replaced with one thoroughly trained in Lancasterian principles, religious instruction was to be introduced, dancing was not to be taught at the company's expense, nor singing 'with the exception of instruction in psalmody', and 'all males as they arrive at the age of six years should wear trousers or drawers'. This agreement, signed in January 1824, led ultimately to the appointment of John Daniel, a master trained in more rigorous monitorial methods, who apparently introduced a course of science lessons in place of some of the dancing.[70]

Although they might object to the role Owen had given New Lanark in his propaganda campaign, his partners could have little complaint about their financial returns from the enterprise. According to the figures compiled by John Wright, who kept the books in the company's Glasgow warehouse after 1810, the third partnership made a gross profit of £192,915 during the period of Owen's management from 1814 to 1825. During the early years of the partnership Allen and Bentham complained both about the delay in signing the article of co-partnership and being kept in the dark about the progress of the business. Whether this can be regarded as evasiveness on Owen's part cannot be discerned from the record for he certainly kept in touch with his partners during his regular visits to London. In any case, the partners had agreed not to draw any profits until the end of 1817, which gave an extended breathing space to the business following its restructure. When they did so, despite the bad downturn in the cotton trade during 1820–21, they were well rewarded with an annual return on capital of over 15 per cent. Wright's figures provide us with a useful overview of New Lanark's continuing profitability, while other data from balance sheets in the Gourock Ropework Company records indicate in more detail how Owen ran his profit account down, no doubt spending heavily on his propaganda campaign. Correspondingly that of John Walker, the next major shareholder, rose, giving his family the largest financial stake and making the Walkers ultimate heirs to New Lanark.[71]

The year 1824 represented a critical turning point in Owen's career and greatly influenced his future direction. He continued to be hounded by critics. Newspapers reported Owen's refusal of school inspections by the members of the Lanark presbytery. According to the reports Owen had said that they had no more right to do so than anyone else and while welcome as individuals, they would not be as an authority. The grudging concession which he had been forced to make on the school curriculum and the use of the Bible was only the first of several major challenges to his authority and presented a setback to his plans for further reform in the village. Indirectly it also damaged his efforts for a trial of the New System. There were other alarming developments in the community, which caused further disquiet among some of his partners. An outbreak of typhoid fever suggested that Owen's hygiene and housing reforms were not as effective as he had claimed and at the very least was evidence of neglect. There was much ill-feeling when

Owen dismissed seven of the workers for objecting to his interference in the friendly society and apparently taking over its assets. Although we do not know exactly what, if anything, happened at New Lanark, the situation was not helped by unrest throughout the Scottish cotton trade as operatives combined to fight for better wages and working conditions. Workers, evidently fed up with the regime, including the dancing, were rumoured to have left New Lanark for work in other mills, notably that at nearby Blantyre. Two books attacking Owen's views, one by the Rev. Aiton and the other by William M'Gavin, reported these events. Both publications highlighted Dale's achievements at New Lanark, called into question some of Owen's reforms, and claimed that the social provision in other Scottish cotton mill villages was just as adequate. McGavin also attacked in the press through the columns of the *Glasgow Courier*, and other papers picked up the stories. Clearly these rumours and attacks did little for Owen's image as a benevolent employer.[72] Worse was to come, for the death of John Walker on 9 May 1824 robbed Owen of his closest colleague and staunchest ally among the New Lanark partners.[73]

Owen's earlier appearance before the Select Committee and his attacks on religion and the law had prejudiced some of his most powerful allies against him. Nor was his case for a trial of the Village Scheme much helped by his constant stress on 'equality', when he ought to have emphasised the importance of 'co-operation'. At any rate when Owen's petition for further consideration of his plan finally reached parliament on 26 May 1824 it was rejected. In the short debate that preceded this decision, one member went so far as to suggest that 'this visionary plan, if adopted, would destroy the very roots of society'. Even his old supporter, de Crespigny, abandoned the scheme, telling the Commons, 'I have asked Mr Owen not to bring it before this House again'.[74] With this window of opportunity closed and his pride again much deflated, Owen again withdrew to his island at New Lanark to take stock and await further developments. Remarkably, his optimism soon returned when more influential visitors to his island, anxious to see what he had built from the resources available there, were able to confirm what he had gradually come to realise: that his New System might be more successfully implemented in the New World.

## NOTES

1. Hazlitt Vol. 8, p. 66.
2. R. Owen, *Mr Owen's Proposed Arrangements*, London, 1819, pp. 21–2.
3. Ibid, pp. 24–5.
4. Ibid, pp. 92–6.
5. Ibid, p. 101.
6. *Glasgow Journal*, 3 November 1819. There was a growing literature on the

United States. Those of Hulme, Melish and Courtauld seem most likely to have been on Owen's reading list.

7. Harrison, pp. 26–42 on prominent Owenites.
8. R. Owen, *Address to the Working Classes*, London, 1819, Everyman's ed. 1972), p. 154.
9. *Life*, IA, Proceedings of the First Meeting, pp. 237–9.
10. Ibid, p. 240.
11. *Times*, 27 July 1819.
12. *Life* IA, Proceedings, 242–3.
13. H.G. Macnab, *The New Views of Mr Owen of New Lanark Impartially Examined*, London, 1819, a very thorough appraisal of the community and its provisions.
14. Sidmouth Papers, Beckett to Sidmouth, 29 August 1819.
15. Ibid, Beckett to Sidmouth, 13 October 1819.
16. See many references in the minutes of the Commissioners of Supply for the County of Lanark.
17. Southey, *Journal*, pp. 259–65.
18. Various accounts survive, notably in *New Existence*, Part V. Lectures on the Rational System of Society, London 1841; *Robert Owens' Journal*, vol. III, p. 191; Podmore, p. 256.
19. *Life*, pp. 151–2.
20. *Life*, IA, pp. 243–8, Address of the Committee, 23 August, 1819.
21. D.E. Ginter (ed.) *Voting Records*, vol. VI, p. 1277.
22. R.G. Thorne (ed.) *History of Parliament*, vol. II, pp. 609–13; vol V, pp. 18–19.
23. *Life* IA, pp. 332–3.
24. SRO, Melville Castle Mun. Owen to Melville, 8 and 13 February 1820.
25. *Life*, pp. 225–6, 230.
26. Lindsay Institute, Lanark Burgh Records, 6, 8, 11 March 1820.
27. *Life* IA, p. 335; Lanark Burgh Records, 6 April 1820.
28. New College Library, Thomas Chalmers Papers, Owen to Chalmers, 24 April 1820; R.D. Owen to Chalmers, 27 Oct. 1824; Glasgow University Archives, Gourock Mss, Visitors Books; S.J. Brown, *Thomas Chalmers and the Godly Commonwealth in Scotland*, Oxford 1982, pp. 148–151.
29. *Leeds Mercury* 28 August 1819.
30. Commissioners of Supply for the County of Lanark, Minute Book, 1 May 1820.
31. Ibid, 16 November 1820; *The Economist*, 7 April 1821.
32. R. Owen, *Report to Lanark*, Glasgow, 1821, p. 63.
33. *The Economist*, 28 April, 1821.
34. *The Economist*, 19 May, 1821.
35. *Hansard*, 26 June, 1821.
36. *Clydesdale Journal*, 4 May, 1821.
37. *The Economist*, 3 November, 1821.
38. *Edinburgh Evening Courant*, 20 December, 1821.
39. Donnachie, 'Orbiston', p. 140.
40. Gourock Mss, Visitors' Book, 2 August 1821; *DNB*, XIV, pp. 757, 777–82.
41. Visitors' Book, 27 September 1821; J. Gallatin, *A Great Peacemaker. The Diary of James Gallatin* (ed. Count Gallatin), London, 1914, pp. 124–5. *DAB* XI, pp. 53–4.
42. Visitors' Book, 9 October, 1821.

43. Sidmouth Papers, Mary Townsend's Letters, 10 October 1821.
44. Taylor, p. 70.
45. *Proceedings of the First General Meeting*, pp. 17–20, 44.
46. Motherwell District Library, Hamilton Collection, Owen to Wilson, 29 December, 1822.
47. See Donnachie, 'Orbiston', pp. 135–67.
48. On the background to the crisis see S.J. Connelly 'Union Government, 1812–23' in W.E. Vaughan (ed.) *A New History of Ireland Under the Union*, Oxford, 1989, pp. 48–73.
49. PP1823 XI Report . . . on the Poor in Ireland, p. 71.
50. Co-operative Union, Owen Coll. Owen to A.C. Owen, 31 October, 1822.
51. *New Existance of Man upon Earth*, Part IX, pp. 12, 16; Podmore, 278.
52. Owen Coll. Owen to A.C. Owen, 3 and 14 November 1822.
53. Hamilton Coll. Owen to Combe and Wilson, 29 December 1822
54. *Freeman's Journal*, 22 January, 1823.
55. Hamilton Coll. Owen to Hamilton, 25 January, 1823.
56. PP1823 VI, pp. 70–103 refers to the itinerary; Owen to Hamilton 25 January 1823.
57. Taylor, p. 71; *Freeman's Journal*, 8 and 11 April, 1823.
58. Ibid, 14 April, 1823.
59. Ibid, 15 April, 1823.
60. Ibid, 22 April, 1823.
61. Ibid, 18 April, 1823.
62. *A Letter Containing Some Observations on the Delusive System Proposed by Robert Owen*, Dublin, 1823.
63. *A Letter . . . re the People of Ireland*, Dublin, 1823.
64. Podmore, p. 281; PP1823 VI, pp. 200–201.
65. R. Owen, *Report of the Proceedings . . . in Dublin*, Dublin 1823 the reports the speeches and discussions.
66. PP VI 1823, pp. 70–103 and 156–8. 'Rules and Regulations of a Community' seen on pp. 71–4 and set-up costs of £30–50,000 depending on location, p. 97. A Memorial of the Hibernian Philanthropic Society is given at pp. 200–201 Dated 1 July 1823, stating that £4,000 had been raised.
67. Macnab, pp. 115–116.
68. ROMM, item 37, Owen to Miss R.K. Carnegy, 30 October 1817
69. *Life*, IA, Address of the Inhabitants, with Reply 7 May 1818, pp. 329–31; Allen, *Life*, vol. I, pp. 344–7. Full reply pp. 348–53.
70. NAS, Register of the Presbytery of Lanark, 14 August 1823; Allen, *Life*, vol. II, pp. 362–3, 366, 374–5; One Formerly a teacher, pp. 9–12.
71. Butt, pp. 199–201, 212–14.
72. W. McGavin, *The Fundamental Principles of the New Lanark System Exposed*, Glasgow, 1824, esp. pp. 51–2; J.Aiton, *Mr Owen's Objections*, Edinburgh, 1824, pp. 36–40; *Glasgow Chronicle*, 17 January 1824.
73. Friends' Library, Registers, London and Middlesex, 9 and 18 May, 1824.
74. Hansard, 26 May, 1824.

# ELEVEN

# Voyager to the West

A mericans showed great interest in New Lanark and its community and from the time of Owen's father-in-law the place received a stream of visitors from the United States. Partly this arose from the commercial links generated by the cotton trade, and partly from wealthy Americans (some with Scottish roots) doing the Grand Tour. Excepting the War of 1812, the flow continued even during the conflict with France, but became a flood after the peace. A few, no doubt, came to have a good look at New Lanark's spinning equipment, hoping to pirate the machinery and emulate its scale and profitability in New England, where some cotton mills were said to show dividends between 20 and 30 per cent. But the majority, like their European counterparts, were middle class intellectuals or reformers curious to see the well regulated factory village set amid the romantic scenery of the Falls of Clyde and to meet its enlightened and benevolent director, whose work was already known in both the United States and Canada.

Apart from Griscom, the Quaker scientist, who was able to tell Owen much about the course of reform in the United States, another visitor with American connections was George Courtauld, a wealthy English silk manufacturer and one of a great dynasty in the textile trade. During a visit to a settlement called English Prairie in Illinois Courtauld had also inspected a second community set up by Father Rapp and his followers at Harmonie twenty miles distant on the Indiana bank of the Wabash. Courtauld was so taken by the country that he had resolved to settle there himself and had just written a pamphlet about an equitable association to buy and work land on the frontier. This was certainly not the first that Owen had heard about Father Rapp and the Harmonie Society, for John Melish, a Scot involved in the Glasgow cotton trade, had earlier provided the public with a description of the first Rappite community in Pennsylvania which included figures demonstrating its commercial success. While this was in itself highly commendable it was the fact that both Melish and Courtauld praised the high moral character, hard work, and docile behaviour of the Harmonists which probably most appealed to Owen.[1]

However, the most influential American by far was William Maclure, a Scottish merchant who had settled in Philadelphia. Having made his fortune he was free to indulge his interest in geology, to which he made a distinguished contribution in his adopted country. He was a key figure in the establishment of the Academy of Natural Sciences in Philadelphia, which attracted many overseas scholars and became a power house for the exploration of the continent. Accompanied on occasion by either Jospeh Cabell, the son of a Virginian planter or by Joel Poinsett, who later became US secretary in Mexico, he travelled widely in Europe investigating all manner of reforms and developed an interest in education. As well as becoming an ardent disciple of Pestalozzi, Maclure set up an experimental industrial school for poor children in Alicante, run on roughly similar lines to von Fellenberg's at Hofwyl. But Maclure described what he found at Yverdun as 'the most rational system of education I have seen'. He provided Pestalozzi with capital, books and equipment, as well as sending over young Americans to learn the method. He also persuaded Joseph Neef, a Pestalozzian teacher in Paris, to migrate to the United States, where he set up a school and published the first American manual on the system. Few thinkers or reformers would be in a better position than Maclure to assess what Owen had achieved at New Lanark.[2]

It is odd that William Maclure's visit to New Lanark in July 1824 was so long delayed, for he had probably met Owen before and clearly kept himself up-to-date with reform movements in his native country. Given his enthusiasm for educational innovation he was familiar with Owen's views on the subject and had known about the educational and other reforms at New Lanark for some time. On an earlier European tour during 1809 Maclure had met Erik Svedenstierna, then Director of Foundries in Sweden, and it is possible that he discussed his host's visit to New Lanark seven years before, not long after Owen's arrival as manager. Maclure, in a letter to Marie Fretageot, another Pestalozzian teacher and later a leading educationist at New Harmony, described his few days at New Lanark as the most pleasant in his life. He was greatly impressed by what he saw. He was captivated by Owen's success on two counts: first, for the good it would produce; second, because it encouraged him in his own ideas for experimental schools in the United States. Maclure was also struck by the number of ladies visiting the school 'from which it would appear that women are more interested in the improvement of society than men'.[3]

Maclure was clearly not only sympathetic to educational reform but was also familiar with community experiments of the kind Owen advocated, such as those of the Shakers, Moravians and Harmonists in the United States. Moreover in his adopted country, as Owen must have known, he was well connected with the intellectual and political elite and consequently could open doors in high places. Of course Owen himself knew plenty of influential Americans, notably Adams, who succeeded James Munroe as President early in 1825, Richard Rush, the US secretary in London, and quite likely Albert Gallatin, the distinguished diplomat, who was a relative of the Pictets. Given Owen's frame of mind at the time he probably discussed with Maclure his long-standing interest in Harmonie and the impending arrival at New Lanark of Father Rapp's agent, Richard Flower. Whether or not a prospective partnership between himself and Owen in the purchase of the Harmonie Society was considered at that stage is uncertain but it is possible. At the very least Owen could take from Maclure's response to what he saw at New Lanark tacit approval of his plans.

Quite when Owen himself developed an enthusiasm for America is impossible to determine but it probably coincided with the second phase of the propaganda campaign to establish a proto-type model community in the early 1820s. While the community would encourage manufactures its domestic economy was to be closely linked to the intensive agriculture advocated by William Falla and enthusiastically embraced by Owen himself. This advocacy brought him into contact with experimental farmers and agricultural improvers, the most distinguished of whom were Thomas Coke of Norfolk and Sir John Sinclair of Ulbster, secretary of the Board of Agriculture. Coke and Owen knew each other and were mutual allies in their attack on Malthus's view on the population explosion and how the rapidly increasing numbers could be employed and fed. Coke also knew many Americans who visited him in London and at Holkham, venue for the famous annual sheep shearing, which Owen himself attended in July of 1821. At a grand dinner one evening he expounded on his plan to a distinguished company, including the Duke of Sussex, numerous lords and MPs, and gentry like Sinclair and Hamilton. Also a guest was Rush, distinguished in Britain and his native country, friendly to Owen and hence a very useful ally.[4]

Altogether more controversial was John Dunn Hunter who arrived in England the following year and was befriended by Coke. Hunter also became Owen's protégé, appearing with him on public platforms. Hunter was a clever young American, whose experience among the Osage Indians and later adjustment to life with his white countrymen, seemed to personify all that Owen had claimed about character formation and the influence of environment on the individual. Hunter had written a book about his abduction by the Indians and his upbringing among them, a wandering existence, which he claimed had taken him as a boy to the very shores of the Pacific. Confronted with the dilemma of joining in the killing of a party of whites, Hunter had chosen instead to escape from the Indians and integrate himself back into white society. He quickly caught up on his education, studying the classics and entering into polite society. While there was always the worry for some of his fellow countrymen and women about his time with the Indians, the noble savage was seen in a different light in Europe, and thus Hunter provided Owen with a splendid example of the influence environment could be seen to exercise on character formation. Race, however, was not an issue Owen then confronted in any detail.[5]

About the same time Owen also became acquainted with another American, the artist, Chester Harding. Harding became a talented portrait painter, who built up a business in the mid-west before moving east and then setting his sights on Europe. When he arrived in England Rush helped him obtain commissions and he rapidly built up a distinguished clientele including Owen himself, the Duke of Sussex, and other members of the aristocracy. At Rush's in December of 1823 Harding heard Owen explain his new system of education and thought it 'thoroughly republican'. Owen told the company that he regarded the United States as the 'half-way house' between this country and his desired object, so it may very well be that even before the events of the following year he was already thinking about the possibility of trying his ideas in the United States.[6]

Owen had established his first direct link with Father Rapp in August 1820. Writing from New Lanark he expressed interest in the Harmonist community, briefly outlined his achievements at New Lanark, and enclosed copies of A New View of Society and other publications. Owen specifically asked for detailed particulars of the Harmonie community and solicited communication with its leader.[7] Although no further correspondence has survived the interest Owen had shown in the community on the Wabash was enough to guarantee that when Rapp decided to abandon Harmonie for a third settlement back in Pennsylvania he informed Owen of his intention to sell. His messenger and agent, Flower, reached New Lanark in August 1824.

Owen invited Harding to New Lanark and when the latter arrived on 11 August he found Flower already there. According to Harding Owen continued to live in some style, keeping open house to visitors. The Owen family he thought very interesting. Harding was also greatly impressed by the school, by the dancing and the music and thought that the domestic arrangements, the store and medical provision for the workers were all of a high order. He was less impressed by Owen's credulity as Flower described the great advantages of Indiana and of Harmonie as a ready made community. Flower, Harding thought, drew a 'long bow', as he worked on Owen to go and see the place. Harding evidently cautioned Owen and advised him to try Massachusetts or 'some of the older states where there is a more crowded population as well as a greater portion of intellect'.[8] Flower himself had his suspicions about Owen but kept them to himself. He too was amazed at Owen's determination to pursue the purchase of Harmonie, regardless of existing business and domestic commitments or the difficulties of pioneering life in the American wilderness.

While Owen must have realised how different Harmonie was from a Scottish mill village he still saw New Lanark as his model. However, Harmonie had another advantage over any other village built afresh on home ground, the price. He was still a rich man, but Harmonie, by all accounts, was likely to be bought cheaply by British or European standards, a third or even a quarter the price, if the estimates for the proposed Motherwell scheme were anything to go by. Like New Lanark Harmonie was a ready-made community and said to be highly profitable.[9] Even if the experiment was a failure he was unlikely to lose out on his investment. If Rapp's experience was anything to go by he might well make money into the bargain and prove once and for all that the community scheme was profitable.

We have explored some of the explanations for this sudden decision, the most compelling being that despite his rebuff by the British establishment he still regarded himself as something of a visionary and believed that the message of New Lanark still had universal application. Owen undoubtedly had expectations of his ideas being embraced with greater enthusiasm in America and had been told that there were likely to be fewer social and legal restrictions in implementing his plan. As far as the law affected him the British parliament's repeal of the Combination Acts, which had hitherto prevented the emigration of skilled artisans, opened up the possibility of enticing skilled operatives across the Atlantic, something Owen had earlier frowned upon but could now turn to his advantage. He may simply have felt that he could do no more at New Lanark, especially since he had so badly alienated his partners and on a personal level lost the one individual among their number who was most supportive of his schemes. As far as his family were concerned, he certainly saw Robert Dale and probably William, as potential successors, and it was clear that both were adequately equipped by their unusual education to play a role in his ventures. His partners knew little about cotton spinning and less about running a factory community, but so effective had his management and delegation been that he could reasonably leave Robert Dale in charge for an extended period. Whatever the explanation, before Flower left New Lanark Owen had made up his mind to accompany him to Indiana and inspect Harmonie.

And so in that autumn of 1824, leaving Robert Dale in effective charge of affairs at New Lanark and once more abandoning the long-suffering Caroline and the younger children, Owen set out for London. There he saw his partners, acquainting them of his plans and possibly also reassuring himself that they, and Allen in particular, would act as guarantors in any financial transactions likely to arise in his prospective purchase from the Harmonists. He then headed north to Liverpool where he was joined by William, by Flower, who was returning to the United States, and by the faithful disciple, Captain Macdonald. Wasting no time the party took ship for the United States. They sailed appropriately enough in the 'New York', leaving the Mersey on 2 October. Hunter had left earlier, bound for

Philadelphia. By this time rumours were already reaching America about Owen's intended visit.[10]

Wealthy passengers could travel in some style and Owen and his party were no exception. Once the inconvenience of sea sickness was overcome, they and their fellow passengers settled down to an entertaining crossing among what was evidently sociable and intelligent company. Macdonald kept a detailed diary of the voyage, recording much of the social life on board. Interestingly, Owen apparently attended all the religious services and on a number of occasions had detailed and amicable discussions about his views with two Anglican clergymen and many of the other passengers. It may not have been obvious before but Owen was clearly greatly attracted to the ladies and went out of his way to spend time in female company. The New Lanark costumes were duly exhibited. Perhaps, given his personal experience he was beginning to develop what, for their time, were quite radical views on marriage and the equality of the sexes. It could be that part of this thinking included uniform clothing for both sexes in the planned communities, designed to reinforce equality. But again, like the birth control issue, he kept these notions to himself or at least confined discussion to those he thought he could trust.[11]

With him he had a copy of William Thompson's recently published book, *Inquiry into the Principles of the Distribution of Wealth*. Owen had met Thompson in 1822 and was a major influence on his writing. Anna Wheeler, the convinced feminist, also exercised considerable influence on Thompson and the book contained a strong plea for legal sexual and political equality between men and women. Thompson not only attacked sexual inequalities, but also the double standards of sexual morality. More radically still, he sought to promote birth control, divorce by mutual consent, and 'free love'. Owen evidently passed the book around and read out passages from it on occasion. Thompson apart, the discussions of Owen's views, like the company, were friendly and even the clergy declared that 'We will support you as far as our principles will lead us'.[12]

When on 2 November land was sighted beyond the lighthouse at Sandy Hook 'Mr Owen looked with delight upon the New World, considering it the field for great improvements in Society'.[13] Although some, including Marie Fretageot in Philadelphia, knew of his coming, his arrival in New York was only announced a few days before his ship docked on 4 November but no sooner had the party landed and cleared customs than Owen was met by the eccentric Edward Page, propagandist for the 'Scientific Commonwealth', and by the Quaker, Dr Blatchley, president of the New York Society for Promoting Communities. Owen's publications had begun to attract attention from 1820 and this society was mainly responsible for disseminating his ideas. There certainly was enthusiasm among some for his benevolent ideas to organise a colony in America, but how widely his interest in Harmonie was known is impossible to tell.[14]

Owen's party spent their first evening with the promoters of 'Commonwealth', 'a dozen middle aged persons almost all Quakers', who told Owen in the course of discussion that some of the 'leading people discountenanced the idea of communities' but that regardless their society intended to press ahead when funds could be raised. More positively Owen learned that Jefferson at least favoured communities 'in a confined manner, as the Harmonists, Moravians, etc, but opposed the idea as a state proceeding'.[15]

From the following day John Griscom, who had written so eloquently about his visit to the New Lanark schools, entertained Owen and introduced him to the intellectual elite of New York City. By the end of his first week at dinners, soirees and even in the lecture hall, he had met most of the leading faculty of Columbia College, including John McVickar, who was shortly to publish *Outlines of Political Economy*, James Kent, author of *Commentaries on American Law*, Jonathan Wainwright, a future bishop of the city, Judge John Irving, brother of Washington Irving, and a clutch of influential newspaper editors, to whom he expounded his new view of society and explained his community building proposals. The British consul also entertained him to dinner, explaining that although it was not customary to make the first call such was his personal admiration for Owen and the benevolence of his views, that he felt it was 'the duty of every man who wished to benefit his fellow creatures to step forward to receive him'.[16] Those he met provided introductions to others of influence, by far the most distinguished being DeWitt Clinton. As governor of New York, to which post a recent electoral success would return him after two year's absence, he had worked to build the Erie Canal, completed the following year. As mayor of New York he had opened the city's first public school. He had become a member of the US Senate in 1802 and was the unsuccessful Federalist candidate in the presidential election of 1812 won by James Madison.[17]

What must have been immediately obvious to Owen, given his earlier relationship with Fulton, was the enthusiasm with which steam navigation had been adopted on the rivers and lakes of the United States. His first experience of an American steamboat was a trip up the Hudson to Albany to make his call on Clinton. Arriving in the state capital on the 11th he arranged to see Clinton the following day and meantime called on another venerable figure, General Stephen van Rensselaer, who had rented 1000 acres of his land to a Shaker community at Watervleit near Niskeyuna. Owen and his party spent four or five hours minutely inspecting this establishment, which had originally been set up by the English Shaker, Ann Lee. Though according to William Owen there were another 150 or so in the neighbourhood, a hundred Shakers lived in the community, sharing their labour and goods, all appearing happy and contented.[18] As they went round Owen reportedly murmured, 'Very right, quite right', but turned a deaf ear to their warnings about setting up a non-sectarian community. 'Of Quakers? Or Jews? Or what? They shook their heads', wrote William, 'when they found it was for all sects'.[19]

Back in Albany Owen, together with Clinton, dined at Rensselaer's, but being short of time was forced to decline another invitation from the incumbent governor, Joseph Yates. On the return from Albany Owen met the first of several influential manufacturers he encountered on his journey. This was Peter Schenck, a fellow mill master, whose cotton and woollen factory at Matteawan Owen duly inspected. He was later taken by Schenck's brother to an exhibition of American manufactures in New York and later sat up half the night discussing his 'new views'. Several other businessmen approached offering to sell him land in either up-state New York or in Ohio, hoping he would purchase from them rather than from the Harmonists. While they and others clearly had their own interests at heart, the majority, if sceptical about his choice of site and wider vision, at least expressed interest in his immediate plans.[20]

More generally during that fortnight Owen moved in the 'most exalted political and intellectual circles of the Empire State', but the people he met, like those of a similar class in Britain, could hardly be regarded as supporters. However, even the most conservative were struck by his apparent simplicity and charm. Such was the view of Supreme Court Justice Joseph Story, who wrote to his wife about his meeting with Owen saying that, 'He thinks property ought to be held in common, and is so benevolent and yet so visionary an enthusiast that he talks like an inhabitant of Utopia. However he is very simple in his manners and pleasant in his conversation, and gave a considerable interest to the residue of the journey'.[21] Like Story, most listeners and observers caught on to the co-operative aspect of the planned communities, an objective altogether more contentious and problematic than the social and educational ones. However, the fact that the elite were prepared to give him a hearing undoubtedly raised his prestige and brought his ideas to a much wider audience, including those of genuinely communitarian aspirations. Owen achieved widespread newspaper coverage which was altogether more sympathetic and positive than anything he had generated in Britain. By the time he left New York his presence and purpose in the United States was widely reported. To William's surprise on the party's return from Albany on the 16th he found their movements reported in the New York press. Although Owen himself did not know it, news of him was reported that same day in the Cincinnati paper – and eleven days later in that of Vincennes, Ind., the nearest town of any size on the Wabash upstream of Harmonie.[22]

Much of the earlier reporting of Owen's plan derived from British newspapers but more accurate and sympathetic reviews based on his personal explanations now began to appear. Reprinted immediately in the Baltimore and Washington papers was an article in the *New York American* which reported that:

> The means to be employed are, that certain communities should be assembled in any given district – each community living in common, though with separate and private dwellings for each family, and cultivating in common its allotted portion of earth, and prosecuting its own manufactures. These communities inhabit a large square of buildings, within which are the schools, refectories, dormitories, and other public rooms. A perfect equality to reign among all – the children above two years old, to be put under the government of the rules, and to conform to the general scheme, so that education may not vary according to inexperience or indulgence of the parents. Mr Owen has with him drawings and plans, carefully made, and exhibiting most ingenious combinations of a square of 1000 feet, presenting four faces outward of these dimensions, capable of supporting a very large number of families, who might subsist in community at a very small proportion of the expense they now separately incur, and become better, as well as more comfortable by the change.
>
> These plans, together with his general views of the subject, it is the intention of Mr Owen to submit to the congress of the United States – and whatever may be thought of their practicability (and on that subject we will not presume to hazard an opinion) the praise of the disinterested and persevering philanthropy [sic] will certainly not be denied to Mr Owen.[23]

This, as Bestor observed, was a succinct and balanced summary of Owen's ideas, with the emphasis on his social and educational objects rather than the economic ones which had been viewed with such scepticism by British audiences. The friendly tone perhaps indicated the personal enthusiasm with which Owen had explained his proposals since he arrived in America.[24]

The party left New York for Philadelphia on 18 November travelling by steamboat to New Brunswick and then on through Princeton to Trenton by stage-coach, where they arrived safely but nonetheless 'prettily shaken'. Philadelphia surprised them as it had many Europeans, as it certainly matched Manchester or Glasgow in its intellectual society. Indeed long before the revolution it was a city of some significance: by 1770 it vied with Dublin as the empire's second city. It was also a city of Quakers, who had founded it, and thus Griscom had many contacts there to whom he provided further introductions. Being a well-respected scientist himself he was also well known to associates of the Academy of Natural Sciences, one of whose founders was the ubiquitous Maclure. So Owen again had no difficulty meeting people of influence, and indeed his visit of five days was to prove another personal triumph.

During a frantic series of engagements from 19 to 24 November he met most of the city's elite. He dined with Dr James Rush, son of Benjamin Rush, the Revolutionary hero, and the brother of his friend, the diplomat, Richard Rush, and breakfasted with Mathew Carey, the publisher and economist. He lectured at the Franklin Institute, discussed his plans with members of the Athenaeum, and at a large tea party explained the New View to assembled guests. Although he was too busy to address a 'Society of Commonwealth' that had been formed in the city (another sign that he was perhaps dismissive of schemes which were not his own) he did cultivate the editor of the influential *National Gazette* to whom he presented a copy of Thompson's *Inquiry*, passages from which had been read out during the voyage from Liverpool. More significantly he met John Speakman, a druggist, and the distinguished Thomas Say and Charles Lesueur of the Academy of Natural Sciences, to discuss their projected community.[25] Finally, there was Marie Fretageot, Maclure's protégé (and possibly also his mistress), the Pestalozzian teacher, who, as charmed by Owen as Maclure had been on his visit to New Lanark that summer, declared herself a convert to his views. All four, and another distinguished scientist, Gerard Troost, were to be future participants in the New Harmony experiment.[26] Owen speculated, rightly in this instance, that if people like these could be persuaded to join him they would put a very different complexion on his project, something he had possibly not thought of up to that point, a community of ideas, partly peopled by an intellectual élite and by educationists willing not only to pursue their interests but also pass on their ideas to others.

Leaving Philadelphia on the 24th they headed for the capital.[27] At Baltimore the proprietor of the hotel where they stayed told them he and others had once tried to buy Harmonie for $100,000 and that in his opinion it was likely to be an unhealthy place. Nothing daunted, Owen and his party then pressed on to Washington. Entering the city they saw the Capitol by moonlight. But otherwise they were not impressed. The city appeared to be very straggling and although the streets were broad few were actually made up and many blocks stood empty. However, Pennsylvania Avenue and those streets off it looked very grand and the vista from the Capitol to the President's House and on to the Potomac beyond were exceptional in William Owen's opinion.[28] In truth, the city that Pierre Charles L'Enfant had laid out on a scale to represent the genius of the new republic had as yet attained little distinction. The party soon found that hotels were expensive and uninviting, the city's most notable hostelry being the 'Indian Queen', which charged as much as the most expensive in London. Yet the civic hospitality for prominent visitors was often lavish and that same autumn and the following summer when the great revolutionary hero, Lafayette, visited he was fêted with a magnificent reception, dinner and balls that cost more than the city's annual school budget.[29]

Owen's fame may have gone before him but he did not command quite the same attention as the national hero. However, the following day, the 26th, and despite the political turmoil caused by an indecisive presidential election, Owen immediately began a round of calls, starting with John Quincy Adams, by then Secretary of State, whom he had met as minister in London. Adams was a powerful figure, soon to emerge from the political crisis as President, and although having private misgivings about Owen, accorded him due respect in public. He then met William Crawford, Secretary of the Treasury, and another presidential candidate though felled by a stroke, and John C Calhoun, Secretary of War, and later Adams's Vice-President. Owen was afterwards granted an interview with President Monroe, 'a plain and intelligent man', who, possibly to deflect more specific commitments of support, blandly told him that 'this country gave more scope for improvements of every sort than any other'.[30]

Improbably, Owen also had a meeting with a group of Choctaw and Chickasaw Indian chiefs, who had arrived in the capital to negotiate with the government. Through an interpreter he explained to them his views of society and also assured them that he, and many people he knew in England, were anxious to see the Indians united. One of the senior chiefs, evidently a shrewd character, said they were already surrounded by French, Spaniards, English and now Americans, so had little alternative but to try and preserve what they could of their way of life. However, the Indians seemed pleased with what Owen had to say about the influence of environment on character. Hunter, who had again joined Owen's party, but had been suffering from toothache, also met the Indians, and was so affected that he longed to hasten westward.[31]

The commerce of Washington and neighbourhood, as Owen soon discovered, had struggled, mainly because of poor communications. For while steamboats had recently multiplied in great numbers on coastal inlets and navigable rivers, land transport was still primitive.[32] The journey to Pittsburgh along a stretch of the Cumberland Road and going via Hagerstown, Hancock, Smithfield, Brownsville, and Washington, Penn. was something of a nightmare. As they speeded on their way they overtook several parties of emigrants heading for the Ohio and passed numerous droves of hogs being transported to market in the east, some from as far away as Ohio and even Indiana. When they arrived in Pittsburgh William thought it 'a smokey, dirty looking manufacturing town', but since John Speakman had gone ahead with news of his impending arrival Owen was again assured a warm and sympathetic reception. Speakman introduced him to a number of communitarians, notably Benjamin Bakewell, a leading industrialist, who later became president of an Owenite society in the city.[33]

Of much greater significance given his ultimate object was his visit to Economy, the new community being built by an advance guard of Harmonists headed by Father Rapp, and located on the Ohio eighteen miles downriver. Owen could not have known that his movements had been closely followed and reported on by Flower and a network of agents in all the cities he and his party had visited en route to Pittsburgh. Rapp must have been pleased to see him since some of the reports from his contacts suggested that Owen might be persuaded to build his community in the east and abandon Harmonie, a state of affairs likely to alarm Flower who stood to gain a handsome commission when the deal was clinched. All this intelligence was passed on to Rapp's adopted son, Frederick Rapp, the community's business manager, who had stayed on at Harmonie and also anxiously awaited Owen's arrival.[34] Owen and his party were extended every courtesy and reassured that the Harmonists were returning to Pennsylvania because they felt that they had done all they could on the Wabash and that they preferred to move on to new locations periodically because of the good that they knew their settlements would do. This was to become a routine explanation, again trotted out by Rapp's son on several occasions. This seemed fair to Owen because in his opinion 'it would show the world what united human beings can do'.[35] But back in Pittsburgh there was further confirmation of the unhealthiness of Harmonie, caused mainly by summer fever, almost certainly malaria. One of the Harmonists admitted to Macdonald that the place was too warm in the summer. They heard many observations about the Harmonists' hard work, but there were inevitably mixed opinions about their adoption of celibacy and aversion to marriage.[36]

On 6 December Owen and the others set off by steamboat down the Ohio, the entire journey being recorded in considerable detail by both young diarists on board. Travelling 'covertly and secretly' was another of Rapp's spies, who reported that Owen was remarkable and seemed to be 'in morals and activity an extraordinarily effective man'.[37] By the 9th they had reached Cincinnati, over 500 miles downriver. Twenty years earlier it had been forest, but by then it had a population of 13,000 and was reckoned 'the most flourishing and best situated town west of the Allegheny Mountains'.[38] At Louisville, Kentucky, where they arrived on the 10th, they were forced to spend several days waiting for another steamboat. This would continue downriver from Shippingport where the rapids could only be crossed at high water. Owen used the opportunity to explain his views and show his plans to local officials and fellow passengers, as well as meeting a party of English MPs, apparently on a fact-finding mission to the Ohio and Mississippi valleys. Interestingly, Macdonald, and possibly Owen, met a merchant who had been in Mexico.

According to his report, the country was still in a chaotic state of military despotism but the government was nonetheless 'introducing schools and endeavouring to educate the people'. The Mexicans were almost in a state of slavery, though not in the formal sense of the numerous blacks the party encountered in Louisville. Owen had his hair cut by a former slave, who working night and day for years had bought his freedom and that of his wife and child.[39]

The party got underway again on the 13th in a packed steamboat which navigated its way down the Ohio, passing between Kentucky and Indiana. Two days later they reached Evansville and further downstream, Mount Vernon, the Ohio river port serving Posey county in which Harmonie itself was located. They were told that both these ports were 'advancing but slowly' and according to Macdonald 'a silence and dullness about them seemed to confirm such an opinion'. However, quitting Mount Vernon on the 16th they pressed on to their objective, Owen and William going by a shorter route and arriving slightly ahead of the rest. From the surrounding uplands they at last looked down on the village of Harmonie, surrounded by its meadows, orchards and vineyards, with in the middle distance the Wabash river and uncleared forest beyond. All of them no doubt felt much like Macdonald who observed that 'to a traveller just emerging from a forest where little or no improvement has taken place, and remembering the many days he has spent wandering through a thinly peopled and badly cultivated country, the view from those hilly pastures down upon a rich plain, flourishing village, and picturesque river winding through a magnificent forest, is highly gratifying'.[40] Owen himself may well have reacted to Harmonie in much the same way as he had when he first saw New Lanark, reminding him again of his birthplace in the upper Severn valley. After a long voyage, Owen, as Crusoe, had reached his new island.

Frederick Rapp, relieved at his arrival, welcomed him and for the next eight days Owen and his party conducted a detailed inspection of the village and its surroundings, the scene of his great experiment. From balconies at Father Rapp's house and on the roof of a second church they were able to look down on the village laid out before them on a rough grid plan, the streets lined with black locust trees and mulberries – the last providing food for silkworms bred by the community. The dwellings were of log, timber frame or brick, each with its garden enclosure and fruit trees. There were four large communal houses, stores, a tavern, a massive stone granary that doubled up as a fort in case of Indian attack, a wooden church, the later (still incomplete) brick church, and, grander than the others, Rapp's own home. Several small factories were scattered round, notably a rope-walk, silk factory, woollen mill, saw mill, dyeworks, oil mill, brickyard, smithy, and a distillery.[41] On the edge of the village was a labyrinth or maze with a meditational gazebo at its centre. This was said to have been designed by Father Rapp to symbolise the wanderings of the soul through the world and finding ultimate peace in communal living.[42]

When not inspecting the village or engaged in negotiations with Frederick Rapp, Owen spent his time riding about the woods, dining on cold meat and Harmonie wine, seated on old trees and 'enjoying this life very much'. He arrived at Albion on Christmas Eve, having guided himself by a map of Illinois he had with him. According to William, writing on Christmas Day, 'the capabilities of Harmony' seemed to appeal to Owen more and more.[43] Rapp followed Owen to Albion and the discussions continued. Owen returned to Harmonie on New Year's Eve and the following night informed William that 'he had decided on the purchase'.[44] However, on the 2nd Owen and Rapp continued negotiations and the latter presented the Harmonists' terms in writing. This somewhat unsettled Owen who promptly wrote a hasty note to George Flower back in Albion telling him that it was 'very desirable that you should be here as early tomorrow as you can conveniently come for important decisions may be made between 10 and 11 o'clock and it is very uncertain whether they will be for or against a purchase'.[45] Flower duly arrived and on 3 January 1825 the papers were signed. This was apparently a binding agreement, though the terms were later to be revised and become the subject of controversy between Owen and his associates. He had at that juncture become proprietor of 20,000 acres of partially cleared land with 180 brick, frame and log structures, comprising the public buildings, factories, stores and housing for about 700 people. The price was to be $125,000, payable in instalments. The first of $20,000 was to be paid as soon as the deeds had been drawn up and delivered to Owen, on or after 1 May, the rest at regular intervals thereafter.[46]

Although he was to end up paying a great deal less there is some evidence that Owen was cheated by Frederick Rapp, not only on what he paid for the village, but also what he had to pay for the stock and stores left behind by the Harmonists. Still even at that price, roughly £25,000 sterling, he got a bargain by British standards, especially when he had recently talked of set-up costs of £50,000–£100,000. When Solms, a Harmonist agent, heard of the sale he wrote telling Frederick Rapp that he was pleased Owen had bought Harmonie, but doubted if his plans would come to fruition. Owen, he said, 'will not experience the happy success in America of which he flatters himself, least of all in Indiana'.[47] Owen had evidently planned on returning to the east immediately after concluding these preliminary arrangements to purchase. That very afternoon, leaving William and Captain Macdonald in charge at New Harmony, he and Rapp, together with '70 to 80 Harmonians', embarked on a keelboat for Shawneetown where they took a steamboat back up the Ohio.[48]

In setting out for the east and emulating the great Napoleon's Hundred

Days, Owen himself spent a hundred days engaged in a propaganda mission of frantic visits, meetings, speeches and lectures. To all appearances his tour was one of the greatest triumphs of his career. He called briefly at Cincinnati and possibly arranged for the reprinting and publication of a recent London edition of *A New View of Society*. By 22 January he was certainly back in Pittsburgh, holding his first public meeting. According to reports the response was so overwhelming that the court suspended its sitting during the period of Owen's address.[49] He probably also called at Economy, the new Harmonist community, for further discussions with the Rapps.[50] Soon after he was in Philadelphia and so enthused were those he met on his earlier visit that Lesueur, Say, Speakman, Troost and the others associated with the Academy of Natural Sciences were allegedly preparing to join him in Indiana. He again called on Marie Fretageot who wrote to Maclure begging him to re-orientate his educational and scientific interests to New Harmony.[51] An even more ambitious plan possibly crossed Owen's mind at that time, following reports of President Monroe's special message on the Indian tribes, delivered to the House of Representatives on 27 January. The United States, suggested Monroe, should 'act with a generous spirit' regarding Indian lands, should seek co-operation with the Indians, and resolve conflicts peaceably. The united tribes, according to Monroe, 'at no very distant day' would be persuaded to play a role in their own government, which would thus preserve order, educate them, and 'make them a civilised people'. For Owen this may well have suggested that the scope of his communitarian and educational experiment was boundless and that his community on the Indiana frontier was ideally placed to be the centre of such an initiative.[52]

Owen's arrival in Washington was propitious. A complex vote had ultimately resulted in the election as President of John Quincy Adams and the capital was still crowded with the American political élite. His visit had been anticipated in the *National Intelligencer*, which had reported that he seemed 'to have had no thought but how to lessen the sufferings of the unfortunate, and better the conditions of the human race, in every quarter of the world'. When he had actually arrived in the capital, the *Intelligencer* was even more fulsome in its praise, asserting that at New Lanark Owen 'realised . . . effects more extraordinary and rational than any lawgiver of ancient or modern times'.[53] 'It is a fortunate event for the United States', the report continued, 'that this gentleman has come among us with the express purpose of establishing an institution, in which all that has been noticed, and more than what is here possible to be described, are meant to be carried into execution'.[54] Such was his reputation that he was readily given permission to use the Hall of Representatives in the Capitol for two addresses, on the first occasion by Henry Clay, the Speaker, and on the second at the behest of Adams, the incoming President.[55]

In private Adams was far from complementary describing Owen as 'a speculative, scheming, mischievous man'. Adams's opinion is clearly important but if his associate, the distinguished Albert Gallatin, is to be believed his judgement was not to be relied on. Adams, thought Gallatin, was 'a virtuous man, whose temper, which is not the best, might be overlooked, but he wants to a deplorable degree that most essential quality, a sound and correct judgement'. Although Gallatin felt Adams could be controlled and checked by others, something Owen could never be, 'he ought never to be trusted with a place where unrestrained his errors might be fatal to the country'.[56] Adams must have set aside these doubts for he himself attended the first lecture on 25 February, personally entertained Owen two nights later, went to the Capitol the day after his own inauguration to hear the second lecture only to discover it had been postponed, and, on 7 March actually sat through the full three hours of Owen's second discourse. Adams' predecessor, Monroe, several members of the cabinet, the Supreme Court, and of the Congress were also in the audience.[57]

The presentation of his ideas to the dignitaries assembled on Capitol Hill was undoubtedly one of the highpoints of his life. Having been rejected by the British and European élites, here he was at the seat of government in the most powerful nation of the New World commanding the attention of its leaders in his New View of Society and his schemes. Not only was he treated with the utmost respect, but almost fêted at every turn. Newspaper reports devoted almost as much space to him as to Adams' inaugural address. Moreover, another edition of *A New View of Society*, published in New York, came to hand in time for him to read extracts from it at his second discourse. This and the Cincinnati edition were subsequently reviewed in the most important newspapers, so it could reasonably be said his triumph in Washington generated widespread publicity about his ideas and plans throughout much of the United States.[58] How much his personal fortune played a part in the campaign is impossible to tell, though those who travelled with him on the trip to Indiana and on subsequent tours, mention the often quite substantial expenses involved. As in the campaigns in England and Ireland, some might have wondered just how much money talked.

Bearing letters of introduction from Adams, Owen in mid-March visited Jefferson at Monticello and Madison at Montpellier. Returning briefly to the capital he then travelled on to Philadelphia where those he had previously met were even more enthusiastic about his project than they had been earlier. Calling again on Marie Fretageot he wrote with her a joint letter to Maclure with news of what had occurred. Madame Fretageot reported that she had listened to 'the best man explaining a plan which is best calculated for human happiness . . . I have heard and seen but what is positive in my mind as well as in the mind of all those who have had the same opportunity. It is that a great change is to take place on this

part of our hemisphere'.[59] She had already made up her mind to join the
great experiment at New Harmony. Pressing on westward Owen met a
similarly enthusiastic reception and two members of a recently formed
Owenite society at Cincinnati actually accompanied him down the Ohio
to Indiana.

To all appearances Robert Owen's hundred days in the eastern United
States had been a triumph. He had been treated with unfailing courtesy
by the most distinguished men and women in the land. His views had
attracted widespread coverage and as his son could testify people were
already rushing to join the proposed community at New Harmony,
which he himself reached on 13 April.[60] While William had explained
the problems of overcrowding and lack of supplies that had arisen in
his absence in the east, he largely chose to ignore them. Writing on 21
April he told William Allen that the results of his campaign 'exceed the
most sanguine anticipations that I had formed'. With millennial fervour
he continued:

> The United States but particularly the States west of the Allegheny
> Mountains have been prepared in the most remarkable manner
> for the New System. The principle of union & co-operation for the
> promotion of all the virtues & for the creation of wealth is now
> universally admitted to be far superior to the individual selfish
> system & all seems prepared or are rapidly preparing to give up
> the latter & adopt the former. In fact the whole of this country
> is ready to commence a new empire upon the principle of public
> property & to discard private property & the uncharitable notion
> that man can form his own character as the foundation & root of all
> evil. For years past everything seems to have been preparing . . . for
> my arrival. This new colony will be filled . . . before the end of this
> [blank] by useful & valuable families & individuals . . . I believe
> the whole district north of the Ohio River comprising all of the free
> States will be ripe for change before the [blank] of 1827 . . . Our
> operations will soon extend to the blacks & the Indians who by
> singular circumstances have been prepared in a peculiar manner
> for the change which I propose.[61]

His final assertion was presumably a reference to Monroe's earlier statement about future relations with the native tribes. As to the crucial words
omitted in his excitement, did Owen mean to say 'month' or 'year' in the
first instance, and 'beginning' or 'end' in the second?

While glowing optimism well described his feelings at that time, it was
still hard to see how this could actually be harnessed at New Harmony.
Nothing he had done, as Bestor observed, really advanced the practical
experiment to which he had committed himself and much that he did was
to prove detrimental. While engaged in propaganda he had attempted

to raise interest in his community scheme with New Lanark as his model. What was required now that he had actually purchased New Harmony was not theory but practice, demonstration that the scheme he had formulated would work. The time for talking was over.

Unfortunately for Owen, he had neither spelled out what his 'plan' intended, nor explained that it was in reality a mere sketch. Two questions required answers. What system of property rights did he intend to implement at New Harmony? And what criteria would govern the selection of members? Given that he was investing a large proportion of his fortune in the community Owen's relationship as owner with potential members investing their own capital and labour was of vital importance. Despite everything he had said and written over the previous decade Owen had never actually made clear his views on property and the possibility of holding it in common. He himself admitted in a speech at Albion on 30 December 1824, four days before he signed the deed agreeing to buy Harmonie, that only that morning it occurred to him that if he purchased the place 'the community might rent the houses and land from him and cultivate the land in common'. Someone asked what members would do with their own property, to which he replied that it might be farmed 'for the private benefit of the individuals of the society'.[62] This answer showed his naive and confused thinking, an expression of 'airy unconcern', as Bestor put it. What settler on the frontier would abandon his land or arrange for someone to cultivate it in his absence? The second option struck at the roots of Owen's system, for how could community of property be reconciled with unearned income received by individuals from outwith the community?[63]

Incomprehensible as it seems, Owen still had no clear idea if the comunitarians were to be regarded as employees, almsmen, partners or tenants of his as lord proprietor of New Harmony.

Each had a place in his earlier experience or proposals, the first at New Lanark, the second in the poor relief schemes, the third in his plans for 'independent' communities. The last, on the issue of tenancy raised at Albion, was too vague to dispel the inevitable ambiguity in his answer. So those who descended on New Harmony in his absence included many who hoped to find work with Owen, others who hoped to live off his bounty, others who thought Owen would pool his vast property and resources with them on terms of equality, and finally a small number who wanted to form their own community groups and lease land from the founder. While Owen had suggested the last arrangement many years before and regarded it as the only way forward by the beginning of 1826, he certainly failed to make that fact clear during his propaganda campaign of 1825. 'His triumph at Washington was his doom at New Harmony'.[64]

Owen, accompanied by two Swedenborgian Owenites who had joined him at Cincinnati, arrived at Mount Vernon on 12 April and the following day was back in New Harmony. He immediately called a meeting for the 20th.[65] The situation itself, as communications from William Owen and Macdonald had made patently clear, required immediate solutions. The place was crowded and even allowing for the space likely to be available after the last Harmonists left was so packed they scarcely knew where to put new arrivals. The log cabins were being fitted up to accommodate them as best as possible. This influx, mainly from the surrounding districts of Indiana and Illinois, but from as far away as Cincinnati, was largely the result of Owen's propaganda. William and Macdonald, left in charge and forced to give *ad hoc* responses to enquiries, had attempted to reduce the flow by issuing an advertisement providing details of the skills actually need at New Harmony.[66]

At the meeting on 20 April, when 600 to 800 people were said to be present, Owen spoke for between two and three hours about the new system, but does not seem to have provided much detail about his proposals for the community.[67] A committee was nominated and began its deliberations on the 25th. In the course of the following week this committee with Owen's guidance,'made many arrangements', among them drafting a Constitution of the Preliminary Society. With only the minimum of alterations this was in fact a reiteration of the 'Rules and Regulations of a Community' which Owen had drafted in 1823 during his Irish tour and quoted in his Washington addresses. These 39 rules gave a deceptive appearance of precision, but on the key issue of property rights were extremely vague and inappropriate in the context of New Harmony. They assumed a carefully selected and organised cohort of members to provide or raise the capital for the initial purchase. Members were to work for the common good and were to be 'fully supplied with the necessities and comforts of life', but whether their labour was to be balanced against their consumption, and how, was left unexplained. The 'surplus proceeds of the exertions of the community' were not to be apportioned among members, but retained for the establishment of a second community, which seemed to infer that members would forego any right to participate in profits on the basis either of their investment or greater productivity. In the case of withdrawal, the only recognition or protection of property interests in the community was a clause authorising the committee 'to allow any such gratuity as the circumstances of the case may require'. Taken alone and at face value, these provisions clearly indicate Owen's thinking on community of property. But, as Bestor showed in his detailed discussion of these rules, there were other clauses which were totally inconsistent with this idea.

Article VI, for example, gave greater powers at the outset to those who invested £100 or more and actually provided for eventual return of the capital advanced, which undoubtedly implied that private ownership of capital would not disappear when the New Society was underway.

Owen's recent public statements in Washington and elsewhere left this issue vague and ambiguous. On the one hand he proclaimed that inequality of wealth, individual competition, and the trading system must disappear, to be replaced by communities of 'common property, and one common interest' On the other, he asked those with capital to join the Preliminary Society as non-labouring members, and he advocated a bookkeeping system which certainly did not seem to provide community of property, for 'at the end of every year, a certain amount, in value, will be placed to the credit of each family . . . in proportion to their expenditure, and to the services rendered by them to the society'. He did not explain quite how these arrangements were to lead gradually to a system of common property, so the economic doctrines underpinning the communities were confused not to say bewildering.[68]

Owen meantime renamed the Harmonist brick church the Hall of New Harmony and on 27 April gave an address there explaining his current thinking, so far as it went. 'I am come to this country' he said, 'to introduce an entire new state of society; to change it from an ignorant, selfish system to an enlightened social system which shall gradually unite all interests into one, and remove all causes for contest between individuals.' The change in the system could not be accomplished at once, hence the Preliminary Society at New Harmony was to be a 'half-way house' between the old and the new. Contrary to his own feelings he would be forced 'to admit for a time, a certain degree of pecuniary inequality'. He himself would direct the experiment during its first year, members would share its control during the second, and thereafter 'at the termination of the second year, or between that period and the end of the third year, an Association of Members may be formed to constitute a Community of Equality and Independence'. Owen then turned to the constitution, which though hastily drafted was more specific in some regards than its predecessor. Members were to provide their own furniture and small tools, but were to be credited in the books with any livestock they might contribute. As at New Lanark, their daily labour would be assessed and recorded, and they would be debited for goods consumed. Pending an annual balance, the society would advance to each member credit of a fixed amount at the community store. Cash transactions would be limited and except in the case of withdrawal members would receive their earnings only 'in the productions of the establishment, or in store goods'. Far from liberal, the terms were at least clear, and might have remained so if Owen had not muddied the waters with ambiguity. 'I now live', Owen concluded, 'but to see this system established in the world.'[69] More practically Macdonald took a draft of the constitution off with him and rode over to Evansville to get it printed.

Although the constitution was plucked from the past, the proposal setting up the Preliminary Society certainly provided evidence of constructive thinking on Owen's part. This 'half-way house', as he called it, provided a sensible way of deferring some of the problems he had brought on himself. As he must have realised it gave him a breathing space of two to three years to produce a plan that might actually work, either by thinking through the fundamental problems he had hitherto ignored, or again by improvising practical solutions of day-to-day management as he had done with such success at New Lanark. However, the problem, for which Owen had only himself to blame, was that New Harmony was filling up with people he had neither selected nor recruited. For months after he purchased the place, he had given no clue as to how he intended to recruit the population for his experiment and he had been able to exercise little control over those who had now settled in the community.

Despite the problems of overcrowding and self-selecting personnel congregating on the place, much was being achieved. Thomas Pears, who had moved with his family from Pittsburgh, felt that the organisation of the schools and the boarding houses, the work of the tradesmen and those employed in agriculture, was going so well that he thought they had been thus engaged for a year rather than just a few months. 'And this', said Pears, 'has been accomplished by one man, who has drawn together people from all points of the compass, various in habit and disposition, to mix together like brethren and sisters'. On listening to Owen, Pears said of himself that he was 'always in the hills'. Although no great orator, Owen appeared to have 'the power of managing the feelings of all at his will'. Owen was a wonderful man, he thought.[70]

Soon after the last of the Harmonists had departed Owen himself announced that he was leaving New Harmony for a while because he did not want to succumb to the summer heat and that he needed a rest. Whether or not these were just excuses, it had clearly been his intention to return to Britain at the earliest opportunity, and his reasons for doing so were more complex than they at first appear. He obviously had to sort out his financial affairs, not only in connection with the purchase from the Harmonists, but also with his partners. As far as the latter were concerned he perhaps hoped to persuade them to back his enterprise in Indiana, which would thus allow him to maintain a substantial stake in New Lanark, even if he was no longer managing partner. Indeed he may well have thought that he could stay on as manager and commute across the Atlantic. Given his intention that Robert Dale join William at New Harmony and that his younger sons would assist in the business as their elders had done, this does not seem improbable. Many years experience of New Lanark's well-oiled machinery had shown that the place worked efficiently in his absence so a proposal of this kind could possibly find favour with his partners. He may also have thought he could play a role at Orbiston, demonstrating personally that his ideas worked equally well in the Old World as in the New. According to a later report in the *New Harmony Gazette* the prime intention was to visit his family and return with them as early as possible, but it was unclear whether this meant the entire entourage, including Caroline and her sisters.[71] He had recently declared his intention of becoming an American citizen, so he was almost certainly thinking about a permanent move both for himself and his family at that stage.[72] Marie Fretageot thought that he was going to gather further support, bringing new settlers and 'part of the children of New Lanark', presumably to get the school at New Harmony off to a sound start.[73] Whatever the explanations for his decision a major consideration was his self-esteem, something he denied, but privately cherished. His experience in America had demonstrated that he could open doors in the highest circles and that his community plan would work.

Owen and Macdonald left New Harmony on 5 June, calling at Mount Vernon, Louisville, Cincinnati, Marietta and Pittsburgh, where his discourses gave enthusiastic impressions of what he had accomplished rather than answering his critics. Thereafter, Owen and Macdonald stopped off to visit Economy, discussing further the financial transactions connected with the sale of Harmonie.[74] It may have been at this juncture that the Rapps agreed to settle for $95,000 in cash, leaving Owen with the option for further purchases of land or goods in future. Deviating from his usual route Owen and Macdonald called at Meadville, viewed the Niagara Falls, and then headed east across New York state by the completed sections of the Erie Canal. He reached New York city on 4 July, travelling on to Philadelphia to lecture again at the Franklin Institute and meet the numerous savants he had previously encountered. He then made a brief trip to Boston, where he met the aged John Adams, to whom Owen's servant, Watson, having met all the other surviving presidents, was also introduced. Adams evidently told Watson that his master was 'a very smart man, and would be of great service to the Human Race'.[75] Owen arrived back in New York on 15 July. Before leaving he met Maclure, who declared himself 'highly delighted and astonished at his success.' Maclure found himself in agreement with most of Owen's ideas but reflected that 'the materials he has to work upon are stubborn, crooked and too often buck in an opposite direction'. Education, he insisted, 'must be the chief support and foundation of the system'.[76] The following day Owen embarked for England aboard the 'Canada' and reached Liverpool on 6 August 1825. While time ticked away, Owen, unlike Crusoe on his island, had turned his back on the reality. The vital experiment at New Harmony had been abandoned to chase the phantom of public opinion on both sides of the Atlantic Ocean.

# NOTES

1. E. Courtauld, *Address to those who may be Disposed to Move to the United States*, Sudbury, 1820; J. Melish, *Travels in the USA, 1806–1811*, Philadelphia, 1812; *Owen's Proposed Arrangements*, pp. 91–100; Taylor, p. 48.
2. On Maclure see *DAB*, vol.XII, pp. 135–7.
3. New Harmony Workingmen's Institute, Maclure Journals, 22 November 1809; 30 July–1 August, 1824.
4. On Coke and the annual gatherings see R.A.C. Parker, *Coke of Norfolk*, Oxford, 1975 and A.M.W. Stirling, *Coke Of Norfolk and His Friends*, London, 1912; R.M. Bacon, *A Report of the Transactions at Holkham*, Norwich, 1821, pp. 61–5, 118–24.
5. Taylor, pp. 76–7.
6. M.D. White (ed.) *Sketch of Chester Harding*, Boston, 1890, p. 59.
7. Owen to G. Rapp, 4 August 1820 quoted in Arndt (ed.), *Indiana Decade*, pp. 89–9.
8. White, pp. 86–8.
9. The most impressive figures were quoted in *An Indication of Mr. Owen's Plan*, London, 1820. Therein the Harmonist Society was said to be worth $20,000 in 1805, but by 1811 to hold land worth $90,000 and stock of $130,000.
10. C.D. Snedeker (ed.) *The Diaries of Donald Macdonald 1824–1826*, Indiana Hist. Society 1942 (reprinted 1973), p. 159.
11. Ibid, p. 169.
12. Ibid, p. 166.
13. Ibid, p. 173.
14. NHWI, Maclure-Fretageot Corr., Fretageot-Maclure, 21 Oct. 1824; A.E. Bestor, *Backwoods Utopias*, Philadelphia, 1950, p. 104.
15. Macdonald, p. 176.
16. Ibid, p. 181.
17. On Clinton see *DAB*.
18. J.W. Hiatt (ed.) *Diary of William Owen 1824–1825*, Indianapolis, 1906 (reprinted 1973), pp. 9–15.
19. Ibid, p. 14.
20. Bestor, pp. 105–6.
21. Quoted in Bestor, p. 106.
22. W. Owen, p. 24; Bestor, p. 107; Bestor Papers, Chronologies 1824.
23. *National Intelligencer*, 16 November, 1824.
24. Bestor, p. 107.
25. On Say, *DAB* vol.XXI, pp. 401–2 and Patricia Stroud, *Thomas Say*, Philadelphia, 1992; on Lesueur, *DAB* vol. XI, pp. 190–191.
26. On Troost see *DAB* vol. XXIII, pp. 647–8.
27. W. Owen, pp. 36–7; Arndt, *Harmony on the Wabash*, Worcester, Mass., 1982, p. 294, J. Solms to F. Rapp, 29 November, 1824.
28. W. Owen, p. 39.

29. Constance M. Green, *Washington. Village and Capital*, Princeton, 1972, pp. 105, 108, 111.
30. Macdonald, p. 217.
31. W. Owen; pp. 42–5; Macdonald, pp. 217–8.
32. Green, p. 114.
33. W. Owen, pp. 49, 51.
34. Arndt, *Harmony* reproduces some of the confidential reports to the Rapps, pp. 295–302, 313–4.
35. Ibid, G. Rapp to F. Rapp 6 December, 1824.
36. Macdonald, pp. 229–32.
37. G. Rapp to F. Rapp 5/6 December, 1824.
38. Macdonald, p. 236.
39. W. Owen, pp. 66–7.
40. Macdonald, p. 40.
41. Initial impressions in W. Owen, pp. 72–4; Macdonald, pp. 243–8.
42. Podmore, p. 287; D. Pitzer & J. Elliott, *New Harmony's First Utopians*, Indianapolis, 1979, pp. 288–9.
43. W. Owen, pp. 82–3.
44. Ibid, p. 92.
45. Arndt, *Harmony*, p. 375, R. Owen to G. Flower, 2 Jan. 1825.
46. NHWI, Branigin-Owen Papers, Memorandum of Agreement, 3 January 1825.
47. Arndt, *Harmony*, p. 474, J. Solms to F. Rapp, 17 March, 1825.
48. NHWI, Pelham Papers, W. Owen to W.Pelham, 22 January, 1825; W. Owen, pp. 94–7.
49. Macdonald, p. 288; *Times*, 9 March 1825; W. Owen, p. 120.
50. W. Owen to W. Pelham, 22 January 1822.
51. NHWI, Maclure-Fretageot Corr., Fretageot-Maclure 11 February, 1825.
52. *Addresses and Messages of the Presidents of the U.S.*, New York, 1847, Vol. 1, pp. 536–8.
53. *National Intelligencer*, 1 December, 1824; reporting his return east, 8 February, 1825.
54. Ibid, 17 February, 1825.
55. Owen's unsubstantiated assertion ten years later in the New Moral World, vol. I, p. 362, 12 September, 1835.
56. R. Watters, *Albert Gallatin*, New York, 1957, p. 319.
57. Published as R. Owen, *Two Discourses on a New System of Society*, Louisville, Ky., 1825 and other eds. in Washington, D.C., London, etc. the same year. Reproduced in Claeys (ed.) *Selected Works*, vol. 2, pp. 1–37. The Second Discourse appends the 'General Rules and Regulations for an Independent Community' and a Statement of the objectives at Harmony regarding 'a Preliminary Society'.
58. Bestor, p. 112 lists the widespread coverage in the press and the various editions of the works which subsequently appeared.
59. Maclure-Fretageot Corr., Fretageot to Maclure, 28 March, 1825.
60. W. Owen, p. 134; Macdonald, p. 292.
61. Co-operative Union, Owen Coll., Owen to Allen, 21 April, 1825.
62. W. Owen, p. 90; Macdonald, p. 260–1.
63. Bestor, pp. 116–7.
64. Ibid, p. 116.

65. Arndt, *Harmony*, p. 520, W. Owen to G. Flower, 13 April, 1825.
66. Co-operative Union, Owen Coll., W. Owen to R. Owen 7 February 1825; 'Notice to Farmers, Tradesmen and Others'.
67. Macdonald, p. 292.
68. Bestor, pp. 118–119.
69. *New Harmony Gazette*, 1 October, 1825 reprints the speech.
70. NHWI, Pears Papers, T. Pears to B. Bakewell, 2 June, 1825
71. *NHG*, 1 October, 1825.
72. Macdonald, p. 294.
73. NHWI, Maclure-Fretageot Corr., Fretageot to Maclure, 11 February, 1825.
74. Arndt, *Harmony*, p. 571, F. Rapp to W. Owen, 21 June, 1825.
75. Macdonald, p. 304.
76. NHWI, Maclure-Fretageot Corr., Maclure-Fretageot, 15 July, 1825.

# TWELVE

# Feudal Overlord

I n Owen's absence in America there had been a number of significant developments, of which the most critical to the success of his
community scheme in the British Isles were a clutch of new Owenite
'co-operative societies', notably that in London, and efforts by some of his
followers to establish communities, particularly that at Orbiston, which
Hamilton and Combe were directing near Motherwell. Perhaps more than
he realised, his ideas had generated continuing interest among a growing
band of followers, although he himself had exercised little direct influence
on the subsequent train of events. The man had become a movement,
modest certainly, but nonetheless some of his most enthusiastic disciples
had actually been inspired to put the precepts of the New System into
practice in the apparently apathetic context of Old Society in Britain.

The co-operative societies, several of which had sprung up in different
guises, were devoted to 'the formation of communities of mutual co-
operation and equal distribution' and attracted mainly middle class and
artisan support. The most influential, the London Co-operative Society,
had inherited much of its agenda from the earlier Co-operative and
Economical Society of 1821, and was then the principal disseminator
of Owenite propaganda.[1] The likelihood is that it was funded directly
or indirectly by Owen himself. From its office in Pickett Street, Temple
Bar, he published the first English edition of his *Two American Discourses*
and a pamphlet detailing the articles of agreement for a community.[2]

Orbiston was essentially the successor to Owen and Hamilton's
Motherwell Scheme and indeed Owen in the interim had sold back
to Hamilton for nearly £15,000 the land he had previously acquired
for the proposed community.[3] Hamilton and Combe had pressed ahead
and were making good progress at Orbiston, where construction work
had actually got underway in the spring even before the legal and
financial arrangements had been completed. Here, according to Scottish legal practice, resort was made to a partnership agreement setting up the Orbiston Company. It was to have a capital of £50,000 in
200 shares of £250 with Abram Combe designated as company trustee. Several of the original subscribers to the Motherwell Scheme took
shares in Orbiston, and using the paid-up share capital and land as
securities Combe had borrowed nearly £20,000 to help finance the project. Initially at least this seemed to the casual observer something
akin to a conventional business enterprise with the partnership acting

as proprietor rather than an individual as Owen was at New Harmony.[4]

Owen's movements during his brief sojourn in Britain are unclear.
There are few clues in Robert Dale's journal as to when exactly Owen
returned to Braxfield to visit his wife and family. The journal records a
long spell of beautiful weather from July to September, during which time
Owen's son was busy 'preparing for our Journey to America'.[5] Subsequent
reports suggest that Owen went directly to New Lanark, afterwards
visiting Orbiston to inspect the buildings for the new community, before
heading south to London, where he arrived on or about 20 August, and
giving a lecture on the 24th.[6] Assuming he returned to Lanark about
the 8th and left there three days before arriving in London, he must
have spent less than a fortnight at home. This may be explained by his
anxiety to sort out with his partners the financial details entailed by the
Harmonie purchase and at the same time try to secure his position as
managing partner at New Lanark. However, there is no evidence as to
whether or not he wished to continue as manager, even if his partners
would have agreed to such an arrangement.

Soon after arriving in the capital he breakfasted with members of the
London Co-operative Society, and later that week delivered another
address to the same body in which he repeated his account of what
had transpired in the United States and progress at Orbiston.[7] He must
have spent the next few weeks negotiating with his partners, since he had
already anticipated withdrawing capital from New Lanark. Indeed, when
Robert Dale arrived in London on 29 June after a visit to Holland, Gibbs,
one of the New Lanark partners, told him that bills for £6,000 in part
payment of Harmonie had been presented at Barclays for acceptance.[8]
Owen's son actually attended the meeting of the partners the following
day when he found that more bills had been presented, totalling in all
£18,000. These and another for £2,000 which was still to be presented,
the partners authorised Barclays to accept, acting as Robert Dale put
it, 'a friendly and liberal part in this matter'. Owen at that point had
therefore paid fourth-fifths of the original sum agreed with Frederick
Rapp. When he knew the bills had been honoured Rapp reported that
Owen 'had almost paid for the purchase of our Society', was clearly a
man of great property and respectability in Scotland, but continued to
doubt whether he would have much success in America.[9]

Owen's withdrawal or dismissal from management at New Lanark
could have been anticipated long before the autumn of 1825. The major
problem was the rift with Allen over religion and education, which had
reached such a low point by 1822, that Allen was suggesting they part
company.[10] In August of that year Allen exercised his right to call an
extraordinary general meeting of the partners 'to take into consideration
the propriety of purchasing Three of the Shares belonging to Robert Owen

on such terms as may be agreed upon . . . and to take *steps* into . . . making regulations for the future conduct of the concern'.[11] It seems unlikely that this occurred, but the following year on 31 July 1823 Allen arranged a meeting at which 'the question of the Continuance of Robt Owen as Manager will be brought forward'.[12] At the end of that year Owen, possibly anticipating his withdrawal, actually proposed to transfer one share each to Robert Dale and William. While the circumstances surrounding his break with his partners are far from clear, he effectively ceased to be managing partner at New Lanark that September. Whether he knew it before he left for America is uncertain. The other important outcome of the discussions was the release of a substantial proportion of his own capital to pay the Harmonists and provide additional funds for other purchases, store goods, travelling and other expenses, which must have been considerable. His personal fortune, though undoubtedly diminished, was still large. And it must be remembered that he retained a personal interest in New Lanark until at least 1831, continuing to derive income from its admittedly reduced profits. Not only that, the family benefited from the shares held by his sons and the interests represented by the Dale Trustees on behalf of his wife and her sisters. Wright, the faithful overseer of much of the New Lanark business, had expressed foreboding at the New Harmony purchase, largely because of the drain on the family's fortunes.[13]

The lives of Owen's wife and family were thrown into confusion by his removal from New Lanark. When they moved out of Braxfield that autumn they did not know if it would be for the last time, and since Dale's house in Glasgow had evidently either been sold or let, Caroline and the family took a house in Holland Place, then one of the most westerly streets in the city. From there she wrote to William saying that while they were all cheerful she herself found the distance separating her from her friends a great trial and 'the absence of a dear husband and children I feel very much'. 'The New System', she told William, 'may bring happiness but it has created a great deal of uneasiness in some individuals.' She had also been amazed to hear that Applegarth, one of the teachers at New Lanark, intended to leave his wife and children and head for New Harmony in the coming spring. 'I shall cease to be astonished at anything now', she concluded sardonically.[14] At New Lanark itself, Jane added, some of the workers and friends of the family wished that 'persons and things were in their old places again'.[15] Wright, in questioning Owen's wisdom in buying Harmonie at all, had gone further. If he did so, Wright warned, it would result in 'many impediments to your own happiness and that of your dear family'. He did not know what financial arrangements Owen had made at that point, but in his opinion, 'on any terms it is too dear'.[16] Jane Dale Owen assiduously kept a scrapbook of cuttings relating to her father's activities, which ends abruptly in 1825 and was later left behind at

Braxfield House when the family were forced to abandon it for less costly accommodation.[17]

Apart from dealing with his financial affairs, seeing various publications through the press, and making travel arrangements for his return to the United States, Owen also commissioned the construction of a scale model 6 feet square of his proposed community. The builder was a young architect and social reformer, Stedman Whitwell, whose sister was a teacher at New Lanark and later at Orbiston. Whitwell had earlier been recruited to produce the drawings and plans which Owen had previously displayed at his lectures and which accompanied him on the first American trip. Over the years Owen had offered many descriptions of his 'parallelograms' which Whitwell worked up into model form, raising the proposed community off the prairie on a platform. Family houses under peaked roofs surrounded the square, while dining halls and communal facilities extended toward a central greenhouse. The corner buildings were to be schools and 'conversation rooms' for adult communitarians. One of Owen's more imaginative ideas, borrowed from New Lanark, was extending bunks from the walls at night and pulling them up to the ceiling to free space by day. Observers could see that the physical environment was to be held in high regard, for industry (not represented on the model) would be located at a distance. It has to be said that while Owen wanted to use architecture to reinforce social design, he, and perhaps his architect, were more concerned with physical display. There is no doubt that the model caused a sensation. Unfortunately, although Owen sensed the power of environmental design as a force for social change at New Lanark, events would prove that he did not really understand how to harness it successfully at New Harmony.[18]

The model was completed in time to be displayed at Owen's lecture on 26 September. The lecture, to a large audience crowded into the theatre of the London Mechanics' Institution, restated his principles and explained the advantages that would result from the general adoption of the New System by 'correcting the present misapplication of the powers of society [and] increase their means of happiness tenfold'. He then moved a series of resolutions calling for the introduction of a new social system ('as proved by the societies of Quakers, Moravians, Harmonists, etc') and the development of an experimental society 'within a short distance of London'. In response to questions about the practical economics of the communities Owen said that 'the property of each community was to be invested in the members of it'. He himself 'would never again invest property with a view to profit'. He continued by saying that 'Whatever he had done or would do in America, he would be content with the simple interest of his capital invested there'. He thought others would do the same and that those who had been lent money would reciprocate and so 'the system would be gradually extended'. He had tried it, he said, and not been disappointed. However, despite the expectations of his followers that he had returned to Britain to encourage others to join them, he cautioned against migration to the United States. America was very different from Europe, migrants could not expect home comforts on the frontier, and the climate would expose them to risk. With these rather thin excuses he concluded that his followers would be better off forming their own communities at home 'where they had greater opportunity of enjoying happiness and doing good'.[19] He evidently tried to impress this point on the Home Secretary personally, but Peel was too busy to see him.[20]

Meanwhile back at New Lanark Robert Dale had been so busy he had no time to keep up his journal but when he did take it up at the end of September he noted that the heavy luggage was being sent in advance by steam packet to Liverpool. This included 'our library of about 1,400 volumes'. Robert Dale left home on the 27th, and possibly accompanied by Macdonald, reached Liverpool the following day. Owen, along with Whitwell and Owen's manservant, arrived on the evening of the 29th.[21] On 1 October the party set sail on the *New York* minus the model and some of the luggage which had been delayed on its way from Greenwich. Schmidt, the servant, stayed behind to ensure its safe passage on a later ship.[22]

On board the *New York* Owen and the party found themselves among a particularly lively group of individuals including a troupe of opera singers headed by the Garcias, a famous Spanish musical family. The singers were clearly versatile, their repertoire embracing not only 'catches, glees and humorous songs', but also a passable imitation of the 'Scotch bagpipes'. Much of the voyage was spent playing games and quizzes, singing, dancing and listening to music. A newspaper, *The Sextant*, was published three times a week. Owen joined in these activities but according to Robert Dale he also had more serious discussion and arguments with fellow passengers about his New System. Writing this aside in German Robert Dale thought that his father did not accomplish much. 'It seems to me', he continued, 'that he expresses himself in too vehement a manner and is too general in his criticism of the present system. Such general criticism is not only unjust but it also irritates almost all those who have other ideas. He tends to fall into the same fault which he criticises in others'.[23] Owen also wrote a letter to the Americans, which was published in the New York papers soon after his landing. Towards the end of the voyage a song entitled 'Ebor Nova' was composed with words by Whitwell and music by Garcia, which was sung on deck in full chorus as the ship entered New York harbour.

Like Washington on his first visit, New York was caught up in a wave of excitement, on this occasion accompanying the opening of the Erie Canal, or 'Clinton's Ditch', as it was popularly known. Owen and the others were

sent tickets for a ball to celebrate the event. They perhaps believed they
had something to celebrate since soon after landing Dr William Price, son
of the superintendent of the Friend's Boarding House at Westown near
Philadelphia, whose brother, a physician Dr Philip Price, had visited
New Lanark and was already at New Harmony, brought news of the
community. Price, who with his family, including his wife's sister-in-law,
Helen Fisher, was to join Owen's party bound for New Harmony, reported
that while things were going along steadily and the place had remained
healthy over the summer, some of the communitarians were idle and this
had created considerable dissatisfaction among the rest. However copies
of the gazette and some letters seemed to confirm that all was well.[24]

On 11 November they travelled to Philadelphia. In the city Owen again
met all the enthusiasts who had earlier embraced the New System and
held detailed discussions with them about arrangements for the journey
to Indiana. The potential communitarians included the Academicians,
Thomas Say, Charles Lesueur, Gerard Troost and other intellectuals
and educationists with whom they associated. Owen also talked to
Maclure, Marie Fretageot, and another of Maclure's protégé's, William
Phiquepal d'Arusmont, about plans for the school at New Harmony,
to which the two teachers had agreed to convey a number of their
pupils. Maclure also promised to secure the services of Joseph Neef,
the first Pestalozzian teacher he had sponsored in the United States, by
then settled in Kentucky. Although he did not actually know what the
situation was at New Harmony, Owen agreed to place an advertisement
for workmen in the local papers.

Having completed details of the journey west, Owen returned to New
York, where he made arrangements to ship the bulk of the luggage to New
Orleans and from there up the Mississippi and Ohio to New Harmony.
Copies of the first edition of the *New Harmony Gazette* were reprinted
and sent to editors and literary societies. Clinton made the City Hall
available and there in their saloon the model was placed for viewing
and on the 18th for a public meeting at which Owen explained his
ideas. This again caused Robert Dale some discomfort for he thought
his father 'criticised hardest the existing system . . . in a too vehement
and absolutely irritating manner'. 'However', he wrote, 'all the people
have accepted it all very well, and have even applauded the parts which
hit them hardest.' The impression created would certainly have been far
greater had Owen 'understood how he ought to talk'.[25]

They set out once more for Philadelphia, making a side trip on 22–23
November to visit Joseph Bonaparte, formerly king of Naples (1805–8) and
of Spain (1808–14), but, like several prominent Bonapartists, now living in
exile in the United States. He was hardly in reduced circumstances since
he had established himself and his family near Trenton in a splendid
plantation house overlooking the Delaware.[26] Owen added another figure

to the list of personalities he had met during his career, including a notable clutch of French republicans, Bonapartists, and Bourbons, all of whom apparently gave his notions a sympathetic hearing. In Philadelphia he gave two lectures to explain his system, both well attended and sympathetic. At the second he responded to a question about the scriptures by saying that in his opinion they were no more inspired than any other book. To Robert Dale's surprise his father's answer was applauded. They found a couple of dozen mechanics had responded to the earlier advertisement, but none were very suitable so their names were taken to be contacted from New Harmony if required.[27]

Owen was by now in a desperate rush to head west and wasted little time pressing on to Pittsburgh, which they reached on 1 December.[28] Some of Maclure's people travelled with them and soon the whole party of men, women and children were assembled on the banks of the Ohio. There they found that the river was too low for steamboats, and this seemed likely to be so for some time. Accordingly Maclure got a keelboat fitted out, all achieved in three days. The craft was 85 feet long, 14 feet wide and moved by six long oars. Below deck was a compartment at the front for the crew, a second cabin for the women, called 'Paradise' by the men, which doubled as the galley, a third for the men, also used for dining, and a fourth at the rear for the children (nicknamed 'Purgatoire' by Lesueur). The quarters were furnished with tiered bunks, crude chairs and tables, and pot-bellied stoves.[29] In these cramped and humble quarters the party made itself as comfortable as it could. On the masthead flew the vessel's flag: on one side 'Harmony' and on the other 'Philanthropist' (spelled in French by Leseuer), which Owen had called the boat in honour of its patron, Maclure. Optimistic though this sounded, no doubt catching the mood of the moment, Owen and the others, like Crusoe and his shipmates, were to make temporary landfall in less than promising circumstances.

Considerable dispute surrounds the passenger list of the *Philanthropist* because a number of individuals either came aboard late or left before the craft reached Mount Vernon. The organisers consisted of Owen and Maclure, the scientists, Say (elected captain) and Leseuer, the educationists, Marie Fretageot and Phiquepal, together with ten of his students, the artists and musicians, Balthazar Abernasser (Obernesser), a Swiss artist, who taught painting at New Harmony, and Virginia DuPalais, ward and student of Leseuer, who was to teach art and music there. Another notable was the physician Dr William Price, his wife Hannah, and their three children. Apart from Owen's son, several workmen and the original crew of eleven, there were eleven other passengers. Among them was the mysterious Helen Fisher, Russian sister-in-law of Hannah Fisher Price. Married briefly to Hannah's brother, Miers, merchant in St Petersburg, she was widowed soon after and eventually migrated to the United States. She had met Owen in Philadelphia and quickly became 'attached to his system'. Whether she had any emotional attachment to him is unknown, though they certainly spent time alone together on the trip to New Harmony. Macdonald and Whitwell, by the by, had stayed in the east transporting the model to Washington where it was shown to President Adams and then put on display. They did not join the vessel until 8 January.[30]

On a cold Thursday, 8 December 1825, the keelboat cast off on its voyage down the Ohio. In two days it made only 20 miles before running aground on some rapids near the Harmonist village of Economy. Here Owen, Maclure, Leseuer and Phiquepal left the vessel to seek Father Rapp's help. Six strong men were sent to free the boat which proceeded the following morning to Economy. Owen and his entourage were entertained liberally by the Rapps, drinking fine wine, the best of which was made with wild grapes picked at New Harmony. Owen's son observed the traits that gave the Harmonists their cohesion in community, knowing 'admirably how to act in concert, to be steady, retired, cautious and industrious, but not to possess superior intelligence or liberality of sentiment'.[31] Owen, like the others, could see the fruits of strong communal organisation in the new town of Economy. He may well have asked himself whether the unanimity of purpose and economic success could be replicated among a more random population at New Harmony. He presumably thought so, even though others already had their suspicions.

At that point Owen decided to return to Pittsburgh to obtain deeds for the New Harmony property and thus missed the most exciting adventures of the *Philanthropist*. For 28 days, 11 December 1825 to 9 January 1826 she was stuck in ice at Safe Harbor only 15 miles below Economy, before being freed to continue on her way down the Ohio. Owen, evidently in the company of Mrs Fisher, who, according to Robert Dale, left the ice-bound keelboat on 16 December, visited Yellow Springs, Greene County, Ohio, an Owenite community 60 miles up country from Cincinnati. This had been established by a Swedenborgian minister from that city, Daniel Roe, who assembled about 75 to a hundred families there from July 1825. It included professional and business people as well as farmers and labourers.[32] Closely modelled on New Harmony, it soon ran into similar problems. According to Macdonald it had already 'partly suspended its operations in consequence of want of funds'.[33] Returning to Cincinnati, Owen saw his agent and then, accompanied by Mrs Fisher, headed off downriver in a steamboat, eventually reaching New Harmony on the morning of 12 January.[34] By 7 o'clock he was in the pulpit of the Harmonists' brick church, now the hall, telling his audience about the merits of unity and brotherly love and that a company of people was following him by river, in a vessel which carried more learning than was ever contained in a boat. By learning, he went on, he did not mean Latin and Greek or any other language, but real substantial knowledge. And so, as others observed, New Harmony acquired its very own ark, and the nickname *Philanthropist* was soon replaced by the slogan Owen invented, the *Boatload of Knowledge*.[35] The *Boatload of Knowledge*, after weeks of adventures, eventually docked at Mount Vernon on 23 January and Robert Dale dashed off on horseback for New Harmony, unfortunately missing William, who had come to meet him by another route. Owen's son, as the very last entry in his journal records, arrived just in time to hear his father addressing the inhabitants.[36]

What did Robert Owen find and what had transpired during his long absence? The first thing that must have struck him, as it did Macdonald, was that although the population was roughly the same as it had been the previous June, there were as many strange as familiar faces. The great majority were young, often with several children, though this was typical on the American frontier. New families had replaced those who left.[37] Many had been turned away because there was no room for them and in some cases because they were known to be shirkers. These last and people who had withdrawn from the society because they were either idle or felt they had been hard done by inevitably spread rumours about the place, but as Pelham pointed out, these invariably had no foundation. A small number had been expelled for drunkenness, conduct Owen personally abhorred as he had made clear to the people at New Lanark. There were problems with poor lodgings, but these had gradually been resolved as more of the older dwellings were fixed up and new ones erected. The major difficulty was that output of manufactures, at which the Harmonists excelled, and production from the farms lagged behind the community's requirements. The shortage of skilled artisans and labourers willing to work was compounded by inefficient management and poor supervision. The recording of credit earned to be set against goods drawn from the store presented the governing committee with continuing headaches and led to murmurs of dissatisfaction. Because consumption exceeded production the Preliminary Society soon ran into debt. Owen is thought to have subsidised the operation's nine month existence to the tune of $30,000, a substantial sum even by his standards.[38] He presumably hoped to recoup this by subsequent payments from members of the community when it embarked on the next stage of its existence.

While Owen might have cause for concern about the disappointing financial situation, the social and cultural life was vibrant. There were regular dances and balls, musical concerts, lectures, readings, and other cultural events. At some of the dances women had appeared in 'uniform dress of American manufacture', apparently to the design of those worn by the girls at New Lanark and brought over on the first voyage.[39] The schools had made progress and by December of 1825 140 children were being boarded, clothed and educated at public expense.[40] Religious toleration and liberty of opinion prevailed and preachers of various denominations had been given equal access to the pulpit. The community had its resident preacher, Rev. Robert Jennings, a Universalist who had become a confirmed Owenite and played a key role in affairs. He was a member of the management committee and also edited the *Gazette*. The intellectual and social life of the Preliminary Society was certainly unusual in the American West, and New Harmony, famed for its industry and productivity under the Rappites, was already beginning to be recognised as a centre of knowledge if not learning. Some found the egalitarianism and communal activities worrying: Sarah Pears for one, expressed reservations about associating with some of the less privileged of her fellow communitarians. On the other hand many, like the avid correspondent, William Pelham, thought it enjoyable and stimulating. Quite how egalitarian these activities were is difficult to determine for it seems many of the poorer, less educated folk were mere spectators at the dances, musical evenings and lectures of the 'better sort' in the society.[41] All of this, setting aside the defects, William, though only 23 years old, had managed and encouraged to the best of his ability.[42] While it had cost Owen dear, his disciples had managed to create a new social environment and proved the success of the Preliminary Society.[43]

Owen had made up his mind to establish the Community of Equality without waiting for the three year delay he anticipated in his original plan. Quite what his motives were in arriving at such a decision are hard to determine. Back in Britain he had seen the first Owenite community at Orbiston launched and established a closer relationship than previously with British radicals likely to support his ideas. He was naturally anxious to see his own experiment initiate what he thought of as complete community for the first time. Pleased by what he saw, he was swept up in the optimism of the more committed members and the enthusiasm of the intellectuals he had persuaded to join him from the East. By this time too he would have heard from Wright that John Walker's son, Charles, had been appointed manager at New Lanark and that his own salary had ceased from September of the previous year.[44] This was bad news, if he had not known it before or anticipated this turn of events, but word was also reaching the United States about a financial collapse in Britain, which, incidentally, affected the fortunes of the Orbiston community.[45] Now that the wealthy Maclure had arrived he might help share the burden of the operation. However any earlier deals between them are far from clear, and their financial relationship remained complex during much of the life of the community. While Maclure was patron to the majority of intellectuals who arrived on the *Boatload of Knowledge*, some of them were not without resources, and Owen might have felt justified in believing that they too would help support the community financially. So despite the fact that he thought the New System was about to sweep all before it, the move was also designed to spread the responsibility and save at least some of his own investment in New Harmony.

On 25 January members of the Preliminary Society resolved to form the Community of Equality. The meeting then effectively became a constitutional convention and elected a committee of seven to prepare a draft for discussion. Although Owen and Maclure secured a high vote in the ballot they were excused the labour of drafting, but both Owen's sons, the faithful Macdonald, Jennings, the preacher, and a young lawyer, James Wattles, joined the committee. Continuity was achieved by virtue of the fact that six of the seven drafters belonged to the core group that had controlled things from the outset. Subsequent debates in the committee and convention took up much of the following fortnight. Views were far from unanimous, but the committee duly produced a draft. Owen read out a series of proposals that differed from the committee's, including a plea for a hierarchy of overseers, like those at New Lanark, to report 'on the whole industry & daily conduct of every individual'. Robert Dale Owen produced his own draft, while Macdonald made a minority report and twice moved that the constitution be rejected. Ultimately on the twelfth day of the convention, 5 February, a revised constitution was adopted.[46]

The constitution began with a statement that the prime aim of the community was the happiness of its members which would be achieved, by among others the following objectives:

Equality of rights, uninfluenced by sex or condition, in all adults.
Equality of duties, modified by physical and mental conformation.
Co-operative union, in the business and amusements of life.
Community of property.
Freedom of speech and action.
Sincerity in all our proceedings.
Kindness in all our actions.
Courtesy in all our intercourse.
Order in all our arrangements.
Preservation of health.
Acquisition of knowledge.
The practice of economy, or of producing and using the best of
    everything in the most beneficial manner.
Obedience to the laws of the country in which we live.[47]

Much of the constitution once more echoed the 'Plan for the Permanent Relief of the Working Classes', but there was greater stress on the Community of Equality acting as one family, eating the same food, wearing the same clothes, and as soon as practicable, living communally. An assembly of all those over 21 would make the laws and an executive council would run the community, which would have six branches: agriculture, manufacture, education, domestic economy, general economy, and commerce, each with its own superintendent.

This all very well in theory but as far as economic principles were concerned the new constitution was even vaguer than that of the Preliminary Society. Earlier provisions which admitted 'a certain degree of pecuniary inequality' (for 'scientific and experienced persons' or 'persons of capital') were dropped, but so too were the credits and debits and bookkeeping which, however deficient, provided a record of the Preliminary Society's day to day operations. Instead each branch would select a number of 'intendents' who would report the 'daily character of each person attached to their Occupation', based on his or her application and productivity. Each week the reports would be presented by the council to the assembly, together with a report on the intendents themselves. This was effectively the silent monitor with a human face, Macnab's 'secret police' translated from the mills on the Clyde to the community on the Wabash. All the accounts would be balanced 'at least once each month'. It was far from clear whether or not members' earnings would depend on the results of the daily inspection, and what the accounts were that would be balanced went unspecified. Members who quit would no longer receive whatever balance stood to their credit but were only promised 'such compensation for previous services as justice shall require'. Nothing was said about the surplus the community was expected to accumulate. And although Owen evidently expected the community to purchase or lease New Harmony from him there was no mention of this fundamental relationship between the founder and its members.[48] Nonetheless by the 8th 300 members had already signed the constitution and Pelham for one anticipated complete success. However, he was more realistic than Owen, saying that he saw the new arrangement as something like 'a second-third of the way' and that the Village of Equality and Independence still lay in the future.[49]

The very day people were signing up to the new constitution the Preliminary Society presented a report evaluating the labour performed by members to date. Thomas Pears, an enthusiastic supporter of the society, was one who was disappointed to learn that the labour credited to his family was inadequate to pay for its board. More generally this dashed any optimism, greatly heightened by Owen's return, that the community would soon produce enough for all. The reality of New Harmony's less than efficient industries combined with relatively low per capita production served to stress, as Owen's original plan had predicted, that the members were entering a period when hard work and meagre living would be the rule. Only by such precepts would a living be earned and the proprietor paid a return on his investment, something that might take years, the secular equivalent for members of forty years in the wilderness. The members of the Community of Equality also realised that Owen's return, so long awaited, would not

after all bring continued subsidy by a rich man sharing his means with
the less fortunate. Rather, many concluded that they would have to
work even harder to provide themselves with subsistence and pay
any surplus to Owen, a situation frontier settlers had headed west to
escape.

In the opinion of some this state of affairs was not a crisis of economics
but rather of morale. The way forward was unclear and there seemed to
be no possible retreat to the Preliminary Society, since Owen had so vigorously pressed Equality upon the community. The faithful Macdonald,
not a theoretician but, reflecting his engineering background, a practical
doer, was one of the first critics. In the same issue of the *New Harmony
Gazette* that carried a report on the organisation of the new departments,
he attacked the system in general and the constitution in particular for
he favoured government by 'open family assembly' and declared himself
suspicious of all 'Creeds or Codes'. A few weeks later Macdonald was
gone, utterly silent about the turn of events and evidently disillusioned
by the man he had supported for the last five years.[50] Meantime the
executive abandoned any hope of making the constitution work in its
existing form and asked 'the aid of Mr Owen for one year, in conducting
and superintending the concerns of the Community' for the next year.[51]
By an agreement effected on 4 March Owen was given sole direction of
affairs until 1 January 1827.

Owen was undoubtedly placed in a difficult position for, as he must
have realised, he needed to demonstrate that his community experiment
would work, and, at the same time recover the substantial investment he
had made in New Harmony. Personal control might make a difference,
but it placed even greater responsibility on him, since failure could not
be countenanced. He now had to face three major challenges: the splits
that almost immediately occurred among the communitarians; the related
economic crisis; and the re-organisation of community that arose after the
effective collapse of the Community of Equality.

The splits which Macdonald observed prior to his departure arose
from the varied interpretations put on Owen's thinking and objectives,
at least so far as they were discernible to the leaders of the cliques
and splinter groups.[52] The first group, whose religious views Owen
would recall from his boyhood as particularly pernicious, were 'native
backwoodsmen, strongly tinctured with methodism', who had refused to
sign the constitution because of its deistic undertones. Community No II
was named Macluria after William Maclure, though members could not
have appreciated that his views on sectarian religion were as strong as
Owen's. Its constitution was as vague as before, but Owen nevertheless
turned over upwards of 1,200 acres of uncleared land (valued at about
$5,000) two miles beyond the village. By mid-March 80 people were
crowded into nine newly erected log cabins. Numbers rose to 150 by

summer. Dissension among members was publicly acknowledged in October and Macluria given up a month later.[53] The second separatist movement consisted of English farmers who had come from Illinois. Owen granted them 1,400 acres of land for $7,000. Community No III's constitution closely resembled that of Macluria but its name was startling different, Feiba-Peveli. This nomenclature, the brain-child of Whitwell, was based on the translation of longitude and latitude into letters, as he explained in an issue of the gazette published at the time. According to his system, the convict colony of Port Jackson would have been known as Filts-Bubep. No III erected frame and log cabins and by devoting their attention to the land and ignoring the dissentions around them continued a group existence until 1828, long after the parent community had succumbed to further splits and acrimony.[54] Last, were the young intellectuals, apparently dedicated to 'perfect equality' among themselves, but in reality less than anxious to share that with others. Some wore a distinctive costume, much as Owen had planned, with pantaloons for both men and women. However, contrary to Owen's notion, this actually marked them off as an aristocracy. Led by Robert Dale, William, and Jennings, the 'Literati', as they became known, were cooled by Owen himself. In a crafty move he offered them a tract of virgin woodland where they could 'cut down trees and build log cabins as fast as they pleased', but naturally this proved to have limited appeal and the proposed Community No IV collapsed. However, in the longer term, the intellectuals were to re-group and set about creating New Harmony's most enduring legacy, as many had come to see their children educated.[55]

It was essential that Owen keep Community No I together given the financial situation he was forced to reveal on 18 March. Owen had paid the Harmonists $95,000, subsidised the Preliminary Society by $30,000 in 1825 and brought with him in January 1826 $15,000 worth of goods for the store. Moreover his travelling expenses had been substantial, especially during his hundred days in the east and on the trans-Atlantic voyages. This may well have amounted to about three-fifths of his private fortune of $250,000, and he still owed the Rapps $40,000 payable in equal instalments on 1 May 1827 and 1828.[56] Although he never revealed the true extent of his assets he did make clear what he had already spent and in accordance with his original plan indicated that he was now willing to turn over to the community part of his lands at a value to be assessed by a committee, payment to be made over twelve years at an interest rate of five per cent. The valuation was put at $126,000 including $88,000 for the land, sums greeted with utter disbelief by the members. Under the Preliminary Society Owen himself had borne the risk, but now all signed up members were being called upon to meet their financial obligations to the proprietor. Given the modest sums involved this presented few

problems to the members of Macluria and Feiba-Peveli, but apart from
people of substance like Maclure and some others among the élite, few
could contemplate these sums on top of paying their board and lodging
by their labour.[57]

Owen, however, immediately set about implementing the new organ-
isational structure by selecting 24 people who were prepared to go along
with him, naming them the 'nucleus' of the permanent community. They
undertook to meet the financial obligations and in return were given
authority to admit new members on the same terms, and apparently
going against any concept of equality, introduce subordinate grades of
membership. By 21 March this nucleus had assumed full authority and
Owen had seen the second re-organisation in two months completed.
He was obviously determined to keep New Harmony intact, some said
the better to sell it. Indeed the deal that Owen attempted to make in
April would have brought him a handsome profit, since he was asking
$140,000 for the town and another $20,000 for credit due to him for
deferring repayment over a number of years. Annual interest would
begin immediately at a rate of $8,000 per annum. This seemed a long
way from being a Community of Equality, especially Owen's role in
it, but was in close accord with the original concept of the Villages of
Unity and Mutual Co-operation described by George Mudie, editor of
the Owenite *Economist*.[58]

Owen remained optimistic, but given the financial situation in which
he then found himself, he was cautious in his assessment of the first
year's progress, delivered on 9 May. 'The great experiment in New
Harmony', he reported, 'is still going on to ascertain whether a large
heterogeneous mass of persons, collected by chance, can be amalgamated
into one community'.[59] As all the evidence indicated this was unlikely,
when Maclure came up with another suggested reorganisation, Owen,
privately, was probably forced to agree. Pushed for money, he had
earlier taken an advance from Maclure to carry 'the sociable system
into operation' and then agreed to lease him for $50,000 an area at the
centre of the village on which stood Rapp's house, the granary and the
first church as well as 900 acres of land. These Maclure would use to house
the School or Education Society. At the same time Maclure suggested
dividing the population into different communities, each consisting of
persons engaged in a particular occupation. The federated communities
would exchange goods and services, and because similar occupations
were working together the labour needed to produce the total output
expected of each community, or at least so Maclure convinced Owen,
might be more justly apportioned. The financial responsibility of each
community would be limited to paying for the property it occupied, a
more realistic sum than before. Maclure's proposals were duly presented
by Owen and adopted on 28 May. Three independent communities were

designated, the School or Education Society, an Agricultural and Pastoral Society, and a Mechanic and Manufacturing Society. They were to be linked by a Board of Union and trading with each other in labour notes, apparently the first application of the scheme Owen had earlier proposed in his *Report to the County of Lanark* and later the currency deployed by the Owenite labour exchanges. However, Owen kept control of both the store and the tavern.[60]

This third re-organisation in four months contributed to the longer-term break-up of New Harmony, giving Maclure and his associates the freedom of action they wanted in the schools, but leaving Owen with much of the responsibility for the rest. His complex financial deals with Maclure were obscured from most, he had substantial assets, and his personal influence was clearly still considerable. The regime which had prevailed under the Preliminary Society was now reinforced by Owen's vigorous espousal of the work ethic. Members of the community were entering the phase he had anticipated during which by hard work and living a frugal existence they would create a surplus to pay the interest and eventually the capital cost of the land. The resulting regime would have been recognised by any resident of New Lanark, Owen's role as proprietor being akin to that of managing partner at the mills.

From then on work dominated the existence of most communitarians. Sarah Pears voiced the general discontent, noting that 'Mr Owen is growing very unpopular even with the greatest sticklers for the system . . . Mr Owen of New Harmony is a very different personage from Mr Owen in Pittsburg, Washington, etc'.[61] The younger children were sent to the boarding schools while boys and girls over 14 were to live together in special houses, a move which scandalised some. Bells rang out the hours of work, but 'instead of 4 or 5 hours of labour being sufficient for one's maintenance, as people were led to imagine by Mr Owen, the bell is now rung at 5.30 to get up, at 6 to go to work, at 7 for breakfast, at 8 for work again, at 12 for dinner, at one to go to work, at 6 in the evening to return home'. Bad time-keeping was reported to the superintendents and sick lines had to be produced. As at New Lanark, withdrawals from the store, particularly 'luxuries', were closely monitored against the work returns. All of this Owen regularly reported every Sunday, reading out the expenditure of each of the two societies, the amount of work achieved by each trade, and the performance of each worker. Karl Bernhard of Saxe-Weimar Eisenach, whose tour of the United States brought him to New Harmony, observed all this at first hand. He thought Owen resembled a feudal baron, allocating tasks, giving rewards, and dispensing justice. Karl Bernhard said many thought their work tedious and disagreeable, and like the genteel young lady he saw sent to milk cows, only performed under protest! An impression was given that manual labour counted for more than intellectual effort, something that did not quite square up with either notions of equality or indeed with the value Owen evidently attached to education. But Maclure had gone his own way, and their ideas on education were beginning to diverge. Talking to Joseph Applegarth, previously a teacher at New Lanark, a participant in events at Orbiston, and who had recently arrived in New Harmony, Karl Bernhard agreed that Owen's Village plan virtually assumed statutory or forced labour. Indeed, Neef, the Pestalozzian teacher, told Owen he had established a feudal barony rather than a community of equality.[62]

However, apart from the hard work and constant turmoil there were compensations in the numerous social gatherings and the success of the schools. According to Paul Brown, a Quaker, who spent a year in the community, there were gatherings of some kind almost every day.[63] Apart from the meetings, lectures, debates, religious services (which Owen did not discourage), there were concerts, plays and dances. The Owens brought with them the music played at New Lanark, many of the notables were talented performers and as a result there was much musical and theatrical entertainment. While all of these activities were attended by a wide cross section of the community, Karl Berhard noticed that at the lectures, 'the better educated kept themselves together and took no notice of the others', some of whom lounged around nonchalantly.[64] Much the same behaviour could be observed at the dances and balls. While the higher classes besported themselves in the community costumes some of the lower class men sat around reading newspapers scattered on side tables. As at New Lanark, ordinary folk, often reluctant participants in organised activities, had their own social life both in and beyond the bounds of New Harmony. How much this was a form of protest against élite culture or for that matter the élites themselves, is hard to determine, but as on the banks of the Clyde, the forest along the Wabash was the locale of regular carnivalesque events, 'frolics' they were called, invariably held in the woods beyond the improved land. This wilderness context was appropriated for drinking, dancing and sex, the sorts of activities that were common in the woods around New Lanark beyond the eyes and ears of Owen's moral police.[65]

The lectures and other means of improvement were largely detached from the most successful feature of the community, the schools. As other scholars have noted, Owen played some role in their organisation and curricula, arguing constantly with Maclure, but evidently to less effect than at New Lanark. Maclure and his associates, Marie Fretageot, Phiquepal and Neef, directors of the schools, largely ran things their own way, sticking closely to Pestalozzian precepts. Robert Dale, increasingly distanced from his father's thinking on this and other things, became for a while superintendent of the Education Society, as well as editing the *New Harmony Gazette*. This meant supervising three schools, which were also centres of production, the sale of goods helping to defray expenses.

Again an interesting parallel can be drawn with New Lanark, since there the profits of the store subsidised the schools, but Maclure himself had visited Fellenberg and tried out his ideas earlier in a School of Industry at Alicante. The educational experiment survived beyond the community experiment, making New Harmony for long unique in the west.[66]

While the members were concerned about work routines and rewards, Owen was increasingly forced into facing the fact that they consumed more than they produced. The numerous reorganisations had made little difference and the deteriorating economic situation placed greater strain on his own finances and his ill-defined business relationship with Maclure. He was also an increasingly isolated figure. First Macdonald and then Whitwell left, Applegarth helped run the School Society for a while and then left for English Prairie, while Robert Dale was more and more circumspect about his father's views. In articulating his social system Owen had always hidden from the public the very thing that Karl Bernhard and Neef had observed after short acquaintance, his own role as paternalistic master, replicating his experience at New Lanark. His belief in his own infallibility bred arrogance and an indestructible optimism, both of which found outlet, as it had before, in attack.[67]

The celebration on July 4 1826 was an occasion of considerable significance in the United States since it was the fiftieth anniversary of the Declaration of Independence. Owen chose New Harmony's festival as an opportunity to make his 'Declaration of Mental Independence' in which he averred 'that man up to this hour has been in all parts of the earth a slave to a trinity of the most monstrous evils that could be combined to inflict mental and physical evil upon the whole race. I refer to private or individual property, absurd and irrational systems of religion, and marriage founded on individual property, combined with some of these irrational systems of religion'. This uncompromising statement was bound to stir up trouble not just in New Harmony, but worse, in the country at large where the three 'evils' lay at the very heart of American family life.[68]

But as Owen soon found, the last thing on the minds of many were high principles. The heat and humidity of the summer made almost everyone lethargic or sick. And the lazy became even more idle, with the result that equality was more difficult to justify. Things went from bad to worse. In August Owen began a prolonged attack on the Education Society. He wanted to see more of the population educated in thrice-weekly evening lectures (with maps, globes and other visual aids) and more critically insisted on replacing the Pestalozzian system with that of Lancaster used at New Lanark. Maclure told Fretageot, who agreed to conduct one of the classes on the New Lanark method, that Owen had 'not the smallest idea of a good education and will not permit any to flourish within his reach. His parrot education to exhibit before strangers as at New Lanark is the whole he knows'. Nor had it ever achieved much, he thought, 'for of all the New Lanark children none got above the merit of twisting a thread of cotton'. Maclure need not have worried for the arrangement lasted only seven weeks before lapsing.[69]

In September Owen suggested abolishing the existing community and starting a new No 1 community, but this was overtaken in October by yet another major re-organisation as the Agriculture and Mechanics societies were replaced by trustees headed by Owen and four of his appointees, to manage and control all the property. The covenant signed by the members had provisions for dismissing those guilty of offences and a number were sent on their way. In another move to recover as much of the property as he could he disputed the right of the Education Society to gather crops from the land it had been assigned, saying these belonged to the whole community. He also disputed the boundaries, attempting to take back some of the land. At the same time it was revealed that the store, although closely supervised by Owen and operating much like that at New Lanark, had almost sold out of the $15,000 worth of goods bought earlier in the year.[70] This was perhaps not surprising, since apart from supplying the community on the work-time principle, it was patronised by all and sundry as the cheapest place for miles around. As a result Owen again needed money, but this time Maclure refused to help. Maclure also thought William and Robert Dale should be informed, since he suspected Owen intended to sell up and leave in the spring.[71]

This proved premature for Owen was forced into a fifth re-organisation since the trust set up in October had been as unable as its predecessors to cope with the situation. Centralisation having failed, decentralisation was tried again, first in the village itself, and then in the outlying areas. In January the population was again divided up by occupation, each cohort having responsibility for its own affairs. At the end of March the *Gazette* claimed this new system was in operation, each occupation supporting itself, 'paying weekly a small percentage towards the general expenses of the town . . . determining its own internal regulations, and distributing or exchanging its own produce'. But, the report admitted, this was hardly Owen's new social system, concluding that 'New Harmony is not now a community; but as was originally intended, a central village, out of, and around which, communities have formed'.[72]

Another projected community, No IV, was announced following the lease of 1,500 acres to William Taylor, an Ohio businessman, to whom Owen also sold many of the of main buildings, notably those which generated income, the store, the tavern, flour mills and cotton works. This was the first public indication of Owen's determination to quit, and it was rapidly followed by what Paul Brown labelled 'Doomsday' on 1 February. On that occasion Owen announced that his support of the inhabitants would cease and a number 'whose services could not be beneficially employed' were given what Brown described as their 'walking papers'.[73] At the same time he was happy to offer leases to any who wanted them 'to form societies of common property, equality & kindness', but there were strict conditions attached. Some accepted, but most departed. In March eighty folk departed by boat up the Ohio to found a community near Cincinnati. The public buildings were soon nearly deserted and the remaining communitarians took their meals in the boarding school. The stage was set, as Bestor put it, for the last act of the tragicomedy at New Harmony.

Although Owen remained convinced of the truth of his views, circumstances again forced him to confront reality. This came in the shape of Frederick Rapp demanding settlement of two bonds for $20,000 each, deferred from 1825 for goods left behind by the Harmonists. Rapp's arrival coincided with the return of Maclure, who had spent part of the winter in New Orleans. While the relationship between Owen and Maclure was far from clear, the former certainly represented himself as being in partnership with the latter. Owen offered to pay Rapp with notes in Maclure's name, which Rapp refused. Rapp then threatened to sue Owen at which juncture Maclure, anxious to protect the interests of the schools, bought the $40,000 worth of bonds. At that time Maclure owed Owen $20,000 as the balance for the school property and $10,000 of losses he had agreed to cover. Maclure offered to pay all he could in return for an unrestricted title to the property, which Owen refused, asking $15,000 more. Maclure was forced to comply or risk losing the $40,000 he had already paid. Arbitration was resorted to and this found that a partnership of some sort had existed. Maclure reckoned that in the end he had paid $82,500 for about a quarter of the real estate and that Owen had made a profit of 300 per cent on the deal. Owen's version, as he subsequently revealed, was very different.[74]

Maclure, like Owen, spent only short spells of time at New Harmony. Despite their disagreements on matters of policy, particularly the management of the schools and the curricula, they remained on good terms. But Maclure, like others before him, had seen aspects of Owen which had made him much more circumspect in his dealings with the man. Maclure was disillusioned and had totally changed his opinions of Owen's capability of success 'in any undertaking on the high visionary ideas that a concurrence of circumstances has engendered in his brain'. He thought Owen was in too great a hurry, not only with regard to the schools, but the community as a whole. Too much faith had been placed on the New Lanark system with Owen ranting on continuously 'in big vague, undefined words, without sufficiently examining the consequences'. Maclure's acolyte, Marie Fretageot, took a more positive view saying that Owen 'is upright in his dealing, knows very well that man is not brought up to understand his true interest, but his patience and mildness are such that he may change them in a short time'. The fact that people wanted to preserve their connections with the 'individual society' was 'a constant check to any improvement' and although Owen managed to counter some of the old habits his actions were not always as prudent as they might have been because his own thinking was so muddled.[75]

Having sorted out what he could of the financial and legal affairs of New Harmony, Owen delivered two farewell addresses which still struck notes of optimism. On 26 May he told his listeners that 'the social system is now firmly established', but more cautiously the following day he slipped into the future tense, asserting that 'with the right understanding of the principles upon which your change from the old to the new has been made, you will attain your object'.[76] Refusing to admit defeat, as Crusoe had done throughout his sojourn on his island, Owen on 1 June left what remained of the community. As he travelled east he was already preparing to counter charges of speculation and to present a defence of the New System, which he had by no means abandoned.

## NOTES

1. On the LCS see Harrison, pp. 31, 48, 74–5, 198–9.
2. *The Economist*, vol. I, pp. 11–16; *Times*, 26 September, 1825; the Discourses are reproduced in Claeys, 2, pp. 3–37
3. Co-operative Union, Owen Coll. J. Wright to R. Owen, 6 May, 1825.
4. Donnachie, pp. 145–7.
5. R.D. Owen, Journal, pp. 223–4.
6. *Times*, 24 August, 1825.
7. Ibid.
8. R.D. Owen, Journal, p. 213.
9. Arntd, *Harmony*, pp. 644–5, F.Rapp to M. Morgan 17 Aug. 1825.
10. Allen, vol. II, p. 238 quoting W. Allen to R. Owen, 27 July, 1822.
11. British Library, Add. Mss. 33545, f570, W. Allen to J. Bentham, 21 August, 1822.
12. Ibid, f629, W. Allen to J. Mill, 25 July, 1823.
13. Co-operative Union, Owen Coll, J. Wright to R. Owen, 9 March 1825.
14. Kenneth Dale Owen Papers, A.C. Owen to W. Owen 13 January 1826; also Elliott, p. 278.
15. Ibid, J. Owen to W. Owen 14 January 1826.
16. Co-operative Union, Owen Coll. J. Wright to R. Owen, 9 March 1825.
17. ROMM, Item 47, Scrapbook.
18. Dolores Hayden, *Seven American Utopias*, Cambridge, Mass. 1976, pp. 21, 34, 66, 196.
19. *Times* 26–27 September, 1825.
20. Co-operative Union, Owen Coll., Sir R. Peel to R. Owen, 25 September 1825.
21. R.D. Owen, Journal, pp. 223, 225.

22. Macdonald, p. 307; R.D.Owen, Journal, p. 226.
23. R.D. Owen, Journal, pp. 227–8.
24. Ibid, p. 229; Macdonald, p. 308.
25. R.D. Owen, Journal, pp. 233–4.
26. Ibid, pp. 234–5; Macdonald, pp. 315–16.
27. Macdonald, p. 316.
28. R.D. Owen, Journal, p. 237.
29. D. Pitzer, 'Original Boatload', p. 5.
30. Ibid.
31. R.D. Owen, Journal, p. 239.
32. Harrison, p. 166.
33. Macdonald, p. 335; R.D. Owen, p. 245; Bestor, pp. 210–13.
34. R.D. Owen, Journal, p. 262.
35. *New Harmony Gazette*, 18 January 1826; Pelham Papers, 8 & 27 January 1826. Taylor, p. 137.
36. R.D. Owen, Journal, p. 264.
37. Macdonald, p. 337.
38. Bestor, pp. 167, 180–1.
39. Pelham Papers, 3 October 1825.
40. *NHG*, 21 December 1825.
41. Lucy J. Kamau, 'Anthropology of Space in Harmonist and Owenite New Harmony', *Communal Societies*, vol. 12, 1992, pp. 68–89.
42. Carmony & Elliott, pp. 168–70.
43. Bestor, p. 167.
44. Co-operative Union, Owen Coll., J. Wright to R. Owen, 10 December, 1825.
45. Donnachie, pp. 155–8.
46. Macdonald, p. 337; *NHG*, 15 February, 1826.
47. NHG, 15 February, 1826.
48. Ibid; Bestor, pp. 173–74. These proceedings are also described in E.B. Lockwood, *the New Harmony Movement*, New York, 1905, pp. 103–111.
49. Pelham Papers, 23 February, 1826.
50. Macdonald, pp. 337–8.
51. *NHG*, 22 February, 1826.
52. Macdonald, p. 337.
53. Bestor, p. 176; Macluria's Constitution in *NHG*, 29 March, 1826.
54. *NHG*, 12 April, 1826.
55. Pears Papers, p. 71, S.Pears to Mrs Bakewell, 10 March, 1826; Bestor, p. 179.
56. NHWI, Robert Owen Papers, Memorandum of Agreement, 3 January 1825; ibid, Branigan-Owen Coll, Bond of F. Rapp And Associates, 25 April 1825; on the controversy over the cost see K.J.R. Arndt, 'Did Frederick Rapp Cheat Robert Owen?', *West Penn. Hist. Mag.*, 1978, pp. 358–365.
57. Bestor, pp. 180–182.
58. Pear Papers, pp. 76–7, S. Pear to Mrs. B. Bakewell, 10 March 1826; P. Brown, *Twelve Months in New Harmony*, Cincinnati, 1827, pp. 15, 19–20.
59. *NHG*, 10 May, 1826.
60. Ibid, 7 June, 1826.
61. Pears Papers, p. 81, S. Pears to Mrs. B. Bakewell, 8 April, 1826.
62. Brown, pp. 35, 109; Karl Bernhard's views in Lockwood, pp. 123–33.
63. Brown, p. 16.

64. Karl Bernhard, *Travels*, p. 430.
65. See Kamau on the dances etc., pp. 82–5.
66. See A.E. Bestor, *Education and Reform at New Harmony*, Indianapolis, 1948; also D.J. Maclaren, 'Robert Owen, William Maclure and New Harmony', *Hist. Of Education*, Vol. 25, 1996, pp. 223–33.
67. Taylor, pp. 148–9.
68. *NHG*, 12 July 1826; the Declaration is reproduced in Pitzer and Elliott, *New Harmony's Fourth of July Tradition*, New Harmony, 1976, pp. 9–13.
69. NHWI, Maclure-Fretageot Corr., Maclure to Fretageot, 21 August, 29 August and 19 September, 1826.
70. Ibid, Fretageot-Maclure, 27/8 July, 1826.
71. Ibid, Maclure to Fretageot, 28 November, 1826.
72. *NHG*, 28 March 1827.
73. Brown, p. 85; Bestor, p. 195.
74. NHWI, Hodge-Fretageot Papers, A Short Account of all the transactions between R. Owen and W.Maclure.
75. Maclure-Fretageot Corr. Maclure-Fretageot 21 August, 30 August, 1826; ibid, Fretageot-Maclure, 21 August, 1826.
76. *NHG*, 30 May, 1827.

# THIRTEEN

# Towards Social Fatherhood

Although Owen had ostensibly abandoned the experiment at New Harmony almost as quickly as he began it, the principles under-pinning it remained central to Owenite ideology. The Village Scheme, so obviously a derivative of New Lanark, but now embracing both co-operation and communitarianism, however ill-defined, was to figure periodically in Owen's thinking for the rest of his life. New Lanark and New Harmony were inevitably linked in public perceptions of Owenism, but Owen himself returned to the former as his model rather than the latter. But in the summer of 1827 he began to investigate other possibilities of implementing the New System in communities, before turning his mind to other projects three years later. During the course of this time he paid another visit to New Harmony, made a remarkable journey to Mexico, returning again briefly to New Harmony, before ascending the Ohio to Cincinnati to engage an American clergyman in a famous debate on religion.

After leaving New Harmony on 1 June, Owen, accompanied by Robert Dale, who was returning home to visit the family, headed east via Louisville, Cincinnati and Pittsburgh.[1] Some of the newspapers were reporting the collapse of the experiment and criticising his own conduct, so he used the opportunity of a public lecture held on 25 June in Philadelphia to refute these claims. He dismissed charges that he was nothing but a speculator, saying that both he and Maclure had agreed to put in $150,000 into the enterprise. Owen seemed to imply that he himself had done so, and that official documents published in the *New Harmony Gazette* would corroborate this view. He then reiterated the familiar benefits of his New System and gave a glowing account of New Harmony, where, he said, a number of small communities outside the town were emerging from a period of hardship, into a time when, with good management, they would become independent and self-sustaining. He felt he had discharged his responsibilities and settled his debts. Much of this was an illusion, for if accounts by Paul Brown, Joseph Neef and others, are to be believed, New Harmony and its satellite communities were rapidly disintegrating. Perhaps Owen was suffering from the condition that Maclure felt had afflicted him when he visited New Lanark, his eyes obscured by a film 'refracting all objects out of their natural place'.[2] However, Owen's explanations were apparently well received by his audience. He held another well attended meeting in

New York 29 June, speaking 'with renewed confidence of his system', which at least suggests that he might earlier have lost faith in it.[3]

Sailing from New York on 1 July Owen and his son duly arrived in Liverpool on 24 July 'in very good spirits, after a very favourable passage'.[4] In the last few days of the voyage he had drafted a paper giving conditions of contracts for the land at New Harmony and this he finalised and signed in Liverpool on the 26th, presumably sending a copy directly back to the United Sates by the first available crossing. The contract reaffirmed the stringent conditions Maclure and others had earlier rejected and this could be taken to indicate that whatever was done at New Harmony, Owen was determined it would still be on his terms.[5] Almost as soon as he landed he was denying rumours reaching England that his projects in the United States had failed. He and Robert Dale then headed north to rejoin the family which was evidently staying at Braxfield for the summer.[6]

Sometime in early August, Owen, on his way to Glasgow, visited Orbiston, which he found 'in a most flourishing condition'. According to one report 300 individuals were then living in the community, all working ten hours a day at their respective occupations. The site occupied 330 acres, 84 arable, the land having cost £20,000, the buildings and other improvements £17,000, the total thus being roughly what Owen had originally anticipated it would cost to get a community going. Owen told members about his American journey and urged them to persevere.[7] Considering that Combe and Hamilton had become enthusiastic converts to Owenism and that Orbiston was right on his doorstep, reached easily from New Lanark or Glasgow, his one curt visit to the place, the first Owenite community in Britain, seems odd, not to say disinterested.

While at Orbiston he learned of Abram Combe's illness and later that he was dying. The morning before he died Combe had evidently revived when told that Owen was expected in Edinburgh. Owen, on 11 August, rushed to his bedside but arrived too late. Owenism had claimed what Claeys described as its first martyr, a victim of 'over-exertion at spade agriculture'.[8] Combe's creation would go the same way as New Harmony, but more quickly and more dramatically, first in social, then in financial disarray, within a year of Combe's death. Nevertheless, the movement honoured its own and Combe was given fulsome tributes in the Owenite press. However, unlike New Lanark and New Harmony his community left no trace, saving its publication, the *Orbiston Register*. But apart from Owen himself there were interesting links between the three communities, notably Joseph Applegarth's presence in all three and Whitwell's sister, who taught in both Scottish villages. Orbiston's most significant legacy was the contribution some of its residents, Alexander Campbell among them, made to the future cause of Owenism.[9]

Owen's movements during the rest of that summer are unclear, but when Robert Dale, presumably on his own, reached London on 25 August he found his father was in town and thought to himself that 'on the whole the true principles are gradually advancing here, though the advance be slow'.[10] To help speed things up Owen on 7 September published his *Address to the Agriculturists*, which, among other points, contained a description of how the labour note scheme might work.[11] The same morning he was guest speaker at a meeting of the London Co-operative Society, among whom, according to one report, were 'several elegant and distinguished females'. After breakfast he was called upon to read from his latest tract and commented on different parts as he went along. He also spoke briefly about what he had been doing in America, but made only one reference to New Harmony, implying it was still 'in progress'. He made a strong plea for the relief of distress, which he said was impossible to understand when a population of 25 million was capable of producing that of 600 million. It was a reflection of the rottenness of society that such misery could exist, and, the working classes could easily rescue themselves from wretchedness by forming small communities of 4 to 20 families. Little capital was required and indeed, he concluded 'good conduct and confidence in each other was certain to ensure success'.[12]

Having completed some business with his former partners, Owen was probably back in Scotland for much of September and October before setting out again for America.[13] Much against their mother's wishes, arrangements had been made for the two younger sons, David Dale and Richard, to settle at New Harmony. Following in their brother's footsteps, both had been to school in Switzerland, afterwards attending Anderson's College in Glasgow. Accordingly on 16 November Owen and his three sons sailed from Liverpool to endure a long and stormy passage before arriving in New York. Owen lectured there and in other cities of the east for some weeks, eventually arriving in New Orleans sometime in early January. There from 18 January he gave another series of lectures, in which he again claimed to have spent more than $500,000 and devoted 40 years to making preparations for the introduction of the New Society.[14] He went on to criticise both the place of the coloured population in society and the role of religion, which must have done little to endear him to Southern audiences. Undeterred and hitting back as he had in Britain, he caused a sensation by announcing a challenge to any American preacher who might care to debate with him on the errors of religion.

He then set off up the Mississippi. On 3 February he was reported at Natchez 'on the way to New Harmony', and the same day issued an address to the inhabitants of New Orleans, reflecting on the issues he had raised.[15] He did not actually reach New Harmony until 1 April. It seems likely that he stopped off to inspect Nashoba, the community for liberating and educating slaves which Frances Wright, the free-thinking reformer and a regular visitor to New Harmony, had established on the

Wolf River near Memphis, Tennessee. While this was only one of many remarkable initiatives in Wright's career it was clearly much influenced by the Harmonists and the Owenites, and while Frederick Rapp had strongly encouraged her, there seems little doubt that she had personally fallen under Robert Owen's spell. The Declaration of Mental Independence with its strong hints at female empowerment attracted her greatly and she both recognised and privately endorsed his views on birth control.[16]

Owen was in New Harmony for about three months, some of it evidently spent unravelling his legal and financial affairs. On 13 April he gave the assembled inhabitants an account of his journey, produced an optimistic report on the progress of the New System in Britain, and 'stated a general opinion on the state of things as he found them on his return'. In a reference to the store and other enterprises, mainly conducted by Taylor, he condemned monopoly as being as evil as competition, presumably having changed his mind on this since he had relinquished his own monopoly over the inhabitants.[17] Soon word reached Owen that Rev Alexander Campbell, a noted revivalist preacher in Bethany, Virginia, had responded to his challenge, agreeing to meet 'the sage philosopher of New Harmony' in debate.[18] The debate then seems to have become something of an obsession, but he also found time to prepare a farewell address to the inhabitants, which with his usual glowing enthusiasm he duly delivered on 22 June. Five days later, and saying that he would be back the following winter, he was heading for Mount Vernon to ascend the Ohio, en route for the east.[19] Before his arrival in Wheeling on 13–14 July he had visited Kendal and Zoar, two small communities in Ohio established on Owenite principles. In the east Owen visited Campbell to make arrangements for the debate. The venue fixed was Cincinnati, the time, April the following year.[20]

Following his now customary practice Owen then left the United States and returned to Britain. It was his intention finally to withdraw the remains of his own and his sons' interest in New Lanark. Although in January 1829 he told Maclure he had done this and was in a position to pay off any outstanding debts at New Harmony, he still had money in New Lanark because he seems to have been deriving income from the company as late as 1831.[21] He got Caroline to sign a deed renouncing any interest in his property in the United States on condition of a bond for £6,000 on Robert Owen & Company to provide an annuity for herself and her daughters.[22] His wife and her sisters also continued to receive some funds from the Dale Trust, though it is unclear how much, or if Owen still had access to it personally. Despite his property in New Harmony, which he effectively made over to his sons in 1832, his wealth was much reduced by costly propaganda, constant travel, and the community experiment, which had cost him dear, in all perhaps three quarters of his assets.[23] So when he heard about the possibility of settling lands on the Texas frontier and trying the community scheme anew, optimistic of success and the chance to recover his fortune, he embraced the project with open arms.

Of all the schemes with which Owen was involved, of all the travels he made promoting the New Society, the journey to Mexico was the most fantastic. The origins of the Texas project are obscure, but Owen may well have learned of opportunities there from Maclure, who, hating slavery, abandoned New Orleans for Mexico as his winter resort. The politics of the new republic were known to be chaotic, but, regardless, the major powers, including the United States and Britain, were anxiously vying for influence over trade, land and mining concessions. Owen knew that avaricious Yankees were pushing west of the Mississippi beyond the boundary delineated by the Sabine River into the thinly populated province of Coahuila and Texas, and that the Mexicans were trying to control settlement through land agents acting for the republic. John Dunn Hunter, Owen's acolyte, who had been briefly at New Harmony, had earlier sought a grant of land in Texas to establish a colony where Indians could live in peace free of white harassment. It is also possible that Owen had intelligence from Joel Poinsett, a distinguished American, who in 1824 published an account of his visit to Mexico and ultimately became US representative there. Poinsett, incidentally, had attended Edinburgh University and almost certainly visited New Lanark. For a while he was one of Maclure's travelling companions.[24]

Setting aside these speculations, the immediate trigger was a letter from one Benjamin Milan who with an associate claimed to have obtained grants of land in Texas and wrote asking Owen if he was interested.[25] No reply has survived, but the news clearly intrigued Owen and he immediately busied himself preparing his own submission to the Mexicans. The *Memorial to the Mexican Republic*, dated 10 October, provided an abbreviated statement of the New System and sought permission to introduce it in a district of Texas set aside for the purpose.[26] Like earlier copies of the *New View* and the *European Memorials* this was widely circulated – in this case to representatives of Latin and South American governments and other authorities he might approach for support. The copy in the Goldsmiths' Library, which clearly never reached its intended recipient, was inscribed to the Emperor of Brazil, Dom Pedro I.

Meantime Owen contacted everyone who might be prevailed upon to open doors, including Vicente Rocafuerte, secretary of the Mexican legation in London. The reply of the 17th, though diplomatic, made it clear that the republic's government, beset by civil strife, would be unlikely to entertain his proposals.[27] Although Rocafuerte had sent on Owen's memorial and recommended it to his government he advised him to abandon the idea of going to Mexico. Characteristically Owen ignored his advice telling him in a letter of the 31st that the New World, in his opinion, was 'ripe for a great moral change' and that

Mexico seemed the best place 'at which to begin new and mighty operations'.[28] Having gathered as many letters of introduction as he could Owen left London on 17 November, sailing from Falmouth on the packet ship *Spey* on the 22nd. He spent much of the voyage either working on his speech for the forthcoming debate with Campbell or preparing a set of laws and regulations for the government of Texas, evidently the same 'laws of human nature' which were also to feature in the great debate. Sharing his cabin was Charles Deare, a naval officer, flag lieutenant to Vice-Admiral Fleming, then commodore of the West Indian fleet, a Lanarkshire landowner with whom Owen was friendly. Deare evidently helped Owen edit his work and assiduously copied it in case the original might be lost.[29]

After a long voyage the ship came within sight of Antigua on 31 December, eventually making landfall on 6 January at St Domingo where mail was put ashore. Owen himself was given a quick tour by someone who had earlier visited New Lanark. He concluded that the freed coloured people he met were better dressed, cleaner, more orderly and polite than any other working people he had come across before. His view of Jamaica, reached on the 8th, was also highly positive. Here again his celebrity could be used to advantage to meet the island's élite and to obtain further introductions from Fleming to prominent individuals in Mexico, including the bishop of Puebla. He was also able to see something of the interior, concluding that the slave population on the plantations seemed to be in better circumstances that the majority of the working class in Britain. He says he saw no slave 'half so hard worked as the manufacturing classes are daily in England and Scotland', further evidence of his continuing equivocation on the issue confronted at New Harmony when the role of persons of colour had arisen.[30]

On the voyage to Vera Cruz Owen heard news of the continuing political and civil unrest in Mexico and fifty miles from the coast met a vessel loaded with rich Spaniards fleeing the country and carrying between them a million and a quarter dollars in gold. However, the country seemed to be quieter, for following a controversial result in the recent presidential election, the intervention of the military led by the great liberator, General Antonio Lopez de Santa Anna, had resulted in the success of the defeated liberal, Vicente Guerrero, an uneducated hero of the wars against Spain. Once landed at Vera Cruz, which struck him as 'truly foreign', Owen, possibly fearing the fever more than public disorder, and leaving behind luggage (which contained infant school apparatus, probably the visual aids, charts, globes, etc), wasted little time setting out for Jalapa, which he reached on the 20th.[31]

Whether by accident or design, Owen found Maclure at Jalapa, apparently unconcerned about the political situation and relaxed in the beautiful climate of the plateau. Maclure was amazed by the letters Owen

carried, the impartiality of their authors, and the people to whom they
were addressed, particularly the bishop. He could not believe that Owen
had any hope of convincing these individuals that 'it is in their interest to
support the new order of things he wishes to introduce, founded on the
divine law of nature that man is the child of circumstance'. However, he
told Marie Fretageot, 'so long as he stops at theory all will be well . . .
but should he attempt practice, the second edition of New Harmony will
be published to world confounding his theories and bringing loss and
disappointment on all that have placed faith and confidence in him'.[32]

As it transpired Maclure could put his mind at rest. After waiting ten
days, on about the 31st, Owen went on with an unescorted party up to
Mexico City. En route, at Perote, he met and spoke with Santa Anna about
the situation in Mexico City and apparently arranged to meet again three
weeks later in Jalapa. Santa Anna provided an escort to Puebla, where
Owen called on the bishop and, carefully avoiding religion, explained his
views and plans. His interpreter was a young German mining engineer he
had recruited en route, and as usual when in the presence of the mighty he
came away feeling that the bishop had appeared interested in what he had
to say.[33] They pressed on through wonderful country, reaching Mexico
City three days later, probably on the 7th. There, evidently to his surprise,
he found the British representative, Packenham, and his US counterpart,
Poinsett, co-existing in mutual suspicion, while the merchants of both
countries eschewed protocol and vigorously pursued land, mining and
trade concessions. Remarkably, Owen also seemed unaware that the most
successful of these individuals, Richard Exter, an English merchant, was
already one of the largest landowners in Texas and on intimate terms
with members of the government. More immediately, he was able to
produce letters of introduction from Lord Aberdeen, Admiral Fleming,
and a clutch of English bishops, and Packenham promised to help him
in his mission.[34]

Owen's account of his stay in Mexico City also reveals his continuing
fascination with the powerful. Packenham on the 9th helped smooth his
way into the presence of the outgoing first president, Guadelupe Victoria,
and his senior ministers. The memorial had preceded him, and through
Packenham as interpreter, he was able to tell the president of his plans,
of his wish for good relations between Mexico and the United States, of
his desire to settle part of the country's northern territory, and try the
community scheme on a larger scale. If, as seems likely, the Mexican
authorities had been warned by Rocafuerte to play along with Owen
in the knowledge that nothing would come of such ambitious plans
in any case, then the president's response was a foregone conclusion.
Indeed, according to Owen, Victoria announced that the government
had acceded to his request for a ribbon of land 50 leagues (200 miles)
wide stretching along much of the Mexican–US border. Once congress had

ratified this, Owen was assured, the legal formalities could be completed without delay. Owen seems to have believed all this, but given what he heard from both Packenham and Poinsett it is hard to credit. Apart from the internal strife, relations with the United States over American settlers moving into Texas were edgy. While the constitution defended freedom of religion, Catholic Mexico hardly welcomed the presence of Protestant Yankees on its northern frontier, far less communities of aetheistic Owenites. Owen, in his narrative, had convinced himself of his success. Even the architecture of Mexico City seemed to confirm the country's adaptability to his schemes. Pacing out the dimensions of one of the grand squares, Owen was delighted to find it measured 1070 by 870 feet, near enough in dimensions to the 1000 feet sides of the proposed communities reproduced in miniature on the famous model. But in Owen's utopian community there would be no street, lane, court or alley, which, he thought, formed 'vicious and unfavourable circumstances, too prejudicial to happiness to be admitted into an approved state of society'.[35]

After promising Victoria to send on the materials for the rational infant school and holding discussions with Packenham and Poinsett, Owen on the 18th set out on the return journey to Vera Cruz. Puebla was reached without incident on the 20th, but his German companion badly hurt his ankle when a wheel of the carriage ran over his foot. On the 24th they arrived in Jalapa, having met Maclure on his way to Mexico City on the journey. The following day, as arranged, Owen saw Santa Anna who listened attentively and apparently had him explain in minute detail all his human laws, by which the proposed settlement in Texas would be governed. Typically, as Maclure noted, Owen took the polite attentiveness of the great general, the bishop, and for that matter the president, as endorsement, even definite encouragement. At that juncture Owen decided he could not wait for the small matter of legislation to be resolved for he was called to higher things in the debate at Cincinnati. Accordingly he set out for Vera Cruz, where Admiral Fleming and the British Navy had obligingly provided a sloop to convey him to New Orleans.[36] Possibly the authorities, thinking that Owen's visit was unlikely to prove successful, were anxious to spirit him away before there was any adverse reaction. At any rate he reached New Orleans on or about the 8th, and after spending some time there set off up the Mississippi on a twelve day journey which brought him to New Harmony about 30 March. He stayed only for a few days, spending the bulk of the time with his sons. Fretageot, on Maclure's behalf, was supposed to receive Caroline's relinquishment of any interest in the New Harmony property, but Owen did not produce it.[37] Owen then went direct to Cincinnati, reached on 10 April. It was remarkable, he thought, that on such a long and complex journey, during which he had so many important engagements, he had managed to stick so closely to his timetable.[38]

The debate with Campbell was another millennial moment and as in 1817 generated misconceptions about his views on religion and brought him considerable notoriety. The encounter, described by Fanny Trollope in her *Domestic Manners of the Americans*, took place over five days and fifteen sessions, beginning on 13 April.[39] It was held in a large Methodist hall, before audiences of 1,200 people, many being strangers attracted to the city 'by the novelty and importance of the discussion'. Trollope thought the whole thing was like a melodrama and was especially struck by Owen's performance. In denouncing religion as a fraud so gentle was his tone of voice, so lacking in harsh expression, so genuine his feeling for 'the whole human family', so strong his apparent wish to be proved wrong, so kind his smile, so mild the expression of his eyes, that he won an astonishing degree of tolerance for views odious to the majority of the audience. While she could see much sense in the Twelve Laws Owen cited as his main contribution to the debate, she concluded that he was an 'extraordinary man and certainly possessed of talent, but he appears to me so utterly benighted in the mists of his own theories, that he has quite lost the power of looking through them, so as to get a peep at the world as it really exists around him'.[40] Judging from the applause Campbell won readily and at the close of the final session only a handful were brave enough to support Owen's position. Trollope thought it could only have happened in America and was not certain it should have happened at all. It was Owen's last major public appearance in the United States and marked another significant turning point in his career.

He stayed on in Cincinnati for several weeks, possibly attending to business connected with New Harmony, and before leaving also saw through the press *A Short Narrative of the Author's Voyage to Mexico*. Afterwards he headed east, stopping in Washington, where he had an audience with Jackson and Van Buren, evidently agreeing to communicate their views on the Oregon boundary question to the British government. He also visited the Rev Campbell, who had undertaken the preparation of their discussion for publication.[41] From Bethany was published the first edition of the *Debates on the Evidences of Christianity*, a book which was to become widely read on both sides of the Atlantic. He arrived in New York at the end of July and after seeing Robert Dale, who had recently moved to the city, sailed for England on 1 August. Three weeks later Owen was back in Britain saying that 'the Americans are not capable of governing themselves' and consequently he had abandoned all ideas of reforming them. But, the newspaper report continued, 'the evenness of his temper does not seem even ruffled by the recollection of the time and money he has thus fruitlessly expended in his benevolent projects on the other side of Atlantic'.[42]

Owen went straight to London where he reported to Aberdeen on his meeting with Jackson and Van Buren and his views on Anglo-American affairs generally, and trade and boundary disputes in particular. By 12 September he was back in Scotland, living with his family at their new home in Hamilton. From there through the *Glasgow Chronicle* he issued a detailed account of his travels to Mexico, a round trip of 15,000 miles and through 'many varieties of climate'.[43] But the Owenites wasted little time urging him to return to his propaganda mission.[44] Owen duly responded, but in circumstances very different to those a decade earlier: it was with a modified agenda. It seems that when he stepped ashore issuing his statement about the ungovernable Americans, he had probably put much of his experience at New Harmony behind him. He certainly put it out of his mind and rarely referred to it either in his speeches or publications. When the communitarian vision shone forth, as it did periodically, it was New Lanark, however inappropriate, that he held up as his model. Even then he often said that his experiment at New Lanark was 'on a very limited scale . . . confined to the establishment of an infant school'.[45]

Robert Owen was not yet sixty and was to fill the rest of his life with further schemes of social reform. Entering what Harrison described as the most radical phase of his career, he was to regain immediate prominence on public platforms throughout Britain espousing the relief of the working class and co-operation.[46] That both were closely related was seen, during his absence overseas, in the success of the consumer co-operatives which had mushroomed to a total of 300 by 1830. These were partly inspired by his ideas, but their aim of selling good quality products at fair prices and distributing profits among members was more limited than his. After failing to persuade the movement to adopt a more Owenite agenda, he moved on in 1832 to the labour exchange, a concept that had been aired in the early 1820s and underpinned the economic arrangements in the new communities.[47] This new phase, providing an escape route from competition and at the same time raising capital for communities, went beyond consumer co-operation by involving producers directly. The means of exchange was the labour note, which had its prototype in the ticket for wages at New Lanark.[48] The National Equitable Labour Exchange attracted perhaps a thousand artisans, Owen personally supervising the largest branch in London. Another branch opened in London, and yet another in Birmingham. At the same time he led the Institution of the Industrious Classes (founded in December 1831), which had similar objectives to the British and Foreign Philanthropic Society of a decade earlier, removing ignorance, promoting education and employment by weekly lectures, provision of schools and the purchase of land. Another important outlet for his ideas was his new journal, *The Crisis*, (1832–34), edited for a time by his son, Robert Dale, who returned briefly to assist his father in his reforms. The exchanges ran into the same difficulties that had arisen earlier in the communities, mainly the twin problems of valuing labour and goods, and were wound up in the summer of 1834.[49]

Meantime, in the wake of the Reform Act, which had failed to deliver the vote to all of the middle class far less the artisans, Owen was swept into the trade union movement and momentarily during 1833–34 found himself playing the role of working class leader.[50] Finding Owenism embraced by growing numbers of local unions, especially in London, Birmingham, Yorkshire and Lancashire, and in the Staffordshire Potteries, he tirelessly toured the country preaching fundamental changes to society.

In November 1833 he joined John Doherty, leader of the Lancashire cotton spinners, and John Fielden, the radical mill owner and MP for Todmorden, in establishing the National Regeneration Society. Its main object was the eight hour day in factories, as a prelude to the elimination of competitive society. Owen was now evidently convinced that the scale of union activity was such that 'the crisis was at last at hand and the old immoral world was about to be swept away'.[51] The emergence in early 1834 of the Grand National Consolidated Trades Union, a loose amalgamation of unions and co-operative organisations, may briefly have confirmed that view. The GNCTU soon claimed a million members, but its success was short-lived, not only due to the setback caused by the sentencing of the Tolpuddle Martyrs to seven years transportation for taking oaths, but also because employers resorted to the union-breaking tactic of forcing workers to renounce membership as a condition of hire. Owen himself briefly headed a mass movement, which he hoped would transform society quickly and peacefully, but by August of 1834 the GNCTU had collapsed and the trade union phase of Owenism was effectively over.

On a personal level the life of a wandering reformer cost Owen dear. Anne, his eldest daughter, died in 1830, followed by his wife, from whom he seems to have been effectively estranged or at least separated by ideology and distance, in 1831, and his youngest daughter the next year. The remaining daughter, Jane, joined her brothers in the United States, where she later married.

Eschewing political action, particularly 'the mania of radicalism' which he saw manifesting itself in the Chartist movement, Owen returned again to communitarianism. While he had largely ignored the efforts of an Irish landowner to set up a cooperative community at Ralahine in the early 1830s he now established what he called the Association of All Classes of All Nations.[52] Founded on 1 May 1835 it later amalgamated with another of his numerous organisations to become the Universal Community Society of Rational Religionists, or Rational Society for short. He also revived the village scheme, which was given considerable impetus by rising unemployment and poverty during the later 1830s. The Rational Society, backed by another Owenite paper, *The New Moral World*, attracted considerable working class support, and claimed 60 branches with up to 50,000 members crowding into weekly lectures by 1840. In 1839 Owen was even presented to Queen Victoria, whose late father, the Duke of Kent, was indebted to him for a loan, not repaid until Robert Dale pursued it after his father's death.[53]

The Rational Society, of which Owen, somewhat reluctantly, became 'Social Father', proved to be one of the most successful Owenite organisations.[54] It was held together by the strength of its branches and the zeal of its 'Social Missionaries', who like Owen himself, toured the country expounding on popular topics. Its funds were used to open 'Halls of Science', where the lectures and soirées were held. The halls were also used for services, during which social hymns praising the virtues of community, including some composed at New Harmony and Orbiston, were sung. Marriages were conducted and children named, sometimes by Owen himself, practices he had began at New Harmony. Not all of the propaganda was his critique of competition and a just social system and his views on religion and marriage continued to provoke fierce reaction in some quarters, leading in some instances to the burning of books and the storming of premises where Owenites met. Nevertheless the Rational Society provided the means for one final community project, begun amid great promise at Queenwood in Hampshire in 1839.[55] Again Owen assumed a paternal role, somewhat negating the social democracy that ought to have prevailed. In 1842 work began on a palatial building, the construction of which rapidly absorbed funds needed for day-to-day operations. By 1844 the project had cost £40,000 and bankrupted the parent society. Members tried to rescue the organisation, but lack of funds, lack of accommodation, limited agricultural skills and poor organisation led to Queenwood's ultimate demise. The Owenite movement slowly crumbled, its members finding outlets in other popular movements of the day, like Chartism, the Anti-Corn Law League, or the revived consumer co-operatives.

Owen was back in the United States by the autumn of 1844, visiting his family at New Harmony, and passing much of the period till 1846 travelling, lecturing and visiting communities. In 1846 he again acted as an intermediary in the border dispute in Oregon between Britain and the United States. He visited Ireland during the famine crisis, and in 1848, the year of revolutions, spent four months in Paris, an experience which seems to have contributed to a radical reappraisal of his views on parliamentary reform in Britain. This typically frantic timetable took its toll on a man now 77 years of age, and though far from inactive, he slowly declined. Converting to spiritualism, a fad of the time, he claimed to be in periodic contact with the spirits of those who had gone before him to the other world. As well as reissuing some of his earlier works he dictated the first volume of his autobiography, published in 1857. In

October 1858 after addressing an audience in Liverpool he was carried off the platform and later set out for Newtown, which he had not visited for more than half a century. Surrounded by Robert Dale and a handful of loyal followers he died there on 17 November, mourned as the lost 'Social Father', and almost immediately transformed by his obituarists and earliest biographers into the 'Father of Socialism'.[56]

Any assessment of Robert Owen is bound to be partial, but this study has emphasised the close links between his personal experience and his social philosophy, which found its ultimate expression in the community scheme and mutual co-operation. Hazlitt's view of Owen as a man of one idea was not wide of the mark. He has rightly been condemned for much woolly thinking, but was at least consistent in articulating the key role that education would play in his New Society. Packed into this were revolutionary ideas about the influence of environment on individuals and how they would relate to each other in communities, where some of the precepts of Old Society regarding the role of women, sexual relations, marriage and religion would be left behind. A few of the ideas that he picked up, like birth control, which, apart from its obvious function, empowered women, were so contentious they could not be given expression, though it was clear he intended population in the new communities to be regulated in that way. While he was muddled in his economic thinking, this could be put down to his failure to realise that the success of New Lanark as a dynamic capitalist enterprise under his management could hardly be replicated in multi-functional villages where the profit motive was secondary to co-operation, and to social and moral improvement. Despite the numerous contradictions in his own life and thought, some of which have been described here, his ideological legacy was profound. Many of these ideas, as Hazlitt noted, did not transmit too well in time or space, but the lessons Owen learned in Newtown, Stamford, London, Manchester and Glasgow certainly had a profound impact on his most tangible legacy, the remarkable if contrasting communities of New Lanark on the Clyde and New Harmony on the Wabash. In both places his ideas on environment, education, social welfare, co-operation and belief have provided a source of inspiration for the revitalisation of these historic communities. Of the many questions that remain to be answered about Robert Owen, perhaps the most intriguing, given the importance he attached to the impact of environment on character, is whether or not these places influenced him more than he did them.

## NOTES

1. *NHG*, 13 June, 1827.
2. NHWI, Hodge-Fretageot Papers, Maclure to Fretageot, 7 January, 1827.

3. *New York Advertiser*, 6 July, 1827; *NHG*, 25 July and 1 August 1827.

4. *NHG*, 3 October, 1827.

5. NHWI, Misc. Mss. Conditions of Contracts for Land, 26 July, 1827.

6. *Times*, 1 August, 1827.

7. *NHG*, 17 October, 1827, copied from Glasgow & New York papers.

8. *Orbiston Register*, 19 September, 1827; *NHG*, 9 April, 1828; Claeys, 'Introduction', xxxxiii.

9. See W.H. Fraser, *Alexander Campbell*, Manchester, 1996 and his articles cited in the bibliography.

10. R.D. Owen's Travel Diary, 1827.

11. R.Owen, *Address to the Agriculturists etc.*, London, 1827 reprinted in Claeys (ed.) *Selected Works*, vol. 2, pp. 105–113.

12. *NHG*, 12 December 1827 reported from the *Courier*.

13. R.D. Owen's Travel Diary 1827.

14. *NHG*, 6 February, 1828.

15. Ibid, 9 April, 1828.

16. Taylor, pp. 172–3.

17. *NHG*, 16 and 24 April, 1828.

18. Pelham Papers, J. Neef to W.C. Pelham 23 May 1828; *NHG*, 30 April, 1828.

19. *NHG*, 18 June, 2 July, 1828.

20. Ibid, 6 August, 1828.

21. NHWI Maclure-Fretageot corr., Maclure to Fretageot, 28 June 1829; ibid, Robert Owen Papers, Bond of 23 July, 1832.

22. K.D. Owen Papers, Deed of A.C.D.Owen 29 October, 1828.

23. NHWI, Branigin-Owen Coll., R.D. Owen to M.J. Owen, 26 September, 1832.

24. On Poinsett, DAB, vol.xx, pp. 30–32; J.R. Poinsett, *Notes on Mexico*, London 1825.

25. Co-operative Union, Owen Coll., B. Milan to R. Owen, 30 August 1828; see generally W.H. Timms, 'Robert Owen's Texas Project', *Southwestern Hist. Quart.*, vol. 52, 1947, pp. 286–93 and L. Garver, 'Benjamin Rush Milam', *Southwestern Hist. Quart.*, vol. 38, 1934, pp. 79–121.

26. R. Owen, *Memorial to the Mexican Public*, London, 1828, reprinted in Claeys (ed.), *Selected Works*, vol. 2, pp. 115–122.

27. Co-operative Union, Owen Coll., V. Rocafuerte to R. Owen, 17 October, 1828.

28. Ibid, R. Owen to V. Rocafuerte, 31 October, 1828, partly reproduced in Podmore, p. 338.

29. The journey is recounted in *Robert Owen's Opening Speech and his Reply to the Rev. A. Campbell*, Cincinnati, 1829 ('Preliminary Statement')

30. Ibid, pp. 189–90.

31. Ibid, p. 191; on the situation in the country National Archives, Washington, D.C., Despatches from US Ministers To Mexico, vol. 4, April 1828 – Feb. 1830, mainly those of Poinsett reveal the underlying tensions in relations between the US and Mexico, and Anglo-US relations.

32. NHWI, Maclure-Fretageot Corr., Maclure to Fretageot, 28 January, 1829.

33. Ibid, Maclure to Fretageot, 18 February, 1829.

34. Owen, 'Preliminary Statement', p. 196.

35. Ibid, p. 210.

36. Maclure to Fretageot, 18 February, 1829.

37. Fretageot to Maclure, 12 March and 8 April, 1829.
38. Owen, 'Preliminary Statement', p. 226.
39. F. Trollope, *Domestic Manners*, London, 1832, (1974 Reprint) describes the debate, pp. 147–53.
40. Ibid, p. 153.
41. *National Intelligencer*, 20/22 July, 1829.
42. Unidentified press cutting 22 August, 1829.
43. *Glasgow Chronicle*, 12 September, 1829.
44. Goldsmith's Library, Pare-Owen Papers ('Robert Owen's Scrapbook'), W. Pare to R. Owen, 26th September, 1829.
45. This quotation is from another unidentified press cutting probably 1832, 'Mr Owen at Dundee'.
46. Harrison, p. 195.
47. See W.H. Oliver, 'The Labour Exchange Phase of the Co-operative Movement', *Oxford Econ. Papers*, vol. X, 1958, pp. 355–67.
48. Donnachie and Hewitt, pp. 70–71, 104, 108–9.
49. Harrison, especially pp. 201–7.
50. On the trade union phase, see Harrison pp. 208–16; W. Hamish Fraser, 'Robert Owen and the Workers' in Butt (ed.), pp. 76–98; also his 'Owenite Socialism in Scotland', *Scott. Econ. & Social Hist.*, vol. 16, 1996, pp. 60–91.
51. Harrison, p. 211.
52. Ibid, pp. 216–32 on the AACAN.
53. Podmore, 503–4; Indiana State Library, Robert Dale Owen Papers, Letters concerning a loan to the Duke of Kent, 1859.
54. Harrison, pp. 218–32 on the Rational Society.
55. See R.G. Garnett, *Co-operation and the Owenite Socialist Communities*, Manchester, 1972; Harrison, pp. 123–4, 172–3, 180–92; E. Royle, *Robert Owen and the Commencement of the Millennium*, Manchester, 1998, is the most detailed study of the last Owenite community in Britain and Owen's personal involvement in its affairs.
56. The best account of his declining years is still Podmore, pp. 575–630.

# SELECT BIBLIOGRAPHY

For a comprehensive bibliography of Owen's writings and works by
Owenites see J.F.C. Harrison's *Robert Owen and the Owenites in Britain
and America* and the modern reprint of Owen's major works edited by
Gregory Claeys, *Selected Works of Robert Owen*.

The catalogue produced for the Goldsmiths' Library of Economic Literature exhibition on *Robert Owen 1771–1858*, London, 1959, also includes
the most important of his works.

## ARCHIVAL SOURCES

*Blair Castle, Blair Atholl*
  Atholl Mss. Letter Book of Robert Owen
*Bodleian Library, Oxford*
  Abinger Papers
  Wilberforce Papers
*British Library*
  Place Papers
*Burgerbliothek, Bern*
  Owen-Fellenberg Correspondence
*Cooperative Union Library, Manchester*
  Robert Owen Correspondence
*Corstorphine Historical Society, Edinburgh*
  Corstorphine Kirk Records
*Devon Record Office*
  Sidmouth Papers
*Edinburgh University Library*
  Cash Book of the New Lanark Institution, 1816–25
  Letters of Dale and Owen
*Glasgow University Archives: Business Records Centre*
  Gourock Ropework Company Mss.
*Goldsmiths' Library, University of London*
Pare Collection, Newspaper Cuttings re Owenite Cooperation from the Library
  of William Pare 1828–42
  Robert Owen Scrapbook
*Highland Council Archives*
  Inverness Burgh Records
*Indiana State Library, Indianapolis*
  Robert Dale Owen Papers

*Library of Congress, Washington DC*
   Department of Prints and Photographs Collection
   Trist Papers
*Library of the Religious Society of Friends*
   William Allen Papers and Records
   Digest Registers of Births, Marriages and Burials
   Quaker Biographies
   Register of Members
*Lindsay Institute, Lanark*
   Commissioners of Supply for the County of Lanark Minutes
   Lanark Burgh Records
   Miscellaneous Records
   Newspaper Cuttings Books
*Mitchell Library, Glasgow*
   Burgesses and Guild Brethern of Glasgow
   Dale-Alexander Correspondence, 1787–97
   New Lanark School Books and Records
   Patent Records
   Plans, drawing and maps of New Lanark
*Motherwell District Libraries*
   Hamilton of Dalzell Collection
   Orbiston Collection
*National Archives of Scotland*
   Abercromby of Forglen Muniments
   Campbell of Jura Papers
   Court of Session Records
   Melville Castle Muniments
   Register House Plans
*National Library of Scotland*
   Advocates' Manuscripts
   Combe Papers
   Dale-Moncrieff Letters
   Liston Papers
   Owen Letters
*National Libary of Wales*
   Galpin Correspondence
*Nuffield College Library, Oxford*
   Robert Owen Papers
*Robert Owen Memorial Museum, Newtown*
   Robert Owen Collection
*Signet Library*
   Session Papers
*National Archives, Washington, DC*
   Despatches from US Ministers to Mexico
*University of Illinois – Champaign-Urbana*
   *Illinois Historical Survey*
   Bestor Papers
   Dorsey-Owen Collection
   New Harmony Records

*University of Southern Indiana, Evansville*
  Center for Communal Studies Collection
*Workingmen's Institute and Library, New Harmony, Indiana*
  Branigin-Owen Papers
  Hodge-Fretageot Papers
  Maclure's Journals
  Maclure-Fretageot Correspondence
  New Harmony Correspondence
  Pelham Papers
  Robert Owen Papers
  Robert Dale Owen Papers


## NEWSPAPERS & PERIODICALS

*Blackwood's Magazine*
*Caledonian Mercury*
*Clydesdale Journal*
*The Crisis*
*The Economist*
*The Freemans Journal*
*Gentleman's Magazine*
*Glasgow Chronicle*
*Glasgow Courier*
*Glasgow Mercury*
*New Harmony Gazette*
*Orbiston Register*
*The Scotsman*
*Scots Magazine*
*Stamford Mercury*
*The Times*


## PARLIAMENTARY PAPERS

1816 III Report from the Select Committee on the State of Children Employed in the Manufactories of the United Kingdom.

1816 IV Reports from the Select Committee on the Education of the Lower Orders of the Metropolis.

1819 IV Digest of Parochial Returns made to the Select Committee on the Education of the Poor. Part III.

1823 VI Report from the Select Committee on the Condition of the Labouring Poor in Ireland.

1824 V Reports of the Select Committee on Artisans and Machinery.
    VIII Report of the Select Committee . . . into Disturbances in Ireland.

1825 VII Minutes of Evidence re . . . Ireland.

1833 XX First Report . . . on the Employment of Children in Factories.

1833 XXI Second Report . . . on the Employment of Children in Factories.

1834 X Report from the Select Committee on Handloom Weavers' Petitions.

1834 XIX Supplementary Report . . . on Children.
1835 VII Report from the Select Commitee on Education in England and Wales.
1837–38 XXVIII Reports of Inspectors of Factories.
1839 XLII Reports of the Assistant Commissioners on Handloom Weavers.
1840 X Reports from the Select Committee on the Act for the Regulation of Mills and Factories.

## BOOKS PRE-1900

Adams, John Q, *Memoirs of John Quincy Adams*, vol. 12, Philadelphia, 1877.

*Addresses and Messages of the Presidents of the United States*, vol. 1, New York, 1847.

Anon, *A Letter containing some observations on the delusive nature of the system proposed by Robert Owen Esq for the amelioration of the people of Ireland*, Dublin & London, 1823.

Aiton, Rev. J., *Mr Owen's Objections to Christianity and a New View of Society, refuted by a plain statement of facts. With a hint to Archibald Hamilton Esq of Dalziel*, Edinburgh, 1824.

Allen, W., *Reply on Behalf of the London Proprietors to the Address to the Inhabitants of New Lanark*, London, 1819.

*Life of William Allen*, London, 1847.

Bacon, Richard M., *A Report of the Transactions at Holkham sheep-shearing . . . containing Owen's Attempt to explain the cause of commercial and other difficulties*, Norwich, 1821.

Baines, E., *Mr Owen's Establishment at New Lanark, a Failure!*, Leeds, 1838.

—*History of the Cotton Manufacture in Great Britain*, London, 1835 (reprint London, 1972).

Beatson, Jasper, *An Examination of Mr Owen's plans for relieving distress, removing discontent and 'Recreating the character of man'*, Glasgow, 1823.

Bell, Andrew, *An experiment in education made at the Male Asylum of Madras. Suggesting a system by which a school or family may teach itself under the superintendence of the master or parent*, London and Edinburgh, 1797.

—*An experiment in education. 2nd edition. To which is prefixed the scheme of a school on the above model . . . and a Board of Education and poor-rates suggested*, London, 1805.

Brown, J., *Remarks on the plans and publications of Robert Owen Esq of New Lanark*, Edinburgh, 1817.

Brown, Paul, *Twelve Months in New Harmony*, Cincinnati, 1827 (reprinted 1972).

Christianus, *Mr Owen's Proposed Villages for the Poor shown to be highly favourable to Chritianity in a letter to William Wilberforce Esq MP*, London, 1819.

Combe, Abram, *An address to the conductors of the periodical press, upon the causes of religious and political disputes*, Edinburgh, 1823.

—*Metaphorical sketches of the old and new systems, with opinions on interesting subjects*, Edinburgh, 1823.

—*Observations on the old and new views, and their effects on the conduct of individuals, as manifested in the proceedings of the Edinburgh Christian Instructor and Mr Owen*, Edinburgh & Glasgow, 1823.

—*The Life and Testimony of Abram Combe in favour of Robert Owen's New Views of Man and Society*, London 1844.

Courtauld, George, *Address to those who may be disposed to remove to the United*

*States of America, on the advantages of equitable associations of capital and labour, in the formation of agricultural establishments in the interior of the country*, Sudbury & London, 1820.

Davidson, W., *History of Lanark and Guide to the Scenery*, Lanark, 1828.

Fleming, G. A., *A Day at New Lanark by the Editor of the New Moral World*, Birmingham, 1839.

Flower, G., *History of the English Settlement in Edwards County, Illinois, founded in 1817 and 1818 by Morris Birkbeck and George Flower*, Chicago, 1882.

Garnett, T., *Observations on a Tour Thro' the Highlands and part of the Western Islands of Scotland . . . to which are added . . . A Description of the Falls of Clyde etc*, new ed. London, 1811.

Godwin, William, *The Enquirer. Reflections on Education, Manners and Literature in a Series of Essays*, London, 1797.

Griscom, J., *A Year in Europe. Comprising a Journal of Observations in England, Scotland, etc in 1818 and 1819*, 2 vols, New York, 1823.

Hebert, W., *A Visit to the Colony of Harmony in Indiana, in the U.S.A. recently purchased by Mr Owen*, London, 1825.

Hulme, Thomas, *Journal Made During a Tour in the Western Countries of America 1818–1819*, in H. Lindley, *Indiana As Seen by Early Travellers*, Indianapolis, 1916.

*Jones' Directory or Useful Pocket Companion*, Glasgow, 1787.

Jones, L., *The Life, Times and Labours of Robert Owen*, London, 1890.

Lancaster, Joseph, *Improvements in education, as it respects the industrious classes . . . and a detail of some practical experiments conducive to that end*, London, 1803.

—3rd edition, *. . . Contains an account of the institution for the education of one thousand poor children, Borough Road, Southwark*, London, 1805.

—*Outlines of a Plan for Educating Ten Thousand Poor Children*, London, 1806.

M'Gavin, W., *The Fundamental Priciples of the New Lanark System Exposed*, Glasgow, 1824.

Macnab, H.G., *The New Views of Mr Owen of Lanark Impartially Examined*, London, 1819.

—'One Formerly a Teacher at New Lanark', *Robert Owen at New Lanark*, Manchester, 1839.

Owen, R., *A Statement Regarding the New Lanark Establishment*, Edinburgh, 1812.

—*A New View of Society*, London, 1813–16.

—*An Address Delivered to the Inhabitants of New Lanark*, London, 1816.

—*Observations on the Effect of the Manufacturing System*, London, 1815.

—*Development of the Plan for the Relief of the Poor*, London, 1817.

—*New View of Society. Tracts relative to this subject; viz a College of Industry . . . a Brief Sketch of the Religious Society of People called Shakers. With an Account of the Public Proceedings*, London, 1818.

—*Two Memorials on Behalf of the Working Classes*, London, 1818.

—*An Address to the Master Manufacturers of Great Britain*, Bolton, 1819.

—*Mr Owen's Proposed Arrangements for the Distressed Working Classes Shown to be Consistent with Sound Principles of Political Economy, in three Letters to David Ricardo, M.P.*, London, 1819

—*Report to the County of Lanark*, Glasgow, 1821.

—*Permanent relief for the British agricultural & manufacturing labourers, and the Irish peasantry*, London, 1822 (Dublin, 1823).

—*Report of the proceedings at the several public meetings, held in Dublin, by Robert Owen, Esq*, Dublin, 1823.

—*An explanation of the cause of the distress which pervades the civilized parts of the world, and of the means whereby it may be removed*, London, 1823.

—*Two Discourses on a New System of Society*, Philadelphia, 1825.

—*Address to the Agriculturists, Mechanics and Manufacturers of Great Britain and Ireland*, London, 1827.

—*Memorial to the Mexican Republic*, London, 1828.

—*A Short Narrative of the Author's Voyage to Mexico*, Cincinnati, 1829.

—*Six Lectures on Charity delivered at the Institution of New Lanark*, London, 1834.

—*Lectures on the Rational System of Society*, London, 1841.

—*The Revolution in the Mind and Practice of the Human Race*, London, 1849.

—*Life of Robert Owen by Himself*, London, 1857 (reprinted 1971 with introduction by John Butt).

—*A Supplementary Appendix to the First Volume of the Life of Robert Owen Containing a Series of Reports, Addresses, Memorials etc*, Vol 1A (1803–20), London, 1858.

Owen, R. and Campbell, A., *Debate on the Evidences of Christianity*, Bethany, Va., 1829 (London, 1839)

Owen, R.D., *An Outline of the System of Education at New Lanark*, Glasgow, 1824.

—*Threading My Way: Twenty Years of Autobiography*, London, 1874.

Owen, William, *Diary of William Owen from November 10, 1824 to April 20, 1825*, ed. J.W. Hiatt (reprint of 1906 Indianapolis ed.), Clifton, 1973.

Philanthropos (J.M.Morgan), *Remarks on the practicability of Mr Robert Owen's plan to improve the condition of the lower classes*, London, 1819.

Poinsett, J.R., *Notes on Mexico . . . Made in the Autumn on 1822*, Philadelphia, 1824 (London ed. 1825).

*Proceedings of the First General Meeting of the British and Foreign Philanthropic Society for the Permanent Relief of the Labouring Classes*, London, 1822.

Sargant, W.L., *Robert Owen and His Social Philosophy*, London, 1860.

Southey, R., *Journal of a Tour in Scotland in 1819*, London, 1929.

Svedenstierna, E.T., *Tour through part of England and Scotland in the years 1802 and 1803*, Stockholm, 1804 (English ed. with introduction by M.W. Flinn, Newton Abbott, 1973).

Trollope, Frances, *Domestic Manners of the Americans*, London, 1832 (ed. Donald Malley), Gloucester, Mass. 1974.

Wilberforce, Robert and Samuel, *The Life of William Wilberforce*, 5 vols., London, 1839.

Woods, John, *Two Year's Residence in the Settlement on the English Prairie in the Illinois Country United States*, London, 1822.

Wordsworth, D., *Recollections of a Tour Made in Scotland A.D. 1803*, 3rd ed., Edinburgh, 1894.


### POST-1900

Anderson, J.R., *Burgess and Guild Brethern of Glasgow*, Edinburgh, 1935.

Andrews, C.B. (ed.) *The Torrington Diaries*, London, 1935.

Arndt, K.J.R., *George Rapp's Harmony Society*, Rutherford, 1972.

Arndt, K.J.R. (ed.), *A Documentary History of the Indiana Decade of the Harmony Society 1814–1824, vol. II 1820–1824*, Indianapolis, 1978.

—*Harmony on the Wabashn Transition 1824–1826. A Documentary History*, Worcester, Mass., 1982.

Arnold, J.E., 'New Lanark: rescue, preservation and development' in D.C. Mays, M.S. Moss and M.K. Oglethorpe (eds.), *Visions of Scotland's Past. Looking to the Future*, East Linton, 2000.

Bain, Margaret I., *Les Voyageurs Francais en Ecosse*, Paris, 1931.

Bazant, J. 'Mexico from Independence to 1867', in L. Bethell (ed.) *The Cambridge History of Latin America*, vol. III, Cambridge, 1985, 423–470.

Beecher, J., *Charles Fourier. The Visionary and His World*, Berkley, 1986.

Belchem, John, *'Orator' Hunt. Henry Hunt and English Working Class Radicalism*, Oxford, 1985.

Bestor. A.E. (ed.) *Education and Reform at New Harmony. Correspondence of William Maclure and Marie Duclos Fretageot 1820–1833*, Indiana Historical Society, Indianapolis, 1948.

—*Backwoods Utopias. The Sectarian and Owenite Phase of Communitarian Socialism in America: 1663–1829*, Philadelphia, 1950.

Bickle, R. and Molly Scott Cato (eds.), *New Views of Society: Robert Owen for the 21st Century*, Glasgow, 2009.

Bindhoff, S.T. (ed.), *British Diplomatic Representatives 1789–1852*, London, 1934.

Blake, G., *'The Gourock'. The Gourock Ropework Company Ltd.*, Glasgow, 1963.

Boewe, C., *Prairie Albion. An English Settlement in Pioneer Illinois*, Carbondale, Ill, 1962.

Brant, Irving, *James Madison. Commander in Chief 1812–1836*, Indianapolis/New York, 1961.

—*The Fourth President. A Life of James Madison*, London, 1970.

Brodie, Fawn M., *Thomas Jefferson. An Intimate History*, New York, 1974.

Brown, S.J., *Thomas Chalmers and the Godly Commonwealth in Scotland*, Oxford, 1982.

Butt, J. (ed.) *Robert Owen: Prince of Cotton Spinners*, Newton Abbot, 1971.

Carnall, Geoffrey, *Robert Southey and His Age. The Development of a Conservative Mind*, Oxford, 1960.

Chapman, S. D., *The Early Factory Masters*, Newton Abbot, 1967.

*The Cotton Industry in the Industrial Revolution*, 2nd ed. London, 1987.

Cherok, R. J., *Debating for God: Alexander Campbell's Challenge to Skepticism in Antebellum America*, Abilene, Texas, 2009.

Claeys, G., *Machinery, Money and the Millennium. From Moral Economy to Socialism, 1815–1860*, London, 1987.

Claeys, G. (ed.) *Selected Works of Robert Owen*, 4 vols, London, 1993.

Claeys, G. (ed.), *Owenite Socialism: Pamphlets and Correspondence*, 10 vols, London, 2005.

Clarke, G. (ed.) *John Bellers. His Life, Times and Writings*, London/New York, 1987.

Cole, G.D.H., *Robert Owen*, London, 1925.

— *The Life of Robert Owen*, with new introd. by Margaret Cole, London, 1965.

Cole, Margaret, *Robert Owen of New Lanark*, London, 1953.

Conway, S. (ed.) *The Correspondence of Jeremy Bentham*, vols 8–10, Oxford, 1988–94.

Cooke, A.J., *Stanley. Its History and Development*, Dundee, 1977.

Cooke, A.J., *Stanley. From Arkwright Village to Commuter Suburb: 1784–2003*, Perth, 2003.

Cooke, A.J., *The Rise and Fall of the Scottish Cotton Industry 1778–1914*, Manchester, 2010.

Cookson, J.E., *Lord Liverpool's Administration. The Crucial Years 1815–1822*, Edinburgh, 1975.

Cullen, A., *Adventures in Socialism. New Lanark Establishment and Orbiston Community*, Glasgow, 1910 (new ed. Clifton, 1972).

Davis, R.A. and O'Hagan, F., *Continuum Library of Educational Thought: Robert Owen*, London, 2010.

Donnachie, I., 'Orbiston: A Scottish Owenite Community 1825–1828' in J. Butt (ed.) *Robert Owen. Prince of Cotton Spinners*, Newton Abbot, 1971, 136–167.

Donnachie, I., 'Robert Owen and New Lanark: The lessons of history' in C. Tsuzuki, N. Hijikata and A. Kurimoto (eds.), *The Emergence of Global Citizenship: Utopian Ideas, Co-operative Movements and the Third Sector*, Tokyo, 2005, 59–79.

Donnachie, I., 'A new moral world? International dimensions of Owenism 1815–1830', in Elizabeth Russell (ed.), *Transforming Utopia: Looking Forward to the End*, Oxford, 2009, 185–193.

Doskey, J.S. (ed.), *The European Journals of William Maclure*, American Philosophical Society, Philadelphia, 1988.

Edwards, M. M., *The Growth of the British Cotton Trade 1780–1815*, Manchester, 1967.

Elliott, Josephine M. (ed.) *Partnership for Prosperity. The Correspondence of William Maclure and Marie Duclos Fretageot, 1820–1833*, Indianapolis, Indiana Historical Society, 1994.

Elliott, Josephine M. (ed.) *To Holland and to New Harmony. Robert Dale Owen's Travel Journal 1825–1826*, Indianapolis, 1969.

—*Robert Dale Owen's Travel Journal 1827*, Indianapolis, 1977.

Farnie, D. A., *The English Cotton Industry and the World Market 1815–1896*, Oxford, 1979.

Fay, C.R., *Huskisson and His Age*, London, 1951.

Ferber, Michael, *The Social Vision of William Blake*, Princeton, 1985.

Fitton, R. S., *The Arkwrights. Spinners of Fortune*, Manchester, 1989.

Fitton, R.S. and Wadsworth, A.P., *The Strutts and the Arkwrghts*, Manchester, 1958.

Ford, W.C. (ed.) *Writings of John Quincy Adams*, vols. V and VI, New York, 1915–16.

Fraser, W. Hamish, *Alexander Campbell and the Search for Socialism*, Manchester, 1996.

Fryer, P., *The Birth Controllers*, London, 1965.

Furneaux, Robin, *William Wilberforce*, London, 1974.

Galen, B., *Rural Disorder and Police Reform in Ireland, 1812–36*, London, 1970.

Gash, Norman, 1984, *Lord Liverpool*, Weidenfeld & Nicolson.

Garnett, R.G., *Co-operation and the Owenite Socialist Communities in Britain, 1825–45*, Manchester, 1972.

Gillen, Mollie, *Royal Duke. Augustus Frederick, Duke of Sussex (1773–1843)*, London, 1976.

Ginter, D.E. (ed.) *Voting Records of the British House of Commons*, Vol. VI Divisions 1810–20, London, 1995.

Gordon, Barry, *Political Economy in Parliament 1819–1823*, London, 1979.

Green, Constance M., *Washington. Village and Capital 1800–1878*, Princeton, 1972.

Green, Daniel, *Great Cobbett. The Noblest Agitator*, London, 1983.

Greig, J. (ed.) *The Farington Diary by Joseph Farington, RA*, London, 1928.

Grugel, Lee E., *George Jacob Holyoake. A Study in the Evolution of Victorian Radicalism*, Philadelphia, 1976.

Hardy, D. and Davidson, L. (eds.), *Utopian Thought and Communal Experience*, Middlesex Polytechnic, 1989.

Hargreaves, Mary W.M., *The Presidency of John Quincy Adams*, Kansas, 1985.

Harrison, J.F.C., *Robert Owen and the Owenites in Britain and America*, London, 1969.

Hatton, Helen E., *The Largest Amount of Good. Quaker Relief in Ireland 1654–1921*, Kingston & Montreal/London, 1993.

Hayden, Dolores, *Seven American Utopias*, Cambridge, Mass. 1976.

—*The Second Coming. Popular Millenarianism, 1780–1850*, Rutgers, 1979.

Hiatt, J.W. (ed.) *Diary of William Owen from November 10, 1824 to April 20, 1825*, Indianapolis, 1906.

Hills R. L., *Power in the Industrial Revolution*, Manchester, 1970.

Hilton, Boyd, *Corn, Cash, Commerce. The Economic Policies of the Tory Governments 1815–1830*, Oxford, 1977.

Hinde, Wendy, *Castlereagh*, London, 1981.

Hindle, G.B., *Provision for the Relief of the Poor in Manchester 1754–1826*, Manchester, 1975.

Historic Scotland, *Nomination of New Lanark for Inclusion in the World Heritage List*, Edinburgh, 2000.

Hollander, Samuel, *The Economics of David Ricardo*, London, 1979.

Holloway, Mark, *Heavens on Earth. Utopian Communities in America 1680–1880*, London, 1951.

Hopkins, James K., *A Woman to Deliver Her People. Joanna Southcott and English Millenarianism in an Era of Revolution*, Austin, Tex., 1982.

Hunt, G. (ed.), *The First Forty Years of Washington Society*, New York, 1906.

Indiana Historical Commission, *New Harmony As Seen by Participants and Travellers*, Philadelphia, 1975.

James, Patricia, *Population Malthus. His Life and Times*, London, 1979.

Jeremy, D. J., *Transatlantic Industrial Revolution: The Diffusion of Textile Technologies Between Britain and America, 1790s–1830s*, Oxford, 1981.

King, James, *William Blake. His Life*, London, 1991.

Kolmerten, Carol A., *Women in Utopia. The Ideology of Gender in the American Owenite Communities*, Bloomington, Indiana, 1990.

Leopold, R.W., *Robert Dale Owen: A Biography*, Cambridge, Mass., 1940.

Lincoln, W.B., *Nicholas I. Emperor and Autocrat of All the Russias*, London, 1978.

Lloyd-Jones, R. and Lewis, M.J., *Manchester and the Age of the Factory*, London, 1988.

Locke, Don, *A fantasy of reason. The life and thought of William Godwin*, London, 1980

Lockwood, George B., *The New Harmony Movement*, New York, 1905 (with new introd. by Mark Holloway, 1971).

Leopold, R.W., *Robert Dale Owen. A Biography*, London, 1940.

Macdonald, D., *The Diaries of Donald Macdonald 1824–26* (ed. C.D. Snedeker), Indiana Historical Society, 1942 (reprinted, 1973).

McLaren, Angus, *A History of Contraception*, Oxford, 1990.

McLaren, D.J., *David Dale of New Lanark. A Bright Luminary to Scotland*, Glasgow, 2nd ed. 1990.

McCoy, Drew R., *The Last of the Fathers. James Madison and the Republican Legacy*, Cambridge, 1989.

Manning, William R., *Early Diplomatic Relations between the United States and Mexico*, Baltimore, 1916.

Marshall, Peter H., *William Godwin*, Yale, 1984.

Meyer, M.C. and Sherman, W.L., *The Course of Mexican History*, New York, 1979.

Middleton, Charles, R., *The Administration of British Foreign Policy 1782–1846*, Durham, N.C., 1977.

Miles, Dudley, *Francis Place 1771–1854. The Life of a Remarkable Radical*, London, 1988.

Morton, A. L., *The Life and Ideas of Robert Owen*, London, 1962.

Muncy, R.L., *Sex and Marriage in Utopian Communities*, Bloomington, 1973.

Nevins, A. (ed.) *The Diary of John Quincy Adams 1794–1845*, New York, 1951.

New, Chester, W., *The Life of Henry Brougham to 1830*, Oxford, 1961.

Niven, J., *Martin Van Buren. The Romatic Age of American Politics*, New York/ Oxford, 1983.

O'Brien, D.P., *J.R. McCulloch. A Study in Classical Economics*, London, 1970.

Pankhurst, R.K.P., *William Thompson (1775–1833). Britain's Pioneer Socialist, Feminist and Co-operator*, London, 1954 (new ed. 1991).

Pankhurst, R.K.P, *The Saint Simonians, Mill and Carlyle. A Preface to Modern Thought*, London, 1957.

Parker, R.A.C., *Coke of Norfolk. A Financial and Agricultural Study 1707–1842*, Oxford, 1975.

Pears, Thomas C. (ed.), *New Harmony. An Adventure in Happiness. Papers of Thomas and Sarah Pears*, Indianapolis, 1933 (reprinted 1973).

Pelham, W., 'Letters of William Pelham, 1825–26' in H. Lindley, *Indiana as Seen by Early Travellers*, Indianapolis, 1916.

Perkins, Bradford, *Castlereagh and Adams. England and the United States 1812–1823*, California, 1964.

Pitzer, D.E. and Elliott, Josephine M., *New Harmony's Fourth of July Tradition*, New Harmony, 1976.

Plummer, A., *Bronterre. A Political Biography of Bronterre O'Brien 1804–1864*, London, 1971.

Podmore, F., *Robert Owen: A Biography*, London, 1906

Pollard, S. and Salt, J. (eds.), *Robert Owen. Prophet of the Poor*, London, 1971.

Pollock, J., *Wilberforce*, London, 1977.

Prentice, A., *Historical Sketches and Personal Recollections of Manchester 1792–1832*, London, 1851.

Priestly, F.E.L. (ed.) *Enquiry Concerning Political Justice and its Influence on Morals and Happiness by William Godwin*, 3rd ed. corrected, 3 vols., Toronto, 1946.

Raistrick, A. (ed.), *The Hatchett Diary. A tour through the counties of England and Scotland in 1796 visiting their mines and manufactories*, Truro, 1967.

—*Quakers in Science and Industry*, new ed. Newton Abbott, 1968.

Renwick, R. (ed.), *Extracts from the Records of the Burgh of Glasgow*, vol. IX 1796–1808, Glasgow, 1914.

Rippy, J.F., *Joel R. Poinsett. Versatile American*, 1935.

Robert Owen Bicentennial Conference, *Robert Owen's American Legacy*, Indiana Historical Society, Indianapolis, 1972.

Roberts, M., *The Whig Party 1807–1812*, London, 1965.

Robertson, A.D., *Lanark: the Burgh and its Councils*, Lanark, 1974.

Roper, Derek, *Reviewing Before the Edinburgh 1788–1802*, London, 1978.

Royle, E. *Victorian Infidels. The Origins of the British Secularist Movement 1791–1866*, Manchester, 1974.

—*Robert Owen and the Commencement of the Millennium. A Study of the Harmony Community*, Manchester, 1998.

Rush, R., *A Residence at the Court of London* (3 vols. 1833), ed. P. Zeigler, London, 1987.

Sack, J.J., *The Grenvillites 1801–29. Party Politics and Factionalism in the Age of Pitt and Liverpool*, Urbana/London, 1979.

St Clair, William, *The Godwins and the Shelleys. The Biography of a Family*, London, 1989.

Sambrook, James, *William Cobbett*, London, 1973.

Schama, S., *Patriots and Liberators. Revolution in the Netherlands 1780–1813*, London, 1977.

Scola, R., *The Food Supply of Manchester: Feeding the Victorian City 1770–1870*, Manchester, 1992.

Silber, Kate, *Pestalozzi. The Man and His Work*, London, 1960.

Silver, H., *The Concept of Popular Education*, London, 1965. (new ed. 1977)

Silver, H. (ed.) *Robert Owen On Education*, Cambridge, 1969.

Slaven, A., *The Development of the West of Scotland 1750–1960*, London, 1975.

Snedeker, C.D. (ed.) *The Diaries of Donald Macdonald 1824–1826*, Indianapolis, 1942.

Soloway, R.A., *Prelates and People. Ecclesiastical Social Thought in England 1783–1852*, London, 1969.

Stirling, A.M.W., *Coke of Norfolk and His Friends. The Life of Thomas William Coke, First Earl of Leicester*, London, 1912.

Stroud, Patricia T., *Thomas Say. New World Naturalist*, Philadelphia, 1992.

Sunstein, Emily, W., *Mary Shelley. Romance and Reality*, Boston/London, 1989.

Syrett, D. and Di Nardo, R.L., *The Commissioned Sea Officers of the Royal Navy 1660–1815*, London, Navy Records Society, 1994.

Taylor, Anne, *Visions of Harmony. A Study of Nineteenth-Century Millenariansim*, Oxford, 1987.

Taylor, Keith, *The Political Ideas of the Utopian Socialists*, London, 1982.

Temperley, H., *The Foreign Policy of Canning 1822–1827*, London, 1925.

Thompson, B., *Devastating Eden: The Search for Utopia in America*, London, 2004.

Thorne, R.G. (ed.), *The History of Parliament. The House of Commons 1790–1820*, vols. I–V, London, 1986.

Tsuzuki, C. (ed.), *Robert Owen and the World of Co-operation*, Tokyo, 1992.

Vaughan, W.E. (ed.), *A New History of Ireland. V. Ireland Under the Union 1801–70*, Oxford, 1989.

Wadsworth, A.P., *The Strutts and the Arkwrights, 1758–1830*, Manchester, 1973.

Wallers, Ronald G., *American Reformers 1815–1860*, New York, 1978.

Ward, J.T., *The Factory Movement 1830–1855*, London, 1962.

Watters, R., *Albert Gallatin. Jeffersonian Financier and Diplomat*, New York, 1957.

Weaver, S.A., *John Fielden and the Politics of Popular Radicalism*, Oxford, 1987.

Weiner, Margery, *The Sovereign Remedy. Europe After Waterloo*, London, 1971.

White, M.D., *A Sketch of Chester Harding, Artist*, Boston, 1890.

Williamson, A., *Thomas Paine*, London, 1973.

Wilson, W.E., *The Angel and the Serpent. The Story of New Harmony*, Bloomington, 1964 (new ed. 1984)

Young, James S., *The Washington Community 1800–1828*, New York, 1966.

Ziegler, P., *Melbourne. A Biography of William Lamb, 2nd Viscount Melbourne*, London, 1976.

—*Addington. A Life of Henry Addington, First Viscount Sidmouth*, London, 1985.


## ARTICLES

Arndt, K.J.R., 'Did Frederick Rapp Cheat Robert Owen?', *Western Pennsylvania Historical Magazine*, 1978, 358–365.

Botscharow, Lucy J., 'Disharmony in Utopia. Social Categories in Robert Owen's New Harmony', *Communal Societies*, vol. 9, 1989, 76–90.

Butt, J., Donnachie, I. and Hume, J.R., 'Robert Owen of New Lanark (1771–1858)', *Industrial Archaeology*, vol 8, 1971, 186–93.

Carmony, D.F. and Elliott, Josephine M.,'New Harmony, Indiana: Robert Owen's Seedbed for Utopia', *Indiana Magazine of History*, vol. 76, 1980, 161–261.

Chaloner, W.H., 'Robert Owen, Peter Drinkwater and the Early Factory System in Manchester, 1788–1800', *Bulletin of the John Rylands Library*, 37, 1954, 78–102.

—'The Cheshire Activities of Matthew Boulton and James Watt of Soho, 1776–1817' in W.R. Ward (ed.), *Palatinate Studies. Chapters in the Social and Industrial History of Lancashire and Cheshire*, Manchester, 1992

Clark, Sylvia, 'Chorlton Mills and Their Neighbours', *Industrial Archaeology Review*, vol. II, 1978, 207–239.

Cooke, A.J., 'Richard Arkwright and the Scottish Cotton Industry', *Textile History*, vol. 10, 1979, 196–202.

—'Robert Owen and the Stanley Mills, 1802–1811', *Business History*, vol. 21, 1979, 106–111

Dean, Russell, "Trading Owenism", Co-operation, Socialism and Capitalism, 1827–34', *Scottish Labour History Society Journal*, 31, 1996, 8–34.

Donnachie, I. 'Robert Owen's Welsh Childhood: Kin, Culture and Environment 1771–c1781', *Montgomeryshire Collections*, vol. 86, 1998, 81–96.

—'Historic Tourism to New Lanark, and the Falls of Clyde 1795–1830', *Journal of Tourism and Cultural Change*, vol. 2, no. 3, 2004, 145–162

Donnachie, I. and Mooney, G., 'From Owenite socialism to Blairite socialism: Utopia and dystopia in Robert Owen and New Labour', *Critique: Journal of Socialist Theory*, vol. 35, no. 2, 2007, 275–291.

Elliott, Josephine M., 'The Owen Family Papers', *Indiana Magazine of History*, vol. 60, 1964, 331–52.

Fraser, E.M., 'Robert Owen in Manchester 1787–1800', *Memoirs of the Manchester Lit. & Phil. Soc.*, vol. 82, 1937–38, 29–41.

Fraser, W. Hamish, 'Owenite Socialism in Scotland', *Scottish Economic & Social History*, vol. 16, 60–91.

—'Alexander Campbell, 1796–1870', *Scottish Labour History Society Journal*, no. 31, 35–8.

—'Alexander Campbell and Some "Lost" Unstamped Newspapers', *Scottish Labour History Society Journal*, no. 31, 39–50.

Garver, L., 'Bejamin Rush Milam', *Southwestern Historical Quarterly*, vol. 38, 1934, 79–121.

Geoghegan, V., 'Ralahine: Ireland's Lost Utopia', *Communal Studies*, vol. 9, 1989, 91–104.

Harding, F.J.W., 'Stringers Welsh Excursions II: North Wales', *Trans. Hon. Soc. of Cymmrodorion*, 1981, 51–78.

Jones, I.G., 'Patterns of Religious Worship in Montgomeryshire in the Mid-Nineteenth Century', *Montgomeryshire Collections*, vol. 68, 1980, 93–118.

Kamau, Lucy J., 'The Anthropology of Space in Harmonist and Owenite New Harmony', *Communal Societies*, vol. 12, 1992, 68–89.

Lewis, G. J., 'The Geography of Religion on the Middle Borderlands of Wales in 1851', *Trans. Hon. Soc. of Cymmrodorion*, 1980, 123–142.

McLaren, D.J., 'Robert Owen, William Maclure and New Harmony', *History of Education*, vol. 25, 1996, 223–33.

—'Education for Citizenship and the New Moral World of Robert Owen', *Scottish Educational Review*, vol. 32, no. 2, 2000, 107–116.

Moore, D., 'Early Views of Towns in Wales and the Borders', *Trans. Hon. Soc. of Cymmrodorion*, 1981, 35–50.

Nicolson, M. and Donnachie, I. 'The New Lanark Highlanders: Migration, Community and Language 1785–c.1850', *Family and Community History*, vol. 6/1, 2003, 19–32.

Oliver, W.H. 'The Consolidated Trades' Union of 1834', *Economic History Review*, vol. 17, 1964, 77–95.

—'The Labour Exchange Phase of the Co-operative Movement', *Oxford Economic Papers*, vol. 10, 1958, 355–67.

Pitzer, D.E., 'The Original Boatload of Knowledge', *The Ohio Journal of Science*, vol. 89, 1989, 128–42.

Pitzer, D.E. and Elliott, Josephine M., 'New Harmony's First Utopians', *Indiana Magazine of History*, vol. 75, 1979, 224–300.

Pollard, S., 'Factory Discipline in the Industrial Revolution', *Economic History Review*, vol. 16, 1963, 254–71

Pryce, W.T.R., 'Wales as a Culture Region: Patterns of Change 1750–1971', *Trans. Hon. Soc. of Cymmrodorion*, 1978, 229–261.

—'Welsh and English in Wales, 1750–1971: A Spatial Analysis Based on the Linguistic Affiliation of Parochial Communities', *Bulletin of the Board of Celtic Studies*, vol. 28, part I, 1978, 1–33.

Robbins, K.G., 'Wales and the Scottish Connection', *Trans. Hon. Soc. of Cymmrodorion*, 1985, 57–69.

Robertson, A.J., 'Robert Owen and the Campbell Debt 1810–22', *Business History*, 11, 1969, 23–30.

Shirai, Atsushi, 'William Godwin and Robert Owen', *Keio Economic Studies*, vol. 7, 1970, 64–76.

Timmons, W.H., 'Robert Owen's Texas Project', *Southwestern Historical Quarterly*, vol. 52, 1949, 286–93.

Volwiler, A.T., 'Robert Owen and the Congress of Aix-la-Chapelle', *Scottish Historical Review*, vol. 19, 1921–22, 96–105

Williams, L., 'A Case Study of Newtown Montgomeryshire: The Socio-Economic Structure of a Small Industrial Town in the Mid-Nineteenth Century', *Montgomeryshire Collections*, vol. 64, 1976.

# Index